A contemporary broadsheet describing the Pappenheimers' alleged crimes and their dreadful execution

Highroad

A Tale of Witchcraft

to the Stake

Michael Kunze

Translated by William E. Yuill

THE UNIVERSITY OF CHICAGO PRESS

Chicago and London

MICHAEL KUNZE, born in Prague, received his education in Germany, studying law, history, and philosophy. His doctoral dissertation, *Der Prozess Pappenheimer* (1981), gave rise to the present book. Since 1970 Kunze has been active as a lyricist and translator as well as pursuing research in legal history.

This book was first published in German under the title *Straße ins Feuer: Vom Leben und Sterben in der Zeit des Hexenwahns,* © 1982 by Kindler Verlag GmbH, München.

The University of Chicago Press, Chicago 60637
The University of Chicago Press, Ltd., London

Library of Congress Cataloging-in-Publication Data

Kunze, Michael, 1943–
  Highroad to the stake.

  Translation of: Strasse ins Feuer.
  1. Witchcraft—Germany (West)—Bavaria—History—17th century. I. Title.
BF1583.K8613 1987   133.4'09433   86-11230
ISBN 0-226-46211-0

"In ages overshadowed by catastrophe men look for someone to blame, and anything that deviates from the norm is blameworthy."

WILL-ERICH PEUCKERT

· Contents

· Preface

The year is 1600. Somewhere in Germany, in a small, Lower Bavarian village, a family of traveling people—husband, wife, grown-up sons, a ten-year-old child—falls into the clutches of the powers that be. For the local authorities it is nothing but a trivial, routine incident. But when the duke's council of state in Munich learns of the case, it shows a surprising interest in it. It so happened that the council was on the lookout for suitable delinquents who might form the subject of a major show trial designed to deter highwaymen, arsonists, and murderers throughout the country. Opinion in the capital suggested that these vagrants, who had been taken into custody, would suit the purpose admirably. This was the decision that determined the course of subsequent events. Instructions were issued for the transfer of the prisoners to Munich.

There they were subjected to extensive interrogation. Their statements, recorded in minute detail by the officiating clerk, constitute the principal source for my account of their fate. They lead the reader into the everyday world of traveling folk, craftsmen, and small farmers who have been dead for nearly four hundred years. From this transcript of their trial, long-forgotten men and women are brought back to life; they talk about themselves, their joys, their fears, and their distresses. Their view of many things differed from ours. They lived within a stable order that distinguished between superiority and inferiority, between heaven and hell, angels and demons. Our judgment of them is bound to be false, for we can no longer think, believe, or feel as they did.

And yet the temper of the age was not so very different from that of our own times. Dark clouds hung over the land, unseen, but manifest to all. A storm is brewing, people thought, and trembled at the prospect. The great war presaged by all the omens would be the most terrible of all, the ultimate conflict to be endured by mankind. Good and Evil were arming themselves for the final battle that was to precede the Last Judgment. In the East stood the Antichrist, armed to the teeth: the Turks, merciless archenemies of Christendom, were threatening to overrun Vienna. Unity in the Western camp would seem to be the most urgent need of the moment, but in fact confusion reigned. Suspicion and strife prevailed among the governments of the West: it was a case of every man for himself. People argued about words, and every party believed it had a monopoly of the truth. In the end, however, it was, as it always had been, a question of power and money. But in this case greed and rapacity were inspired by a higher purpose, a sacred idea, the true faith, so that every means to that end was reckoned legitimate, every sign of restraint regarded as reprehensible. Self-interest sported a halo and no longer needed to feel ashamed. If we become wealthier and more powerful, the rulers claimed, we may yet avert the disaster that threatens us. People took note of their words and clung to that hope.

But that did not suffice to dispel their fears, and so they devised ways of escape. They plunged into dissipation, indulged in sumptuous feasts, reeled and reveled in dances that grew ever wilder—or else they hoarded, scrimped, and saved. Men cursed or mocked their Lord, or else they donned sackcloth and ashes, joined one of the new sects, prayed and did penance. Some attempted to dissect the chaos around them with the power of ideas, to explore it and reduce it to a system; others put their trust in occult powers, clung to murky superstitions, hoping for the aid of spirits and demons. Above all, however, people looked for scapegoats. To those whose hearts are struck with terror it is a relief to stand in the midst of a seething mob, to point to a "culprit," and to cry "Burn him!" The age of fear is the age of fire and the stake. But the relief gained by the threatened mob from the victims' screams and the crackling of the fire is short-lived. The dense smoke that rises from such conflagrations serves only to make the sky darker, to render the general menace all the more obvious.

This is the background against which we may observe the principal characters of our tale as they tread the path which leads to the fire. I have attempted to reconstruct their lives. Nothing in this story is invented, no matter how much it may remind us of a novel. My "heroes" speak for themselves; they tell us what they felt and thought, what they put their faith in, and what inspired their doubts; they tell us of their remedies for poverty and sickness; they tell us how they played and laughed, suffered and dreamed. I have amplified their story discreetly by adding such explanations and discussions as seem to me necessary for an understanding of the age in which they lived.

This amplification also entails a scrutiny of those who operated the levers of power, the officials who sat in judgment on our prisoners. By reference to old letters, notes, and dusty files, I shall attempt to describe their thoughts as well as their actions. To understand the judges within the context of their historical limitations is, of course, more difficult than to sympathize with their victims. But we should not judge too hastily. The educated sensed the imminence of disaster even more acutely than ordinary people, and they felt themselves threatened. Fear turns wise men into simpletons, makes the just unjust, the pious wicked, and the meek ferocious. Learned councillors, in no way less intelligent than modern civil servants, blindly followed the "prevailing opinion" of contemporary jurisprudence, which grappled with witchcraft as a real crime and thought it merited scholarly investigation.

Was this nothing but an unfortunate aberration on the part of a young science, an ineptitude it has long since mastered? We have no occasion to assume an air of superiority: there are now, as there were then, any number of lawyers prepared to accept uncritically whatever view happens to be current. In our universities the niceties of an "academic approach" foster the capacity to accommodate common sense to legal realities that give cause for concern. A philosopher of the twentieth century, Hannah Arendt, remarks somewhere that the worst thing about intellectuals is that they can think of an argument in favor of absolutely anything. This remark was aimed at the intellectual acrobats who sought to justify the Nazi regime, but it also applies to the judges who tried the case described in this book, and generally to the typical modern intellectual. The nursery of this intellectual type was the University of Bologna, where jurisprudence came into existence in the twelfth century as the earliest of the secular disciplines. Bound by the established authorities of the Roman corpus juris, the students were taught from the very start to demonstrate that contradictions in legal tradition were apparent rather than real, and to resolve inconsistencies by means of interpretation and fresh arguments. This juggling with concepts, this scholastic tightrope walking, succeeded in turning the new legal profession into an instrument that could be employed in any political system by any authority whatsoever. The profession was able to discover logically impeccable arguments for anything that was represented to it as "law." This ability is still highly esteemed today. Legal training has not changed in principle down to the present day; patterns of thought and argument established in Bologna have left their mark on legal commentaries, journals, and the judgments handed down by our supreme justices.

The reader should bear this in mind when he learns how legal authorities transformed the superstitious belief in witchcraft into a refined and dogmatic criminal code. In Dr. Fickler and Dr. Wangereck, leading characters in our story and adversaries to our tramps, artisans, and peasants, the reader will recognize representatives of an intelligentsia to which most of us belong. Judicial torture and witchhunts were the early products of a "modern" mentality and not, as is sometimes claimed, the monstrous offspring of the allegedly benighted Middle Ages. It was only the emancipation of the intellect from the emotions that allowed human beings to practice inhumanity with an easy conscience. The four hundred years which separate us from the events described here should not obscure the fact that these events took place in the dawn of our own era. Duke Maximilian, who governed the fate of our vagrants and villagers from Lower Bavaria, was imbued with an idea of the state which did not come into its own until the present century. He envisaged total surveillance of every citizen, supreme authority over the citizen's conscience, and control of his life. Had the duke possessed the technical facilities of our own day, he would not have needed the crude device of a show trial. So the comforting reflection that such things could not happen now is hardly justified.

I ask the indulgence of experts in the field. My book represents a great deal that is common knowledge, and it also attempts to make what is new comprehensible to as wide a circle of readers as possible. Those who are seeking a more strictly scholarly account of these events I would refer to my dissertation, *Der Prozess Pappenheimer* (Ebelsbach, 1981). My concern here is to rescue the fate of my principal characters from oblivion. The more people know of this fate, the better. For this reason I thought it justifiable to adapt quotations from my sources so that they conform to our modern orthography, without, of course, changing the sense. Doubts and uncertainties that still defy investigation are responsible for numerous phrases like "presumably," "more or less on these lines," and "perhaps." Many readers may be irritated by these and other tentative expressions, but unfortunately there is no other way of drawing distinctions between speculation and authentic source material.

For the most part this book recounts incidents ignored by historical studies: they were of too little significance to affect the general course of events. Anyone who regards history as a series of political acts, a stage on which heroic figures perform, or a storehouse of edifying examples will attach little importance to what I have to relate here. Major political issues are peripheral to my story, and my "heroes" are distinctly dubious characters. The lessons of this book consist of truisms to the effect, for example, that even the most erudite stupidity is still stupidity. Why do I think the story is still worth telling? Because history is made up of many stories—a few "major" stories and innumerable "minor" stories. This is one of those minor stories. We should listen to it not because we are eager to learn something but simply out of curiosity. I propose to recount how these people fared; I am not out to prove anything, to achieve some particular end, or to stir up emotions. I merely want to follow in the footsteps of these people, to accompany them a little way along the path that led them to the stake.

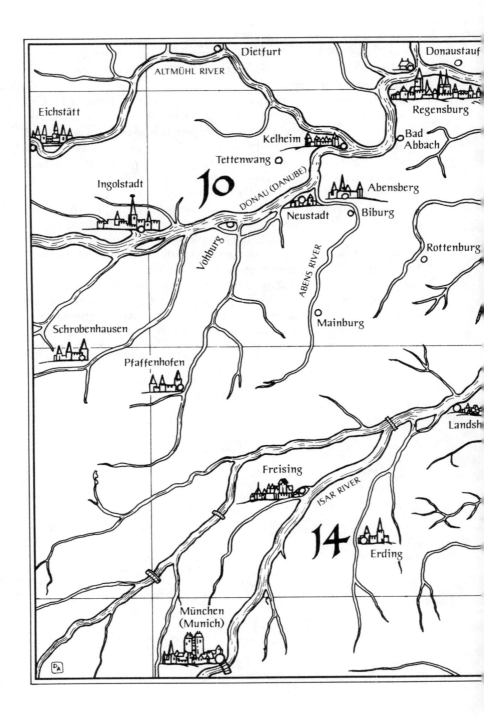

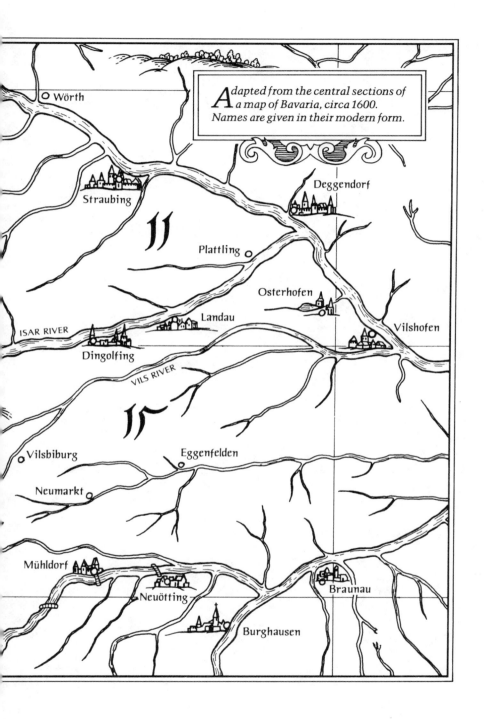

○ Wörth

*A*dapted from the central sections of
a map of Bavaria, circa 1600.
Names are given in their modern form.

Straubing

Deggendorf

Plattling ○

Osterhofen

Landau

Vilshofen

ISAR RIVER

Dingolfing

VILS RIVER

Vilsbiburg ○

Eggenfelden

Neumarkt ○

Mühldorf

Neuötting

Braunau

Burghausen

CHAPTER · 1

The Falcon Tower in Munich (drawing by G. Steinlein, Munich City Museum)

⋅ The Tower

One afternoon toward the end of April 1600, an open cart drawn by a pair of horses rumbled along the uneven, swampy cart track that once passed for the highway linking Nuremberg and Munich. Day in, day out, caravans of traders, peddlers' carts, and merchants' coaches lurched along the deeply rutted road, screeching and creaking under their loads of spices, silks, and glasses from the celebrated commerical center of Nuremberg, sumptuous cloth from England and Flanders, wines from the Rhine and the Main. They were bound for the capital city, whence they would set out northward once more, laden with Styrian copper, pewter from Carinthia, sacks of salt and grain, wax, Tyrolean wine, and bales of loden cloth. The rumbling cart that opens our story, however, was carrying a different sort of freight: riffraff of the most disreputable kind, miscreants under arrest. They were sitting chained together on a wooden bench—an elderly couple, two young men, a boy. In front of the cart rode the sheriff of Altmannstein and Abensberg. Every now and then he looked back at the cart bearing the prisoners, staring past the wretched offenders at the two constables who brought up the rear.

The walls, towers, and steeples of Munich had long since come into sight. The highway from Nuremberg led through meadows green with the first flush of spring, crossing a broad, flat plain studded with still leafless bushes and pollarded willows. On either side of the highway, cows and horses, sometimes sheep and goats, grazed behind fences and gates: cattle belonging to the duke. Travelers could gaze on the splendid prospect of Munich from a mile or so along the road[1] without seeming to make much progress toward the city.

3

A medieval wall encircled the town, together with a pair of moats filled with flowing water. A patch of ocher flecked with red and specks of yellow, green, and blue, the city rested on its green-and brown-checkered plain. To the east, a pallid glint of pebbles, the River Isar flowing unconfined, divided as it wound through straggling shoals of shingle. Gentle, wooded hills veiled in the afternoon's blue haze formed the background to the west. A contemporary, seeing the city thus, noted enthusiastically in his diary: "The city could scarce be fairer nor more lovely, more radiant in the limpid air, a beauty deriving no doubt from its situation in a broad, resplendent plain."

And what a skyline! The twin onion towers of the Church of Our Lady, and the tower of St. Peter's, massive in its lower part, delicately proportioned higher up, dominated the other buildings and showed the approaching stranger where the heart of the city lay. From the sea of houses spread out below, tall, narrow gables jostling together, other spires soared up into the sky: the New Collegiate Church, the Fair Tower, the Old Palace, and the mortuary chapels of St. Peter and Our Lady. Ranged against them the squat bastions of the city's fortifications, planted foursquare in the earth, marked the city limits. They looked like the keeps of medieval castles, bristling like them with pinnacles, loopholes, and spouts for the discharge of boiling tar.

An astounding sight, even for the captives in their cart, who had never before been in the Bavarian capital. They looked on its splendors, it is true, with doleful thoughts and downcast hearts. This was the city in which they were doomed to die. The husband and wife at least were certain of their dreadful end. And even if the two young men and the child sitting with them in the cart might still believe in a favorable outcome, this was scant comfort for their elders, for their fellow prisoners were their own sons. It was an entire family that the sheriff of Abensberg, acting on instructions from the highest authority in the land, was escorting to Munich on that April day. For the ducal council, apprized of the nefarious deeds of these evildoers from Lower Bavaria, had ordered their transfer to the capital. The wretched vagrants who sat chained together in that cart lurching and creaking its way toward the Schwabing Gate were the objects of the duke's personal interest.

This may have occurred to the sheriff as he turned round from time to time to look at the prisoners and their escort. He was responsible for the safe delivery of this important cargo. Fortunately, his task would soon be done. He had brought the prisoners from Abensberg to the capital over bumpy and perilous roads and had made sure they were securely lodged in the city hall at Pfaffenhofen, where the party was obliged to spend the night. Now he would hand them over, along with the official documents, to the duke's officers, find himself a lodging for the night in Munich, and return home next day with the empty cart. The fate of these people would no longer be any concern of his. How would the business end? He had frequently talked to his prisoners and had found them less depraved and fiendish than gossip suggested. Not that his impression counted for much: everybody knew that the Devil lost all his power over his creatures the moment they were in the hands of the authorities. So it would be with those five individuals in the cart who, by all accounts, had been on the most intimate terms with Satan.

The prisoners looked like a poor peasant family. Their outward appearance is described by the author of a contemporary pamphlet,[2] who tried to give an accurate impression of them with the help of some woodcuts. In these we can identify the father as a broad-shouldered, stocky individual. Beneath a narrow-brimmed hat of black or gray material, gray hair hangs down below his ears; his eyes are set far apart, his nose is narrow, and the lower part of his face is covered by a full beard, its wiry curls standing out a couple of inches from chin and cheeks. He is wearing a coarse jacket over his linen shirt, faded breeches, knitted stockings, and laced shoes. His hands are large and shovel-shaped, evidently capable of a firm grip. Beside him is the mother, rather a thin woman, taller than her husband, with straggly, grayish-yellow hair falling to her shoulders. Her mouth is severe and thin-lipped, her eyes deep-set and framed in wrinkles. She is wearing a dark dress, its hem almost touching the ground. Both the young men have long, fair hair under peasant hats like their father's; the elder of the two has narrow features like his mother, otherwise he is as burly and well built as his younger brother, who generally resembles his father. Finally there is the boy, clad like the adult males in breeches, linen shirt, and jacket, also wearing a hat over his long, lank hair. Outwardly, these prisoners had nothing to distinguish them from the common folk we see in other illustrations of the time. But they were lying fettered in a cart that rumbled across the bridge over the city's outer moat, passed the watchman's hut on the far bank, and then turned right to make for the Schwabing Gate.

There, the sheriff, who had ridden on ahead, showed the sentries his official papers, explained his commission to them, and was allowed to enter with his unusual cargo. The cart rolled across the arches of the stone bridge that spanned the inner moat. On the city side of the bridge, the causeway was flanked by rectangular towers, battlemented, and with loopholes at a height of some twelve feet; between them was a fifteen-foot wall pierced by the rectangular outer gateway, which was not much wider than the cart. They rode into the gloomy inner courtyard, hemmed in by high walls surmounted by gangways, the crunch of the iron-rimmed wheels and the hooves of the horses resounding loudly. But only for a moment; then the cart with the prisoners was already passing through the gateway itself, the inner gate, rumbling through the short tunnel below a huge rectangular bastion that joined the city walls on either side, its battlemented summit rearing some sixty feet into the air.

The Schwabing Gate[3] gave entry to the city at the point now occupied by the Odeonsplatz—on the south side of the square that now forms an open space in front of the Feldherrenhalle. Emerging from the dark recesses of the tunnel beneath the tower, we would have been confronted at that time by one of the most imposing buildings in the city, known as the Bauerngirgl, or "Farmer George," a broad, three-story structure with two turrets at its corners, each crowned with the typical onion-shaped roof. To the left of this splendid patrician dwelling lay the Hintere Schwabinger Gasse (now Theatinerstrasse), which led to the Marienplatz and the town hall. The cart with the prisoners veered left on the square facing the Bauerngirgl, however, and then turned almost at once into the Vordere Schwabinger Gasse (now known as the Residenzstrasse). This was the shortest route to the Falcon Tower, the duke's prison for those accused of capital offenses, where the sheriff of Abensberg and Altmannstein was to hand over his captives.

THE CITY

In the year 1600, Munich, of which the criminals from Lower Bavaria had seen nothing but a few streets and rows of houses on their way to prison, bore no resemblance to the present-day metropolis of that name. Barely 24,000 people lived in the capital of the duchy of Bavaria; fewer than half were citizens, that is, subject to the jurisdiction of the city council. In 1596, complaints had been voiced in the town hall that the citizens were only a tiny group in comparison with the court and the clergy.

Had he heard these complaints, the duke might well have been mortified at such ingratitude. It was barely a hundred years since his forebears had chosen the town on the Isar as their permanent residence and thus conferred on it both wealth and status. Munich was in no position to rival commercial centers like Augsburg, Nuremberg, Regensburg, or Passau; nor could it claim to be a religious center, given its proximity to the venerable archiepiscopal city of Freising. Since the whole of Bavaria had been ruled and administered from Munich, however, the city had managed to acquire political importance. The court attracted foreigners: traders eager to sell their wares, artists keen to display their talents, diplomats seeking to exert their influence. As a result, there were plenty of pickings for the townsfolk—not least from the commissions that issued from the ducal household itself. All the available bricklayers and carpenters, painters and masons had recently been enlisted to build the Jesuit College, while extensions to the Neufeste, the ducal residence, were already underway. Provisions were required for the duke's kitchen; his servants had to be clothed. The court warmed and mothered the citizens of the town like a hen her chicks.

The citizens not infrequently had the impression that they were being smothered rather than mothered—in 1587, for instance, when Duke William V deprived the city of its right to trade in salt; or in 1598, when his son Maximilian rescinded sundry time-honored prerogatives and privileges *"ex plenitudine potestatis,"* by virtue of his sovereign powers. The ducal council treated the city council more and more frequently as an inferior authority, and even went so far on occasion as to fix the butchers' prices and to rebuke the city fathers as "agitators and demagogues" when they protested, thus imposing restrictions on them which had not previously existed. Unmoved by the citizens' complaints, the duke had whole streets of houses torn down in order to erect churches, monasteries, and mansions. There was no doubt about it: he, and no one else, was master in Munich.

That feeling was shared not only by the patricians who sat on the city council but also by ordinary people. The innkeepers, for example, had to fill out four registration forms for every guest from outside the city: one for Duke Maximilian, one for his father, who had abdicated, one for the duke's chamberlain, and one for the mayor. When the church bells rang out the Angelus in the evening, every inhabitant of Munich was required by ducal decree to kneel down in the street. Once a year the duke's officers went from house to house collecting certificates of confession; anyone who had failed to go to confession ended up in jail.

The air of Munich, then, did not confer quite the same degree of freedom as that of many other cities. Yet people lived well enough. There were forty-two wine shops in the streets and lanes, besides fourteen alehouses, which were often the scene of wild carousing. When the duke tried to prohibit the singing and bawling that issued from these hostelries, the city council pointed out that it was a popular custom and could not be suppressed by decree. The same may well have been true of the dozen public bathhouses in the city, in which men and women frankly and cheerfully assisted each other in their ablutions, and also ate, drank, gambled, and made music together—in defiance of all the duke's puritanical decrees.

A contemporary wooden model has preserved, as in a snapshot, the appearance of the city at that time.[4] The houses, generally of two or three stories, are either pinched and narrow or broad and rambling; some have narrow pitched roofs, others are commodious; some are sleek, adorned with bay windows, others have only mean and narrow casements; some are pompously ornate. They follow the often tortuous lines of the streets, crammed together, seldom in regular rows. At one point a building towers above its neighbors, thrusting a gallery or a bay window far out into the street; at another point a workshop with its stall obstructs the thoroughfare at ground level. Nothing is uniform: every house has a different angle to its roof, its own characteristic window shape, pinnacles, ornaments, outhouses. All the roofs have dormer windows, skylights, random turrets, and decorative gables—but not a single chimney, for they had not yet been invented. It was an angular jumble of walls and corners; yet it formed a single entity, a city. The alleys were narrow and gloomy, the main thoroughfares grand and spacious, often widening into open squares. Most of these squares contained a water source—thirty-six wells and eighteen fountains supplied the population with water. The courtyards were filled with vegetation and flowers. There was scarcely a house without its vegetable patch, and streams flowed everywhere. There were wooden foot-bridges, sheds, barns, stables, and higgledy-piggledy wooden fences.

However accurately the wooden model may have reproduced

each individual house, it still shows us only half the truth. It tells us nothing, for example, of the state of the streets. The major thoroughfares were paved with "gravel," round gray-and-white pebbles taken from the nearby river Isar. The street level was lowest in the middle, where there was a kind of gutter that collected the drainage from fall pipes as well as the waste from kitchen windows.

Munich at that time hardly smelled sweet. Even the better class of dwellings had middens and rubbish heaps. People often simply flung their filth and garbage into the street, where it was eagerly turned over by stray dogs or by the pigs that were driven past every so often. In fact, one should not ignore the peasant aspect of urban life in that age. Hens scratched among the cobbles, sheep found their way from rural backyards onto the street, cows were led down to be watered at the wells.

The city's music was made up of bells pealing solemnly or jangling officiously, the voices of choirs drifting through open church doors or monastery windows, women gossiping at the wells, children shrieking, a cock crowing, a peddler crying his wares. From the open workshops of the craftsmen came a medley of sounds: planing and hammering; clanging, filing, and forging; seething and hissing. There were thirteen mills at work in the city, driving small forges where all sorts of utensils were manufactured from copper and other metals amid incessant clatter. Snatches of this symphony must have come to the ears of the criminals who were being conducted to their prison on that afternoon toward the end of April.

Passersby no doubt stopped to stare curiously at the fettered prisoners, asking their neighbors what sort of evildoers these might be. Street urchins probably ran yelling behind the cart. Someone may well have cried out in astonishment: one of the criminals was no more than a child. But the cart was already turning the corner. People resumed their former pursuits: the shopkeeper went back into his shop, the children returned to their game. This, or something like this, was the scene in the capital city of Munich when the prisoners from Lower Bavaria arrived.

PRISON

The prisoners' destination was situated to the northeast, on the outskirts of the city, roughly the same spot where formally dressed opera goers today mount the broad flight of steps leading up to the

9

National Theater. In the year 1600, the site was occupied by the Falkenturm, or Falcon Tower,[5] part of the city's defensive wall. Built about 1450, the tower was originally one of the numerous strongholds erected on the walls encircling Munich. It was equipped with loopholes and projecting turrets that were reached by gangways. The Falcon Tower was distinguished from other similar buildings on the city walls by an elaborate superstructure incorporating sloping gables that rose on all four sides with projecting bays; these bays occupied the entire width of the roof ridge, perching on the walls of the tower like outsized dovecotes. The tower had once offered an uninterrupted view of the broad plain that the cart bearing our prisoners had crossed in its approach to the city. For some decades now, however, the view in this direction had been obstructed by new buildings put up by the duke. The Falcon Tower had running water on two sides. To the north, the waters of the town moat, some thirty feet wide, flowed sluggishly past, following the line of the city walls. To the west, the Pfisterbach gurgled out from an opening in the wall and crossed the moat on a kind of aqueduct.

Almost from the time it was built, the tower had served as a store for the implements the duke needed for the pursuit of falconry. Since about 1520, however, birds of another feather had been caged in the tower: prisoners awaiting the gallows who could not be accommodated elsewhere. The change paid off: the tower turned out to be totally secure. In those days towers were frequently used as jails. A mere hundred yards or so to the east of the Falcon Tower, just in front of the gate known as the Kosttor or Wurzetor, stood a round tower in which petty debtors were confined. The so-called Pocket Tower, or Taschenturm, in front of the Boatman's Gate (Schiffertor) on the east side of the city wall, was used as a military prison. Another tower, which guarded a corner of the city wall not far from the Falcon Tower, was surrounded by all sorts of legends: it was called the Witches' Tower, a name it acquired in the mid-seventeenth century, when this little corner tower too was turned into a jail because the witch trials ordered by the duke had become so numerous that the Falcon Tower could no longer house all the accused.

The cart carrying the captive family turned left by the "Oat Bin" in front of the entrance to the ducal stables, rumbled past the Witches' Tower and a short way along the little frequented alley by the city wall, coming to a stop about fifty yards farther on, in front of the Falcon Tower. Here the sheriff of Abensberg probably leaped from his horse and called for the "ironmaster," supposing the latter had not already been drawn to door or window by the sound of hooves and the rumble of the cart.

"Ironmaster" was the name given to the warden of the Falcon Tower.[6] In 1600 the incumbent of this post was Sebastian Georg. Master Georg was more than just a jailor or prison warden. He was, rather, an entrepreneur, who ran the Falcon Tower as if he were an innkeeper, by virtue of a lease from the duke's treasury. For every prisoner put into his keeping he was paid a stipulated subsistence allowance by the treasury. In return he was responsible for housing and feeding the inmates. The temptation to water down their soup was considerable: the cheaper the fare, the greater the profits of the business. The ironmaster's children lent a hand as well, supplying the prisoners with fresh straw from time to time and sweeping out the cells. The master himself had to guard the criminals and keep them in such close custody that they had no chance of escape. And, unfortunately, he was also required, at the behest of the ducal commissioners, to administer torture. This was the main reason for the hostile looks he encountered as he went around Munich, for the fact that his children were hounded through the streets by the catcalls of their fellows, and for the ordeal his wife had to face every time she went shopping. The ironmaster and his family were considered beyond the pale; they were outcasts, with whom no respectable citizen would wish to have dealings.

Master Georg could not read the document that the sheriff from Lower Bavaria presented to him, so he would have been told by word of mouth what kind of people the prisoners were. Perhaps he immediately dispatched one of his children to the Old Palace to inform the office of the chief justice that the detainees had arrived. At any rate, the escort made the family get down from the cart and led them in their clanking chains into the tower, where they ascended the stairs to the cells that were popularly known as *Keuchen* or "chokey." The males in the family were separated, except for the child, who was locked up in the same cell as his mother. The officials from Abensberg removed their fetters, carried the irons back downstairs, and flung them into the empty cart. In the meantime, Master Georg was putting the offenders back in chains. On their wrists he fastened heavy manacles, the last link in a massive chain that was cemented into the wall. Those were the regulations: every prisoner had to be fastened in such a way that he could not bring his hands together. Care also had to be taken that the manacles were not too loose—which would have allowed the prisoner to free himself—or so tight that they would "cut into the flesh and cause the arms to swell."[7] The criminal who was thus fettered was able to sit down on the straw spread on the floor by the wall, and might even lie down in an uncomfortably contorted posture. He was forced to perform his natural functions on the spot—the straw was changed every day, as in a stable. The only way to cope with the stench was to open the cell window. When the ironmaster's wife brought the prisoner food, she would, at his request, let in some fresh air; in the cold season, that entailed a further reduction in the temperature of the unheated sties, so that many of the inmates no doubt preferred to do without fresh air.

There they sat and waited, each in his own cell, surveyed their new quarters, probably called out to father, mother, or son, whom they rightly supposed to be nearby. The mother will have comforted her child, taken him in her arms—the two of them had been spared fetters—as darkness began to fall outside and the noise of the city gradually died away.

THE PREFECT

A thick wad of closely written papers, court transcripts from Abensberg, statements by the detainees as to their identity and the charges laid against them, had arrived in Munich long before the cart with its fettered prisoners. A mounted courier from the prefect of Abensberg and Altmannstein had handed over the file in the council offices in the Old Palace, probably with a covering letter from the local magistrate asking for instructions on the further conduct of the case. The documents had been passed as a matter of course to one of the learned councillors, who was required to make a brief report, together with recommendations, to a full meeting of the council. Then a vote would be taken and instructions issued as to whether the malefactors should be subjected to further and more severe torture, or whether a judgment should be pronounced. We already know that neither of these courses had been prescribed, but a third and more unusual procedure: the scoundrels were to be dispatched forthwith to Munich and the subsequent conduct of the case left to the council of state.

A strange decision. After all, the young duke in Munich, a notorious miser and skinflint, had instructed his councillors and officials never to spend a cent more than was strictly necessary. What prompted him to institute criminal proceedings against individuals who were virtually destitute? It would only cost money, apart from all the trouble of carrying out the sentence. We can visualize Alexander von Haslang zu Haslangsreut, Grosshausen und Ried, the prefect of Abensberg and Altmannstein at the time, reading the council's instructions with some surprise. He was pleasantly surprised, of course, being only too glad to be rid of the whole business, because of the expense and the bother, for one thing, but also on personal grounds. For Haslang was no dry jurist but a swashbuckler, "Captain of the Bodyguard," a born warrior, colonel, and cavalryman.[8] He soon found life too dull in his Lower Bavarian bailiwick; in 1601 he moved to Hungary as lieutenant-colonel, never to return to his old county. He died in 1620, at the beginning of the great war, as a prisoner in Bohemia. His heart was certainly not in the practice of law—especially when it brought him nothing in return.

One might ask, then, why he had assumed responsibility for the judicial district of Abensberg and Altmannstein. To put it plainly, it was because a county court, a so-called prefecture,[9] was a source of ready cash as well as payments in kind. Of the eighty-five administrative districts into which Bavaria was divided at the time, most served simply as benefices for the duke's most deserving henchmen. A disconcerting thought, when we learn that the prefectures were not only centers for the administration of criminal justice but also served as the lowest tier of government; that is, they represented the authority of the state for all the inhabitants of that particular region. In Duke William V's time, when the finances of the state were in poor shape, the monarch actually handed a number of prefectures over to his creditors. So it will come as no surprise that certain of the prefects knew their districts by name only and never put in an appearance there. The work was done by someone else, the procurator. Even he was not a civil servant in the modern sense; he received no salary from the prefect whose duties he performed, but worked on his own account. He had to be content with the official fees, for his superior retained the perquisites of office, which might be very substantial: twenty-five pounds of prime fish, sixty bushels of oats for the four horses on his establishment, and an annual retainer of two hundred and fifty gulden. This traffic in public appointments caused widespread resentment. At one point the citizens of Wasserburg even refused to obey the procurator: only the prefect himself was entitled to give them orders, they claimed. These refractory subjects were quickly put in their place, and nothing was changed.

It is clear, then, that economic considerations were paramount in the administration of the Bavarian prefectures at that time: it was the return on capital that counted. Criminal proceedings offered some prospect of profit only if they were brought against delinquents who owned property that might be confiscated. The prosecution of penniless vagrants was a judicial obligation that had to be reckoned on the debit side and, consequently, an obligation to be evaded wherever possible. This was done, for instance, simply by bundling the offenders over the border. We have reason to believe that Haslang was prevented from taking this way out in the case of the arrested family. Presumably they had been apprehended on orders from higher up. In any case, correspondence on the matter had been officially registered in Munich from the very outset.

In Wörth, a small town between Regensburg and Straubing on the northern rim of the Danube valley, a thief by the name of Geindl had been hanged in the summer of 1599. Before he died, he had, among other things, made a statement to the effect that the "tinker lads" had abetted him in the murder of seven pregnant women. These tinker lads, Michel and Gumpprecht, were the adult sons of old Pappenheimer. The latter allegedly traveled about the Danube area with his wife, child, and all his belongings, never spending long in any one place, stealing from the peasants and killing wayfarers. This was the gist of it—we do not know the details of Geindl's denunciation.

We can only speculate on the subsequent course of events. The authorities in Straubing probably wrote to their colleagues in Munich, asking them to mount a search for those dangerous vagrants, the Pappenheimer family, in those Danube prefectures that were under their jurisdiction; they themselves would keep a sharp lookout in their own area. A little later, no doubt, Alexander von Haslang received his instructions from Munich. These he passed on to his officials, who constantly traveled around the country, talking with the peasants and sitting with them in the taverns after they had inspected the markets.

One February day in 1600, when snow lay thick on the ground, the authorities learned that their quarry was to be found in Tettenwang in a barn belonging to a farmer called Ulrich Schölz. That same evening, a sleigh bearing the sheriff of Altmannstein escorted by a number of horsemen made its way to the village. They were directed to Schölz's farm, where the arrest was effected. It probably happened roughly as follows: the barn is surrounded, the wooden door yanked open. Searching questions, startled replies. Eyes blinking in the light of lanterns held aloft, bare feet stumbling in the snow, arms seized and bound. Five figures, bewildered by the suddenness of events, gape at the sheriff and his men; the adults are bundled onto the sleigh, the child howls. The man with the lantern goes back into the barn so that the sheriff can see to search the tramps' sleeping quarters. The prisoners' belongings are also flung on to the sleigh: bundles of shoes and clothing, a leather pouch, glazier's tools, a huckster's basket, tinker's lead. Then off into the night, to Altmannstein, to jail.

A ten-year-old boy remained behind, weeping, and their host's wife looked after him as best she could. Next morning she took him to his parents, who were imprisoned in the Altmannstein town hall, since she could not think of anything else to do with the child. The boy was allowed to visit his mother and was soon going freely in and out of her cell. Altogether, things did not seem too serious at first. The conditions of their confinement gave the arrested family grounds for hope that the final outcome would not be too dire. At that point they could easily "have made a run for it," as Gumpprecht said later. He had been secured with "a handcuff from which he could easily have pulled his hand free. What's more, two or three hours had often passed without anyone coming to look at him." But there was no attempt at escape. The captives still had no idea of the terrors and torments that were to be their lot.

Haslang had obviously reported the arrest of the wanted family to Munich. But since he had no prospect of getting rid of the vagrants otherwise than by finding them guilty and passing sentence on them, he began to question them. It rapidly became clear to him that it would not be easy to dispose of the case satisfactorily. They all denied having committed any crime whatsoever. The thief who had been hanged in Wörth had denounced them out of sheer spite. They had known Geindl, yes, seen him at fairs from time to time. But since he was a notorious thief they had wanted nothing to do with him, and he had been well aware of that. Once he had wanted to know why they kept out of his way. "Leave me and my children alone," old Pappenheimer had replied; "You're up to no good, so we've heard." Then Geindl had lost his temper and threatened him. No idle threat, as they now saw. Such statements were no good to anyone, so Haslang had had recourse to torture during the next interrogation. Examination under torture led to answers that were better calculated to support a judgment. The accused suddenly confessed to thefts, arson, armed robberies; their testimony was not consistent, nor was it corroborated, but there was plenty of it. And, above all, the "tinker lads" admitted having practiced witchcraft.

At about this stage in the interrogation, the prefect of Abensberg and Altmannstein thought it appropriate to dispatch a transcript to the council of state in Munich. He may have had an ulterior motive, possibly seeing in the suggestive term *witchcraft* some hope of getting rid of this expensive and troublesome case. Alexander von Haslang, who had been educated as a page in company with the present duke, was aware of the special interest his princely master took in witchcraft and other diabolical practices. And even if the case against the vagrants was not yet a witch trial, it could easily become so by virtue of that confession of witchcraft.

Possibly Haslang had hit upon the right course of action. Be that as it may, he received instructions to have the entire family transported to Munich. He must have been astonished, all the same, for the duke's court was meeting expenses that would otherwise have been borne by the prefecture of Abensberg-Altmannstein. There must be weighty reasons for this step, reasons only incidentally and indirectly linked to these wretched vagabonds. But that was no longer Haslang's business: he had got the case off his hands. His sheriff had delivered the family to the Falcon Tower, and the papers had been passed on to the council of state. That was the end of the affair, as far as the prefect of Abensberg and Altmannstein was concerned.

FICKLER

In those days the nights were darker than they are now—and not only for those who, like the vagrants from Lower Bavaria, were trying to sleep, wretched and shivering with cold, their minds filled with dark forebodings, chained in excruciatingly uncomfortable positions to the walls of the Falcon Tower. Not a gleam of light reached the windows of their cells. There were no street lamps, and the feeble glow of tallow candles, rush dips, or the wicks of crude oil lamps that served the sleepless in their homes or the tipplers in the taverns scarcely struggled through the bull's-eye windowpanes. From time to time the lantern of some belated

16

wayfarer swayed through the silent alleys but the taverns closed at ten o'clock, and no respectable citizen ventured onto the streets after that hour.

People went to bed early, but they rose at the crack of dawn. Everything happened during the morning. Lunch was eaten at noon, and work ceased at three o'clock in the afternoon. Ten o'clock in the evening—it seemed like the middle of the night. That late in the evening, scarcely anyone was still up and about in Munich. No one but the sacristan of St. Peter's and the excise watchmen on the towers by the city gates, who kept a sharp lookout, particularly for signs of fire and for thieves.

But there was someone else prepared to forgo sleep: in a patrician house on Dienerstrasse an old man sat by the light of a tallow candle, tracing black letters on a sheet of paper. Like the night watchmen he was performing a duty, although in his case it was a self-imposed duty. He had sat like this all his life, late into the night, writing—and now the duty had become a habit, the snuffing of the candle and the sharpening of the quills was a beloved ritual. His days had been crammed with urgent business on behalf of lords both spiritual and temporal, with the conduct of correspondence and the drafting of important documents in elegant Latin concerning political missions and even the education of a prince.[10] He had worn himself out in these tasks, devoted, obsequious, humble. But his nights had been his own—hours in which he could labor with scratching pen to preserve his name for posterity. He had written books—voluminous, learned, larded with quotations, in the style of his time. Some of these nocturnal pieces had even been printed: German translations of Latin works, learned treatises on jurisprudence, pamphlets and lampoons aimed at the members of the Protestant and Reformed churches, whom he despised.

His laborious nights had scarcely established his reputation, but they had, after all, gained him a teaching post of the highest rank. In 1588 the Bavarian duke William IV had enticed him away from the archbishop of Salzburg, his employer at the time, and appointed him to the University of Ingolstadt. This was partly on account of his books, whose titles at least were familiar to his new master. They proved him to be not merely an expert in jurisprudence and in Latin rhetoric but also a doughty warrior in the Catholic cause. This was precisely how the duke of Bavaria visualized a tutor for his son Maximilian—erudite and widely read but also a devout Papist. The diligent nocturnal scholar had friends among the Jesuits who were closely associated with the duke in Munich. They may well have brought their influence to bear. Certainly, the duke never had cause to regret his choice. His son learned a great deal from the teacher who had been brought from Salzburg: the Institutes of Justinian; the common law of Bavaria; Greek; Latin; political science. And his teacher too was delighted: he had gained a model pupil. How well he had learned his lessons was already apparent by 1600. The young duke had ruled the country single-handed for no more than three years, and already the world was astounded at his statesmanship. His teacher should have had every reason to be proud of him, if only—yes, if only he did not have the bitter feeling that hardly anyone really appreciated his services, no one was willing to acknowledge that he had had a hand in shaping this paragon among princes.

He had followed his pupil to Munich when the young man's father declared that his studies in Ingolstadt were now completed. His erudition would still be of service to the prince: he was given a seat and a vote in the council of state. And for some time to come he would still be summoned to the residence in the Neufeste, where father and son ruled jointly. There he continued to give his pupil private tuition in languages and the law, was consulted from time to time in connection with intricate problems of a legal or political kind, and was generally held in high regard. But once the old duke had retired and handed over power to his son, younger advisers had replaced the aged tutor. He was now approaching sixty-six, a great age in those days. That was taken into account: messengers no longer knocked on his door without warning in order to conduct him to the young duke. He was not made privy to important affairs of state, nor was his advice sought when difficult decisions had to be taken. Worse still, when the duke insisted in council that economies must be made, the treasury suggested that he should dismiss his old teacher. Fortunately, Maximilian would not hear of it. All the same, he gave the old man to understand that his presence was no longer necessary at the daily council meetings and entrusted him simply with the compilation of catalogues and indexes to the state archives.

During that April night, however, the old councillor was engaged in a different task. We cannot say with any certainty what he was writing. We do know, however, that he was trying, in the spring of 1600, to write a brief account of his life.[11] So it may well be that at that very moment, by the light of his tallow candle, he was inscribing the title of his autobiographical notes: "A true and circumstantial Record of the Genealogy and Affiliation of Myself, Doctor Johann Baptist Fickler, insofar as I have been diligent to compile the same from the Report of my beloved Parents and others of my Kith and Kin, since departed this Life, and also as thereinafter communicated unto me by my elder Brothers and Sisters, together with a Tabulation of the Degree and Manner in which this, my Kindred, has further been enhanced and augmented through the Bonds of Holy Wedlock."

We can describe pretty accurately the appearance of this same Johann Baptist Fickler as he committed his monstrous sentences to paper. He was not, of course, one of the great men of his time who gave portrait sittings to celebrated painters or whose likeness was captured by adroit engravers. But in 1601, as the duke's secretary, he took part in the so-called Religious Conference in Regensburg and figured in an engraving which recorded that event for posterity. A skilfully colored print has been preserved, pasted into an album belonging to the Donauer family.

In this picture we see the participants in the debate sitting at long tables in the Regensburg town hall, observed by four princes who have taken their places on a dais draped with velvet. Our man is sitting on the left, at the extreme end of the Catholic table, totally absorbed in writing down what others more important than himself have to say. His delicate features are barely concealed by a sparse, curled beard which comes to a point at his chin, exposing a mouth that is thin-lipped and a shade too small. A finely formed, pointed nose between large, close-set eyes, a tinge of darkness marking the bags beneath them. His forehead is distinctly high, his temples broad; the sparse gray hair that falls to the nape of his neck scarcely covers his skull. The old man's right hand is holding the pen, his left rests on the open minute book—long-fingered, narrow hands, suggesting sensitivity, tenderness, vulnerability.

Those hands wrote down many vicious words: shy and retiring individuals are often capable of putting on paper acid or trenchant sentences that no one would have credited them with. Frail and delicate as he appeared, Johann Baptist Fickler was nevertheless a militant character, even if his battles were fought with pen and ink during the watches of the night. He deluged his archenemies, the Lutheran preachers, with bucketfuls of scorn, calling them vile and filthy swine and claiming that "for some years now they have learned their lessons from quacks, cheats, mummers, sharpers, rogues, and scoundrels." And in learned Latin he demanded the ruthless persecution and eradication of witches and sorcerers throughout the land. The mischief wrought by such spawn of the Devil was one of his favorite topics, the academic and legal implications of which he had often discussed with his princely pupil during their sojourn in Ingolstadt. He was an expert in the field. It is true that his instructions to judges and lawyers on the punishment of witches and magicians, worked out in his nocturnal sessions, were numbered among those works for which no publisher could be found. Nevertheless, he was to list them in his autobiographical notes along with all his other works, no doubt concerned that nothing should be lost to posterity.

An April night in Munich. In the Falcon Tower the newly arrived prisoners tossed and turned on their unyielding beds of straw. Barely five hundred yards away an old man sat in the grudging glow of his candle, scratching away with his quill. He had nothing to do with the accused vagrants; his influence on the course of events was minimal. And yet without him we could not tell this story. At the conclusion of the trial it was on Johann Baptist Fickler that responsibility for preserving the records was to fall.

THE COUNCIL OF STATE

At dawn the following day, Karl Kulmer, the duke's chief justice, made his appearance in the Falcon Tower, accompanied by his clerk.[12] This routine visit was for the purpose of registering and checking the current state of the prison. By virtue of his commission, the chief justice was required to inspect the condition of the cells, the prisoners' diet, and their accommodation, and to receive a report from the ironmaster on any particular incidents. He visited prisoners newly committed to custody, questioned them on personal matters, and opened a file on each case.

This is what was done with the family of vagrants from Lower Bavaria. It was in the person of the chief justice that these prisoners were confronted for the first time with a representative of the court that was to decide their fate. For Karl Kulmer was not only a kind of chief commissioner of police, he was also a member of the council of state. Hence the early hour of his visit. He had to go straight from the Falcon Tower to a meeting of the council.

These meetings took place every morning in the Old Palace, formerly the duke's official residence in Munich. They began with divine service, attended by all the councillors, in the palace chapel, the hour specified being six in summer and seven in winter.

The council was presided over by its president who was required, in accordance with ducal decree,[13] to ensure "that each and every one of our councillors who is required to attend sessions of our council should be present at the appointed hour, viz. from St. George's Day to Michaelmas at six o'clock in the morning, without fail, that they should forthwith begin to deal with the current business of the council and continue thus with all due diligence and prudent application at least three full hours together."

The time was short enough: the agenda could scarcely be covered in three hours. It began with the discussion of civil actions, the first hearing of disputes involving privileged persons, or with appeals against judgments of the lower courts. Individual councillors who had studied the relevant documents reported briefly on the facts of each case and recommended a judgment. Then a vote was taken and the judgment dictated to the clerk in the form of a brief instruction. In this manner about ten or twenty civil actions could be dealt with each day—an inadequate number, for while the caseload increased constantly, the membership of the council scarcely grew at all.

The next item on the agenda concerned "the implementation and maintenance of public order and other matters of manuduction." This phrase masked an attempt to regulate the daily lives of the duke's Bavarian subjects down to the very last detail and to ensure that the decrees issued to this effect were observed. Fresh edicts had to be drafted, generally at the request of the duke: against ostentatious dress and excessive drinking, against the marriage of young Catholics into Protestant communities, against the sale of non-Catholic books, against mixed bathing, against dancing in the evenings, against extravagant weddings, against card games and skittles, against an unbridled increase in swearing and blasphemy, against fortune telling and superstition, against vagrancy and highway robbery.

Commands, ordinances, edicts, prohibitions. It was not difficult to issue them; to enforce them was often impossible. A uniformed police force, such as the modern state employs to superintend its subjects, was unknown in the year 1600. Under William V, therefore, a system of informers had been set up.[14] Agents and spies were recruited whose duty was dutifully and diligently "to note and report" all infringements of the duke's edicts. These secret agents in the pay of the authorities sat incognito in the taverns, eavesdropping on peasants and townsfolk; frequented weddings, dances, card games, and skittle parties; dogged the footsteps of farmhands and servant girls, pried into living rooms and closets. The reward for eventual denunciations: a share of any fines imposed and favorable consideration when it came to the allocation of official posts—which speaks volumes concerning the qualities of character required of a Bavarian civil servant at that time. To preclude the risk of unfounded or partisan denunciations—a risk that was, after all, taken into account—the informers were subject to supervision by even more secret observers. The reigning duke thought very highly of this system of surveillance, recommended that it be still further extended, and, despite his usual tightfistedness, even instructed his officials to spare no expense to that end. He could see no other way of forcing his subjects to observe his decrees. He felt he had a duty to do so, believing he was answerable to God for the temporal and eternal well-being of the subjects entrusted to his care.

In one area at least the system of informers was a manifestly ineffective weapon: in the battle against the hazards of the highways in the duchy. Merchants were attacked where no watchers were posted, farms set on fire when no witnesses were present. All the decrees issued against "masterless vagrants, tramps, beggars, hucksters, gypsies, and suchlike godforsaken rabble" failed to reduce the number of murders and robberies—a fact that filled the duke and his council of state with impotent rage. The situation was grotesque. On the one hand, every utterance offensive to the Catholic faith, every absence from Mass was punished, the length of women's dresses was prescribed, every banquet considered too opulent was liable to be penalized. On the other hand, arson and murder were perpetrated with impunity on highway and farm. In 1598 the sovereign noted "with especial displeasure and most gracious disapprobation" that all his ordinances designed to curb the general insecurity of his realm were in vain. He once more gave instructions that officers should be sent out on patrol to restore order. A hopeless enterprise: the country was huge, the state of the roads catastrophic, a mounted courier the most rapid means of communication. By 1599 at the latest, the authorities in Munich had to resign themselves to the fact that even the ordinance instituting a "regular and general patrol" was a fiasco. No doubt the duke and his councillors were racking their brains at this time to think of some other remedy—and there was only one that could be put into practice: these pestilential robbers and arsonists would have to be deterred by a show trial involving one or more of them. This may well be how the idea of setting an example by means of a large-scale, sensational show trial was conceived at a full sitting of the council in 1599: one or two members of the "godforsaken rabble" would be picked out and given such exemplary sentences that the whole duchy would be talking of nothing else.

No minutes were kept of such discussions in the council of state. For that reason I cannot guarantee that the idea of a show trial was the reason why the Pappenheimer family were brought to the Falcon Tower and their case made the concern of the duke himself—but I can see no more plausible explanation.

If it is correct, then the chief justice's announcement that the malefactors from Altmannstein had been committed to the Falcon Tower the previous day would have reminded the council of the security considerations that had prompted this step. Oh, yes, that bunch of vagrants, the councillors will have thought. They were not familiar with the details of the case; they knew only from the Altmannstein transcripts that it suited their purpose. They were ignorant as to the guilt or innocence of the prisoners. Nevertheless, the Pappenheimers' fate had been sealed simply by the fact of their transfer to Munich, for they had been brought there only for the sake of the hoped-for effect their gruesome punishment might create.

Now that the family of vagrants had arrived, they would have to be questioned at length and convicted of as many as possible of the crimes associated with such itinerant folk. For this purpose a commission had to be formed which would carry out the interrogations in the Falcon Tower. One of the commissioners chosen from the membership of the council would also have to act as chief investigator, familiarizing himself with all aspects of the case, preparing interrogations, and reporting the results from time to time at full sessions of the council.

Allocation of this kind of responsibility was a matter for the president of the council. The procedure was no doubt much the same as it is nowadays when one member of a group of busy people has to be saddled with a troublesome and time-consuming task. Wolf Konrad von Rechberg must have glanced at his list of assignments and then looked round his colleagues in some perplexity.

None of the aristocrats within the council[15]—Ernst von Roming, Albrecht Pronner, Hans Winkelmair, Ulrich Speerstein, Martin Haimbl, Martin Rieger, and Theodor Vischpecker—wanted anything to do with criminal cases. Most of them owed their seat on the council to their membership of the duke's entourage; few had any legal training. One of them might possibly serve as the

23

second member required by law to be present at any examination, but none was competent to act as chief investigator. Except for one: Ernst von Roming, but he was treasurer of the Munich exchequer, was responsible for supervising thirty prefectures, and had to go on circuit annually throughout his administrative area, passing sentences in criminal cases which were his delegated responsibility. The prosecution of the vagrants certainly fell within his jurisdiction, but, given his other obligations, he could scarcely be expected to deal with it in any detail. This is exactly what he said when he was asked whether he would take on the business.

So someone had to be picked from among the scholars on the council. All those who sat there were doctors of law: Johann Gailkirchner, Christoph Rumbler, Johann Baptist Fickler, Manfred Poitzhaim, Johann Simon Wangereck, Otto Forstenheuser, Franciscus Soll, Matthaeus Pittelmair, Wilhelm Wailheimer, Christoph Gewold, Georg Jobst, Jakob Hainmüller. We can imagine how the president's gaze must have moved from one to the other, as they, well aware of his scrutiny, busied themselves with the documents on the table in front of them and studiously avoided his eye. Old Fickler—supposing he was actually present at that meeting of the council—may perhaps have expressed an interest in assuming this responsibility, but was probably informed, not without a certain amount of embarrassment and apologetic evasiveness, that, however much they esteemed his learning and zeal, they would not wish to expose him to the rigors of such a task. Johann Gailkirchner, on the other hand, might well be in the running—he too was a recognized legal expert, although no longer as young as he might be. But he was not at all keen to take on a criminal case—he had specialized in civil actions, from which he profited in obscure and devious ways. And Christoph Gewold, the schemer, still in his late thirties and already in a position of the greatest influence, would obviously refuse. The duke burdened him with all kinds of major political assignments, he would have no time for the Falcon Tower. And so it had to be Johann Simon Wangereck, a rabble-rouser. It would not be surprising if it was he who had first raised the idea of a show trial. He had a good deal of experience with criminal cases, at any rate. He certainly knew how to make such riffraff talk. And, what was more, he enjoyed the full confidence of the duke.

For these or for other reasons, Wangereck was chosen as chief investigator in this case. The subject of the vagabonds confined in the Falcon Tower had been disposed of for the present.

But the meeting continued. There were other criminal proceedings at a more advanced stage that had to be discussed. After that there were matters of government policy on the agenda, for the council of state was not simply a central administrative body supervising the local authorities of Burghausen, Landshut, and Straubing; it also had to perform all the functions of government, controlling trade and commerce in the fiscal area of Munich, fixing the annual beer tax, keeping the local clergy in their place, ensuring proper discipline in the local monasteries, exhorting Protestant noblemen to convert to Catholicism, taking decisions on petitions submitted to it, and so on and so forth. It had any number of matters to deal with, and the decision concerning the prosecution of the vagrant family in the Falcon Tower was certainly looked on as one of the less important issues.

AN EXAMINATION

Master Georg had been expecting the visit. On this 17 April in the year 1600, in spite of the early hour, his living room on the ground floor of the Falcon Tower had already been put in order for the worshipful gentlemen. The commissioners delegated by the council—Doctor Wangereck, Doctor Hainmüller, and Treasurer von Roming—entered, accompanied by a clerk, and took their places on the rough wooden chairs set out for them. The ironmaster was ordered to "bring in the small boy who had been brought from Altmannstein."

So the child was first: that was good legal practice.[16] Legal scholars taught that "the most feeble and timid" in a group of malefactors should always be questioned first. You open an oyster at its weakest point. And so the boy, fetched by Master Georg from his mother's cell and brought downstairs, found himself gazing into the stern faces of the gentlemen assembled in Master Georg's living room. Councillor Wangereck was holding a sheet of paper containing the questions he proposed to ask. At the other side of the table, we may suppose, sat the clerk, with paper, freshly sharpened quills, and a portable inkwell set out in front of him. As Wangereck, after a brief glance at his list of questions, proceeded to ask the boy his name and his parents' names, we can visualize the clerk at his table dipping his pen briskly into the black fluid and noting down the answer.

It was as follows: he was Hänsel ("Johnny") Pämb, now aged ten or eleven. His father was Paulus Pämb from Ansbach, who earned an honest living emptying privies, which was why he was called Pappenheimer (the name given to those who performed that lowly service). His mother was called Änndl ("Annie"). They were both imprisoned here, as were his brothers, Michel and Gumpp. He had always lived with his parents, and knew how to make knitted bonnets. Hans Scheiflinger, an innkeeper on the River Lend near Regensburg had been his godfather. His parents were well acquainted with Scheiflinger and had often stayed at his inn. The last time had been in the winter just past, when they had been emptying the cesspools at a noble gentleman's castle not far from Regensburg.

Had they always had enough to eat at home? the councillor wanted to know. Yes, said the boy, as far as he was concerned it was always enough: bread, milk, thin broth, meat only rarely. His father had not earned a great deal emptying privies, but they had mostly had enough to eat. Sometimes they could even afford a beer or a measure of wine, which his parents had had sent into their quarters. It was his mother who managed the household. Whatever his father earned emptying privies and his brothers earned as glaziers, they handed over to her, and she bought the essential provisions. His eldest brother, Gumpp, however, had not been able to contribute very much because he was often sick and had the fever.

Whereupon the councillor asked: Where had they been the previous summer? In and around Kelheim, Abensberg, and Altmannstein, the child replied. They had gone on emptying privies even during the summer, although it was anything but a pleasant job in hot weather on account of the stench and the flies that pestered them. But if a privy was full, then it just had to be done. The brothers had done a bit of glazing as well, and his mother had gone begging. The councillor: Hadn't they also gone to fairs? The child: Not often, because you met all sorts of bad company, folk they had steered clear of for fear of ending up like them. His brother Michel had once told him that one of these shady fellows often carried four or five guns or other weapons around with him. But they had never had anything to do with that sort of riffraff, and had gone their way as honest folk should. They had not charged people too much for their work, either, so that people were glad to see them wherever they went. And they had never spent the night in fields, in woods, or at the roadside, like common tramps, but had always had a roof over their heads.

How often had he been in Arbach? Never. He had never heard

the name, at any rate. And even supposing they had ever been there, they had certainly never done anything wrong. Many people had said of them that they wouldn't be wandering round the country in such rags and tatters if they were up to no good. After this prelude it seemed to the councillor that the time had come to put questions that were more directly to the point. Did he know Geindl? No, said the boy. Wangereck: It was time he stopped this barefaced lying. The child answered hesitantly, yes, it was true; he had seen Geindl from time to time at fairs, but his parents had always kept well out of his way. The councillor: He might as well admit that Geindl had been an accomplice of theirs and had drunk and caroused with them. The child: He knew nothing about that. Even if his peole had drunk and enjoyed themselves in Geindl's company, they still hadn't done anything bad in his company. Perhaps Geindl had said that about them, and that was why Herr von Haslang in Altmannstein had asked them about it, but it wasn't true.

The councillor: Why was he denying things that his brothers had long since admitted? There were ways of making him talk. The child: If he said a lot, it would be the death of his whole family. He couldn't say anything anyway. His brothers had told him about their confessions: that they had stolen money and clothing from a farmer near Straubing. But none of that was true, and so it had turned out when inquiries were made. Apart from that, they had been tortured so much that they had confessed to fourteen murders—and that was a pack of lies as well. When they had been brought here from Altmannstein, his mother had said he should tell the truth, and his brothers had said the same. The councillor: Hadn't he seen the severed hands of dead children in his brothers' possession? The child began to cry, looking desperately from side to side. The councillor: Out with it! Where were the children's hands? The child: Never saw any.

What followed we can imagine more or less: the councillor rises angrily to his feet and orders the ironmaster to take the child to the place where he will be subjected to questioning under torture. The warden takes the struggling child from the room and leads the way down into the vaults beneath the tower. The other gentlemen also stand up. The clerk picks up the page on which he has just been writing and waves it in the air to dry the ink; then he gathers up his paper and pens, puts the stopper back in his inkwell, crams everything into his leather pouch, pushes back his chair, and stands up. The party leave Master Georg's living room, exchanging a few remarks such as "What a hard-boiled little scoundrel!" and "Maybe he really doesn't know anything" or "It's getting on for midday, perhaps we should stop soon." And so they go down the steps into the cellars. The conversation ceases: it is not easy to find the next step in the gloom. The door to the vault is ajar. Master Georg has lighted the tallow candles in the two holders.

In the dank chamber stands the trembling boy. Chains on the walls, a winch fastened to the ceiling. He knows what these implements are for—and the stone weights on the shelf, too. A hearth, with iron pincers hanging on hooks nearby. In the corner is a pile of ropes of various thicknesses. On the wall above, a selection of rods and birches. The worshipful gentlemen enter the vault one after the other, the door bangs to behind them. They sit down on benches and stools at the massive wooden table. The clerk unpacks his pouch.

Councillor Wangereck calls the ironmaster over, murmurs instructions to him. The boy's linen shirt is removed. He begins to cry. His hands are bound in front of him, he is pushed across to the wall, and the free end of the rope is fastened to an iron ring. So now the wailing child stands with his arms stretched above his head and fastened to the wall, his eyes turning anxiously to Master Georg. The ironmaster chooses one of the rods from his stock, shows it to the councillor, and, at a nod from him, steps up to the boy. Wangereck raises his hand to indicate that the torture may begin. The jailor draws back his arm, then the rod strikes the child's bare back. A scream of pain, red weals on the slender body. And now another blow. And another, and another, again and again. The child sags, whimpering, but he cannot fall down, for his wrists are tied to the ring in the wall. The councillor makes a sign to the ironmaster once again; he puts down his rod, unfastens the rope from the wall, helps the sobbing child onto his feet, and leads him back to face the worshipful gentlemen. He has now learned, Wangereck says to him, where his lies will get him. He has told the ironmaster to desist so as to give the boy a chance to confess. If he continues to be so stubborn, they will have to go on flogging him until he thinks better of it. He will ask once more whether the boy has seen children's hands in his brothers' possession, and what they had done with them? The boy, in tears, replies Yes, yes. He has seen the hands of seven children in his brothers' possession. The councillor: And where had they gotten these hands? The child: In three cases they had cut them off beggar children.

The councillor: How had they gotten the others? The child: They had simply murdered big-bellied women who might give birth at any time, slit their bellies open—and hacked off the children's hands. The councillor: And what had they used the hands for? The child: For all sorts of magic. In the first place, you could heal sicknesses with the children's hands, but you could also inflict harm on other people. And finally they could be useful for murdering or stealing. He himself had seen Geindl giving his brothers dried and crushed children's hands to eat, hidden in a freshly baked roll. Not to make them ill, but so that they could murder people more easily. And this was how they began to commit murders right away. They had told him they could not help themselves, once they had eaten that roll: they simply had to do it. But the moment they were arrested and taken to Altmannstein, they said, the effect stopped. They could no longer commit such atrocities, even if they had been set free straight away. The magic had vanished from their heads.

The child falls silent. Wangereck looks at him searchingly and says nothing. Then he tells the ironmaster to put the prisoner back in his cell, they have done enough for today. Master Georg frees the boy's hands, tells him to put his shirt back on. The heavy door swings open, the child is pushed from the room. Master Georg takes him back to his cell.

So it must have been, more or less. The gentlemen will have risen from their seats, exchanged a few words to break the tension. As he rose, Wangereck presumably handed his list of questions to the clerk, who put it with the pages of notes he had written in the course of the morning and concluded his transcript with the line: "It being then the twelfth hour of noon, he was let go for the time being." We are familiar with the course of this first examination because the record of it, along with the record of all the other interrogations, has been preserved. Nevertheless, there is more that we might wish to know. For instance: what went on in the hearts and minds of the men who were present at the examination?

WANGERECK

Let us take a closer look at one of these men. He was in his mid-thirties, uncouth yet learned, a committed zealot, arrogant and fawning. His name: Johann Simon (some sources call him Johann Siegmund) Wangereck, or Wangeregg, or Wagnereck;[17] he himself wrote his name now this way, now that—orthography was not at all important in those days. The chief investigator, hence the crucial figure in the prosecution of our vagrants, was a Lower Bavarian through and through, with the sluggish blood of his breed, which could nevertheless seethe with sudden passion.

He was born, as far as we know, in Neuötting, by the green waters of the Inn, where the fields are fertile, the meadows lush, the churches numerous, and the people Catholic. The germ of insurrection that had been rife even in many parts of Bavaria during the sixteenth century had never perplexed the minds of those who dwelt in this region. During their childhood, Johann Simon and his brothers had never heard from the mouths of their father, their preacher, or their schoolmaster anything other than virulent condemnation of the Lutheran heresy, which, thank God, had spared their little town. Edifying and heart-warming tales were told, on the other hand, of the God-fearing Duke Albrecht, who held court up in Munich and down in Landshut, accompanied by a tame lion, surrounded by painters, musicians, and mentors in clerical garb. It was told how with saintly cunning and pious deception he had enticed to Munich the renegade Count von Ortenburg, who had thrown his estates open to the heretical preachers. There he had imprisoned the count, seized his land, and placed him on trial—a luridly embroidered tale that served as an introduction to the Bavarian politics of the age. The Wangerecks were subject to this artful zealot in two senses: he was both their monarch and their employer, for Wangereck senior had been appointed customs officer under his rule. He retained his post when Albrecht V died in 1579 and was succeeded by a son, William V, who much resembled him. Wangereck was even promoted, kept his authority to collect tolls, and, in addition, assumed the honorable burden of a seat and a vote in the ducal administration of nearby Burghausen. People in high places were graciously inclined toward the Wangerecks; that was shown repeatedly through the years. Duke Maximilian consented to the transfer of the customs appointment to Johann Simon's elder brother while Wangereck senior was still alive; and a little later the duke elevated the family to the nobility in recognition of the exciseman's forty years of service.

What was the reason for so much grace and favor, a benign rain in which Wangereck's sons too were destined to flourish? There were plenty of honest officials in the duchy, but very few were elevated to such remarkable eminence. We are inclined to think that the special gratitude of the duke was somehow connected with

30

the minor trade war Bavaria was waging at the time against her neighbor, Salzburg. Wangereck senior was a kind of skirmisher occupying a strategically important position, for his customs post controlled the stream of goods that flowed—more hither than thither—between the Salzburg town of Mühldorf and archbishop's principal territories on the Salzach and the Inn: mainly salt from Hallein, but also copper and lead, Italian spices, oils and cloth, wine and herring, almonds and rice. Many a well-lined purse tempted the exciseman to turn a blind eye, but it seems that Wangereck was steadfastly loyal.

His loyalty soon paid dividends as far as his son Johann Simon was concerned. Everything points to the fact that he was permitted to attend the Jesuit college in Munich, perhaps not from the beginning but certainly from the secondary-school level onward. There he seems to have acquired his knowledge of Latin, a stilted kind of pulpit German, and the fanatical religious faith propagated by the Jesuits. The lush rustic delights of Neuötting were succeeded, then, by lean years of cramming verbs and learning by rote. No other path led to the ducal court, and that was the only place where it was possible to better oneself socially. The next step followed on 12 March 1585 [18]—entrance to the University of Ingolstadt. He registered as "Joannes Simon Vnagger Eckius studiosus iuris" and was not exempt from the matriculation fee of 14 kreuzer, which suggests that his father, although he may have kept his eyes open as he collected his dues, had not remained poor. His son's studies cost him a good deal: the expenses of a year's study were reckoned to be at least 250 gulden, which was equivalent to the starting salary of a state councillor. A contemporary who, it is true, had studied in Italy as well as in Ingolstadt estimated the total cost of his studies at 15,000 gulden, although he had "studied assiduously" while "paying his fair share as student custom required." [19]

Student custom: there was no room for the fastidious here. Our hero from Lower Bavaria no doubt enjoyed this mode of life more than the respectability of his strict Munich college. "A good many parents would sooner permit their children to go off to war than see them go to Ingolstadt": no less a personage than Duke William V described student life in Ingolstadt in these terms. "Bestial guzzling and boozing," gambling and general hullabaloo late into the night—these were the more innocuous varieties of student custom. Taverns demolished from sheer spite and nocturnal pranks played on nervous townsfolk in terror of the swords the students wore—that was even worse. But it didn't stop there. Brawls, stabbings, saber duels were the order of the day, and there were deaths almost every term. We have reason to suppose that Wangereck, dour as he was but prone to fits of sudden rage, was much attracted by this aspect of academic life. He was not the man to stand aloof when quarrels broke out, much less to mediate; he surely took sides and thus formed many lasting friendships, acquired many bitter enemies. Jakob Hainmüller, for instance, the councillor who had sat next to Wangereck during the examination of little Hänsel Pämb, was an old classmate from Ingolstadt. It was there, too, that Wangereck had made the acquaintance of his colleagues Christoph Rumbler, Martin Rieger, Franciscus Soll, and Christoph Gewold, who later turned out to be a notorious schemer. A few terms senior to Wangereck, Gewold was presumably his much admired model; at any rate Wangereck was his devoted disciple and doughty comrade-in-arms.

The law faculty at Ingolstadt in those days was hardly an illustrious one.[20] The only teacher who enjoyed any sort of renown was an Italian, Andreas Fachineus, but Wangereck would not have come across him until his concluding terms. Otherwise the standard was embarrassingly mediocre; nevertheless it seems to have sufficed for the legal knowledge required of a councillor. Training in criminal law was based—as was the whole course—on the Corpus Juris, the imperial Roman law; it was conducted in conformity with a section of that classical legal authority known as "the terrible books." Otherwise, the students were supposed to familiarize themselves with the penal code promulgated by Emperor Charles V in 1532. They had ten years to do this, the average length of the course. Apart from the lectures there were various other academic exercises arranged by the professors when they had nothing better to do. Occasionally there were day-long debates, discourses held in the Auditorium Maximum and followed by discussion. Whether Johann Simon Wangereck learned a great deal in Ingolstadt it is hard to say. His graduation with the degree of Doctor proves nothing: it involved no proper examination but was simply an exorbitantly expensive formal ceremony, the purchase of promotion up the social scale, a welcome supplement to a professor's salary. University teachers were not everywhere such mediocrities as they were in Ingolstadt, where the term *professor* was taken rather too literally: every teacher had to swear an oath annually on the Professio Tridentis, the current creed of the Catholic church. Europe's better minds refused to accept this constraint and steered clear of the Bavarian academic domain.

Scarcely had Wangereck paid for his doctorate, thanks to the fiscal labors of his father, when he found himself once more in the genial radiance of ducal favor. This may be taken literally, for he was one of the chosen few who were permitted to accompany the twenty-one-year-old Duke Maximilian to the Imperial Diet in Regensburg on 9 May 1594. No doubt someone had given him a helping hand, and it looks very much as if that someone had been Dr. Christoph Gewold,[21] the admired hero of his rowdy student days. In the intervening years, Gewold—a convert, incidentally, from the reformed town of Amberg—had been recommended to the duke by the Jesuits and taken into the service of the court. He had already wormed his way into the entourage of the reigning duke and his heir apparent; had made an impression by reason of intelligence, resourcefulness, and an obsequious manner; and had already begun to devise schemes, work out long-term plans, and recruit devoted accomplices. Johann Simon Wangereck became one such accomplice.

The exciseman's son joined the council of state immediately as a freshly graduated doctor, and seems to have rapidly made his name there. He was soon numbered among those councillors who were asked for an opinion in difficult legal issues. He was reckoned to be widely read and erudite, at least among those colleagues who were his friends. Others called him a hothead, an opinionated numskull. We can tell that there were factions within the council of state that had very little time for each other.[22] The group around Gewold, to the inner circle of which Johann Simon Wangereck belonged, usually stayed behind after the meeting and discussed a great many matters. It was said that the more experienced among them helped their less talented associates draft the reports they had to present to the full council. They also recommended each other for various special appointments on the grounds that they were learned, upright, and zealous Catholics. They had not a good word, on the other hand, for those councillors who did not belong to their circle.

Wangereck was given to fits of rage during meetings; he adopted an offensive manner and an implacable stance. Malicious rumors claimed that he was mixed up in various shady deals: he was wont to accept payment for legal advice given to individuals who were parties to actions that were to be decided by the council. He was allegedly both judge and a secretly commissioned advocate: in other words, venal. These allegations were never clarified; an inquiry set up at the instigation of two attorneys came to no conclusion.

In the field of criminal law, Wangereck was particularly interested in the crime of witchcraft. He possessed a volume of Martin Delrio's legal manual on witchcraft entitled *Disquisitiones Magicarum*. From this and other relevant literature he derived the firm conviction that witches and sorcerers should be prosecuted ruthlessly. Once, when an alleged witch had endured every degree of torture without confessing her guilt, one of the learned councillors proposed that she should be set free as having been "purged." Wangereck, on the other hand, demanded that fresh grounds for suspicion should be sought as justification for a resumption of the torture. This would be illegal, declared the other councillor, for, in accordance with established judicial procedure, suspicion had to precede the application of torture, and not the other way round. In any case, it appeared that the prisoner was "a simplicitas or simpleton," a harmless, crazy woman.

At that point, so we are reliably informed,[23] Wangereck leaped to his feet, interrupted his colleague, and proceeded to upbraid him in front of the whole council: he had no need to be coached in the law; after all, he was himself a Doctor of Laws and, what was more, a full member of the duke's council of state. His colleague, on the other hand, obviously had no idea of the true nature of such sorcerers and was not aware that they merely pretended to be simple-minded. He ought to consult the authorities on the subject more carefully. And, anyway, what did he mean by "crazy" in this context? And much more in this vein. With the result that the council decided to admit the original grounds for suspicion as justification for a new inquisition. The simpleton was sufficiently intelligent to commit suicide in time to avoid this.

When this incident took place, the prosecution of our vagrants was already underway. No doubt there were differences of opinion here as well. Wangereck was always prudent enough, when he went to the Falcon Tower, to take with him both the treasurer and another councillor who was well disposed to him. That was the case with Dr. Hainmüller and also with Dr. Vagh, both younger fellow students from Ingolstadt and members of the Gewold group.

At the time of the trial, Wangereck was married to a wealthy woman and was father to a five-year-old son. The family occupied a house on the Dienerstrasse,[24] just around the corner from the Old Palace. Ducal favor continued to flow to the exciseman's son from Lower Bavaria in the form of gratuities and honorable assignments, a gracious stream that was never to dry up. The manner in which this phlegmatic and irascible expert on witchcraft pounced on the case of the vagrants from Lower Bavaria may well have demonstrated once more to the duke that he had not squandered his favors on someone who was unworthy of them.

THE GRAVEDIGGER'S DAUGHTER

Early on the morning of the 18 April, Wangereck, Treasurer von Roming, young Councillor Hainmüller, and the clerk assigned to assist them, Sebastian Steinwandner, reentered the ironmaster's living-room in the Falcon Tower. Immediately afterward the prisoners heard steps on the stairs, the jangle of keys. Master Georg opened the door of the cell in which the boy was lying with his mother. He had to be questioned again, the jailor said, or words to that effect; the worshipful gentlemen who had come yesterday were here again. Whatever his words, he certainly dragged the boy away from his mother and through the door, which was locked once more. How might the mother have reacted? That kind of thing is not recorded in any transcript. Perhaps she hammered hysterically on the oaken planks and screamed; perhaps she called after her child as he was led away; perhaps she just sat there listlessly on the straw. It is hardly possible to reconstruct emotionally what was going on in her mind as they led the child away to be questioned again, the same child they had brought back tortured and lacerated from the previous day's hearing. There is much to suggest that she buried her pain within herself, bore it in bitter animosity, too numbed by suffering to revolt.

She was an old woman who in all her fifty-nine years had been on the losing side. She had come into the world as Anna Conz in what is now the Franconian town of Ansbach but was then the capital of the margravate of the same name. Her father was a gravedigger and hence, according to the opinion of the time, a social outcast. Even as a child she was forbidden to associate with the children of "respectable" citizens. There could be no thought of education or social advancement. Later on, it was difficult to find a husband. The children of such outcasts were not permitted to take part in balls or dances arranged for the benefit of respectable folk. And even laborers and servant girls thought themselves a cut above the gravedigger's daughter and excluded her from their parties. She was already twenty when she finally met Paulus, a worker in the Ansbach brickyard.

He too was an "outcast," doubly so, in fact, and a foreigner into the bargain, as his Swabian dialect revealed. He came from

35

Hüttlingen, a small place between Ellwangen and Aalen, where his father had worked as a linen weaver—a trade that was also despised. His other blemish was worse still: he was an illegitimate child, although it is not clear whether his blood bond was with his mother, Agatha, or with the linen weaver. He himself maintained that he had "been fathered out of wedlock," although by that he may not have meant his mother's husband, for he called himself not only "Gämperl," which was the linen weaver's name, but also "Pämb" or "Pämbs," which may have been his mother's maiden name. In any case, he was the black sheep of a family that was itself looked at askance. That was made clear to him at an early age by a number of stepbrothers, whose disdainful sneers made his childhood a torment. There was no comfort to be had of his parents; that they had treated him "ill and a mite harshly," was how Paulus characterized such domestic brutalities. He could scarcely walk before he ran away from the teasing and the torments, wandered about, as he said, "like any young shaver," was recaptured and brought back home, where he got a good thrashing. He put up with his lot as a stepchild for a time, then absconded once more; wandered about for days on end, his empty stomach rumbling; slept in the hay; picked wild berries on the banks of the Jagst; went begging, tattered and grimy, for a morsel of bread in Jagsthausen, Westhausen, or Lauchheim; trudged back home half-starved and suffered the beating he had earned by his flight. Until one day, when he had "grown somewhat stronger," he turned his back for ever on the linen weaver's cottage that he detested, determined only to get as far away as possible. On the way, the fourteen-year-old boy asked peasants for work, which he was ready to do in return for a meal and a place to bed down in the barn. In this way he sometimes "herded pigs," mucked out stables, drove the muck cart. And then he moved on, doubtless propelled by sheer restlessness but also because, tempted by a favorable opportunity, he had pocketed a spoon, a platter, and a cloth he found in an unlocked chest, trifles which might be exchanged in the next village for something useful or edible.

Some years later—he was eighteen—he apparently came to rest. He found work in the Ansbach brickyard, settled down, became hardworking and honest. Soon he met a young woman. She also had suffered from the contemptuous looks and the turned-up noses of her neighbors, although she had always had the comfort of loving parents. She was two years older than the laborer in the brickyard; she took him under her wing and tried to put him on the right path.

Her father was asked to help his future son-in-law, and hence to help his daughter, whereupon he nominated the foreigner with the Swabian twang as his assistant. Work on the brick kilns had been hard and ill-paid. Now Paulus Pämb could be seen digging graves with the old man and sharing the night watch. Soon he married Anna—a pauper's wedding, to be sure, but one that offered the prospect of a calm and secure future. For when Anna's father retired, his assistant could move into his place and have an income for the rest of his life that was secure, even if despised by most people.

At that point Anna probably thought that she had overcome the blindly irrational power of destiny. In fact, she was once again on the losing side, and should have known it. Still, for three or four years everything went well. By day, Paulus shoveled the soil of the graveyard as required, by night he did his rounds as watchman. Anna had children in rapid succession, the young family grew. And then disaster struck.

They had ventured on a journey to Nuremberg, possibly to visit relatives of Anna's. The occasion was a cheerful one, at any rate, for they were in high spirits. After a few days in the imperial city, however, traces of ill-humor manifested themselves in the case of the young husband, who reckoned that his wife's gaiety was somewhat overdone. There was a soldier for whom Anna showed more partiality than was good for the wavering self-confidence of a newly married assistant gravedigger. There were wordless glances that told the jealous husband more than he could stomach. Then Anna withdrew in a conspicuously discreet manner and was absent for an inexplicably long time. And then, finally, there was a local milliner, who surprised the soldier, whom she regarded as her own, in a less than ambiguous situation with the wife of the Swabian from Ansbach, whereupon she hastened forthwith to the cuckolded husband and revealed everything. Fury seethed up in Paulus Pämb-Gämperl—the anger of a man who had constantly been rejected, baited, despised, mingled with the dismay of one betrayed and deserted. When his wife returned to the inn, he tackled her. She probably defended herself, or put on an air of injured innocence, which must have infuriated the deceived husband even more. Voices grew shrill, chairs crashed over, a body slumped to the floor.

When Paulus came to his senses again after his violent outburst and saw his young wife lying senseless on the floor, he realized what had happened. In his fury he had seized an iron pan filled with red-hot coals that was standing by the hearth and had hurled it at his wife's head. No need to call for help: the noise had already alarmed the neighbors. They laid the unconscious woman, who was scarcely breathing, on the straw mattress, applied a crude bandage, and felt sure she would die. The milliner was among those who had rushed in. She, the talebearer who had instigated the quarrel, urged the stupified husband to make good his escape before the authorities learned of his reckless deed. She would give him a hunk of money if he would get out of Nuremberg as fast as possible. For she readily admitted that she too had an interest in keeping the details of the business dark. All this she whispered insistently into the ear of the man who had been so cruelly brought to his senses.

But he pushed aside the purse that was offered him and would not hear of flight or escape; he was going to stay with his dying wife. He tended her as best he could in the days that followed. As though by a miracle, and possibly also because of the care lavished on her by her remorseful spouse, she survived the attack. She was quickly reconciled with her husband while they were still in Nuremberg. But she never recovered her health. Following this assault she suffered from sudden seizures, which afflicted her "often scarcely more than once a month, sometimes three times a week or a day," and was liable to lie unconscious for up to an hour. When she had fits of this kind, her husband and children forced "a little drop of wine" between her lips. They knew of no other remedy for this ailment, which they called "the falling sickness." It was probably epilepsy.

Apart from these attacks, Anna retained a scar on her cheek as a lasting memento of the Nuremberg incident. Nor was her life the same after that, for her husband had changed.

This became clear following the next misfortune that befell them shortly after they had returned home to Ansbach. There the young couple, who had in any case returned home considerably less elated than they had left, found the old gravedigger on his deathbed. His death was apparently the signal for Paulus to abandon for all time the thought of a tranquil and humble existence as gravedigger in Ansbach. His restlessness grew within him, like a disease, driving him out into the world, just as it had done when he was a boy. He made no attempt to take over the office of gravedigger: the last grave he dug was his father-in-law's. Possibly there were difficulties about taking over the job, but, if so, why did he not mention this motive for his departure, which would have shown him in a better light? I am inclined to think that he made a sudden decision, packed up his belongings, told his wife to get the children ready for the road, and became a vagrant henceforth.

Anna may or may not have protested, but she probably had no choice other than to accompany her husband. How could she ever feed her children by herself? Her father was dead and obviously she had no one but her husband. And so she had to travel the roads with Paulus, the children and their ludicrously meager possessions.

At the time of their arrest the marriage had lasted for thirty-seven years, and Anna had spent most of that time on the road. She had nonetheless borne seven children and managed to keep three of them alive. Given the circumstances of the time, this was remarkable, for even in middle-class households the infant mortality rate was almost as high.

Michel and Gumpprecht, who now lay shackled in separate cells in the Falcon Tower, had been born while the family was still in Ansbach; but only Gumpprecht, the elder son, had been baptized there. They were now twenty and twenty-two respectively and had some skill as glaziers and tinkers. Little Hänsel would not reach his eleventh birthday "until next Michaelmas." Clearly he was his mother's favorite.

But he had been taken away from his mother to be questioned once more. A dreadful misfortune had befallen the family, and there was yet worse to come. The old woman had no illusions. After all, she had all her life been on the side of those who were bereft of hope.

CHAPTER · 2

The winding cart tracks that passed for highways (woodcut of 1539)

· The Road

They left the margravate of Ansbach in 1580, so much is certain, although we do not know at what time of year. It was probably in May or June—a time when a great many individuals before Paulus Pämb-Gämperl, and after him, have been seized by wanderlust. We can see him and his Anna walking along the dusty highway beside the Schwabbach; he is carrying a bundle with their belongings on his shoulder and leading three-year-old Gumpprecht by the hand, while she carries little Michel. They were following the same road as before, when they had set out in blissful ignorance to visit relatives, for their destination was Nuremberg. Anna may have hoped, and Paulus may have persuaded himself, that they would find new contentment and a modest living there. An illusory hope and a vain attempt to allay their own fears. It ended badly, as we well know.

At first, however, the imperial city enticed them with its motley crowds and ostentatious prosperity. A sturdy young fellow might make his fortune there. The memory of a soldier and a fateful fit of fury might have been calculated to cast a dark shadow over such thoughts, but any man who sets off into the world is seeking to escape the past and is convinced that he has his face to the sun. Who thinks that far ahead in such circumstances? Prudence and planning ahead had no appeal for the young assistant gravedigger who craved only freedom. He had no idea what he and his family would live on while they were on the road. Perhaps the problem would solve itself in the wealthy city of Nuremberg.

It did not solve itself. They may have lodged for a time with their relatives there. It is difficult to imagine that these belonged to a different social stratum from Anna's own, have-nots crammed together in tiny rooms and barely able to feed themselves. Paulus never claimed subsequently that he had looked for honest employment in Nuremberg, and the search would in any case have been fairly pointless. The city did not tolerate "paupers" from elsewhere within its walls for any length of time. Too many rootless, unskilled starvelings crowded into the city, enticed by its brilliance and the chink of gulden, as children are drawn to the fairground. There they loafed about the streets, mingled with the chattering citizens who haggled in the markets, sprawled on the church steps, traveling folk, despised by the townspeople, looked on with suspicion by the authorities. And now the Gämperls belonged to this fraternity, were forced to associate with them and learn all kinds of wiles and ruses in order to escape starvation in this city of plenty.

They did not join the mercenary soldiers, that drunken, brawling, heavily armed gang who were waiting to be recruited anew and in the meantime practiced their martial trade on trembling merchants in ill-lit back streets. Nor did they join the somersaulting, fire-spouting, rope-dancing guild of entertainers and jugglers. They shunned the vociferous tribe of quacks, tooth pullers, and soothsayers. They did not acquire from itinerant tradesmen the art of card sharping or picking pockets. They joined the beggars on the church steps.

Begging was a profession in those days;[25] indeed, many people called it "the golden trade." In 1574, seven hundred beggars were registered in Nuremberg, a number far exceeding the members of all other professional groups. These registered almsmen were but the privileged municipal nucleus of the mendicant population. The majority, to which Paulus and his family belonged, consisted of outsiders who could remain in Nuremberg only as long as they were tolerated there. If they were expelled, they moved on to some other town.

In those days several thousand of them hung around taverns and private houses or loitered by the doors of churches and monasteries. They accosted the citizens in droves, wringing their hands, wailing and tearing their hair, so that their victims were forced to push their way through men kneeling in their path, children clinging to their legs, and women kissing their hands. These importunings were systematically organized: each morning the army of beggars was divided into groups and dispatched in accordance with a strategic plan to occupy all the suitable locations.

Beginners like the Pämb-Gämperls, of course, were assigned initially to the less lucrative sites—they had first to prove themselves. In this connection it was probably very useful for them to have two small children. For the art of begging, which is based, like every true art, on talent as well as practice, consists in the power to arouse pity. Given that proviso, begging as practiced in the circumstances of those days offered an extraordinary range of creative possibilities.[26] Some pretended to be blind, groped for the church steps with their sticks, gazing into the void, their palms stretched out before them. Others, fearfully deformed, their features contorted by pain, hobbled up to churchgoers, dragging a leg behind them. Some had lost both legs and pushed themselves along on little carts; others stalked up on crutches, dragging their limp bodies and displaying the sores in their armpits caused by the cross-pieces on their crutches. Others pulled faces, wordlessly, desperately gesticulating to indicate that they could neither hear nor speak. Others rattled rusty chains hanging from neck and wrists and proclaimed loudly that they had escaped from Turkish bondage. There were some who sidled up, bent double, to a well-dressed respectable couple, then rose whimpering and wailing in their path, baring their breasts to show the bleeding and festering sores of leprosy. To escape this repulsive sight and the supposed danger of infection, people hastily threw down a coin. Many of the beggars cast their eyes up to heaven, put a cross repeatedly to their lips and kissed it, scattered ashes on their heads, sang hymns or murmured prayers, all of which was supposed to prove that they were pious pilgrims. A few threw themselves into the path of hurrying passersby, writhing in convulsions calculated to arouse the onlookers' pity, deathly pale and foaming at the mouth. There was no limit to the ingenuity shown here. We may suppose that our couple from Ansbach were among those who displayed all the symptoms of people doomed to die of starvation, and that they held their pitifully bawling children up to the passing churchgoers.

The Nuremberg city council described the situation in the streets of the imperial city in 1588 as follows: "The general citizenry here is excessively inconvenienced by vagrants, beggars, and tramps, especially by the screaming and bawling of children both day and night in the streets and before the houses, boys and girls alike, and particularly in the winter season."[27] Everyone knew, of course, what Sebastian Brandt had written in his popular *World's Mirror, or Ship of Fools:* "Beggars befoul every land." Did the councillors expel these wretched creatures from the city, then?

Not exactly: they had no desire to get rid of all of the wringers of hands, the cripples, and the scatterers of ashes; they merely wished to have their number and the scale of the nuisance rather better controlled. The professional beggar, like every other tradesman, satisfied a need, the need for "charity." Christian charity and pious compassion could, after all, not be displayed publicly otherwise than with the assistance of these histrionically gifted scoundrels. For these virtues must indeed be displayed publicly. People needed a visible sign for everything that was real but not tangible. That applied to things like justice, honor, property, and abstract entities of that sort. Even such a common legal transaction as a purchase, conducted innumerable times daily, acquired its validity only through symbols. The ordinary citizen could hardly refrain from demonstrating his Christian convictions by outward show— not because he was a hypocrite but because, for the people of that age, genuine piety could not be visualized without some concrete expression of it. And so townsfolk and beggars needed each other: the former gave hard cash, the latter gave an easy conscience in return. The transaction also had an educative side effect: the public display of such wretchedness showed the meanest servant and the outcast shunned by his fellows how relatively well off they were in the urban community.

In the evening, this guild of scoundrels met to count the takings in some squalid tavern. Paulus and Anna, along with their children, would have been there as well, counting the coins they had begged, and paying for a hot meal and a jug of wine with the proceeds. While one of the assembled beggars pulled a flute from his doublet and began to play, another took a lute from the wall and strummed a few chords, one or two drinkers began to sing, many others joined in, beating time on the heavy wooden tables, rattling the jars and wooden plates. With the company in such high spirits, "Oh, then you might a wonder see: the blind regained their sight, the dumb began to talk, the crippled and the halt—they all began to walk: the mirth's complete, and then perchance, the beggar-folk begin to dance." This is how the scene was described in 1597.[28]

How long Paulus and his family remained in the fraternity of Nuremberg beggars we do not know. Certainly more than a few days but hardly longer than a month or two. There were close contacts with the authorities: one of the Nuremberg poor-law guardians had served as godfather to Michel. He would hardly have

46

urged the expulsion of the strangers, even if their name was not on the municipal list of registered beggars. It almost looks as if the restless father had set out on the road again of his own accord. Perhaps the little family joined up with other beggars on their way (via Neumarkt) to Regensburg, the next imperial city that tempted them with its splendor and the chink of gulden. There they started all over again wringing their hands, holding out their pathetic, crying children, who were well rehearsed by this time, begging tearfully for alms for the innocent creatures. That display may have prised open many a well-lined purse, but it did not open the hearts of the Regensburg poor-law guardians who, in the absence of that leniency derived from personal acquaintance, quickly dumped the foreign beggars outside the city gate.

As far as I can gather, Paulus, his wife, and his children now moved on down the Danube, entering Lower Bavarian territory for the first time. People of his sort were not particularly welcome there. The duke of Bavaria occasionally decreed "most solemnly, that henceforth all foreign and alien beggars, lepers, mendicant Jacobin friars, and suchlike that do roam and rove from one land to another, together with pilgrims and palmers that are not known or have elsewhere their known dwelling or have no lawful permit or license, be not suffered to remain in our realms but be evicted wheresoever they be found."[29] The duke's prefects and officers will have read these stern words with a sigh, and then put the document away with other decrees to the same effect. His Grace was asking for the impossible; the land was large, its frontiers long, the roads too many.

THE BEAT

The first town visited by our vagrant family of beggars in what was then the duchy of Bavaria was Straubing. It could not compare with the magnificence of an imperial city, but here too was the lure of hard cash. The town on the Danube had recently experienced a wave of ostentatious prosperity arising from a combination of political circumstances. The ragged strangers must have gaped in astonishment as they made their way across a marketplace overflowing with precious wares.[30]

There were merchants from the distant Netherlands with a rich variety of materials spread out in front of them, brightly embroidered or brilliantly colored, diaphanous or sumptuously warm; Brussels lace; English broadcloth; textiles from Mechelen, Louvain, Arras, and the Wetterau. Stalls stacked high and almost swamped with merchandise from the Levant and Venice jostled for space: chests with cinnamon; bags of saffron and ginger; bales of cotton; casks full of figs, bitter oranges, and exotically scented candied lemon peel; baskets full of locust pods, almonds, and mace; sacks of sugar and pepper; casks of wine; wooden sandals tied together in strings; writing tablets and boxes of chalk, great rolls of writing paper; braid trimming; veils as flimsy as spider's webs; velvet and silk. And that was not all: from Bohemia there were leathers in every shade of brown, copper foil that gleamed like gold, drinking glasses, bottles, and jugs of green glass, ocher-colored lumps of beeswax; from Russia there were herrings in open crates; from the Tirol, wine in little scarlet kegs. In a rectangle fenced off with hurdles, oxen that had been driven up from Hungary were bellowing; next to them, horses were being offered for sale. Here, there, and everywhere were stalls with Regensburg pottery, elaborately stacked mounds of local fruit and vegetables, seed for the farmers, and pewter plates for the townsfolk. At one point stood a salesman vociferously extolling his sheep and goats; at another, someone was holding up a cage containing an exotic oriental bird. A hubbub of voices, cackling, screeching, bellowing, and bleating! There was haggling and wavering, measuring and weighing, waving of arms and shaking of heads! Peasants in their Sunday best, craftsmen, townsfolk of the meaner sort made up the crowd of curious spectators, but there were also wholesale merchants from Regensburg, Nuremberg, and Augsburg, sampling a fig here, sniffing a tub of mace there, fingering the textiles, holding up a glass against the light. There were even ladies of the upper class with their servants, while gentlemen clad in velvet with white walking-sticks made their way through the throng, greeted on all sides by deep bows and the doffing of hats.

There were old acquaintances, too. In recesses round the marketplace stood the clowns, the quacks, and the fortune-tellers, each surrounded by a cluster of onlookers. In disreputable hostelries and at gaming tables sat the saber-rattling, beer-swilling, foul-mouthed soldiery. Pickpockets and cutpurses darted through the crowds of gaping spectators, and here and there in small groups were wailing beggarfolk. In the midst of such a seething mass of people there was room of course for our family of beggars.

After this first visit they continued to turn up at the Straubing fair more or less regularly for some twenty years. For Paulus Pämb-

Gämperl went no farther. Not that he put down roots in this thriving commercial center of Lower Bavaria: he merely cast anchor here, and circulated round the town for two whole decades, as though on a long chain. He and his family never came to rest, never settled down, but always remained within the area which they had now chosen as their own. They traveled down the Danube as far as Passau and upstream as far as Ingolstadt; they followed the course of the Danube's tributaries—the Altmühl as far as Eichstätt, the Ilm as far as Pfaffenhofen, the Naab as far as Schwandorf, the Isar as far as Landshut, occasionally returning to the Danube via Eggenfeld and the valleys of the Rott and the Inn. This was their "beat"; in this area they knew almost every village; they had friends everywhere with whom they could spend the night. The restless Swabian seems after all to have found something like a home here. At any rate, he always returned to this district from the few "excursions" to Ansbach, to which his wife was apparently drawn by memories of her childhood.

The Danube was the most important thoroughfare in the whole area. It rolled lazily along its unmade bed, which it was prone to alter capriciously and without warning. It was unpredictable by nature, dwindling in times of prolonged drought to a mere trickle among grayish white pebbles, swelling overnight into a mighty torrent that carried uprooted trees and boulders along with it. Indeed, it was generally a dangerous nuisance, gurgling over its banks, submerging the scrub-filled hollows with its muddy brown waters, finding its way into the cellars of houses, and carrying planks, crates, and barrels all the way down to Austria. Its fury lasted several days; once the fit was over, it reverted to its familiar sluggish ways.

This was when a very different sort of bustling activity came into its own. Rafts cast off from the river banks and nosed their way into the Danube, coming from the Ilm, the Isar, and the Inn, from the Altmühl, the Naab, and the Regen. Floating islands of tree trunks, laden with all sorts of useful freight and steered by expert hands, sped through rapids, whirlpools, and muddy shallows or labored upstream at a snail's pace, buffeted and obstructed by adverse currents, holding their own and dragged forward only with the help of hawsers attached to teams of sturdy oxen on the bank. How brisk this traffic was is shown by the ledgers of the tollhouses.[31] In the year 1590, almost 600 rafts passed through Donaustauf, between Regensburg and Straubing: 140 with casks of salt, 116 with sacks of grain, 79 with mixed cargoes, 63 with barrels of wine, 27 with sheet iron, 18 with hides, 15 with building stone, 5 with wood and barrel-staves, and 106 with planks, timber for building, and firewood from the Bavarian Forest.

In Straubing this stream of goods proceeding from east to west intersected a main arterial highway that ran from north to south, and this was what accounted for the prosperity of the town. Heavily laden carts from Venice and Genoa, Prague, and Breslau lurched along the road from Munich to Cham. Apart from this much used highway, a number of other important trade routes traversed the area frequented by our itinerant family: the road from Schärding to Regensburg, from Kelheim via Landshut to Burghausen, from Regensburg via Geisenfeld to Augsburg, from Mühldorf via Braunau to Passau. The Gämperls traveled on all these roads as well as on others in the area, which connected the smaller towns. They were familiar with every milestone and every toll bar, every bridge and wayside cross. The roads were truly their home.

These roads, however, had practically nothing in common with the highways we nowadays call roads.[32] It is not enough simply to imagine modern roads without their tarmacadam surface. It was not until later, in the eighteenth century, that durable highways with proper foundations began to be built on the French model. Such *chausées* began to appear in Germany in significant numbers only after Napoleon's engineers understood the technical problems involved in road building and developed constructive solutions. It was officers of the great revolution, then, who first brought this technical advance to the Rhine and the Danube. At the end of the sixteenth century, the "roads" were still narrow cart tracks, winding stony ruts, and swampy trails leading through the undergrowth. Their route had evolved in a more or less natural fashion as the product of two often conflicting needs: the shortest route between two places or, on the other hand, the most viable route. Since roads in valleys turned into quagmires in wet weather and became unusable, the highways generally tended to seek the high ground. There the soil was firmer and better drained.

But even the most ingeniously planned route could not overcome the fundamental shortcomings of these highways: even on the most frequented stretches, coaches and carts often sank deep into the mud, bogged down to their axles, and could be dragged free only with the greatest difficulty. The "repairs" which were sometimes attempted were limited to sinking logs or bundles of brushwood into the swamp; by the following spring at the latest that same stretch of road was once more impassable. Travelers had no alternative but to make a detour over the fields or meadows bordering the road, much to the disadvantage and annoyance of the peasants who had to put up with it. Avoiding traffic coming in the opposite direction was also likely to result in damage to crops. Although the causeway was supposed to be sufficiently wide "for one vehicle to pass by another," that was little more than a pious hope.

People grumbled about this state of affairs.[33] In his principality of Bavaria, complained the duke, a "decay and an erosion" of the roads had occurred, and he commanded his customs officers to "ride the length of roads, paths, and highways personally" at least twice a year and to inspect them diligently. They were then required to see that the damage they had noted was dealt with. Not that this was the task of the duke's exchequer, which in fact collected the tolls; it was the responsibility of those tenants whose land adjoined the road and who were subject to socage—and who, often enough, were the very people who suffered most loss and damage from the passing traffic. The roads provided evidence of a certain indignation at so much injustice inflicted on the road repairers.

It was not only muddy potholes that obstructed traffic but also projecting branches and rampant undergrowth. Sometimes the coachman had to jump down from his seat to open a meadow gate, and then close it again after passing through. Serviceable bridges were few and far between, so the roads had to pass through neck-breaking fords. The greatest peril that threatened the traveler, however, came from the robbers and murderers who might lurk behind every bush, in the darkness of the forest, in the narrow defiles of sunken roads. Wherever they were not afraid of being surprised by unexpected witnesses, they fell upon the wayfarer, the trader's waggon, or the coach; slew their victims; rifled pockets, purses, and chests; and disappeared in the empty countryside without anyone being any the wiser.

THE PAPPENHEIMERS

During the first few months of their stay in Lower Bavaria our family made a living by begging—not a very secure source of income, for the prefects' officials checked up on such traveling folk from time to time, particularly in smaller towns. It was thus advisable to have an official document that certified the holder as a beggar licensed by the authorities. Paulus possessed a "begging letter" of this kind for himself and his family quite early in his career, and was to acquire a number of others during twenty years of itinerant existence. Of these documents only one was genuinely official.

The bogus beggar's licenses were written for the vagrant with the Swabian accent by an unemployed schoolmaster from Wegscheid, who traveled from place to place with the beggar folk from Lower Bavaria, in spite of being lame in one leg—"a man advanced in years, with a limp, and a short brown beard, but not yet gray." For drafting a document of this kind he asked half a gulden, roughly equivalent to a lavish dinner with several glasses of wine. The seals which gave the document the necessary official appearance were probably no cheaper. These Paulus obtained from an itinerant engraver of seals by the name of Hans von Hofkirchen, who frequented "all the markets by Straubing and round about those parts" and engraved seals to order, "both for thieves and villains and for honest folk." Or else he got them from an old beggar who called himself Schwabhänsel, or "Swabian Jack," who carried "some five sorts" of seals about with him for the benefit of his numerous customers. It was obviously not difficult to acquire such forged begging licenses.

We might think the forgeries would have been easily detected, but in an age of almost universal illiteracy this was apparently not the case. It is true that the vagrant Pappenheimers once had a licence taken from them and canceled during a check on their credentials. On the other hand, they succeeded in having one of their bogus licenses officially extended.

Anna possessed, as she admitted when questioned in Munich, a begging license from her native city of Ansbach. During one of the family's excursions to her old home, she went to the "office in the town hall," boldly presented her forged certificate, and demanded an extension. It was refused, not in fact because the expired document was detected as a forgery but because they "did not wish to put the beggar woman on a better footing." She should "manage on her old license," the official told her. Anna, in no way discouraged, instantly succumbed to "her sickness, the cramps"; that is, she feigned an epileptic fit: she writhed screaming on the floor of the town hall until she was removed. The same scene was repeated the following day and ended once more with her being thrown out of the building. Then she had a new idea: she asked a crippled beggar to help her. This "mightily infirm" individual, whom they called "Krepshänsel, the fellow with the crutch and sack," was so stiff and deformed that he could move about only on all fours: a most wretched and pitiful figure. Our Anna, determined to achieve her end, hoisted him on her back and staggered, panting, a third time to the town hall, where she dragged her accomplice into the office. Here, on her back, she cried with heart-rending sobs, she was carrying her poor husband so that the worshipful gentlemen might see for themselves what a wrong they were doing her. Her performance had the desired effect. They did not even check whether the cripple the woman had brought into their office really was her husband but simply issued her with a fresh begging license—possibly only in order to get rid of this persistent customer.

In spite of such safeguards, Paulus was already tired of begging during his first year in Bavaria. Now aged thirty-eight, he thought he was still too young to live on alms. In the vicinity of Abensberg he made the acquaintance of an elderly man about this time, and the two quickly became friends. The man, called Wolf Dachdecker, roamed round the country like the Pämb-Gämperls. He was not a beggar, however, but "a hard worker and an honest man" who emptied privies for a living. It was hard work, and irksome, he explained to his new friend, but there was a living to be made at it. Would Paulus care to become his assistant? Dachdecker himself was not as robust as he once had been and was willing to teach him the trade and share the work and the earnings with him. This offer appealed to Paulus, who got Dachdecker to tell him what the business was about, how to open the cesspits so that the evil-smelling excrement could be removed, where to take the full buckets, and, of course, how much a man might earn at the business. The following day he was already hard at work. The former gravedigger and trained beggar had become an "emptier of privies."

This noisome trade was to be his profession and chief source of income until his arrest. At first he emptied privies as assistant to the old man. When the latter died, he carried on with the help of his sons, Michel and Gumpprecht, who had grown up in the meantime. His occupation was so closely associated with his person that people up and down the country soon referred to him only as "the Pappenheimer." At first the name simply denoted his profession, but, as frequently happened in those days, it tended more and more to become a family name and was soon attached to his wife and children. That suited Paulus: his new name freed him from the name of the linen weaver who had thrashed him and whom he had called father in the days of his unhappy childhood. It was not a derisory nickname; he bore it with a certain pride and used to introduce himself as "Pappenheimer."

It was a name that did in fact suggest the best possible associations: after all, it was borne by a noble family whose hereditary seat was on the upper Altmühl, at the extreme limit of Paulus's beat. Although these counts of Pappenheim would have been horrified at the very thought of any family connection with our vagabond, there was no denying that they were his professional ancestors. This distinction they owed to the favor and trust of the emperor at a time when the glory of the empire was at its most brilliant. It was then that they had been accorded the honor of ensuring that the setting for imperial visits was appropriately dignified. Whenever the emperor announced his arrival in the imperial city, therefore, Count von Pappenheim rode through the streets some days before the great event and ordered his servants to remove anything that might offend the nose or the eyes of their illustrious guest. There was a considerable amount of such matter: in the Middle Ages city streets were used literally as elongated garbage dumps.[34] Dead animals, scraps of food, and stable manure were piled high and rummaged through by dogs as well as the pigs that ranged freely through the streets. Apart from that, there were no privies or cesspits in the houses until well into the sixteenth century, and people relieved themselves in the street or in corners. It is obvious that the streets were cleaned only on the occasion of imperial visitations and as a result of the count's inspection. That is why the men who removed the refuse and filth were simply called "Pappenheimer." The people of Nuremberg were to use this term for garbage collectors right down to the twentieth century.

Since his new name really did have something to do with the counts of Pappenheim, Paulus was justified in bearing it with a certain pride. His occupation was offensive only in a literal sense; otherwise it was useful, laudable, and modern, for cesspits were a great advance in hygiene when compared with conditions prevailing in the Middle Ages.[35] From the tenth until the thirteenth century, even in the most aristocratic castles and palaces, lords, ladies, knights, and lackeys performed their natural functions in open, projecting bays, beneath which the walls were spattered with faeces. Chamber pots were unknown: anyone who had to relieve himself during the night did so in the corridor outside the bedchamber. When night crockery became the rule in the fourteenth century, it proved to be a somewhat dubious improvement, for townsfolk threw the contents of their chamber pots out of the window, so that the streets remained more or less in their former condition. In castles and palaces these vessels were found to be so convenient that it was not thought necessary to construct privies or cesspits. There was, for example, not a single privy in the duke's Munich residence, and His Grace used a commode without a thought as to the disposal of the excrement generated by his numerous courtiers. In short, the farms, middle-class households, and castles where Paulus emptied the cesspits were relatively progressive as far as hygiene was concerned. Because of the nature of his work, this emptier of privies presumably came into contact with people who were otherwise outside his social circle.

Our Pappenheimer's work consisted in removing excrement from the cesspit by means of buckets lowered on a rope, and then spreading it on the fields or getting rid of it in running water. The second method was naturally the less disagreeable way of disposing of the stinking feces, which may well be the main reason our family of vagrants tended to stay close to the waterways. Because the air was polluted while the pits were being emptied, many customers required the work to be done during the night, and for the same reason they usually tried to arrange it during the winter months.

Paulus therefore had little to do during the summer. At that time of the year he and his sons usually turned to glazing, carrying the necessary implements in a basket on their back. In larger places like Cham they occasionally used to buy lead and bull's-eye window panes. Gumpprecht and Michel were also able to patch up leaky pots and pans for the farmers' wives. If they could not earn their living in any of these ways, then the family would join forces to make brooms or knit bonnets, which they would try to sell at the next fair. In one or two of the larger places, where the family stayed rather longer, Anna sometimes found work as a maid or kitchen help. Later on, Paulus possessed an extra source of cash in the form of a collapsible gambling table which he had bought from another vagrant. He used to set this up at fairs and other village festivities where there was a crowd, and on good days he might earn a few gulden. We do not know what sort of game he played, but Paulus claimed it was only for entertainment and not for the sake of the money. He probably knew all about the relevant prohibitions on gaming. In one way or another, then, the Pappenheimers kept their heads above water, and took to begging only when they were on the verge of starvation.

ANOTHER EXAMINATION

On 19 April, as on the preceding days, Councillors Wangereck, von Roming, and Hainmüller and their clerk again made their appearance in the Falcon Tower. This time, however, they did not first sit down in the ironmaster's living room but asked Master Georg to take them straight down the dark stairs into the dank vaults, the scene of horrific suffering. Candles were lighted; the clerk unpacked his paper, pens, and inkwell and arranged them on the table; the gentlemen pulled up chairs and sat down. Wangereck ordered the ironmaster to bring in the father of those tramps from Lower Bavaria; shortly thereafter, the accused, Paulus Pappenheimer, appeared before the ducal commission.

Before Wangereck began the examination, he ordered Master Georg to take down the carved crucifix that was hanging in a corner of the room and to hold it up in front of the prisoner. This was done. The councillor addressed the offender in a stern voice: Did he know who was gazing down at him from the cross? Paulus nodded. Wangereck: It was the immutable will of God that he and his sons should now be lying here in prison. It was because the blood of the innocent people they had injured and slain was crying out to heaven, and God was no longer content to witness their killing, robbing, and burning. And so he should now submit to his fate, accept the pain and suffering that his sin and his evil deeds had brought upon him in the hope that he might once more be blessed with the infinite mercy of God. But this could happen only if he told the authorities the truth.

After this exhortation we can imagine how Wangereck instructed the ironmaster by a wave of the hand to return the crucifix to its place. The examination began with questions about Paulus's life and family, and these the gray-bearded vagrant answered readily enough. His business, by which he earned an honest living, was the emptying of privies, and he had been thus engaged in the weeks before his arrest; he had been working in a manorhouse in Regensburg and in the district round Abensberg, Altmannstein, Vohburg, and Kelheim. The councillor replied: There was evidence, however, that he and his sons were anything but honest folk; in fact, a felon since executed had named them as his accomplices. Paulus: He knew very well who was to blame for the fate that had befallen his family—that Geindl, the thief who had been executed in Wörth. But he had never had any dealings with him; he had merely seem him from time to time at fairs, at Irlbach, Michelsbuch, and Eltenbuch, for example, where that ne'er-do-well had been beaten by his son.

Wangereck consulted his list of questions. Following the next question was the note "Torqueatur," which meant that a satisfactory answer was to be elicited by torture, if necessary. What had his sons done with the infants' hands, and how many had they had in their possession? Paulus knew nothing about infants' hands. In response to a sign, Master Georg began to tie the accused's hands, while the councillor continued to admonish him. He should bear in mind that he had not been brought to this torture chamber for nothing. He still had time to take thought and tell the truth before they began to rack his limbs. Paulus: But he and his family were totally innocent and had never had any such hands in their possession. Wangereck gave another sign. Master Georg began to jerk the hemp rope around his victim's wrists to and fro so that it tore his skin like a fine saw with a thousand tiny teeth. The old man screamed. He would gladly tell the gentlemen whatever they wanted to hear, but he knew nothing of children's hands. Unmoved, the councillor ordered his tormentor to begin the torture proper. The latter untied the prisoner's wrists, but only to pull his arms behind his back, binding them painfully once more, and attaching a thick rope to his wrists. This rope hung down from the ceiling, where it passed over an iron drum, and was fastened by its other end to a hook in the wall. Master Georg pushed the old man, still protesting his innocence, under the windlass, unfastened the free end of the rope from the wall, and began to pull. Paulus let out a pitiful scream, for his arms were pulled up behind his back, his shoulder joints twisted backwards, his chest dragged to the sides. His legs slipped back behind him, and he hung in midair, revolving slowly, a yard or more above the floor. Would he tell the truth now, asked a familiar voice from beneath him. He had been telling the truth all along, groaned the panting victim. In the meantime the torturer had lashed the rope to the hook in the wall once more and stood by, awaiting new instructions. For five endless minutes the contorted body of the whimpering victim swung in midair; then, at last, they let him down. With trembling knees he sought a footing on the floor, the bones of his upper arms snapped back into their sockets as the rope slackened. Would he tell them the truth without more ado? demanded Wangereck. But truly, he could say no more than he had already said, panted their victim. Once more a sign to the ironmaster, and the accused was swinging from the rope once again, five minutes, ten minutes. The councillors, conversing in low tones, took no notice of his coughing, groaning, and wailing. At last the man hanging on the rope called to them, yes, yes, he would confess everything, everything, if only they would release him from this torment. It was only then that Wangereck nodded to the jailor and had the broken man lowered to the floor.

The clerk dipped his quill into the inkwell and noted: "Although at first he would by no means confess of his own free will, or admit that he knew anything of any infants' hands, he then, on being earnestly admonished and put twice to the strappado, did state that he had seen four or five hands in the possession of his sons."

The councillor was not satisfied with this but wished to know where the vagrants had concealed those infants' hands and what spells they had wrought with them. Each time Paulus hesitated to reply, the ironmaster was given the order to pull on the rope. No, no, screamed the accused at once, and gave rapid and voluble answers. Now he seemed to be in the right frame of mind for a brisk continuation of the examination.

The next question on Wangereck's list was again tagged "Torqueatur." How many murders had he and his sons committed? A jerk on the rope sufficed to make Paulus talk. The first time had been three years previously when he and his two grown-up sons had met a peasant they did not know, in broad daylight, by a clump of trees somewhere between Geiselhoring and Multhofen. They had thought they might find money on him and so had killed him with a club. He had had three gulden in his pocket; they had taken these and hidden the body behind a hedge. Second, they had killed a peasant on the road between Abensberg and Neustadt and stolen four gulden. Third . . . fourth . . . fifth. Pappenheimer admitted to twelve murders as he stood there beneath the windlass, before assuring them that he knew nothing more. Whether, and whom, his sons had murdered on their own he could not say. If they had acquired money by armed robbery of this sort, they must have frittered it away in gluttony and gambling, for he and his wife had never seen any trace of it but had always lived in poverty and by begging. Little Hänsel, he could say for sure, had never been present at any murder and was therefore totally blameless.

As far as the murders were concered, the councillor was satisfied for the moment. He now wanted to know how many villages they had set on fire. Quite a number, Paulus hastened to say before the torturer could get to work again. To wit, when he and his whole crew had wanted to spend the night on a farm in Geltofling during the summer some three years previously, the farmer had chased them away. In order to get their own back, they had taken burning coals from an oven, thrown them into some straw, and in this way had burned down the entire village and the castle as well. They were also to blame for two other villages going up in flames in the same manner. They had sometimes taken the embers in the presence of other people, who thought they needed them for their glazing or for cooking. Wangereck: How often had his wife and Hänsel laid fires? Paulus: Never, they were totally innocent.

Now Wangereck, still threatening renewed torments, forced the accused to give an account of when and where he had stolen from the local inhabitants on his "beat." In the course of confessing to these crimes, Paulus got them confused, regarding dates and times, with the felonies he had already admitted to, explaining lamely that he was not really sure when the thefts had taken place. Even this inconsistency enraged the councillor, but he did not finally lose his temper until Paulus denied that he and his family had robbed offertory boxes and whole churches. Medical knowledge suggests that the pain-racked man's shoulder joints were already raw and torn internally, blue and swollen externally, but Wangereck was relentless and had him hoisted aloft a third time, until he declared in a pitifully feeble voice that he was ready to stop lying. When he had been let down, he confessed to having used sticks smeared with gum to extract twenty pfennig from the offertory box in the Holy Cross church in Kelheim, similarly in Aunkhofen, in Sankt Gilgen, near Abensberg, in the chapel of Our Lady in Vohburg, and St. Catherine's church in Altmannstein. But he had never broken in, or climbed in, for the churches had been open all the time.

Wangereck had almost reached the end of his list of questions. There was only one other thing he wanted to know: Whether his wife was not a witch or a sorceress. He did not believe that was so, replied Paulus with the logic of the simple man; if his wife were a wicked sorceress or subject to the Devil, she would certainly have killed him long since.

THE VILLAGE

There were good days and bad days in the life of the vagrants. There were days of hunger and cold when they knocked with numb fingers on farmstead doors and were driven off with harsh words. There were good days in early summer, when the air was balmy, the countryside green, and life easy. On one of those good days in the year 1592 we can observe our family making its way along a narrow, grass-grown track through the countryside of Lower Bavaria in the soft morning light.

The boys were leading the way: Gumpprecht, then fourteen, already had his glazier's basket on his back and a tinker's hammer hanging from his belt. He and his twelve-year-old brother may have run on ahead of their parents, as children do, starting a hare here, chasing a lizard there. Then their father, squat and stocky, walking with a measured pace. From time to time he stopped, turned around, and waited for his wife Anna, who was following him, leading two-year-old Hänsel by the hand and bowed down under the weight of the bundle of belongings on her shoulders. The five of them could have been taken for a family of itinerant peddlars, because the bearded head of the family was carrying a heavily laden wooden framework on his back. In his hand he held a long, heavy stick of hazelwood with a rugged knob at its upper end. In an emergency it might serve as a cudgel, but it was not the only weapon carried by the wayfarer. A broad-bladed dagger almost as long as a sword hung from one side of his belt, a short hunting knife from the other; in the waistband of his breeches and hidden by his doublet was an "iron handgun." That was in keeping with the general impression: traveling hucksters, small traders, and craftsmen went about armed, which was justified by the insecurity of the roads and hence permitted by the authorities. The only remarkable thing about the father was his face: his broad, graying black beard and, above that, in the shadow of his hat brim, the scars on forehead and right cheek, which gave the old man a rakish appearance.

They were on their way from Kelheim and, as always, had not taken the most direct route through the wild and gloomy forest but had kept to the course of the Danube as far as Hienheim, where they had spent the night in a barn. Next morning they had set out very early, no longer traveling upstream in a southerly direction, but heading northwest. Now, as the shadows preceding them grew shorter, they had already passed Laimerstadt and were just approaching a small rise from which they could see their destination.

Then as now, the village lay on the crest of one of those gently rolling ridges so characteristic of Lower Bavaria. It consisted of thirty or forty houses and shacks clustered around a roofless rectangular tower. The pale gray masonry of this building stemmed from time immemorial; it was older than any of the dwellings around it, and its original purpose was obscure, but it had ultimately been dedicated to a sacred purpose and served as a belfry. It was a belfry in appearance only, and purely as a symbol of dedication, for it had no bells and could not be entered. To its right and left lay the houses, brown, yellow, and white amid the luxuriant foliage of their gardens. They were mostly built entirely of wood; their variegated roofs were pitched at all sorts of angles and covered with straw or shingles. Fields, meadows, and fallow land spread over both sides of the ridge and covered its slopes, a rectangular patch of green and brown tints crossed by horizontal lines of shady hedges. Centuries of clearing and charcoal burning had forced the forest to retreat in a wide circle, and it now lay in a dim blue haze almost half-an-hour's walk from the village. Small herds of sheep, horses, cattle, and pigs grazed on enclosed pastures on either side of the last stretch of road, which wound downhill and then up again. This was all that now separated the Pappenheimers from the mighty lime tree at the entrance to the village.

Their approach was observed with feelings that were not entirely friendly. The distrust that peasants long settled on the land felt for "gypsies," as they called all traveling people, was too great for that. Still, the Pappenheimers were known in the village: they had friends there—only among the famished and the poverty-stricken, of course. The wealthier peasants would have nothing to do with such riffraff; at most they would get them to empty the stinking cesspits, a job beneath the dignity of the local farmhands and day laborers. And even then they remained suspicious, locked their chests and closets when the tramps carried their buckets of excrement across the yard or sat by an open fire, hammering away at leaky pots and pans. They were only too glad to see the ragged crew depart after they had paid the old man a few kreuzer. The Pappenheimers could not stay any length of time on the larger farms. They lodged with one of the poorer peasants, whose fields were too small to support a family and who therefore had to hire themselves out to earn their daily bread, or else pursue some trade or business. These smallholders were called *Blosshäusler*, or mere cottagers, simply because they possessed little more than their cottages, which were not called farmsteads, crofts, or fiefs, like the larger holdings, but simply "plots." It was to such a cottage plot that the traveling family was on its way. It belonged to Ulrich Schölz, whose barn they could lodge in, although not without payment. This was their regular lodging whenever they came to Tettenwang. In the village it was well known that Schölz harbored all sorts of riffraff. That was one of the ways in which he scraped a living. The wealthy and respected farmers in the village might well despise him for that reason: they had no need to make money on the side in that manner. Their contempt made little difference to the cottager since he was not respected anyway. In church he sat at the back with other paupers, while the pews at the front were reserved for the farmers and crofters in their satin-trimmed fustian cloaks.

Yet these large farmers owned nothing either, in the strict sense of the term.[36] Whether they farmed lands reckoned as forty or as only four days' tilth, they still did not own their soil. The fields and pastures, the meadows and woods, the farmsteads and holdings were merely on loan. Over on the other side of the valley, in the castle of Hexenagger above the Schambach, dwelled the real owners of Tettenwang, the lords of Muggenthal. Their ancestors had once handed the land over to the peasants so that it might be plowed, sowed, tended, and harvested. It was not the intention that this transfer of property should be a gift or that the land should belong permanently to the recipients: it was a provisional arrangement and subject to all sorts of conditions, qualifications, and reservations. Those who plowed and planted were to hand over a share of the produce from the land they had been lent; that was understood. And the landlord could determine the interest unilaterally; that too was understood. The question whether the right to exploit land belonging to someone else was a personal or a hereditary right—that was a more complicated matter, as was the question whether the lease might be terminated at any time or only on certain conditions. These provisos were laid down in each case in brittle, yellowing documents, which could be deciphered only by experts and which were carefully preserved in every farmstead. It was clear beyond all doubt, nevertheless, that the peasants were liable to render service to their landlord, quite apart from the tribute they had to pay. On the other hand, the extent of this socage to which tenants were subject was a matter of endless controversy. And from whom should the peasant take his orders? From us, said the Muggenthals of Hexenagger, exercising their rights as landlords. From the duke, said the prefect, Alexander von Haslang, in Abensberg. There were indeed two different authorities, which might well have come into conflict had not the duke long since proved to be the more powerful. The country's landlords, the so-called territorial estates, were already politically pacified and required from their peasants nothing that ran counter to the duke's ordinances. As far as the government of Bavaria was concerned, they had, like the cottagers in church, long since taken a back seat.

For the peasants of Tettenwang this distribution of power and influence meant that the duke could protect them against abuses by their landlord. Whether he did so or not, depended, of course, on what he stood to gain. But the ruler did take note of complaints made by village communities against the nobility. On the other hand, the landlord was not in a position to improve the situation of his tenants if this ran counter to the duke's interests. This is why, for instance, there was no interest in Munich in the promotion of trade and commerce in the countryside. All attempts to achieve this end on the part of local squires, abbeys, and bailiwicks were invariably blocked by the duke, for he was determined to have no rivals to the towns and markets which paid dues directly to him. That is why country dwellers were not even allowed to trade in cattle but had to conduct their business in the nearest town.

The peasants were worst off when both their masters wanted the same thing from them without either feeling at a disadvantage.[37] This was the case with socage, which was expected of the villagers. It was not only the lord of the manor who demanded free labor from his tenants; their ruler too would draft peasants for such tasks as road repairs. Landlord and duke also agreed that hunting, their favorite pastime and jealously guarded privilege, was more important than the peasant's concern for his crops. The only concession the peasants were granted was permission to fence in their fields and to keep dogs, provided that the dogs were "hobbled," that is, prevented from hunting by having a stick tied around their necks. And when it was a question of meeting extra expense, there was never any argument about who was ultimately responsible. "Of the small quantity of grain that the peasant scratches from the soil," grumbled the duke's chancellor, Simon

Eck, in 1571, "he has to give some to his ruler, his landlord, the parson, his tithe-lord, the prefect, the magistrate, the beadle, the bailiff, the forest ranger and his men, the verger, the miller, the baker, the beggars, tramps, and hucksters."

FARMERS AND COTTAGERS

If the peasants of Tettenwang were nonetheless doing well in the year 1592, it was because prices for their produce were rising. The people who profited most, of course, were the farmers and small-holders, who consumed only part of their produce themselves and were in a position to sell the rest. In those days they reckoned with ten days' tilth of good soil per person, which means that roughly seven and a half acres of land was necessary and sufficient to support one peasant. The farmsteads had significantly more land, seventy-five acres was not uncommon. Half of this served as pasture; the other half was cultivated with plow and harrow, al-though only two-thirds of this arable land was planted with grain (wheat, rye, oats, barley) or, less commonly, with rape, flax, hemp, or hops. The other third of the fertile land was left fallow each year. Potatoes and turnips were totally unknown.

In the meadows there were more oxen grazing than cows—cattle were used less as dairy animals than as draft animals, no doubt because of the difficulties of transporting such perishable goods as dairy products. Nevertheless, there were horses on every farm, for they raised the status of their owner. If the nobility and the patricians in the towns had their coaches drawn by horses, the prosperous peasant had no desire to come on the scene with a pair of oxen. The cattle were seldom stabled. As long as the frost was not severe, the beasts were left outside day and night—as were the pigs, which were herded like the customary large herds of sheep. The peasants provided themselves with firewood and timber ei-ther from woods belonging to the farm or from the landlord's for-est, by virtue of long-standing agreements.

Property of this kind justified those villagers who sat in the front pews of the church in Tettenwang in trimming their fustian cloaks with satin. There were other ways, too, in which they liked to flaunt their wealth whenever opportunity offered—at wed-dings, christenings, and wakes, for instance, when they would in-vite half the village to sit down at festively decorated tables. Mu-sicians brought in from Kelheim would play; game and poultry, all

64

kinds of boiled and roasted dishes, were served up; beer and wine flowed. It was with a certain amount of displeasure that the duke heard tell of such opulence, gluttony, and extravagance on the part of his rural subjects. In 1617 he issued a decree to the effect that a common countryman might not invite more than fifty guests to a wedding, not counting the musicians, and that he might not serve "fish, crawfish, or choice wines." This had little effect.

Needless to say, the Pappenheimers knew this kind of high life only from hearsay. They had practically no contact with the wealthy farmers and crofters of Tettenwang; they associated only with the cottagers and smallholders, who, instead of fustian and satin, wore only wool and goatskin.[38] Unable to live from their little plots of land, most practiced some trade or craft. Among the cottagers of Tettenwang there was a blacksmith, an innkeeper, a piper, a messenger, a shepherd, a glazier, a bread delivery man, a barber, a cooper, and several weavers. At harvest time, no doubt, they all worked as day laborers in the fields belonging to the bigger farmers. Even so, they and their families generally had too little to satisfy their hunger and barely enough to ward off starvation. They could not accumulate any reserves, so that every failed local harvest struck them with the force of a famine. In such cases grain, and consequently flour and bread, sometimes became so expensive as to be beyond the reach of wage earners. In 1582, for instance, when life in Tettenwang became exceedingly "dear and high-priced," the cottagers "fell into such straits that they were close to despair." Over and over again, in the years following, there were times when "they had neither bread nor money in the house and suffered great distress." They had nothing but bran to eat, and neither milk nor lard for their children. To save themselves from starving they baked a dough from oats, acorns, and sawdust, mixed with water and animal blood. The rise in the price of grain affected all other foodstuffs: the butchers complained that there was no livestock to be had. The poverty in the households of the cottagers was such that many of them sold their last few possessions to the wealthier farmers, or exchanged them for provisions, and took to the road with their families, like the Pappenheimers.

But even when the harvest was abundant and trade flourished, the poor of the village were still badly off. They were squeezed into a spiral of wages and prices that threatened to throttle the life out of them, for while the prices of basic foodstuffs went on rising steeply, wages remained relatively low.[39] In the course of the sixteenth century the price of barley rose by 850 percent, of wheat by 560 percent, and of rye by 430 percent, and by 1621 beef and lard cost five times as much as in 1505. On the other hand, in industry and agriculture, ducal regulations laid down maximum wages, which were enforced by legal penalties. In this way the duke sought to keep down production costs in trade and industry, apparently overlooking the fact that such measures led to an emigration of labor and the reduction of many cottagers to the status of proletariat. Without identifying this as the cause, a ducal decree of 1599 deplored that "the wealth of the country was in decline."

At the beginning of the sixteenth century an unskilled day laborer could earn his annual supply of grain in an average of forty days; by the end of the century he needed eighty days. In a village like Tettenwang there was, of course, practically no work in the winter, and little enough in spring and summer. The demand for the services of small tradesmen, given a population of about three hundred and fifty souls, was very limited indeed. For that reason alone, therefore, the cottagers of Tettenwang would scarcely have managed eighty working days in the year. And, quite apart from that, people rarely worked more than three days a week on account of the numerous church holidays.

Supposing he did find employment, a cottager could earn twelve to eighteen kreuzer a day as an unskilled manual worker or as a day laborer. In normal times a pound of beef cost four or five kreuzer, a pound of mutton three kreuzer, a pound of lard twelve kreuzer, a bushel of wheat twelve gulden, that is, 720 kreuzer. If we bear in mind occasional essential expenditure on clothing and tools, we may wonder how the poor of Tettenwang and their families ever managed at all. They were certainly worse off than the farmhands, who were fed by their employers and not forced to spend their wages on expensive foodstuffs.

On a day early in the summer of 1592, the family of travelers was approaching Ulrich Schölz's cottage. Perhaps he was already expecting them and was standing in his front yard, calling out a jocular greeting to the new arrivals. They addressed each other by their given names, cordially, as good friends do who meet all too rarely. As the cottager took the travelers to the barn and watched them throw their bundles into the hay, the first questions were asked, the first tidbits of gossip exchanged. This is how the outcast with the Swabian accent was received in Tettenwang—like a man who had come home.

Another stranger from Swabia was beginning to feel at home in Bavaria during that summer of 1592. This was the prince's tutor and state councillor, Johann Baptist Fickler, who has already been mentioned. At that time he was proudly carrying away from Adam Berg's printing press in Munich the first copies of his latest pamphlet, "Reply to that second, spurious, and idle Prattle of Dr. Jacob Heilprunner, Court Preacher to the Elector Palatine at Neuburg on the Danube, as being his alleged Refutation of Dr. Fickler's etc. Vindication directed against his, Heilprunner's Sermon, in which he hath assailed the true Catholic *Concilia* and Invocation of the Most Blessed Virgin and Mother of God, Mary, the same thereafter having been given under the Press." The title had turned out somewhat on the short side, given the current fashion for adorning both learned and popular literature with almost endlessly convoluted sentences. But that did little to diminish the pleasure he felt on seeing his name once again in print. Not only for the sake of the fame it would bring him but also because that heretical fellow Heilbrunner would not now have the last word. With this publication he had established himself in the Electoral city of Munich as a scholar, and not simply as a tutor. What was more, the duke would finance this pamphlet and possibly future publications. But he was pleased above all because his book was to play no small part in grandiose political plans.

Great and far-reaching political plans.[40] He himself, indeed, had planted the germ of these plans during his years in Ingolstadt when he had traveled to the neighboring principality of Pfalz-Neuburg with Prince Maximilian and his brothers. Count Palatine Philipp Ludwig had invited his relatives who were studying in Ingolstadt to join what seemed like an innocent hunting party. Fickler believed, however, that he had sinister ulterior motives. For the count of Pfalz-Neuburg was a Lutheran, his land a Protestant stronghold. Would he not be tempted to draw the seventeen-year-old prince and future duke of Bavaria onto his side by seductive argument, the closeness of their kinship, and questionable logic? It would have had incalculable, indeed catastrophic, consequences for the Catholic party if this congenial neighbor and hunting companion had succeeded in corrupting Maximilian's youthful heart with his heretical poison. That there could be no question of this was due above all to the prince's austere and steadfast character, his precociously developed political sense, and his loyalty to his father, Duke William, and his confessor, Gregor. But it was due also in some degree to Fickler's insistent warnings against such heretical intrigues. How right he had been became apparent at Grünau Castle, when the cunning count invited his young hunting companions to listen to the court preacher's sermon on the feast of the Visitation of Mary. But he was severely rebuffed. They would rather be hacked to pieces, said Maximilian's brother, than listen to such Lutheran blasphemies. But Fickler had ventured into the snake pit, listened attentively to the words of the court preacher, Jakob Heilbrunner, and made notes. During the hunt that followed, the count had ridden up to him and asked him how he liked the sermon. The answer was somewhat impolite. He felt quite capable of refuting the errors he had heard that morning without the slightest difficulty, the prince's tutor said. Heilbrunner no doubt learned of that; at any rate, his sermon appeared in print forthwith. Fickler saw that as a challenge and wrote his reply in long nocturnal sessions by the light of his tallow candle, his pen racing across the paper to record his forceful phrases.[41] And now he was carrying it home fresh from the press, hoping to use it as part of far-reaching political schemes.

For now it was up to Maximilian to turn the tables. The count palatine also had a son and heir with a youthful heart that might easily be swayed. The young prince would some time pay a return visit to Munich, where he in his turn would have the chance to attend divine service and be cured of his errors. For such a conversion, with its vast political significance, Fickler's polemical treatise was intended to pave the way. The fanatical scholar was far from suspecting that the young count palatine, Wolfgang William, would one day be drawn into the Catholic camp, not by theological and legal arguments, but by the tender glances of the fair sex: Maximilian's sister Magdalena was destined to turn the Neuburg heir's head and persuade him to convert secretly to Catholicism, an act that was to break his father's heart. But all that was to happen long after the events described here.

During that summer of 1592, at least, Fickler might well think that he had achieved an important aim with his little book. After all, it isn't so important to *be* eminent; what matters is to be *regarded* as eminent. The prince's former tutor, who had just been appointed councillor of state, had gained a notable place in Munich court society; he had reached the climax of his career and had even succumbed to the illusion that he might rise still higher. He was receiving an annual salary of five hundred gulden, plus allowances of one hundred gulden and secretarial expenses amounting to seventy-five and one-half gulden. That was more than twelve gulden a week, about twenty times as much as a Tettenwang cottager earned when times were good. Over and above this, Fickler might expect gratuities from his prince on appropriate occasions and for special purchases. He would never have to eat bran. And he had no knowledge of the outlaw's world inhabited by Paulus Pappenheimer—its ingrained filth and tingling frost, its wealth of cunning, its misery and endless diversity, its balmy summer breezes.

But he too had traveled a long way. As a homeless outcast with a Swabian accent in the midst of strangers, he too had suffered distress—emotional distress, it is true; he had succumbed to the wiles of others and had himself had recourse to guile. His life had never been free and filled with balmy summer breezes—but, on the other hand, he had never suffered privation and frostbite.

He had been born in May 1534 in the Württemberg town of Backnang, in wedlock, naturally, and his father had not been a hungry, dishonest linen weaver but a highly respected civil servant. And if he too had been obliged to flee during his childhood, it had not been in the manner of Paulus Pämb-Gämperl, "like any young shaver," but more like Moses in the basket of rushes,[42] or Jesus on the arm of Mary: the Protestant Duke Ulrich had returned to his realm and had dismissed Fickler's Catholic father from his post. He quickly moved with his family to Weil der Stadt, which was still Catholic, to avoid further reprisals. Thus, Johann Baptist had been removed from the Lutheran dust while still an infant in his cradle, which he considered throughout his life to have been an act of divine providence and a miraculous escape. In the ancient little imperial city he spent his happy and sheltered childhood, coming to love not only all its nooks and crannies but also the world of the mind. His mother had a command of Latin, read a great deal, played a musical instrument, knew the Holy Scriptures well, and was not only wise but capable of witty retorts in any arguments she might have with Protestants. It was a warm and propitious nest. And yet this Swabian, too, left his parents' home at the age of thirteen and was deprived of his homeland: his father died young, and when his mother remarried, the children were scattered among various relatives. Johann Baptist was sent first of all to a school in Freiburg in Breisgau, then to relatives in Würzburg, where he was put in the care of Catholic canons. In

1550, when no more than sixteen, he made his way to Ingolstadt to study.

He registered in the faculty of "liberal arts," but was mainly interested in jurisprudence, becoming assistant to the celebrated Italian professor of law, Zoanetti, in his very first year of study. He was no doubt something of a bookworm in other ways too, anything but a drunken bully and nocturnal rowdy, like almost all the students there. Within four years, at the age of twenty, when most students were just starting, this model scholar was able to complete his studies as "Magister artium et philosophiae."

He now set out on his travels again, this time to Basel, where he took up a post as secretary to the dean of the cathedral. A trying time: his employer, Ambrosius von Gumppenberg, in spite of his spiritual calling, was worldly and rapacious; he loved high living and womanizing. The newly graduated arch-Catholic paragon of virtue was dismayed: he had thought that only heretical preachers were capable of such behavior. He could take no pleasure in his duties, which were "full of bustle and labor, what with writing and traveling, and beset with perils, both indoors and out." Fortunately, he had his candle-lit hours. In fact, it was then that he discovered them. Night after night, his pen scurried over the paper. All his energies were devoted to a polemical treatise in Latin which he was translating into German: *Dialogi de vera et falsa religione*, by a Pole, Martin Kromer. Almighty God at once vouchsafed him His grace and the chance to use his manuscript discreetly as a recommendation for a better appointment. Fickler took it with him when he accompanied his detestable dean to the Imperial Diet in Augsburg in 1559, and sent it to the Archbishop of Salzburg, who was present, not without first dedicating his translation to the recipient. The archbishop was flattered, deemed the young secretary's qualifications entirely adequate, his industry and courtesy remarkable. In short, he instructed his chancellor Höflinger to inquire whether Fickler was inclined to enter the service of Salzburg. Fickler did not wait to be asked twice.

This is how the homeless Swabian came to Salzburg. He devoted himself with respectful zeal to a service he felt to be worthy of him. But if he had thought he would be less busy, then he was mistaken: the archbishop's new Latin secretary was more often on his travels than in his office. In 1560/61 he had to travel across the Alps on behalf of the cathedral chapter—in the depths of winter, at that. In 1562 he was sent as a member of the Salzburg delegation to the resumed Council of Trent, where he remained for nearly two years. When he finally returned to Salzburg on 5 February 1564, he was already planning another journey, this time on his own account.

Although he was now thirty and successful in his career, he wished to return to the university. He was planning to finish his legal studies, so as to improve his professional competence, he explained to the archbishop. This sounds too much like an application for a scholarship to be altogether credible. Fickler, who had not spared the midnight oil while in Trent and had written a voluminous history of the Council, was obviously aiming to become a renowned author and politician. It may have become painfully clear to him at the Council of Trent that he lacked the higher academic qualifications that were essential for his purposes. In the first place, a course in philosophy at Ingolstadt was not calculated to make the son of a civil servant from Backnang into a highly respected authority; second, he could in no way hope to achieve his ambition without first acquiring the title of Doctor. The University of Bologna, on the other hand, was the cradle of modern political science and jurisprudence. When the secretary was granted leave, it was here that he completed his legal studies and took his doctorate. Although the heyday of the "Studium Bolognese," renowned throughout Europe, was long past, Fickler could not have found a better place to advance his career. A doctorate in law from Bologna was a recommendation that was highly regarded everywhere.

It was not until he had this recommendation in his pocket that the Swabian thought of starting a family. He married in November 1566, that is, more or less at the same time as Paulus Pämb-Gämperl. And, as with the latter, it was his father-in-law who helped him on in his profession, for he was distantly related to the Archbishop of Salzburg's chancellor. Fickler became a councillor of state, but that still did not satisfy his ambition. His wife was only twenty and no doubt found it hard to understand why her husband scribbled away for whole nights on end. His labors were soon disturbed by the crying of children in the house, for his daughter Benigna was born in 1568 and his son Johann Christoph in 1570. Concordia followed in 1573, and Hans Georg in 1578. The hardworking councillor does not seem to have devoted much time to his children. In this respect at least, Pappenheimer's sons were better off.

For a long time it seemed that Fickler's abstinence, his scholarly zeal, and the frantic scraping of his quill were to be in vain.

The archbishop was not favorably disposed toward him or—even worse—appeared to ignore him. Fickler's massive literary nocturnes remained unprinted for lack of financial support. His requests for raises in salary were turned down. When superior posts fell vacant, others were preferred to the foreigner with the Swabian accent. He was anything but idle: he wrote to friends, put out feelers, ingratiated himself with his superiors. It was not until 1580, however, when he was in his late forties, that Fickler was at last appointed protonotary to the archbishop.

In this capacity he made the acquaintance of official guests of the archbishopric of Salzburg. These included on one occasion the entourage of the Bavarian princes Philipp, Ferdinand, and Charles, who were obliged to spend some time in Salzburg so that they might qualify for election to the archiepiscopal throne, should the occasion arise—a hope that the duke of Bavaria had not yet entirely relinquished. Whenever he had the chance, Fickler talked to the Bavarian officials about his dissatisfaction with his Salzburg appointment and about the possibilities of a move to Munich, not forgetting to hand the gentlemen a list of his published and unpublished works.

His diligence was rewarded: what he had hardly dared hope for came about. On 5 November 1588, Ulrich Speer, secretary to the duke of Bavaria, arrived in Salzburg, called on Fickler, and handed him a letter from William V, explaining that the duke wished to employ Dr. Baptist Fickler as tutor and mentor to his eldest son, Maximilian. What a distinction! A humble reply was hastily penned; Fickler submitted his resignation to the archbishop, packed his belongings, and set off for Ingolstadt. A few weeks after Speer's visit to Salzburg, Fickler arrived in the university town.

Homeless he might be, but the assiduous nocturnal scholar had finally achieved his elevated goal, after so many years. His mission in Ingolstadt had since come to an end, but his Bavarian service continued. Now, in the summer of 1592, he had found the place where he would remain. Munich, the duke's capital city! It wasn't a home; he was lonely, lacking friends and family. His wife had died young, without ever having understood this devotee of the midnight oil. The children had scattered to the four winds. But there was a monarch who was well disposed to him, and a prince he had educated and who would soon be duke himself. There were men of intelligence and taste who were able to appreciate his erudition. The proof of that erudition he was now carrying under his arm—the first copies, fresh from the press, of his "Reply to Dr. Heilbrunner's idle Prattle."

CHEERFUL COMPANY

Pappenheimer was not as lonely as Dr. Fickler; he even had friends. We can imagine these friends sitting with him, his wife, and his children at Ulrich Schölz's table, the afternoon sun shining through the cottage window. 1592 was a good year; there was work and bread in Tettenwang. Schölz's wife would have served bacon and cheese; no doubt a loaf of bread was passed round; there may even have been a jug of wine. The room was blackened with smoke, but it was pleasantly illuminated by shafts of light, and the whole company gorged, and gulped down their wine. There was a cheerful clamor of voices, a story everyone listened to, then an uproar of shouts and laughter, twice as loud as before.

The master of the house was a man of about sixty with a curly white beard. It was becoming more and more difficult for him to find work as a day laborer, but he contrived to scrape a living on the side as an innkeeper. As the Pappenheimer family moved around the country, they used to tell other traveling folk that they were well looked after at Schölz's house, and other guests began to turn up from time to time. Schölz charged ten kreuzer for a week's accommodation in his barn, with food extra. What he was doing was illegal: his sort were referred to as "hole-and-corner" landlords because they carried on their trade as innkeepers clandestinely and without supervision, so that all kinds of shady characters sought shelter in their obscure hostelries. The white-bearded old man, however, had more than just a commercial relationship with Paulus Pämb-Gämperl. He had known the Swabian for ten years, had seen his sons grow up and Paulus and his wife grow gray. He had children of his own, a few years older, who had now grown up and left home, but in years gone by they had romped around Tettenwang with the vagrant's boys. Schölz's wife had made friends with Pappenheimer's wife and used to sit with her for hours when the family came to visit them. The cottager did have his doubts about sheltering them. Other villagers, particularly the farmers, pestered him, telling him he ought not to take in such gypsy trash—which was true, for there was a strict order issued by the duke. Schölz might have been reported to the prefect's officials, who used to sit in Kaiser's inn from time to time. But he had always dismissed such misgivings. He could not manage without the extra earnings, and besides, he had known the Pappenheimer family for a long time and was not prepared to turn them away from his door.

There were a number of other Tettenwang cottagers sitting around the table. One of them, Hans Stumpf, had the nickname Glashänsel, or Glazier Jack. He was in his mid-forties and, like Michel and Gumpprecht, used to earn a few kreuzer by doing minor glazing jobs. Presumably it was he who had taught the two lads this craft. Glazier Jack had started life as a weaver and still earned a meager living in this cottage industry.

Another member of the company had also taken a special interest in the Pappenheimer boys, teaching them to play cards. Augustin Baumann, at twenty-three the youngest of the adults present, was conscious of a close bond between himself and the Pappenheimer family generally. He himself had been a vagrant until a few years before, when a stroke of good fortune made him the owner of a cottage and a plot of land. I am inclined to believe this stroke of luck came clad in petticoats, for Augustin Baumann was something of a lady's man. Many of his tales, which prompted loud guffaws and much slapping of thighs in the family circle, were concerned with maids and country wenches he had encountered in kitchens or stables while he was delivering bread. For this was his job, and he went from house to house with a pannier of loaves on his back. Not every day, and not at all when times were bad, so that he and his family had to earn a living with all kinds of "irksome labors." From time to time he used to get freshly killed hares, pheasants, and deer on favorable terms: the Tettenwang poacher, Jakob Gulden, was a friend of his. Of Gulden we learn that he was caught some time after this summer evening, and had his hand chopped off in Kelheim.

These three Tettenwang cottagers—Schölz, Glashänsel, and Baumann—were friendly not only with the Pappenheimers but also with each other. People in the village used to say that if you saw one of them, the others were not far away; and if you fell out with one, you had to reckon with all three. The bread delivery man and the weaver were stepbrothers; Schölz was godfather to Glashänsel's children, and vice versa. Their Tettenwang friends and acquaintances, who tended to take their side, included almost all the cottagers in the village: Kaiser, who kept the inn in Tettenwang; Georg the shepherd; Georg the horseman; Benedikt

74

the scarfweaver; Mathes the barber; Bastl the blacksmith; Math
the cooper; Resch the piper; and the slater and weaver, Erl.

One of their best friends was a relative who did not live in the
village but only came to visit them from time to time, as he had
done that afternoon. This was the tailor, Georg Schmälzl, who
had known the Pappenheimer family for a very long time. The
pale little man sat at the table, tucking into the food and chatting
with his friends. He lived in the nearby village of Prunn on the
River Altmuhl, beneath the picturesque castle which still looks
down into the narrow valley, as it did then. Georg Schmälzl was
related by marriage to Baumann and Stumpf, although he left his
wife at home when he set out on his trips to Tettenwang. Heaven
knows what prompted him to go there. He seemed to have little in
common with his uncouth companions: he was slightly built and
puny, bowed from stitching countless pairs of breeches, a comic
figure and yet courageous, as was to appear later. The perfect
model of the "little tailor." He was forty-two years old, honest and
poverty-stricken. In this circle of vagabonds and of cottagers who
were anything but affluent, he was the poorest of all. They all
knew that, and when the time came to settle up, the tailor did not
even need to turn out his empty pockets: he was their guest.

And so they must have sat then in the room warmed by the
sun—Paulus, Anna with Hänsel on her lap, Gumpprecht, Michel,
the weaver Hans Stumpf, Ulrich Schölz, his wife, the bread delivery man Augustin, and Georg Schmälzl, the little tailor from
Prunn—all in the best of spirits.

In those days they knew better how to enjoy themselves than
we do nowadays. The jokes were cruder, manners more relaxed,
the women's shrieks and the men's guffaws louder. They slavered
as they ate, grunting and belching; they drank deep drafts and
great quantities of wine and beer; they indulged all their senses
without the least restraint. The austere duke was only too well
aware that "all wine, mead, and ale houses" in his land "were full
both day and night," and that "the people consumed not according
to their need but did revel to excess and did with utmost shame-
lessness shout and sing and make merry and gamble." He could
not prevail, however, against his subjects' high spirits, which were
not just typical of Bavaria but a general feature of the age throughout Europe.

In the hostelries of the time, an average modest repast would
have consisted of five or six cooked courses, including either "two
dishes of good meat" or "a good dish of boiled or dried fish and one

of fried or baked fish."[43] Along with this there would be offered "two kinds of decent wine" and, to round off the meal, "cheese or fruit, but no manner of confectionery." It is said that the landgrave Moritz of Hesse joined with some of his fellow princes in 1601 to found an Order of Abstinence which required that no one should drink more than seven cups of wine at a meal. It was normal to drink several times that amount. It is true that "common men of no great means" and artisans were not permitted to go drinking in taverns more than one afternoon a week, and drinkers were not allowed to remain there after dark. On Sundays, alcohol was not served until after church services were over. To prevent people drinking away their property, the public-order regulations specified that no landlord might allow an indigent farmer more than two gulden credit for food and drink; the limit for the affluent was four gulden. But the regulations were not as stringent as they might appear, for whatever wine or beer householders ordered from a tavern "for their own needs" was exempt both from the prohibition on drinking and the restriction on credit. Behavior at the customary drunken parties was anything but genteel. Even in aristocratic circles it was quite normal to hurl the empty earthenware drinking vessels against the wall so that they shattered into a thousand fragments, to the accompaniment of a chorus of shouts. Table manners also sanctioned spitting on the floor, delousing oneself during the meal, or blowing one's nose into one's hand.[44]

The prevalence of hard drinking was liable to mar the celebration of weddings, as appears from a decree issued by Duke William V on 30 April 1587. It had come to his knowledge, wrote the prince, that the conduct of the rural population was disgraceful and wicked. When country folk celebrated a wedding, they would all get so drunk at the traditional wedding breakfast when the bride was fetched from her home that the wedding party would "not arrive at the church until eleven or twelve o'clock, all crazed with drink and making such a din with hilarity, shouting, and other scandalous conduct." Thus, "as, alas, always happens with excess of drink," the house of God was desecrated.

Such were the customs of the time, so that those who were stuffing themselves in Ulrich Schölz's cottage might strike us as relatively well behaved. After the meal the boys no doubt got up and ran outside to play with the cottagers' children in the dying light of the day. Pappenheimer's wife probably put Hänsel to bed in the barn and then helped Schölz's wife clear away and wash the dishes. And the men? Naturally they took out a pack of cards, or dice, or some other game and began to gamble. And so they carried on, cursing, shouting in triumph, banging their fists on the table, and roaring with laughter until the sun sank behind the willow woods and the darkness crept in through the window.

FROM PLACE TO PLACE

The family stayed in Schölz's barn for two or three weeks. Every day the old man went off with his adolescent sons to do the rounds of the farmers, emptying a cesspit here, patching a few pots there, putting a bull's-eye pane in the window of one of the larger farms. Then, early one morning, farewells and departure. Half a gulden pressed into the white-haired cottager's hand, an embrace for Schölz's wife, the carrying frame heaved up on to the man's back: the Pappenheimers were on their way once more.

Their way led down through the wood into the valley of the Schambach, where Tettenwang's abbey mill clattered and suspicious eyes followed the family on their way. They continued past the grayish white cliffs, topped by the Muggenthalers' castle, and down a gentle incline beside the brook, through the Hexenagger wood to Riedenburg in the Altmühl valley. There was a cottage there, too, where Paulus and his family would find shelter. Everywhere on his beat there were farmers and cottagers who, like Schölz, were his friends, and villages where he felt as much at home as in Tettenwang. And so he made his leisurely way with his family up the Altmühl valley as far as Eichstätt, taking the old Roman road from there via Kösching to Ingolstadt, following the Danube downstream, remaining a few days in Vohburg and in Neustadt before turning east toward Abensberg and then moving along the Abens to Siegenburg, where he crossed the wooded heights in the vicinity of Rohr and descended into the Laaber valley, finally reaching the Danube again at Straubing, via Schierling and Aufhausen.

His movements were not simply a matter of whim. He visited many places because there were fairs or markets there where he could set up his gaming table and where Anna could go begging. How he knew when a fair or carnival was due to be held I cannot say. Did he have, illiterate as he was, some sort of pocket calendar in which he had noted the previous year's dates? Did he simply have a good memory? Or did he merely follow other travelers who were attracted in crowds by the noise of any festivity?

The latter was probably the case, for the Pappenheimers were seldom by themselves in the stables and barns where they spent their nights. Peddlars, hucksters, beggars, fiddlers, journeymen, gamblers, touts, and all kinds of vagabonds made for the well-known "hole-and-corner" taverns. When there were fairs in progress, many of these were packed with guests—the cottage belonging to the tailor Hundsschlager, for instance, by the long bridge in Ingolstadt. A great deal of "guzzling and drinking" went on there, as we know from our vagrants, although there was less hulla-balloo than in licensed inns and taverns. For when spirits rose and threatened to erupt in the usual kind of racket, the cottagers, who earned a little extra by housing the vagrants, used to put their fingers beseechingly to their lips and beg their ragamuffin clients not to venture too often into the street. They were afraid the authorities might learn of their hospitality and raid their premises.

The prefect's officers knew very well that not all visitors to the fairs spent the night in recognized inns and taverns. "Foreigners," that is, peddlars and unlicensed traders from outside Bavaria, tramps, hucksters, alien beggars, and actors were not allowed to make their appearance at fairs, and certainly not to lodge overnight. But there were plenty of farmsteads and cottages where these undesirable guests might go to ground; and the laws governing the rights of city and country dwellers to serve beer and cider or to provide "dry hospitality" for couriers or carters were in any case far too complicated to be properly enforced. Nor should I conceal the fact that a good many officials used to eat and drink their fill in illegal taverns and apparently neither see nor hear anything untoward. There was hardly a householder who took in this riffraff for charitable reasons or from sheer recklessness. "There are people," it was reported to the duke on one occasion, "that shelter the beggars only on account of the alms they bring, share with them the bread they have begged, and, in a manner of speaking, are supported by the beggars." Pappenheimer knew many of that sort—Hans Wachter in Eggenfelden, for example, a poor cottager with a wife and four children. Wachter took the vagrants in so as to "share their meat and drink with them," without making any other charge. Those hosts who exploited their customers' situation by pushing up their prices were even worse. Georg Mair of Eggenfelden was one of these; he was not a proper brewer but used to brew illegally, "sometimes stout and sometimes light ale," which he offered his guests, "taking them in" in more senses than one. He encouraged the gang of vagabonds to drink to their hearts' content and then charged them three times the normal price, also demanding a hefty tip from each of them "by way of deduction." His guests could hardly point out that there were maximum prices for food and drink laid down by law; indeed, they had to be glad that they were allowed to lodge there at all. The brewer Mair with his shady, out-at-elbows clientele was better off, as far as that went, than any honest innkeeper in the town: for twenty kreuzer an innkeeper was required to serve a meal consisting of three meat dishes and three other courses, as well as fruit and cheese. He was not permitted to charge anything for the room; a guest was required to pay for his lodging only if he stayed longer than two days. Given constantly rising prices and a steady decline in the value of money at that time, it is easy to imagine that earning a living from a legitimate hostelry was something of an art. For that reason, many illegal hosts were disillusioned former landlords of licensed taverns: given favorable conditions, it was easier to make a go of it that way.

There was, it is true, a certain risk.[45] Anyone who "secretly fed and lodged nefarious vagabonds and idlers" was to be punished by "the appointed magistrate," i.e. by the imposition of a fine. Any repetition of the offense incurred banishment for a period of three years, while a third offense could be punished with torture, corporal punishment, and lifelong exile. In order to "eradicate vagrants the more quickly," the prefects received instructions from Munich "to conduct a general inspection and inquisition" in each judicial district in order to establish "which of our subjects is so bold as to harbor foreigners and persons unknown, without the permission of the authorities." Objection was raised to this order on the grounds that it was a pointless exercise, since "that manner of illegal lodging might not always and every day be inspected and raided by the authorities, the district courts being often far removed from such places." The duke, with his passion for regulations and his sense of divine ordination, was in any case highly incensed by what went on in country districts; consequently he was not to be fobbed off with arguments of that sort. He announced even more emphatically that "the lodging of persons unknown in this our realm and not here resident is utterly and expressly forbidden to all, whoever they may be, whether dwelling in towns or markets, in villages or in wastelands." Exempt from this prohibition were "hostels and taverns situated on regular highways," but these were required to report guests of the above-mentioned kind to the authorities without delay. The response was typical: here, as in similar cases where the duke's resolve to impose law and order turned out to be impracticable on account of difficulties of communication and enforcement, the gracious monarch in Munich behaved like an obstinate child. In a sense he was saying in midsummer: It must snow. When they tried to explain to him that it was impossible, we can imagine him stamping his foot pettishly and saying: That's just why I want it to snow.

In the twenty years of their travels, the Pappenheimer family lodged with illegal landlords of this kind in every town or village they visited. Not one of them was ever affected by the ducal ban. It was only when the vagrants had betrayed hundreds of their hosts in the Falcon Tower that one of them was made an example of: the cottager Staidl "from Hornsdorf close by the bridge across the Danube at Straubing" was banished by the duke's administration.

Paulus and his family did not depend solely on such hole-and-corner innkeepers. In a number of places they lodged with friends—in Gänkhofen, for example, with "Beindlkramer" ("Bone merchant") the village gravedigger; or in the vicinity of Rottenburg on the Laaber with the peddlar Ulrich, who had once been a tramp himself; or with a farmer called Michel in Rettenbach, whose brother had been executed by the authorities and who thus made common cause with a family that was the object of so much persecution.

When the first hoarfrost lay in the mornings on the gentle hills in the land through which they traveled, and the boys shattered the thin ice on the puddles, Paulus began looking for winter quarters. He called at the poorhouses in the larger market towns and in the cities, begging for pity's sake to be taken in and saved from freezing to death. This he did, for instance, in Kelheim, where he knew the custodian and often found shelter from the bitter winter winds.

Such establishments, called hospitals, were actually shelters for the poor, supported by charitable townspeople and farmers or by monasteries and abbeys. As a rule, the Pappenheimers accepted only the free lodging for themselves and their children and continued to earn their keep with all kinds of odd jobs. As soon as the days grew longer and the snow on the meadows melted, the family would depart suddenly and without warning.

He and his wife grew old and weary on their travels; the two elder sons grew up into young men; and young Hänsel succeeded them as the one who ran on in front, starting hares and catching lizards. Twenty years is a long time. It adds rings to tree trunks and engraves wrinkles in human faces.

CHAPTER · 3

SERENISSIMVS MAXIMILIANVS COMES PALATINVS RHENI · SVPERIORIS AC INFERIORIS BAVARIAE DVX ✥

DOMINVS VIRTVTVM NOBISCVM

*D*uke Maximilian
of Bavaria

⋆ The Heights

On the afternoon of 20 April 1600, Dr. Johann Simon Wangereck was sitting at his desk in Munich's Dienerstrasse, surrounded by paper, some of it blank, some covered with writing. He was engaged in preparing the list of questions for Gumpprecht Pappenheimer's examination. We see him glancing through the record of previous interrogations until he finds a particular statement. He then extracts the page with the relevant note from the pile in front of him, selects one of the pens from the inkwell on his right, wipes off the surplus ink on the metal rim of the inkwell, and proceeds to underline the passage he has just read. Then, perhaps struck by a sudden thought, he abruptly lays down his pen and begins to leaf through another bundle of documents—the files from Abensberg-Altmannstein.

Wangereck's list was probably not very long at this point. He had headed it "Interrogatoria relating to Gumpp Pämb, the tinker lad," and had written down nine questions as to the accused's person, his whereabouts and movements, and his manner of earning a living. Preparing these examinations was an irksome business. Wangereck had been sitting in council all day, debating and casting his vote, and now, perhaps with the mild spring air wafting through his window, he had to organize his "items" for tomorrow's interrogation. Strictly speaking, it was already too late. According to the letter of the law, he ought to have read out his questions in council and had them approved. As if the council had nothing better to do than prepare interrogations for a bunch of tramps! Why burden the entire committee with the details of the case? Wangereck had been appointed to conduct the investigation and was consequently empowered to pursue it to the point where a judgment could be reached. "The individual questions are to be read out in council beforehand," the regulation stated, and that was laudable and entirely justified, as far as it went. But of course it was also open to interpretation. Tacit agreement in advance on the part of the councillors to all questions that Wangereck deemed relevant—that was certainly tantamount to a formal reading. If only the law was construed in the right spirit, then there was no difficulty in complying with it.

The art of interpretation—how well Wangereck had mastered it! The law read: "The itemized questions shall be drawn from previous evidence, they shall be distinctly and intelligibly framed, and the arrested person shall in no wise be prompted, nor have suggested to him what he is to say." This, too, was laudable and to the point, in principle. In practice, however, it could not invariably be applied without qualification. In a case like the Pappenheimers', how could you coordinate the statements of five different members of the family without nudging them gently in the direction of the truth? It was not simply a matter of loosening the criminals' tongues with the help of Master Georg. From terror or sheer malice they would often confess to imaginary crimes and conceal those they had in fact committed. But if a number of statements by different suspects tallied, that was a sign there might be some truth in the confessions. And in order to obtain such corroboration as quickly as possible, surely exceptions to the rule about prompting suspects had to be permitted from time to time. There was no need even to speak of exceptions, for if the suspect was confronted only indirectly with the statements of his accomplices, the principle had not been breached. A clever lawyer had only to read the law correctly in order to comply with it.

We see Wangereck pick up his pen again, dip it in the inkwell, and write the number "10" on his sheet of paper. Alongside it he writes down the question he has been trying to frame all this time: To what use had he, Grumpprecht, his father, and his brother put the children's hands that had been found in Tettenwang? He no doubt read the question through once more to double-check it, and then amended it to include the mother of the family as well. Finally, he wrote beside it the note, "Torqueatur—apply torture!" The question was a trap, an expedient falsehood by which Wangereck hoped to disconcert the prisoner. No children's hands had in fact been found in Tettenwang. They had searched for them all right, several times, in Schölz's barn and in his vegetable patch, but in vain. Perhaps there was some kind of devilry involved in the

84

disappearance of such vital clues: mischief of that sort, after all, was often attributed to the Archenemy. Wangereck thought it perfectly possible that the powers of darkness had forestalled Haslang's men in their attempt to secure incriminating evidence. But that—so his thoughts probably ran—that would not help the scoundrels. After all, he need not show the evidence to the accused, he need only claim to have it in his possession. A bluff, but useful and to the purpose. It would be to the prisoners' own advantage to realize how pointless all their denials were.

Tricks and ruses were essential if progress was to be made in this case. We see Wangereck leafing through the reports from Abensberg again and again, and then throwing them down in exasperation. The evidence was thin and not really sufficient to satisfy the theory of corpus delicti, with which every lawyer was familiar.[46] This stated that prosecutions might not be brought against one or more suspects until it was clear beyond all doubt that a crime had in fact been committed: *Judici ante omnia constare debet de delicto*. According to this principle, no person could be arrested as a thief or murderer if there was no evidence of actual theft or murder. Mere rumor was not enough, suspicion must be based on a proven act. Thus, ill repute could serve as grounds for arrest only if the person concerned had been present in a place where a corpse had been discovered or a church plundered. Any law student in his first semester knew that, and also knew that a subsequent confession on the part of an arrested person could not serve as a substitute for missing proof of a criminal act. If a person of ill repute admitted to a murder, that did not in principle bear upon the legality of detaining him. The murder to which he had confessed must be known and proven beforehand. This principle of *constare de delicto* was expressed in a provision of Emperor Charles V's penal code that "no person might be examined under torture unless sufficient evidence has first been found of the criminal act being investigated." The confession was meant to prove the perpetrator, not the act: the criminal could not be brought to book before the fact of the crime had been established.

This, then, was the principle; it was laudable and fully justified. We may well suspect that Wangereck will apply it correctly to the Pappenheimer case, conforming to it without complying with it too slavishly. All the same, he must have been exasperated that the evidence was so flimsy. There was evidence, in fact, of no more than a single crime, namely the claim by Geindl, the thief who had been hanged in Wörth, that the two tinker lads had aided and abetted him. They had helped him murder pregnant women for the hands of their unborn children. Evidence of a sort, it is true, but really no more than a denunciation. There was no proof: the women's bodies had never been found, nor had the severed hands turned up so far. The further claim by Geindl that the Pappenheimers "went around killing people" referred merely to the alleged criminals and not to any actual crime. The same was true of the evil reputation that tramps and vagrants enjoyed among affluent farmers. Such a reputation was calculated to render the family highly suspect, but it was no substitute for the corpus delicti. That is why Wangereck had written again, a few days earlier, to the prefect of Abensberg-Altmannstein and requested him to have Schölz's cottage searched once more—and more thoroughly this time. He could hardly hope for any more clues from Wörth concerning the alleged murder of the seven women. These cases had been allowed to lapse when no evidence was forthcoming: Geindl's execution could be carried out on the grounds of his other crimes. Supposing the renewed search for clues in Tettenwang failed to unearth a corpus delicti, then it looked as if they would have to manage without one.

A lawyer of Dr. Johann Simon Wangereck's stamp would not be much dismayed by that prospect. "In the case of particularly grave and heinous offenses," ran one of the procedural regulations, "it is permissible to depart from customary procedural and legal principles." Applied to the Pappenheimer case, this meant in effect: the vagrants were suspected of particularly evil offenses; they were, in fact, "notorious killers, robbers, and arsonists." In dealing with crimes of that kind, no account need be taken of the theory of corpus delicti.

How could this be? Anyone who tries to grasp the legal logic of that age with the help of mere common sense will think: what nonsense! In the case of major felonies like murder, robbery, and arson, is not the actual deed sufficiently plain and easy to prove? And is it not precisely in such cases that the potential punishment is most severe, and the risk of a miscarriage of justice most acute?

We only have to construe the law correctly in order to understand. True, it was not possible at the outset to charge these suspects, the Pappenheimer family, with actual crimes. But the fact that the crimes of which they were accused were taking place daily throughout the length and breadth of the land was, after all, a regrettable truth. There were any number of corpora delicti: they lay in the ditches in the form of corpses, and loomed up in the

86

form of charred ruins. Who could be held responsible for these vicious crimes if not the tramps, hucksters, beggars, gypsies, and other such idle, depraved travelers on the highways? At any rate, the prisoners in the Falcon Tower belonged to that wicked crew and therefore were immediately suspected of the crimes mentioned above. What was more, they had been incriminated by a convicted thief. The principle of *constare de delicto* had certainly not been framed for the benefit of such riffraff, who had for long been given short shrift; but it could still be applied, provided it was correctly construed. The legal mind was fully capable of resolving any apparent paradoxes.

It was on lines such as these that a Doctor Juris like Wangereck would have discussed the procedural problem offered by this case. Not that he had any call to do so: nobody at that time doubted that the Pappenheimers' arrest was justified—apart, that is, from their friends among the cottagers of Tettenwang.

But *they* were "nobodies." That is why the busy councillor could devote himself solely to the compilation of his list of questions, without worrying too much about the correct interpretation of the statutes. He had filled four folio pages with questions when he arrived at number 62: Was it true that his mother really had the falling sickness, or was she merely pretending? At this point he thought it proper to add the note, "Can be tortured to the limit so that he incriminates his mother."

Dusk must have fallen while the list of questions was being drawn up for the following day's examination. Perhaps Wangereck interrupted his work briefly to glance through the window and note that the trees and shrubs in the gardens and courtyards were already showing the first hint of tender green. Spring was on the way. However, the councillor had no time to spare for the contemplation of nature. He had to finish his list, and then compose another letter to Alexander von Haslang, requesting the prefect of Abensberg and Altmannstein to arrest the Pappenheimers' friends in Tettenwang and have them brought to Munich. That would incur more expense, of course. But the duke was keen to set an example, and Wangereck was determined that nobody should accuse him of doing his job halfheartedly.

THE YOUNG DUKE [47]

In a dank vault, dimly lit by the mystic blue and red light that filtered through tall Gothic windows, a solitary, slender figure was kneeling on an unyielding wooden bench and passing a black rosary through his clasped hands. The lofty chamber was filled with the fragrance of incense and the distant murmur of a priest reading the liturgy at an altar illuminated by a flickering candle. The solitary man's lips moved silently as he knelt there: Hail Mary, full of grace . . . His face was pale, gaunt, and solemn; the severely trimmed dark beard and the mustache with its ends turned slightly upward contrasted oddly with the sunken, languishing eyes. His lumpy, irregular nose with its blunted end and narrow, elongated nostrils hinted at sensuality and self-indulgence, an impression belied by the short, vertical furrows between the eyebrows and the high brow merging into incipient baldness. The young man's sparse, dark brown hair stood out in an unruly curly forelock, baring his ears, which were delicately formed but a shade too prominent. A white ruff trimmed with exquisitely delicate lace framed this equivocal countenance and descended over a black velvet doublet fastened with little copper buttons. From the doublet there emerged the full sleeves of an ornately embroidered blouse. The bulging folds of his baggy, dark red damask breeches came down only to his thighs and revealed the full length of his thin legs clad in silken hose.

The man who knelt there at evening prayer was the supreme judge of the Pappenheimers, master of their fate: Maximilian I, by the grace of God Count Palatine of the Rhine, Duke in Upper and Lower Bavaria. He had celebrated his twenty-seventh birthday a few days earlier, but this was a man who had never been young. After seven years in the care of nurses he had been surrounded by an entourage in the Spanish style while still a child, confined within the gloomy precincts of the Old Palace and subjected to a strict regime of tutors, preceptors, and confessors—the object of an educational experiment. His father, William, already dubbed "the Pious" by his subjects, had tried to turn the skinny, pallid youth into an ideal prince. It is not uncommon for fathers to wish that their sons might become something they themselves are not. Seldom, however, has a child been so much at the mercy of his parent's will. Like Kaspar Hauser in his dark cellar, Maximilian was doomed to degenerate into a psychological cripple in his dungeon of a palace.

Not that his father was hard-hearted; he was simply weak. He was well aware of his own weakness and constantly in fear of it. Never once had he given way to a natural predilection for the carefree pleasures of the senses, perpetually denying such indulgence and waging painful war against his own fondness for all that was

88

beautiful. He wished to spare his son this battle by stifling at birth any tendency to indulge in the sinful pleasures of life.

If it is true that boys often take after their grandfathers, then Maximilian had a good many ominous proclivities, for his paternal grandfather, Duke Albrecht V, had been, to put it bluntly, a gross drunkard. Not a drunkard of the cheerful, epicurean sort, not a witty, rakish bohemian, but one of the melancholy kind, a victim of his appetites rather than a devotee of sensual delights. We have heard of this prince from time to time because he usually figures in heart-warming tales in which he appears, accompanied by a tame lion, in the character of the pious monarch. This image in no sense corresponded to the reality, and nobody knew that better than his son William. Albrecht passed his days in dicing, gambling, card playing, eating, drinking, and listening to music. His collections of books, objets d'art, and curios swallowed up vast sums of money. The court orchestra, led by the Dutchman Roland Lassus, who Italianized his name as Orlando di Lasso, was Albrecht's incredibly extravagant private indulgence. This reprobate of a grandfather had no time at all for administrative duties, and not much more for the practice of government, leaving politics entirely to his councillors and chancellors. In only one respect did fanatical concern come in the course of the years to run counter to his general indifference—and that concern was the Catholic faith. Since the religious settlement of Augsburg had given to each secular authority the power to determine which denomination its subjects should belong to, the prince had begun to hunt down the members of other faiths with a gusto that he otherwise evinced only in the chase. This vigorous assault on local heretics led to increased support for the Jesuits throughout his realm and for the strictly Catholic advisers and sycophants who thronged to his court.

There is no doubt that even Albrecht V, who, like all alcoholics, deplored his own mode of life, had every intention of turning his son into an ideal ruler. William was to learn precisely what his father lacked: a capacity for hard work and self-control. He could well use both: hard work, because he was somewhat intellectually dull; self-control, because he had inherited certain of his father's tendencies. At the age of eight the prince was put into the charge of strict tutors, whose task was to eradicate any trace of childish imagination by means of regular religious exercises and an unrelenting timetable of studies. The child was made to struggle against his own artistic and sensual nature. He was not naturally assertive, in fact, and had to force himself to acquire regular habits and a taste for hard work. From an early age he sought refuge in a sentimental kind of religiosity, finding a substitute for forbidden childhood dreams in the officially approved mysticism of the saints. That was to remain the case throughout his life. Aware of his own weakness, he clung to superior authority; having too little confidence in himself, he relied totally on the advice of his confessor and the commandments of the only true church. He observed painstakingly the daily ritual prescribed for him by the Jesuits, with its masses, devotions, and periods of work, its soul-searching and spiritual exercises. This slavish, monkish obedience betrays his sheer terror of sinning through taking his own decisions, the horror of failure felt by a man who knows he is not equal to his responsibilities. It was his mediocrity that made William the very model of a Catholic prince, turned his court into a monastery and the ruler himself into an ascetic penitent and self-flagellating pilgrim. At the cost of enormous financial sacrifice he built in the heart of his capital a palace for the Jesuits that contemporaries compared to the Escorial in Spain. In agreement with his spiritual advisers he continued his father's battle against heretics at home and abroad, but he also stepped up supervision of his subjects, since he had been persuaded that he was responsible to God for the welfare of their souls. A great politician he was not. Unlike his dissipated father, he did not shirk matters of state but, being hesitant and slow on the uptake, he tended to follow the suggestions put to him by others. By brutally suppressing the aspirations of his Protestant subjects he sought to present himself to his people as a strict but just father figure, while in foreign policy he had no eye for long-term developments. He was most determined and most successful where his wish to augment his domestic authority happened to coincide with the interests of the Catholic church: thus he succeeded in obtaining the bishopric of Cologne and a seat in the electoral college for his brother Ernst. Possibly he deluded himself into thinking that he was not only a saint but also an important statesman: at one time he appeared to be pursuing a fanciful plan to become Holy Roman Emperor. At heart, however, he must have suspected that prayers, pilgrimages, and hair shirts do not make a saint any more than the defense of the Catholic position in the empire would make him a great politician. Above all, he could no longer turn a deaf ear to the complaints of his chamberlains: donations to the Jesuits, bribes to Cologne, and the costs of the war had brought the state to the brink

of bankruptcy. Although still in the prime of life, William, overtaxed as he was, began to look around for some way of escape. His
son Maximilian was to be placed in a position to take over responsibility as soon as possible. That is why he had the shy, slender
child trained from his tender years to be a prince.

The black rosary slipped through the duke's clasped hands as
he prayed: Hail Mary, full of grace. He had been instructed in the
love of the Virgin Mary early in life, too. By the time he had
learned to read he already knew the Officium Beatae Virginis by
heart and repeated it several times each day; he also knew the
Laurentian Litany and the five verses of the Corona quinque-
genaria, an early form of the rosary customary today. His eager-
ness to learn was soon noticed: "He rode his pony down to the
meadow," we read in his tutor's report to his father; "then he went
through the meadows with us as far as Thalkirchen and joined in
the singing of the Latin litany; at Mass he said three rosaries and a
special paternoster together with the Ave Maria for all of those
specially included in his daily prayers." At that time Maximilian
was seven years old. When he was eleven, he was enrolled in the
Munich Congregation of Mary, a Jesuit society dedicated to "the
revival of trust in the intercession of Mary." In 1581 his father had
dedicated his capital city to "the Virgin of Altötting" and in 1585
had gone on a pilgrimage to Loreto. The cult of the Virgin Mary
was the provocative response on the part of the Jesuits to Protestant criticism of the adoration of the saints; it became enor-
mously popular in Munich during Maximilian's childhood and set
its stamp on the child's religious imagination.

Piety was the first virtue that the boy, as future prince, had to
acquire. In second place came reading and writing, Latin grammar
and rhetoric, an acquaintance with Ovid, Horace, Cicero, Plutarch,
and Livy. Such erudition was not intended to be an end in itself: it
was seen as a means to the knowledge of God and the true faith,
and was correspondingly tinged with religion. The third subject in
the curriculum was Justice. How might that be learned? "Through
examples," ran the instruction. The prince was to be shown "that
princes and authorities are ordained by God in order to defend the
true service of God and the true, unadulterated faith, to rule their
subjects justly and fairly, and to maintain public peace and order."
Since the ruler, according to the opinion of the age, was no more
than the father of his people, he had to take a personal interest in
all matters. Consequently he had to be familiar with laws and leg-
islative processes, administration and the constitution, finance

and military matters—a considerable load. Here again, his tutors were less concerned with his knowledge as such than with the right use of that knowledge. The boy was taught that a prince was a warrior in the cause of Christ who had to lead heretics "back into the fold." When he was seventeen, he made a note in his notebook, "If thou art a truly Catholic prince, then thou hast a duty to lead thy subjects unto the true Catholic faith, as far as that may be possible . . . Therefore be not lenient, but moderate in all things." A model pupil.

Holy Mary, Mother of God, intercede for us sinners. Slowly a rosary slipped through lean, bony fingers. He had not found it easy to repress his yearning for light, love, and life. No doubt he would have wished to be lenient, had he dared, but he was forced to conceal his diffident nature behind a studied gruffness. All that was weak, tender, and heartfelt in him was to be eradicated. Only in the sentimental adoration of the incomparable Virgin Mary might it be permitted to emerge. This is why the hours of his private devotions were very important to the duke. Like his father, he fled from a world that demanded a chilly austerity of him into the mystic gloom of a church fragrant with incense. A different character might have revolted and burst the fetters laid on his soul by zealous tutors. Not Maximilian; he tried to meet the demands made on him, he was industrious to the point of self-denial; he held his breath, as it were, in the cruelly strait-laced corset he had been forced to don as a child. He was bright, not dull like his father, intelligent, determined, witty—but a rebel he was not. He was notable for composure and self-discipline, not for any yearning for liberty and self-assertion. Later, Bavarian historians were to bestow on him the title "the Great." That was to some extent justified, but not on grounds of his character: he was, after all, a petty-minded man. He lacked charisma, the aura of genius: he emanated nothing but the chilly, slightly pungent odor of the sedulous pedant.

Hail to Thee, Mary. The rosary would be finished any moment now, his devotions punctually completed. The young duke kept strictly to his daily program, which began well before daybreak and continued until nightfall. This was the only way he could cope with the tasks that had to be performed. Three years earlier his father had placed the entire burden of government on his shoulders, partly of his own free will, partly because he was forced to. Although it seemed shameful to be ousted from office on account of financial mismanagement, it was nevertheless tempting

92

to escape once for all the demands he could not meet, and henceforth to lead the life of an affluent holy man. Maximilian, on the other hand, could hardly wait to take over the reins of government, for he wished to prove that he could be first among his peers in practice as well as in theory. To put the state finances back on a proper footing, and to get a grip on the administration: those were the main priorities. He had long since realized that, and now it was a matter of putting his plans into effect, step by step. Above all, he must see to things himself, and not leave them to be dealt with by dilatory and stubborn chancellors and chamberlains. At the same time it was important to take over the public-order regime his father had introduced with the aim of suppressing sin and immorality, and to develop it into a system of universal surveillance of his subjects. He was determined to take measures to provide security in the country at last. An end must be put to arson, murder, and robbery on the highways. Since decrees and police patrols had proved ineffective, he would deter the villains by ruthless prosecution. He had given instructions for a show trial to be prepared in his capital city. A few days previously he had been informed that a case had been found which would provide a suitable example, and that the culprits were already lodged in the Falcon Tower. This was the gist of one of the many hundred documents that passed across his desk each day. His measures had begun to take effect, the stranded ship of state was once more afloat. He had been at the helm for barely three years, and his competence was already obvious to all. No doubt he was filled with the pride of the top boy in the class who had once more shown what he could do.

The young duke had completed his devotions. He raised his eyes, gazed up into the dim heights of the vaulted roof for a moment, transferred the rosary to his left hand, made the sign of the cross with his right, rose quickly to his feet, and left the creaking pew. His knees, calloused from childhood by pious exercises, hurt as they always did. But after a few stiff strides his body grew taut as he pulled himself together: it was not Maximilian's habit to give in.

GOD AND POWER

It is astonishing how little the Pappenheimers were affected by the major issue of the age, the conflict of religious confessions: in all their examinations, no one ever asked them to which church they belonged, and, as far as they were concerned, they apparently did not think it worth mentioning. There is scarcely any doubt, however, that our vagrants were Lutherans. Paulus and Anna came from areas that were solidly Lutheran; the elder sons were baptized in Ansbach and Nuremberg, therefore according to the Protestant rite; Hänsel was taken by his parents to be baptized in Regensburg, the only Lutheran city on their beat. It is remarkable that religion seems otherwise to have played hardly any part in their lives— neither in their association with the cottagers of Tettenwang, nor in the choice of their itinerary, nor in their search for accommodation. Nowhere did they encounter any problems on account of their faith, and were presumably not even asked about it. On the lowest social level, religious denomination seems not to have been a real issue.

On the highest level it certainly was. Just as with the present struggle between communism and capitalism, the denominational conflict of the sixteenth and seventeenth century led to a Gordian knot in which ideological motives were entangled with the struggle for political power. Martin Luther's ninety-five theses of 31 October 1517 were like a spark falling into dry hay: fuel of a tangible, down-to-earth kind was ready to hand, although it was the Wittenberg professor's intellectual spark that set it alight. Who can say whether the flames that soon flared up everywhere came from the burning material or from a spark that had taken on material form?

Contrary to present-day appearances, Luther's words had not fallen on deaf ears, even in Bavaria.[48] This was true in the country at large, and it was even true of the dukes William IV and Ludwig X, who were joint rulers at the time. When the pope threatened to excommunicate Luther and his followers in his bull "Exsurge Domine" of March 1521, they were in no hurry to act as instruments of the Vatican's fury. Their motto was "proceed cautiously" and wait and see. The pros and cons of any decision must be carefully weighed.

This was because religious emancipation from Rome was closely linked from the very beginning with a parallel issue in the political field.[49] The emperor had once had the power to foster the Roman faith and had used it, possibly from Christian conviction but also because the united church helped to unite the many peoples of the empire. That power, however, had been lost or frittered away, and the circumstances of the time favored new and smaller units, with territorial princes everywhere setting up their own

94

small monarchies, consolidating their power at home, and throwing off the imperial yoke. In practical terms, too: the Church was one of the intermediate powers in the territorial states which obstructed stricter central government. To eliminate the Church was to remove an irritating obstacle on the path to absolute rule, but it also implied access to church livings and the domains of monasteries, ecclesiastical foundations, and bishoprics. And, finally, there was the chance to gain control of their subjects' conscience by founding their own churches under the monarch's control: tempting prospects.

On the other hand, the barons, the lesser nobility, knights, squires, and cities opposed the growing power of the territorial princes, were determined not to submit to it, and saw the Protestant movement as an expression of their own struggle for independence. As a result, the new doctrine soon won friends in these circles. Although the Church had made common cause with the other estates against increasing control by the territorial princes, the clergy were obliged to take the side of their natural enemy. Threatened by the flames of the new doctrine in their own ranks, the Church was forced to raise the white flag and to desert to the territorial princes in their search for aid: better to lose a measure of freedom than to perish altogether. This suited the territorial ruler very well. Commissioned by the highest authority of all, and invested with the halo of a savior of the one true Church, he could force to their knees the rebellious estates who stood in his way. The only problem that remained was how to preserve his own independence vis-à-vis emperor and pope.

That is not to say that William IV and Ludwig X were not concerned with questions of conscience and faith when they met in February 1522 at Grünwald Castle in the Isar valley to discuss the situation. The Bavarian dukes' discussion of religious issues was, however, conducted very much in the light of reports of religiously motivated uprisings in the country. The Lutheran doctrine, they feared, might lead to "rebellion, tumult, and violence." Apart from that, there were considerations of foreign policy to be taken into account. As next-door neighbors of the Habsburgs, it seemed unwise for the dukes to provoke the emperor by a break with the Roman church. On the other hand, the position of Catholicism in the empire was so threatened, that a high price might be exacted for their loyalty: the beleaguered church in their domain had already been compelled to seek some kind of protection from the princes.

In short: there were advantages in remaining Catholic. That is why the dukes' consciences, guided toward what was politically sensible via the shadowy realm of the subconscious, gave preference to the "Catholic solution." From that time onward the Bavarian rulers consistently opposed the Lutherans in their realm. There was, for instance, Magister Arsacius Seehofer from Ingolstadt, who was condemned for his "Lutheran mischief" and narrowly escaped the stake. The preacher Leonhard Kaiser was not so fortunate: he was publicly burned in Schärding in 1527. The early persecution of Protestants in Bavaria was one reason the country was not involved in the great Peasant War of 1525–26. That in itself confirmed the usefulness of the decisions taken at Grünwald.

But the policy paid off in other respects as well. Forced to rely on Bavaria as a bulwark of the faith, the Roman Curia soon left the control of the local church to the princes' government. As a result, the duke was hardly worse off than the Protestant rulers who had formed their own Protestant state churches. It is true that he had to leave Church property unmolested, but he was able to break the resistance of the clergy by the influence he brought to bear on ecclesiastical appointments. He obtained some return for refraining from a policy of secularization: political support from abroad, as well as money, came via Rome. At the same time their imperial neighbor, whom they had no wish to strengthen, had been obliged to adopt a benevolent attitude, for the emperor needed the most powerful Catholic state in the empire as his ally. But it was within its own frontiers that the Bavarian ruling house reaped the richest return for its loyalty to the old faith. There were still a few imperial territories within those frontiers, ugly stains on the map of the principality, which were difficult to eradicate without breaking the law: Ortenburg, near Passau; Haag, near Munich; Waldeck on the fringe of the Alps. When the authorities in these territories underlined their independence following the religious settlement of Augsburg in 1555 by adopting the *ius reformandi* and putting Lutheran preachers in the pulpits of their tiny realms, the duke of Bavaria was in a position to intervene rapidly and seize—in the name of God—the booty he had coveted for so long. The religious scruples and the political interests of the Bavarian dukes continued to coincide in a similarly advantageous fashion in the course of subsequent history—in the struggle for the episcopal throne of Cologne, the occupation of

Donauwörth, the acquisition of the Upper Palatinate, and the seizure of the electoral mandate from their Palatinate cousins.

The reactionary character of the decisions taken at Grünwald later manifested itself in the struggle against uncatholic tendencies amongst the duke's subjects. It was no accident that this campaign involved the suppression of all opposition on the part of the estates and the city authorities. Opposition there certainly was, as is shown by a spontaneous demonstration that took place in Munich. One Sunday in June 1558 the congregation in the church of St. Augustine suddenly began to sing Lutheran hymns. Father Seidl's sermon, in which he was defending the pope against heretical attacks, was constantly interrupted by hecklers and raucous laughter. We know of this incident because of the stringent inquiry to which it gave rise. It shows how widely disseminated the new doctrine was among the citizens of Munich, and how very strongly those citizens felt that conformism in religion inevitably led to the abrogation of political rights. A good many of the worthiest citizens avoided the threat by moving to Protestant cities like Augsburg, Regensburg, and Nuremberg, taking all their possessions with them. Others sought refuge in a kind of inner emigration, formed secret sectarian groups, and lent each other prohibited Protestant books. It proved impossible to eradicate these last vestiges of resistance by means of house searches, inquisitions, or the collection of certificates of confession, but such methods left their mark on the self-confidence of the city's inhabitants, which was no doubt their true purpose.

Ever since 1563 there had been Corpus Christi processions, counterdemonstrations ordered by the authorities in response to occasional angry flare-ups among the Munich population. The common people stared open-eyed and open-mouthed at the spectacle. Tableaux vivants from the Old and New Testament paraded past; St. George's battle with the dragon was performed in mime; banners, statues, magnificent baldachins were carried past. The sight of such wondrous things banished rational argument: bread and circuses. All citizens of a political persuasion, the city councillors, patricians, the educated class, were obliged to take part in the processions, as were the civil service and the court. Anyone who did not join in invited suspicion and had good reason to fear unpleasant consequences. In such ways the prince utilized the defense of the established faith in order to discipline his subjects and to extend his new-found authority.

He could not cope so easily with the country's hereditary aristocracy, the knights, counts, and barons, for many of them thought themselves the equals of the prince—with good reason, and on grounds of their ancient descent. According to legend, as venerable as it was plausible, God had conferred the fertile lands of this earth as a fief on the emperor, with the power to pass them on to others. The emperor had subsequently availed himself of this power and allocated the land entrusted to him to his officials and to deserving warriors. In this way the landed aristocracy came into being. If the emperor then also chose to entrust certain of his vassals with additional administrative functions—by making Wittelsbach duke of Bavaria, for instance, in 1180—that did not affect the status of the others. All of them owed their fiefs to the emperor, and to the emperor alone. They regarded the duke as their peer, and his special position simply as issuing from the imperial authority. When the ducal dignity became hereditary as a result of shrewd political maneuvering, the issue whether it might be termed imperial or inherent was reduced to an argument about words. The power of the noble family that supplied the ducal nominee grew greater in the course of the centuries, much to the annoyance of the other imperial vassals, who found it of less and less avail to insist on their theoretical equality.

The duke was in fact now vindicating his superior rank without recourse to the emperor. It was quite correct, he reassured his peers, that he was on the same footing as they were as far as his enfeoffment was concerned. But what did that count for in comparison with the divine will, which had, after all, elevated him to princely status from the ranks of those same peers? It was obvious that it was God Himself, and not the emperor, who had raised him up. If He who guided the universe, the supreme Landlord on earth, had not wished to confer on him his dignity and authority as duke, then it would not have been granted, or certainly long since revoked. Looked at in that light, the emperor had merely acted as the instrument of a greater power when he appointed one of his vassals to be duke. The ancestors of the present ruling prince could only have fought their way to supremacy in their land because they were acting with the tacit consent and the miraculous succor of the Supreme Power. In short: since everything that comes to pass corresponds to the will of God, this must also be true of the enhancement of the duke's authority. As a visible effect of that idea, the duke added the words "by the grace of God" to his title, thus making it clear that he owed his rank neither to the emperor nor to the consent of his estates.

Nonetheless, traditional rights still existed which could not be thus swept away by political theories, no matter how ingenious. In particular, the duke had to proceed cautiously in his dealings with the estates because of their power to sanction taxation. It took centuries to subdue them altogether. William V and Maximilian I pursued their policy step by step, paring away the privileges of the aristocracy, forcing them into economic dependence, keeping a close watch on their mode of life. As far as the last was concerned, the princes' position as defenders of true Christianity once more proved extremely useful. They even availed themselves of it against the clergy: monasteries and ecclesiastical houses were also subject to supervision by the duke's Spiritual Council.

The Pappenheimers knew little or nothing of all this. And yet the power structures of the land they traversed were a decisive factor in determining their fate. The prosecution brought against them was not designed simply to deter the ruffians who infested the highways; it was also meant to prove to the aristocracy and the cities who it was that held sway over life and death in the principality. It was a matter of demonstrating the ducal authority.

THE SOUND OF BELLS

We find Gumpprecht Pämb lying on the straw of his cell with limbs torn and bruised, listening to the sound of the bells drifting through the open window. For two days running the twenty-year-old youth had been questioned and tortured down in the vaults of the Falcon Tower. The previous day he had been spared, but he had learned from the ironmaster's wife that Councillors Wangereck and Hainmüller and Treasurer von Roming would return the following day to torment him once again. The joints of his arms, his elbows and shoulders, were misshapen and swollen, the skin discolored by green and blue bruises. The slightest movement caused him agonizing pains in his back, chest, and arms. It is likely that the bowl of soup and piece of bread by his side had not been touched: he would hardly have dared reach for them for fear of the pain: he had been savagely abused.

Yet he had been willing to say anything the gentlemen wanted to hear, except that he had not always known immediately what they did want to hear. He had confessed and lied, described murder and manslaughter, robbery and theft, arson and pillage, until he himself could no longer tell truth from falsehood. When the question about the children's hands was put, he had still been plucky enough. The first application of torture holds the least terror for the victim, since he can contemplate it with unscathed limbs and cannot imagine its unspeakable agony. But after they had hoisted him up the first time, "because he was loath to speak out and tell the truth," he had been concerned only to give the councillors satisfactory answers—often in vain, for he could not always guess what his tormentors were after. And when at last they had been satisfied with a statement, Dr. Wangereck had glanced at his list and asked another question.

The bells flooded the dreadful chamber with their familiar sound. Very like the bells that had pealed from the belfries of the villages and towns that lay on the Pappenheimers' beat. Bells had been the first sound that greeted them when they saw their destination from afar, and bells had conducted the travelers out of each place as they continued on their way. Throughout the length and breadth of Bavaria, they could hear bells pealing, booming, clanging, jangling, tinkling, chiming, now singly, now in concert, over and over again, wherever there stood a house of God. Peasants in the fields would cross themselves—or not, as the case might be; townsfolk knelt down and said a prayer—or ignored the bells.

It all depended. If there was reason to fear the duke's spies, people put on the appearance of piety. At the Munich court it was obligatory to go to Mass daily, to pray five times a day, to go to confession once a week. Out in the country, which Gumpprecht knew so well, there was no great show of piety. As we have seen, religion played little part in the world of the Pappenheimers. The Church's sheep grazed in the wilderness, free of all constraint and in childish innocence. There is no question that the shepherds were negligent.

There were bells that rang in parishes where the pastors were violent drunkards or sexual offenders. Reliable sources suggest that this kind of behavior was the rule rather than an embarrassing exception.[50] A ducal commission summed up the findings of a large-scale inspection of churches as follows: "Most of the priests are topers, drunken sots, who lie day and night in the wineshops, playing at dice and at cards; their attire is that of ruffians, grooms, or the brutal soldiery." In a report on the condition of the Church in the administrative district of Burghausen, written in the year 1583, we read "that the vicar Virgilius of Feldkirchen came upon the simpleminded daughter of the verger as she was ringing sext, and committed a sexual offense with her in the little side-chapel by the outer altar; that he had frequently entered the innkeeper's house by night and had had his way of the servant girl; that he had long lived in adultery with a day laborer's wife from Ansbach; and that he was a gross blasphemer, a drunkard, and second to none as a brawler." Of Vicar Leonhard from Taubenbach we are told, in the same report, that he used to go very frequently to Braunau, where "he would remain six and more days together in the taverns," getting so full of drink that he would "unlace his breeches" and sleep off his debauch "thus disarrayed and soiled." And so on.

Of course, there were others of a different sort. The good shepherds are not mentioned in official reports. And not every priest who had a concubine and children was necessarily a bad parson: cohabitation with a woman in fact made good economic sense, and was often a sheer necessity, a fact the authorities were well aware of. The office of the vicar-general in Passau, for instance, considered clerical marriages not only permissible but even desirable as a means of "restoring derelict and abandoned country livings and homesteads." From the multifarious sound of bells across the Bavarian countryside, a wayfarer passing through the villages learned little about true piety.

There were bells that rang out from monasteries where the vow of chastity was not taken all that seriously. Abbots cohabited with the daughters of better-class families, abbesses paraded publicly with their lovers, monks carried on affairs with the young girls of the villages, nuns took their pleasure with their own confessors. No one took much exception to all this; on the contrary, they thought the duke's campaign against this state of affairs presumptuous. Under the very eyes of the prince, in a convent in Munich, a Franciscan abbot who was living with his veiled charges like a pasha in his harem stubbornly refused to tolerate any interference on the part of the duke with this mode of spiritual life. The piety which had so recently been ordained from on high was felt to be alien, patronizing, and preposterous.

There were bells sounded at the behest of bishops who approved of the traditionally loose morals of the country clergy simply out of opposition to the duke's policy. The priests reported by government functionaries for their drinking, brawling, and whoring were in fact subject to ecclesiastical and not temporal jurisdiction. Certain bishops, instead of disciplining clergy who were reported to them for punishment, would reward them by transferring them to better livings—as a mark of defiance against state intervention. It is understandable that the duke tried to fill ecclesiastical thrones and other high clerical appointments with individuals who would be amenable to his wishes. It is true that he also had a financial interest as far as the lucrative archbishoprics were concerned: since the establishment of primogeniture in Bavaria there had been younger sons in every generation of Wittelsbachs, and they had to be provided for. What could be more obvious than to endow them with church livings?[51] That relieved the ducal purse and also secured for the prince a political influence on the archbishoprics, which were often of great importance. He might even extend this influence beyond the frontiers of Bavaria by nominating incumbents to bishoprics in imperial territories. Albrecht V had already secured the bishopric of Freising for his second son, Ernst, brother of William V. The new bishop was exactly eleven years old when he assumed his high office. What did that matter? The thing that did matter was the income that went with the office. That was the reason for the accumulation of such offices: Ernst became bishop in no less than five large sees. His nephews, Maximilian's brothers, supported by a grateful pope, had similar distinguished careers in ecclesiastical vestments. Philipp William was nominated as Bishop of Regensburg at the age of three, and by the time he was twenty he wore a cardinal's purple. Ferdinand was nominated dean of Strasbourg Cathedral; coadjutor to the deanery of Würzburg; canon of Cologne, Trier, Salzburg, Eichstätt, and Passau; coadjutor to his uncle Ernst in Cologne, Münster, Liège, and Malmédy; prince deacon of Berchtesgaden; finally bishop of Paderborn and, as successor to his uncle, archbishop of Cologne. Another member of the family, Franz Wilhelm von Wartenberg, was the son of William V's brother, Duke Ferdinand I of Bavaria, who had contracted a morganatic marriage: he received the bishoprics of Minden, Verden, and Osnabrück. Thus richly were the Wittelsbach family rewarded by the Church they helped to sustain.

Unfortunately, the bishops who had achieved their plurality of ecclesiastical appointments in this manner were generally lacking in the godliness that might have been desired. While Duke William V was doing his best to become a saint, and Maximilian I spent many hours daily praying on painfully calloused knees, the bishops of the family spent their youth in riotous living, and their behavior even in their more mature years could hardly be termed saintly.

The bells which could be heard pealing in Gumpprecht's cell were those of the Church of Our Lady, the New Collegiate Church, St. Peter's, and St. Michael's Church. In these houses of God a spirit prevailed that was different from that in the country at large. Since the time of Albrecht V there had been Jesuits in Munich, and their number grew each year. The Bavarian dukes quickly recognized the qualities of the Society of Jesus, which had been expanding since the 1540s: the society offered wide-ranging education, training in rhetoric, discipline, flexibility, and single-mindedness. An attempt had been made to achieve the desired indoctrination of the people in the interests of the state with the help of the local clergy, but evidently this had soon been abandoned. William IV had already begun negotiations with Pope Paul and Ignatius de Loyola, founder of the order, with the aim of recruiting Jesuits trained abroad for service in Bavaria. An advance guard of this elite corps arrived in Ingolstadt in 1549. In 1556 the first Jesuit college was founded there, and in 1559 the Augustinian friars had to hand over part of their Munich monastery to the Spanish order. In 1563 the Society of Jesus took over the university in Dillingen. The Munich parishes were occupied by Jesuits, and only Jesuits were appointed as confessors at court. The majority of these priests who were so energetically promoted by the authorities were, of course, foreigners. This was not the only reason, however, why they were invariably treated with reserve by the duke's Bavarian subjects, often, indeed, with suspicion, and in many cases with open hostility: the people were very well aware that an attempt was being made to discipline them by means of religion. And no one cares to surrender a part of his freedom, even if it amounts to little more than slackness and muddle.

The sound of bells. In his cell, Gumpprecht would have heard nothing in that sound with which he was not familiar. Memories reverberated in the chimes: visions of a broad, gently rolling landscape; visions of villages and hamlets in the evening light, of many-towered cities in the brilliance of the morning, of the freedom of the highway. But here in Munich there were many who could detect an ominous undertone in those chimes.

MISGIVINGS CONCERNING THE PROFESSION OF ARMS

In those spring days of 1600 there had been an ugly scene in Fickler's home involving the old councillor and his younger son, Hans Georg. The latter had spent the last two and a half years studying in Ingolstadt—or, rather, he was supposed to have been studying there. Unfortunately he had not the slightest desire to become a scholar; his ambition was to make his reputation as a soldier. The topic had cropped up during a visit the indolent student—for financial reasons, of course—had paid to his father in Munich. The old man may have reproached the youth with his wretched performance, pointing to the good example set by his elder brother, Johann Christoph. Whereupon his unpromising offspring, not in the least abashed, had declared that he would never become an ink-stained, pettifogging lawyer like his paragon of a brother. He hated the musty smell of dingy chambers and the quibbling about Latin definitions. He was not cut out for that sort of thing: he was born to be a man of action and a warrior. This declaration aroused in Johann Baptist family memories that were not calculated to soothe his paternal fury.

His brother Hieronymus, although exhorted and, indeed, at first compelled to study, had also deserted his books one fine day and had enlisted for a soldier, from curiosity and a lust for adventure. Under the great emperor Charles V, he had taken part in the siege of Magdeburg. That was no great honor: the starving out of the last center of resistance held by the League of Schmalkalden had redounded to the glory of the imperial and Catholic cause and had led both to the humiliation of the Protestant party and to the downfall of the Saxon elector in the capitulation of Wittenberg in 1547. But a great feat of arms it was not. What was more, everyone knew that the treacherous Moritz of Saxony, entrusted by Charles V with the execution of the interdiction pronounced on the stalwart city, had turned his military triumph into the first act of a shameful conspiracy against the emperor. Fortunately, Johann Baptist Fickler was certain that his brother had at least not aided the Protestant treachery, although he had, alas, taken part in campaigns by the imperial army in Piedmont and France, as captain of the Protestant contingent from Nuremberg. Thereafter he had fought under the command of the duke of Alba against the heretics in the Netherlands, something our councillor was inclined to put down to his credit, in spite of the notorious bloodthirstiness of his leader. He was less inclined to give his brother credit for his exploits as a mercenary in the service of Protestant cities like Nuremberg and Augsburg—although it had to be conceded, thought Fickler, that he had been steadfast in the faith. As a Catholic he must have been frequently urged by his superiors, friends, and comrades to join the Lutheran sect, and he had been obliged to make his home for a considerable time among heretics in cities like Nuremberg. A good many of his predecessors had been deplorably seduced. Hieronymus, however, remained unmoved, either because, as his brother believed, he had imbibed the Catholic religion at his mother's breast, as it were, or else, as we might suppose, because he was as little interested in the religious squabbles as the Pappenheimers were.

The councillor was concerned that his son Hans Georg might prove less steadfast in resisting such temptations: in a basket of rotten fruit even the soundest apple will not long remain unaffected. A soldier could not choose his leaders or his comrades, that was a fact of life. He had to hire his services out to anyone who happened to need soldiers. The personal beliefs, nationality, or religion of the individual soldier were irrelevant: he fought for anyone who paid him, and not even our aged lawyer could object to that. What upset him was the danger of infection to which his wayward offspring was exposing himself. The Lutheran infection was rife everywhere, and a youth might so easily succumb to it. And even if he remained strong in the faith, he might still come to a sad end, as the gallant Hieronymus had. In 1575 he had died peacefully in the city of Augsburg, a good Catholic and captain of cavalry—or captain of horse, as they said in those parts—when something dreadful happened to him. The Catholic clergy were on the point of burying him in the cathedral chapter when his Protestant superior burst in upon the ceremony and took it upon himself to remove the coffin and hand it over to "those vermin, the Protestant preachers." This was last-minute retribution for his friendship with the heretics: they thought they were doing their Catholic comrade a service when they buried him in St. Stephen's graveyard, alongside the Lutherans who were doomed to eternal death. "It is true that his body lies there," Fickler consoled himself, "but at the Last Judgment his soul will doubtless be separated from those sectarian goats and placed with the Catholic sheep. Amen." In spite of this consolation, our councillor was well aware of the moral of the story: those who associate with heretics come to a bad end. That is why his gorge rose when he heard his son talking of doughty deeds and adventure.

Although he naturally feared above all for his child's soul, he was also concerned for his physical welfare and safety. To a political intelligence like Fickler's at a time like this, the reek of war was obvious—a dreadfully destructive, protracted battle between the religious parties. This was no time to allow his son to become a soldier.

The peace that had prevailed in Germany since 1555 was more apparent than real.[52] The settlement in Augsburg had merely draped the imperial flag over the conflagration: the fire went on smoldering underneath, and the slightest incident might cause it to flare up again even more violently than before. This was no true peace; certain controversial issues had never been clarified, for example the question of ecclesiastical reservation—whether the clergy who converted to the Lutheran faith should forfeit their property and livings as the Catholic party demanded, a demand the Protestant faction repudiated. The whole agreement, in fact, lacked the most essential element: the willingness of the contracting parties to respect it in the long run. At first dissatisfaction was voiced only furtively, or in informal conversation with people of similar views. In the meantime, however, popes like Paul IV and kings like Philip II had declared quite openly that the Holy War must be resumed and heresy totally eradicated from the earth. It will be no surprise to find that the Bavarian duke echoed these sentiments with all his heart. Among young Maximilian's favorite books was a work entitled *De Autonomia* by Andreas Erstenberg, secretary to the imperial council; here, the toleration proclaimed at Augsburg was termed godless, nay, diabolical, and the peace based upon it declared to be worse than any war. But the Protestants also looked with disfavor on the treaty, hoping to gain more ground in the empire at the first opportunity. If even those involved in it regarded the peace simply as a breathing space, those who were excluded from it were bound to despise it all the more. It granted toleration to the Augsburg confession but not to the Reformed church; to the monarch but not to his subjects.

The situation, then, had barely been defused by the Pax Augustana. It was a dangerous settlement because political, constitutional, and ideological tinder formed that highly explosive mixture that is all too familiar to us nowadays. The battle for influence and liberty was dubbed a war of religion; the struggle for the true religion was also a war of conquest and liberation. Holy wine was mingled with political water and intoxicated even the most prudent minds. This happened in Germany, where the inglorious departure of Charles V was a victory of the Protestants over the Catholics but also a victory of the territorial princes over the imperial power. It happened in France, where the argument between the aristocracy and the king was conducted as a struggle between the Calvinists and the old Church. It happened in the Low countries, which regarded their war of liberation against the Spaniards as a holy war. It happened in England, in Bohemia, in Hungary and in Siebenbürgen—all over Europe, in fact.

The assault on old power structures prompted by denominational differences turned out to be all the more complicated and dangerous because of the ramifications of European diplomacy. This diplomacy was directed principally against Habsburg hegemony, which posed a threat to all the other princely houses. Since the time of Charles V, the Spanish line had dominated not only the Iberian peninsula but also, besides the duchy of Milan, the vice-kingdom of Naples, Sardinia, and Sicily, amounting to half of Italy; the duchies of Brabant and Luxembourg; and, temporarily anyway, the county of Burgundy. In this way France was almost entirely surrounded, and her kings were bound to defend themselves. Untold treasures, veritable streams of gold and silver from her overseas colonies, made it possible for Spain to conduct a policy backed by money, to finance unrest, and to influence the elections and decisions of other states by means of bribery. For the first time a monarch was able to afford a powerful standing army. By means of his money and his soldiers, Charles's successor, Philip II, attempted to extend his rule throughout Europe, to secure the French throne, to marry England's great Queen Elizabeth. But gold and weapons can achieve nothing without something the Spanish despot lacked: the intelligence of a statesman.

That was fortunate for his neighbors. For decades, total mastery of Europe by the Habsburg family seemed to be within their grasp, for the younger, Austrian line ruled over a domain scarcely smaller than that of their Spanish relatives: besides the Archduchy of Austria it included the duchies of Styria and Carinthia; the county of Tyrol, extending at that time from Kufstein to Lake Garda; the kingdom of Bohemia; the duchy of Silesia; the margravate of Moravia; Carniola; and Austrian Hungary. There were vassal states, too: the kingdom of Hungary; Siebenbürgen; Bosnia; Bulgaria; and Wallachia. Germany's princes felt themselves hemmed in between the two Habsburg superpowers, as did the pope. This is how strange, tenuous horizontal links came into being: Bavaria's dukes maintained active contacts with France; France, for her part, formed pacts with German Protestants and the (Calvinist) Reformed church in the Netherlands, as well as with the Roman pope and Bavaria—all in an attempt to break the Spanish stranglehold.

Nor were relations between Austrian and Spanish Habsburgs on anything like a fraternal basis, as would have befitted members of the Catholic faith. The Austrians observed the wealth and ostentation of their relatives with a certain amount of envy. Protestant England was decidedly anti-Spanish and in 1588 had inflicted a humiliating defeat on the proud Armada. All the same, she was eyeing France with some suspicion since that country had grown more powerful with the accession of Henry IV. While France had remained Catholic in consequence of Henry's conversion, powerful Protestant monarchies were flourishing in Sweden and Denmark. Germany's Protestant princes and municipalities, particularly in the north, observed this development with mixed feelings, sensing that the covetous gaze of their coreligionists was directed toward them. But the confusion did not end there: since 1593 the Turks had been threatening Christendom again, forcing the hostile parties to combine in common defense; the Habsburgs, being most directly threatened, were forced to pay for assistance by concessions to their internal adversaries. And to make the muddle even worse, the Netherlands claimed with some justice that their Spanish oppressors were contravening imperial laws and demanded imperial—i.e., Catholic—Habsburg assistance. For family and confessional reasons, however, the emperor would not consent to this, while the German Lutherans spurned the support of foreign Calvinists. The stark contrast between the Lutheran and the Reformed factions was often the subject of more vicious and acrimonious dispute than that between the Lutheran and Catholic parties generally—and that tended to make the issue even more complicated.

All these threads, spun from interests, ambitions, and fears, lay like a tangled skein across the political map of Europe. Here, there, and everywhere, fanatical proponents of every faith and despotic monarchs crouched, each tending his own brew and refusing to look beyond the rim of his plate. At some time, perhaps soon, a great war with changing coalitions was bound to come. And there was no doubt that the battleground would be the ramshackle German Empire.

Since this is the way things were—or even worse—can we blame Dr. Johann Baptist Fickler for not wanting his son to become a mercenary soldier? The father could no doubt see further ahead than Hans Georg, who yearned for the adventurous life and returned in high dudgeon to Ingolstadt following a bitter argument. Of course, everyone knows that only a man of vision is capable of common sense. And that was precisely the problem of the age.

IN THE SPANISH STYLE

The chamberlains entered the young duke's bedchamber before dawn. Freiherr Wolf Konrad von Rechberg, chamberlain-in-chief and president of the council of state, was dressed in the Spanish style, complete with sword, his cloak thrown back over his shoulders. He approached the prince's bed and wakened him with the prescribed form of address. As Maximilian rose from his bed, one of the chamberlains handed von Rechberg a clean undershirt, which the latter passed on to the prince with a courtly phrase, receiving in return the prince's nightshirt. In the same precisely prescribed manner the duke, shivering in the chilly chamber, accepted his woolen outer shirt. Now the chamberlain-in-chief stepped back a few paces as the prince's personal barber and a valet approached Maximilian, bowing deeply. The former rubbed the duke's face, arms, and legs with clean towels, whereupon the latter attired him in linen socks, silk stockings, breeches, shoes, and slippers. Then one of the chamberlains, either the chief equerry, Astor Leoncelli, or Captain Giulio Cesare Crivelli, put down in the prescribed place the washbowl that had been brought in by a footman. A second valet approached with the duke's mouthwash, while the barber brought his tooth powder. The president of the council, who had meanwhile covered his hair with the obligatory kerchief, took these articles and proffered them to the prince.

Every movement, every ministering gesture, was specified down to the last detail in elaborate instructions; nothing was left to chance, so that the entire scene must have had an oddly unreal effect, like a play that has been performed many times, stiff, stilted, stylized. This ceremonious performance in Munich, as almost everywhere else, was in emulation of the etiquette practiced at the Spanish royal court, which in Charles V's time had also been an imperial palace. The spirit of Spain pervaded all of Europe in those days. In the course of the centuries the cultural focus of the continent had shifted from east to west and had finally reached Madrid. Spanish taste governed fashion, literature, warfare, diplomacy, manners, and painting. No one who wished to keep up with the times could afford to ignore it. This general trend toward the adoption of the Spanish style by educated people was already on the wane, but in Munich it was reinforced by political orientation toward the most powerful of the pope's allies. The policy of restoration and reaction that was pursued in Bavaria took Spain as its model, which explains its fanaticism and its brutalities as well as the strange mixture of extravagant pomp, asceticism, and mortification of the flesh. It was no coincidence that the dukes had chosen a Spanish order to implement their domestic policy. The public-order measures introduced into Bavaria by Albrecht V, perfected by William V, and made more stringent by Maximilian I, were essentially Spanish: a system of censorship, spying on subjects and officials, denunciations, penalties for emigration, vicious persecution of heretics. Spanish, too, were the officialese, the rank bureaucracy, the scriptomania, the pettifogging pedantry. Spanish were the totalitarian despotism, the omnipresent state, Maximilian's attempt to keep a personal check on absolutely everything, from the confession certificates of his officials to the sexual morals of farm laborers. This was connected with another characteristic of Spanish monarchs—suspicion.

Many things that appear to cast a shadow over Maximilian's character simply reflect the style of the age, an acquired Spanishness: his hypocritical diplomacy, his duplicity and slyness, his tactical maneuvering, his cowardly evasions, the ruthless exploitation of the predicaments of others to his own advantage. All this was considered part of statesmanship and was practiced not only by the Spaniards, although they were preeminent in the art. The popes too were adept at it, as were German Protestant princes such as Moritz of Saxony and Ulrich of Württemberg.

Maximilian, however, was Spanish in a very special way: in his abrupt, chilly attitude to others; in his abhorrence of personal contacts; in his fervent adoration of the saints and his tendency to take refuge in prayer; in his favorite color, which was black; in his inability to show his feelings and his power to remain unmoved; in his fondness for the heroic pose; in his mania for collecting and his appreciation of art; as well as in his deeply felt need for spectacular display, which ran counter to his notorious meanness.[53] We are reminded in an almost uncanny fashion of the character of the Spanish king Philip II, who died in Madrid just as Maximilian assumed power in Munich.

Such affinity may be mere chance, but there is an explanation which seems to me plausible. One of the most impressive personalities encountered by Maximilian in his adolescent years was the great theologian Gregor of Valencia.[54] This learned Jesuit, who was active in Ingolstadt from 1575 to 1597, was regarded, so to speak, as the principal theoretician of Catholicism in that age. In his book *De rebus fidei* he systematically refuted all the attacks that had ever been launched against the doctrines of the Church. But that was not the only reason he was admired and respected: he was noted for his personal charisma and for the clarity and vivacity of his rhetoric. A sturdy man of medium height with a massive head, broad brow, and bushy beard, he was thirty-eight years old when he took the fourteen-year-old heir apparent into his care as tutor, constant companion, and father confessor. It is difficult to overestimate his influence. He came from Spain, from Castile, in fact, the royal, ruling province; he had studied in Salamanca, had entered the Society of Jesus when he was twenty-four, and had not been in his homeland since. When he left in 1572, Philip II was at the height of his power, a dazzling paragon among Catholic princes: Philip had declared his purpose to be the complete restoration of the old Church and the eradication of heresy in Europe. With the image of this ruler in his heart, the young Maximilian's fatherly Spanish friend was able to describe to him a living example of the Christian monarch rather than simply speaking of an abstract ideal, as his teachers did. That is why I believe that the affinity between the despotic king and the future Bavarian duke stemmed from a half-conscious attempt at emulation.

The chamberlain-in-chief handed the duke his doublet. Only aristocratic members of his retinue were worthy of the honor of attiring the prince: his servants were not permitted to help him into breeches, belt, and shoes; that was the chamberlains' privilege. Under their ministering hands, Maximilian assumed the outward appearance of a Spaniard: starched ruff, padded sleeves, false potbelly, galligaskins stuffed with horsehair, spidery, black-stockinged legs in narrow boots. Finally, the noble chamberlain-in-chief and president of the council handed his master his cloak, his velvet cap, and his Spanish sword.

The Spanish sword—what a symbol! The idea of the crusade, born in Spain, had once swept the whole of Europe along in a wave of enthusiasm. It had given way in the meantime to more fruitful ideas, but in the land of its origin it was still alive. From the very beginning it had consisted of that combination of religious fanaticism and worldly rapacity that was once more in vogue. In the Iberian peninsula, militancy is always religious, and religion always militant. The wars against Moors and Jews were waged as crusades. The Spaniards' wars against alien cultures were holy wars, hence bestial; an expression of God's will, hence fiendishly cruel; sanctified, hence ruthless; noble, hence vile; honorable, hence predatory. Fire and incense, blood and cash—a mystic lava poured out over peoples who were different, and consequently inferior. The dreadful idea was propelled in a radically different direction when Pope Innocent III (1198–1216) employed it as a weapon against Christians of other denominations. In 1209, he proclaimed a crusade against the Albigensians in the South of France, and the gruesome lava buried and burned a flourishing stretch of land in the center of Europe. Since the holy war was not being waged against enemies of a different race and a different tongue, but against Christian fellow countrymen, locating and identifying the adversary offered certain difficulties. These were solved by introducing the Inquisition, an investigative procedure conducted by ecclesiastical courts that took rumors and denunciations as its starting point and arrived at confessions by means of torture.

The resemblance between this method and those used against our vagrants is not merely coincidental; the ecclesiastical procedure used by the Inquisition against heretics was subsequently adopted by the secular courts.

It was Spanish despotism once more that first deliberately employed the idea of the crusade and the Inquisition to increase its own power and further its political interests. In their fight against the aristocracy and the privileges of the estates, Charles V and Philip II used the ecclesiastical courts as a weapon. Every suggestion of resistance to the king's absolute authority was regarded as evidence of heresy, which set the Inquisition in motion. Torture led rapidly to "conviction" and elimination of the troublemaker. The clergy readily allowed themselves to be used as the king's henchmen, which indicates, on the one hand, their heavy dependence on royal favor and, on the other, their blind, hysterical fear of heresy.

The typically Spanish interlocking pattern of ecclesiastical and secular interests provided an unfortunate model for the early phase of absolutism in Bavaria. It is hard to say which partner profited more from this symbiosis. It is true, both Spanish and Bavarian princes were devout to the point of monkish asceticism, but they were also assertively self-confident. In spite of their religious fervor, they seldom lost sight of their political responsibilities. But how can the two be separated? It would be wrong to see in Philip II or Maximilian I nothing but willing tools of militant Catholicism, but equally false to see the Church merely as a means to an end in establishing princely power. These rulers of the Counterreformation were neither bigoted servants of the Jesuits nor calculating cynics. The situation was such that the service of God served their own purposes at the same time. The interests of Church and State coincided from the moment when the pope proved willing to leave the supervision of the Church in Catholic territories to local rulers. Given that identity of interests, the princes could afford to trust in God and follow their religious consciences, while prelates and preachers were in a position to heed the secular rather than the ecclesiastical authorities. Conflicts simply did not arise. If we attempt to analyze the results from our modern point of view, we may be struck by the fact that the state religion of the Bavarian dukes William V and Maximilian I, with its Jesuit complexion, obviously served as a state ideology. It seems that totalitarian states are not viable without some such doctrine of salvation—we know that from the communist and fascist dictatorships of our own time. Control of thought and opinion is no doubt an indispensable part of political absolutism: the subject is disciplined by unrelenting ideological coercion, and the spirit of opposition is crushed. At the same time the official ideology glorifies the vast and boundless power of the state, which has a fondness for decking itself out in apocalyptic imagery. This basic pattern of monocratic government was characteristic of Maximilian's state, although I am not implying that the Spanish brand of Catholicism was deliberately adopted as the ideology of early Bavarian absolutism. There was no need for such positive steps, given the inherent affinity. In Bavaria, common interests ensured that the early absolutist state and the theology of the Counterreformation formed a stable marriage.

The coercion exerted by the state through the persecution of heretics and ecclesiastical surveillance did not invariably prove effective. It was a matter of degree. If the yoke became too oppressive, it was cast off in sheer desperation. That was the experience of Philip II: in the seventeen provinces of the Netherlands religious persecution became so utterly unbearable that respectable merchants, fishermen, and farmers, as well as an inherently loyal aristocracy, were left with no alternative but to fight for their survival. This event gave the Bavarian duke no particular food for thought. In William of Orange's fight he did not see the revolt of a tormented nation but simply the confirmation of his view that heresy led to mutiny and rebellion. Philip II's bloody rule in the Netherlands and its miserable failure did nothing to diminish Maximilian's admiration for the Catholic king or to render outmoded the Spanish style at his court.

Maximilian, now fully clothed, signaled to a waiting valet, who announced to the chamberlains in a loud voice that His Grace was about to leave the bedchamber. This was the signal for the chamberlains to bow, turn, and precede the duke from the room. The principal tutor, the chamberlain-in-chief, and the father confessor who was present at the ceremony left the room after the duke, followed by the valets.

OLD LETTERS

His star was not burning as brightly as it once had; Johann Baptist Fickler sensed that. Since the young duke no longer required the services of his old teacher, the Swabian councillor's life had grown quieter. Since the printing of his "Reply to Heilbrunner's Idle Prattle" he had been able to pick up three more works from the printer, Adam Berg: the German translation of a Latin "Lament on the pernicious Loss of Christendom to the reprobate Turk" by Master Aeneas Silvius Picolominaeus; the German version of his "Sincere Admonition to the Estates of Regensburg, from which may briefly be divined the staunch Assiduity with which his Holiness the Pope commends to them a proper Concern for the Christian Commonwealth, as regards the Necessity in these Times of Peril to take up Arms against the Turk"; and, finally, the republication in German of his "Guide to the True Doctrine," the appendix to the *Theologia Juridica*, which he had written in his youth. The subsidies from the duke that made possible these publications had dried up since William V had abdicated and handed over authority to his miserly son Maximilian. The latter probably felt that his former teacher's tracts and pamphlets did not justify his digging into his exchequer. There were less expensive and more useful ways of rewarding the old councillor for his services. Maximilian sponsored the nomination of Fickler as *eques aureatus*, a high distinction conferred on thinkers and writers, and otherwise confined to the nobility. He made it possible for Fickler's eldest son, Johann Christoph, who had graduated as a Doctor of Civil and Canon Law from Ingolstadt in 1597, to embark on a career as state councillor. And he had entrusted his venerable instructor with the task of compiling a descriptive catalogue of his art collection and, later, with arranging and describing his collection of coins and medals.

Perhaps these tasks were intended to be a form of occupational therapy. Certainly Maximilian, like any pupil who has outgrown his teacher, was disinclined to allow the authority that had governed his childhood to have any influence on his own decisions. Anyone putting into practice what he had learned would be bound to feel insecure with his old schoolmaster looking over his shoulder. It was precisely because he had taught the young duke so much that Fickler could not continue to be his adviser: the duke's need for self-confidence demanded that the old man be banished to the archives.

Not that the old councillor objected to that kind of employment. Scrutinizing and assessing, comparing and listing, weighing and valuing, collecting and sorting objets d'art, curios, and medals was very much to his taste; he had already performed such tasks in his youth as secretary to Ambros von Gumppenberg. As far as he was concerned, this assignment, whatever the motives behind it, was not to be taken lightly. Shortly before, on 1 March 1600, Fickler had even written to an old acquaintance, none other than Gregor de Valencia, now resident in Rome, requesting that he obtain papal license for him to read the relevant historical and numismatic reference books, which, like almost all scholarly works of the day, were included in the Index. Fickler was certainly interested in compiling records: what offended him deeply was the feeling that he had been dropped and was no longer being called upon to take part in the daily business of government. It had also come to the old gentleman's ears that opinion at court regarded his work in the archives as calling for "no great exertion or labor of the mind" and his employment there as no more than an oblique expression of the duke's favor. Although he was a good deal fitter than many younger than himself, he had already been put out to grass.

Fickler's evening hours were now spent summing up his past life, by the light of his tallow candle. His best years he had spent as the prince's tutor, there was no doubt about that. He had a book containing copies of important letters he had written in the course of his life,[55] and may well have browsed through it from time to time and revived old memories.

"Saturday, 29 August 1589. Most Illustrious, noble Prince. Most Gracious Lord, may I assure Your Grace of my most humble and obedient service. Albeit we have had from Your Grace no express instruction that Your Grace's young Master should seek his recreation outside Ingolstadt during this present vacation . . . Duke Maximilian has conceived a desire to essay whether there might not be some game to be shot in the preserves of these parts (which he himself holds to be no mean diversion) . . . And thus, on the Wednesday next following, we journeyed by water to Neustadt, early in the day, the weather being fair and lacking all wind, taking breakfast en route with the pastor in Föhringen (who received and entertained His Grace with humble cordiality, insofar as his kitchen allowed). Thereafter we pursued our way to Neustadt, disembarking twice in the meadows, where we sought our ease in the shade of verdant pastures. The pastor twice prevailed upon us to fish, albeit not much of any worth was to be caught but for some Föhringen sausages, which the pastor slyly cast into the nets. By suppertime, His Grace had come to Neustadt and partook of supper in a garden. On that evening the Patres Jesuitae entreated His Grace's servant to take breakfast the next day in their monastery of Biburg, to which place Prince Maximilian came also, having been stalking already at dawn, but without success so far. His Grace took his ease at breakfast cum patribus, having no inclination to do aught else, on account of the very great heat. In the evening His Grace returned to Neustadt. In the meantime the chief keeper of the forest prepared a battue, whereby three beasts were started, of which one was shot by Lord Maximilian, a second being trapped in our net. Thereupon His Grace dined with the Prefect, and was right well served, as befitted the time. Since Duke Maximilian could by no means come by any quarry, however, there being, according to the keepers some dearth of game, His Grace set out once more on the morning of Friday, and came hither, having breakfasted at the inn at Vohburg, and, the great heat being by then passed, arrived in this place, God be praised, safe and sound at six of the evening. In passing I should most humbly inform Your Grace that on Monday past Duke Maximilian was afflicted with a griping in the bowels, being the whole day confined to his room. Et consultato medico Doctore Mencello it was found that he had partaken somewhat to excess of fruit, such as strawberries and cherries, whereof a cruditas of the stomach arose that caused the said griping. The same passed away over night, however, and he felt himself, God be praised, once more in good spirits, as he is at this time. But on the morning of Thursday, when he had been at the battue, his teacher of French, Astor Leoncelli, who had accompanied him, reported to me that His Grace had come near to swooning, complaining that his breast could not suffer the motion of riding, especially at the trot; on coming to Biburg, His Grace lay down half an hour upon a bed, but sine somne, that is to say, without sleeping, and took his ease, where-upon he partook of breakfast most cheerfully with the other gentlemen, and has not further complained. But I remain never-theless of the opinion that he ought to refrain at this time of great warmth from physical exertions and exposing himself to the sun, except for such gentle motions as may be performed in the shade. Which Astor also holds to be prudent. We mean to send straight-way for Doctor Menzel and to consult him concerning the pain in His Grace's breast. Your Grace's most humble Councillor and ser-vant Jo. Bapt. Fikler, his hand. Post scripta. Most Gracious Prince and Lord. This very moment the doctor came and inspected uri-nam Duci Maximiliani, and declared it lacks nothing, and there is no cause for concern, God be praised . . . The which it was my humble duty to add in haste post scripta, that Your Grace might be free of care and be assured that His Grace will be well cared for in this as in all things."

"Ingolstadt, 9 September 1589 . . . Most Gracious Prince and Lord. I am continuing with my instruction in history and the law, in that we are construing in turn Xenophon and the Chronographia of Genebradus. The first book of the Institutiones (of the Roman Corpus iuris civilis) we have, God be praised, completed today. On this Monday we shall, God willing, begin with the second book, and revise in the weeks that are to come what we learned in the first book . . . so that His Grace may the better commit to memory all those matters. Whatever there may be found in Your Grace's Bavarian Code of Law touching each problem I duly apply in the course of our lessons on the law, explaining also to His Grace as I proceed the regulas juris civilis . . ."

"Ingolstadt, 29 February 1590 . . . Your Grace's letter concern-ing Duke Maximilian's learning the Italian language I most hum-bly acknowledge, being content to comply most obediently with the views of Your Grace. Each Saturday I read to him a lesson from an Italian book of sound and choice language, entitled 'Ricordi del M. Saba Castiglione, Cavalliere etc.' wherein all manner of ser-viceable political teachings and documents are contained, also such of a Catholic and spiritual kind, the whole being diverting to read. And we have already so far progressed that His Grace pretty well comprehends what he reads . . ."

"Ingolstadt, 3 March 1590. Most Gracious Lord. Whereas this week there was held a disputation in materia testamentorum (on the law relating to wills), Your Grace's beloved son, my gracious master, Duke Maximilian, once more held forth by way of exercise opponendo et argumentando; Your Grace will receive herewith a copy of his arguments. His Grace bore himself so confidently and without faltering in this affair that the fathers who were present at the disputation, and, indeed, all others there, were most pleased and astonished, so that His Grace earned no little praise . . ."

"Ingolstadt, 5 May 1590. Most Gracious Lord . . . The catarrh that afflicted Duke Maximilian in Munich has now abated. On his doctor's advice His Grace remained a day or two in his lodgings and has until now abstained from wine: it is in no wise dangerous . . . In keeping with medical advice I desisted one day only from learning and the practice of writing. Now that matters have improved, we are pursuing our customary course of studies, as the Holy Spirit directs us. I wish to pursue the matter with all speed and with God's help, so that His Grace may the sooner be done with the Institutionibus."

"Ingolstadt, 2 September 1590 . . . I may report otherwise that all things, both regarding His Grace's health and his studies, do prosper most excellently, but that the open sore on Duke Maximilian's thigh is healing but slowly. We are in hopes, however, as it appears, that it may be cured within two or three weeks. We neglect nothing in tending it most assiduously and binding it up. May God give his blessing."

This is the tenor of the letters the prince's tutor had written to Duke William V. On rereading them, Fickler no doubt looked back with some sadness on those days as guide and mentor which had passed so swiftly away. He knew the young duke a great deal better than did his present advisers. One hot day in late summer on the Danube, he had actually heard him laughing heartily at the trick with the sausages that the pastor from Föhringen had put into their net. Who, apart from this white-haired keeper of the records, could speak of such memories? It was a long time since Maximilian had laughed.

FURTHER ARRESTS

Ulrich Schölz had panicked when the prefect's men had hammered on his door that February evening.[56] By the light of torches and lanterns he had made out a sledge and mounted men in front of his house, heard the barn door being forced open, and seen through a chink in his door his bewildered lodgers being dragged from the straw. So what the farmers in the village had often predicted, what his wife had always feared and he had dismissed with a shrug of the shoulders, had come true. Someone must have denounced him as an illegal landlord. He ought not to have taken the ragamuffins in, even if it meant dying of starvation; now he could see that such earnings on the side were a dangerous business, but it was too late to regret it. They would take him away, along with the Pappenheimers, expel him from the country, old man as he was, or, worse still, execute him. Occupied with such thoughts, the aged cottager may have pulled on his old coat and laced his boots so as to slip out at the yard gate while the authorities were still occupied with the vagrants.

Out and away: through the kitchen garden, across the little brook, often sinking to his knees in the snow. Down the misty white meadow, under the clear, starry sky, stumbling over the hard frozen furrows, panting, driven on by the noises behind him, the hubbub of voices, and the rattle of chains that came ever more faintly from the direction of the village. Now and again he looked round at the flickering lights, to discover with relief that no one was pursuing him. He tramped on all the same, seeking the shelter of the dark woods. There he wandered around, weary and soaked to the skin, finding a charcoal burner's fire to warm his clammy hands. Toward morning he risked going back, crept through the icy mists to the village up on the ridge, and knocked on the window of his cottage. We see his wife shuffle to the door and let him in, greeting him with reproaches and remarking that he had run away for nothing; nobody had asked about him or wanted anything of them. The officials had only been seeking the Pappenheimers; after arresting them they had rummaged through the barn and the vegetable garden by the light of their torches, but then they had left the place. And when the old cottager let the latch fall with a sigh of relief, his wife probably told him in a whisper not to make so much noise, the boy was asleep in the backroom. The horsemen had simply left the poor little chap behind, so she had had to take him in.

Everything appeared to go quite smoothly. On the following day Schölz's wife took the child to Altmannstein and handed him over at the town hall. If the authorities had imprisoned the parents, she said, then they ought to take care of the boy as well. After his wife had returned unmolested, Schölz considered the episode closed as far as he was concerned. It was only weeks later, in March, that officers turned up at his house once more—by day this time, and without the uproar of the previous visit. They searched the barn and the garden once again, and told the old couple that the Pappenheimers were in bad trouble; they were sorcerers, robbers, and murderers. The officers had then departed forthwith, having found nothing. They seemed not to be concerned with Schölz, who no doubt felt that fate had been kind and spared him.

He rejoiced too soon. Primroses and anemones were blossoming by the brook behind the house, and the first tender green shoots were showing on the birch twigs, when the horsemen from Altmannstein returned. By day, certainly, but with an ominous clatter, sharp commands, piercing glances, and no inclination whatever to gossip. They laid rough hands on Schölz and his wife and bound their wrists, as they had done earlier with the traveling folk. Once again they rummaged through the barn, smashing down dividing walls; they dug over the garden, trampling down lettuce and the fresh shoots of flowers; at the same time, Hans Stumpf, the weaver, and Augustin Baumann, the bread delivery man, were brought in bound by other officers and thrown together with the cottager and his wife. All four were thrust onto a cart, which set off on its creaking way, guarded by horsemen and escorted to the outskirts of the village by the speechless and awestruck inhabitants.

The Tettenwang cottagers were not told the reason for their arrest, only that they had been apprehended on the very highest authority and that they were criminals answerable to the duke himself. They were lodged initially in separate cells in the town hall on the bridge at Altmannstein. The weaver, Hans Stumpf, who not only had cause to lament the misfortune of his arrest but suffered also from a "loathsome disease," was taken on the following day to the jail in Abensberg, while Schölz and his wife were dispatched to the Falcon Tower in Munich. Augustin Baumann remained in Altmannstein.

They constantly asserted their innocence to those who guarded, fed, and transported them, and had scarcely any idea as to what they were accused of. The sick weaver in his cell in Abensberg complained loudest of all, finally softening the hearts of his jailers, who allowed his son to tend the sufferer with cold compresses and clean towels. The poor wretch lay in the straw of his cell and entreated his youthful nurse to fetch help. He was to run to Tettenwang next day and go to his neighbor, Georg Reiter—or, better still—go to Prunn, to his brother-in-law Georg Schmälzl, the tailor—or, best of all, to both. They could go to the town hall, perhaps get as far as the prefect himself, declare on oath that their friend was innocent, and clear up this dreadful misunderstanding. And, of course, they should do what they could for Schölz and Augustin as well. But they must intercede quickly, before they set about the prisoners with torture and forced them to make confessions that would be false, but fatal nevertheless.

Thus instructed, the lad left the sick man the following day and hastened to Tettenwang. Toward evening he came into Georg Reiter's room. Reiter was not alone; Bastl Baumann, brother of the arrested Augustin, and the tailor from Prunn, Georg Schmälzl, were also sitting there. They were all discussing the situation in great excitement. Now that their friends had been arrested, were they themselves perhaps in danger? Should they flee? Was there any way they could help their friends who had been taken away? Glashänsel's boy, no doubt restored with something to drink and a crust of bread from Reiter's wife, faithfully passed on the weaver's plea. The argument went back and forth. A pledge, and an appeal to the prefect—that might end with their own arrest. After all, did they know what it was all about? Might they not invite suspicion by doing a friend such a favor? On the other hand, something must be done to help the prisoners; they could hardly just sit there over their wine and do nothing while their friends languished in prison. And if the three of them were to appear before the prefect, respectful, with clear consciences, concerned for their friends—surely that could not be held against them. Such were the arguments, more or less—and in the end the decision was taken to risk it, together.

The next morning the three of them set off for Abensberg—this must have been the course of events, according to the trial record—stood undecided for some time in front of the prefect's offices, then bravely mounted the stone steps one by one, and were admitted by the court clerk. With downcast eyes, turning their hats uneasily in their hands, they spoke to him in turn about innocence, friendship, and mercy. Whereupon he gave the three cottagers the following reply: He very much doubted whether their friends were in fact harmless, but it was none of his business for he was not competent to deal with their petition. The prisoners Schölz, Stumpf, and Baumann had been arrested on the instructions of the council of state in Munich, which no doubt had its reasons. Even supposing he, the prefect's clerk in Abensberg, believed them and wanted to help them, there was absolutely nothing he could do for them. If the three of them wished to submit a formal petition it would have to be done in Munich, not here. But whether it was worth making the journey, he would take leave to doubt. He had nothing to do with the case, however, and they could do as they liked as far as their obligation to their friends was concerned.

After being thus brought down to earth, the three looked at each other in some perplexity, totally at a loss. But the prisoners were here, weren't they? That didn't mean anything, was the answer; they were criminals answerable to the duke, and only the council of state in Munich had authority over them. In any case, one of them, Schölz, along with his wife, had already been moved to the capital; the others would no doubt follow soon. The friends began to understand. One of them inquired boldly whether they might at least visit Augustin Baumann in prison, seeing that they were here anyway. The clerk looked at the supplicants, perhaps not entirely unmoved by their mission, and nodded his head.

CLOISTER, PALACE, FORTRESS

Before Maximilian's father resigned his office, he had built himself a private monastery, where he meant to live the rest of his life as a holy man. It was a palace built at the same time as the Jesuit college and next door to it. Later called the "Maxburg," it was a rambling building, connected by a roofed arch with the Church of St. Michael and the Jesuit monastery. Other covered ways linked it to the Pilgrim House on the Rochusberg and the Capuchin monastery. It was a vast complex, much too lavish for a man who intended to spend the rest of his life in prayer and atonement. In fact, William V had built himself this stately residence in order to install a kind of associate, or even superior, regime there. The overtaxed monarch certainly wished to be relieved of responsibility, but had no wish to relinquish his authority. An active man of fifty, he saw himself as a gray eminence, devout indeed, and relieved by his model son of all the tedious, trivial business of every day, with its penny-pinching economies. His abdication had been halfhearted and not devoid of pique.

Torn between injured pride, frustrated ambition, and voluntary renunciation, William V was incapable of finding inner serenity, even after his abdication. Certainly he fed twelve paupers at his table each day and, like Jesus, even washed their feet occasionally; he chastised himself and mortified his flesh, and spent many hours each day in prayer. But he also kept a close eye on his son's policies, with the censorious expression of the know-all, and tried time and time again to exert a decisive influence on those policies—either openly or by way of intrigue. He maintained close links with his son's confidant, Christoph Gewold, by profession confidential secretary and state councillor, by nature a born schemer. Certainly he shared his palace with a couple of Carthusian monks, but he made them live in an artificial grotto, so that they gave the impression of being just another curiosity in a building crammed with relics, antiques, and works of art. Certainly his table was furnished only with earthenware rather than with gold and silver services—even, indeed especially, when eminent guests were present. He still dreamed, however, of a mighty mausoleum for himself and his wife, and could not manage on his allowance of sixty thousand gulden. William V remained halfhearted, even in his hair shirt: in 1623, when he was seventy-five and was considering "withdrawing as far as may be from the affairs of the world . . . immuring himself for the remainder of his life in the Carthusian monastery in Regensburg," he wrote to the pope for permission to eat meat there, which was otherwise prohibited in Carthusian houses— and urged His Holiness to reply speedily, since he would not enter the monastery until he had this permission.

Now, in 1600, the devout duke still had no thought of isolating himself from the world. No longer pestered by calculating and argumentative officials, he was able to devote himself to issues that were much more important for him. There was one matter in particular that constantly occupied and worried him. It was a family affair but also of a highly political nature, private and yet a matter of public interest: the question of an heir. Maximilian had been married for five years to his cousin, Elizabeth Renata of Lorraine, and the marriage was still childless. That might well change, of course, but if no heir apparent were forthcoming, what then? William had frequently thought about this problem and devised a solution. His youngest and favorite child, Albrecht, the only one of his later male offspring who was not consecrated to the Church, would have to marry and thus secure the succession. Maximilian, of course, wanted nothing to do with any such precaution and appealed to the will that his father had drawn up in 1597, according to which none of his brothers might marry until Maximilian had remained childless for fifteen years. In any case, an heir would turn up: his wife was healthy and prevented from conceiving only by some evil spell.

That argument carried weight with his father. He was in any case inclined to ascribe any misfortune, any illness or other evil to the machinations of sinister forces. The duchess was bewitched, he agreed. He had persecuted the heretics in his realm too zealously, shown too little mercy in burning witches, served the cause of Christ too plainly not to incur the bitter hatred of the Devil on himself and his family. William V had faith, nevertheless, that the Cross would prove more powerful in the end than the pentagram. If the spell could not be broken by prayers and devotional exercises, the general of the Barnabite friars, Michael Marrano, might be brought to Munich. He had successfully exorcised Duke John William of Jülich and was a celebrated expert in removing spells from princely personages.

The abdicated duke knew all about the mischief wrought by witches.[57] The bewitching of his daughter-in-law was actually one of the more harmless exploits of that brood. They destroyed crops and cattle, ruined harvests, brought pestilence and sickness into the country, wrought death and destruction, but, above all, they were an affront to God, which might bring down His wrath on Bavaria. That was why William had very early on exhorted his prefects and their officials to root out such vermin. Under his rule there had been epidemic persecution of witches in Schongau and the Werdenfels area, with one hundred and fourteen convicted witches dragged to the stake. He had given the most rigorous orders that only those that repented might be strangled before they were burned, while the unrepentant were to be roasted alive in the Spanish manner. The screams of his victims did not rouse him from his sleep; he was better off than France's Catharine de Medici, who had been haunted by the ghosts of murdered Huguenots. He had taken precautions to ward off that sort of fiendish commotion: his palace was linked by connecting passages with churches and monasteries and packed with instruments of salvation—relics, crucifixes, and stoups of holy water. The whole devilish clan might rage before his gates, the holy man's abode was impregnably fortified against Satan.

It had been William's wish that his son should carry on the battle against witches in his realm, for it was obvious to the pious monarch that his drastic measures would provoke Lucifer, and that the fiendish brood would go on trying to harm his flourishing principality. One reason why he had chosen Dr. Fickler as his son's tutor was that Fickler had written a book about witch trials. Maximilian should be warned betimes about these ogres. The seventeen-year-old prince had in fact taken an informed interest in a witch trial that was staged in Ingolstadt while he was a student there. "Yesterday a woman was apprehended," he wrote to his

124

father on 1 March 1590, "that was in the judgment of many and by general repute reckoned to be a witch."[58] William then replied that his son should continue to observe the affair and report on it. That was done on 14 May: "As concerns the woman that was here imprisoned, Your Grace commanding that I should inform Your Grace most humbly how the matter might turn out, I herewith most humbly inform Your Grace that it has not proved possible, neither with soft nor harsh words, nor yet with torture or by other means, to draw from her as much as one word. As I myself have seen, she was pulled up in due form twice, and also burned the once, and notwithstanding not only did not make confession but mocked us, neither crying out Oh nor Woe, nor seeming to suffer any pain. Only when she once more touched the ground she did once cry out. Those that pulled her up say that when she was lifted from the earth she grew so light as if they were lifting up an empty sack. Who makes her so light, only God knows. It seems plain that she does not feel any pain. Should the fire not serve its turn, then it will not be easy to draw anything from her. Last Friday there was taken into custody another woman who is answerable to the townsfolk. Her son, who is but a small boy, told many fair and honest pranks concerning his mother, such that I do believe they will soon put her to the question as well, albeit the town council have little stomach for it. What reasons they have, I do not know . . ." On 12 August, Maximilian finally wrote: "With these wicked monsters they go forward apace, and, as I understand, five of them are already ripe for the fire."

In this respect, too, William had good reason to be satisfied with his son, it would seem. He had no inclination to feel sorry for these frightful foes of mankind, and that was no doubt to the credit of Fickler and de Valencia. So it was to be hoped that Maximilian would prosecute the accursed vice of magic and witchcraft as mercilessly as his father had, and that the Devil would continue to rage in vain. Prayer would also help, and the extravagant ascetic in his monastic palace devoted himself to this practice with great zeal and persistence. He was moved to prayer by fervent piety and, it appears, an unselfish concern for his realm—but perhaps also by fear of the ghosts of those he had burned.

CHAPTER · 4

*P*reparations for the form of torture used in the Pappenheimer interrogations (contemporary woodcut)

· The Valley

A DARK CLOUD

One summer day in the year 1590 a large crowd of people had gathered at the foot of a grassy mound outside the gates of the little town of Ellingen. Stakes and piles of firewood had been set up on top of the mound. Guards armed with pikes kept the over-curious at a respectful distance. The tolling of bells from the nearby church of the Teutonic Order mingled with the clamor of voices that rose from the assembled thousands, with coarse shouts, shrill laughter, the shrieking of children at play, and the barking of dogs. Eager spectators had made their way to this town between the Altmühl and the Rednitz, which was the principal seat of the order; they came not only from Weissenburg, Treuchtlingen, and Gunzenhausen, but from as far afield as Ansbach, Schwabach, Eichstätt, and Wemding. Farmers with their families and hired hands stood in groups, taking advantage of the occasion to ex-change gossip about the sowing and the weather; local craftsmen fell into conversation with a Protestant merchant from Donau-wörth; some monks from Eichstätt lounged in a circle, dicing to pass the time until the spectacle should begin; there were masters and servants, rich and poor, God-fearing men and heretics, young and old, the elegant and the out-at-elbows; there were monk's hab-its and leather jerkins, linen and loden, silk and rags. In the midst of this colorful throng, in a group of traveling folk, were the Pap-penheimers. They were craning their necks to catch a glimpse of the cart with the condemned victims, which was greeted by a howl from the mob as it made its appearance on the road that led from the city gate to the place of execution.

The word had gone round that there was to be another burning of witches in Ellingen.[59] The worthy knights of the Teutonic

Order had already sent close on fifty of these monsters to the stake during the last few months. The pious prior had tracked down a whole nest of such limbs of Satan about a year previously. It was pure chance: a poor servant girl, unwilling to stay in her present position, had looked for employment elsewhere. This she had confessed to her mistress in the course of a conversation that took a distinctly unedifying turn. A woman who lived nearby and happened to be present joined in the argument, telling the girl that she would be sorry she had left, and that she would have no luck from that day hence. If there was ever a case that proved it doesn't pay to interfere in other people's quarrels, this was it. For the very next day the servant girl complained of terrible pain in her arm, which she could only attribute to the fact that the wicked neighbor had slipped across the intervening garden into her bedchamber and had pinched her viciously. At any rate, that was what she reported to the authorities, who arrested the neighbor on suspicion of witchcraft. No doubt they managed to loosen her tongue with the aid of thumbscrews, and the result was what might have been expected. Not only did the wicked neighbor confess that she herself was a sorceress and possessed by the Devil; she also revealed to the court the names of numerous other witches in the town. Among them was a wealthy, wellborn widow, who, to all appearances, led a respectable Christian life. In no way deceived by these appearances, and in spite of her frenzied denials, the prior had the old lady thrown into prison and ordered the thumbscrews to be brought out once more. They loosened the secret witch's tongue, so that she admitted her dreadful crimes and was duly condemned. At the same time, however, the torments inflicted on her during the trial moved her to such remorse that, before she went to the stake, she bequeathed no less than one thousand gulden from her estate for the express purpose of rooting out the witches of Ellingen. Thus the financial foundation was laid for an extensive campaign of burnings: there was no end to the fires that were lit in the domain of the Teutonic Order. The more confessions there were, the greater the number of new suspects: every convicted witch instantly denounced her confederates. Some people even expressed concern that the entire population of Ellingen would be wiped out before all the witches were finally smoked out.

With each judgment day, spectators came in greater and greater numbers, and from farther and farther away. Wherever so many people congregated, there were pickings for Paulus and his like. In the summer months particularly, when he could scarcely scrape a living by mucking out cesspits, he could find no public better suited to his gaming table, while his wife could have no ears more receptive to the plaintive importunings of herself and her children. They had heard of the burning of witches in Ellingen while they were in some dosshouse or other. After all, other tramps were always talking of ways of earning a few kreuzer—by honest labor, or else by begging and trickery. Often such folk banded together and moved across country from one fair to another like a kind of tattered army. In this way they cowed the peasants, who tended to look askance at the "gypsies," and enjoyed other advantages as well. In the company of such fellow travelers, Paulus had for once risked leaving his customary beat, and he now stood craning his neck as he waited for the gruesome spectacle to be staged before the gates of Ellingen.

Our vagrant was in company, then—if not particularly choice company. There was a fellow they all called "the Lamprey," a gaunt individual in his late forties, with a forbidding manner. His shirt was black, as were his breeches, black the broad-brimmed hat, black his trim beard. His face was disfigured by scars, and when he spoke or laughed, he revealed ugly gaps in a row of yellowed teeth. He wore a leather apron in the manner of a tinsmith or tinker, with the customary pointed hammer hanging on a leather thong. The traveling folk used to say of the Lamprey that "he could do something to a woman, so that she couldn't bring herself to leave him." He had a perpetual following of several women, seldom the same ones for any length of time. There must have been something impressive about this somber figure, for his word was respected, his quickness in repartee disarmed opponents, his arguments carried conviction. He had collected a kind of retinue, tramps who nearly always traveled in his company. They too were watching the scene on the mound, occasionally shouting comments on the witches to their leader. One of them was a tall, skinny individual in his late thirties, with sunken cheeks and deep-set eyes, a skimpy red beard, and a few thin strands of hair on his bald pate. He was called "Nine-fingers" because he had only four fingers on his right hand, which was paralyzed. His sole "profession" was begging. Another of the Lamprey's companions was carrying a basket like Paulus Pappenheimer's and was apparently a peddler. They called him Abraham or Jack the Cooper—a name that indicated the trade this footloose fellow had pursued before he took to the road. From a story told by little Hänsel Pappenheimer we learn that Jack sometimes used to go in for reminiscences about his previous, "respectable" calling. Whenever he came across a barrel, he would rap on it and perform all sorts of comic tricks with any mallet that happened to be handy. Of the others, we know only that one was called Resch the Pig-sticker, a thickset man of average height with a ruddy complexion and a broad, yellowish beard, and that other members of the gang answered to names like Gilg, Hans Braun, and Sugar Bun. They too looked like peddlers or hucksters, and almost all of them had children of various ages.

An open, horse-drawn cart, bearing the four witches condemned to be burned that day, had reached the top of the rise. The executioner dragged the first witch down and pulled her on a rope across a plank to the stake assigned to her. The spectators kept up a running commentary in the form of "Oh's" and Ah's," coarse laughter, and crude jokes. The victim's arms were bound to the stake that rose from the bundles of kindling. The other three condemned women were treated in the same way. An official clambered up onto the empty cart as the sound of the bells died away with a final clang. A murmur ran through the crowd, then ceased abruptly as the man on the cart raised his right hand, drawing a paper from his doublet. From this paper he proceeded to read in a loud voice the so-called shrift, a summary of the confessions made by the condemned persons. The four wretched sinners had admitted entering into a pact with the Evil One, breaking into cellars by night, and taking part in a witches' sabbath. They had allegedly murdered innocent, unbaptized children, cut off their hands, and ground these down to make a powder, with which they had harmed people and cattle and summoned up hailstorms. For all this the worshipful court had condemned them to death by fire. This was the gist of the long statement, which was accompanied by murmurs of surprise among the listeners and concluded with an assurance of safe-conduct to the executioner, should he incur the wrath of the mob by some technical blunder. The priests and monks stationed between the stakes immediately started sprinkling holy water, swinging their censers, and reciting Latin prayers, while the bells began to toll once more. In a trice the executioner had strangled the first witch by means of an iron collar, an action greeted by the crowd with a roar of blood-curdling savagery. The four piles of brushwood and faggots were already well kindled, with flames leaping up and enveloping the four corpses. Four pillars of black smoke rose up into the blue sky, forming a dark cloud.

The people suddenly grew restless. Pent-up tension was released in a torrent of words, jocular sallies, squabbles, and laughter. Crowds jostled round the tables where wine was being poured and cheese offered for sale. Now the hour of the traveling folk had arrived. Children raced through the crowd begging with plaintive cries; the halt, the blind, and a band of yelling females joined in a jumbled lament, in which Anna Pappenheimer played a leading part. Someone was peddling a lurid broadsheet, in which those who could read would find an exact account of the gruesome doings of the witches. Another individual, a monk of tatterdemalion appearance, was busy preaching in strident tones and with threatening fist, prophesying the imminent end of the world and the advent of the Antichrist,[60] who had but recently been born to a wicked woman in a certain province of Babylon. This child, he asserted, had the teeth of a cat and was abominably hairy; a mere eight days after his birth he had been able to speak clearly and claimed to be the Son of God. But this was blasphemy, to be sure, as was proved by the fact that, on the occasion of his birth, horrible serpents and divers other monsters had rained down from the sky at a number of different places. This was accordingly the very hour of destiny; only repentance and sacrificial offerings could ensure salvation. He, the speaker, who was privy to all these things, was prepared, as it happened, to undertake a pilgrimage to the Holy Land and would intercede there for the salvation of any such as provided funds for his journey.

Paulus Pappenheimer also profited from the generally felt need to be distracted under the shadow of that dark cloud. As always on such occasions, he had set up his gaming table and instantly collected a crowd of inquisitive onlookers and keen gamblers. So it is unlikely to have occurred to him to ponder the crimes of the women who had just been put to death. After all, witches were being burned all over the place. A year earlier he had witnessed a similar execution in the county of Wiesensteig, and there, too, had listened as the shrift was read out. As he urged the crowd to join in the game at his table, he could hardly have thought that he himself would one day be forced to make such confessions. He was certainly in no doubt concerning the guilt of the victims. Probably he thought no more about what he had heard and seen but seized the opportunity to make what hard cash he could.

MARAUDERS

In no other country were there so many infamous scoundrels as in Bavaria, claimed Michel Pappenheimer during one of his interrogations. It is true that this eighteen-year-old youth had scarcely traveled outside Lower Bavaria, so that his remark merely represented a prevalent view. Of course, traveling people were liable to come across dangerous characters in the course of their travels. "Around Straubing," Gumpprecht told his judges, "there's thieves and villains in as fine attire as any nobleman. From a single robbery they get as much as a thousand or six hundred gulden, or thereabouts, for sure. And if the people they're robbing won't say where the cash is, they do them in or fry their hands in boiling fat."

At that time organized bands of robbers were waging a virtual guerrilla war against lonely farms, villages, and market towns.[61] In 1565, raiders set fire to four large villages in the area of Pfaffenhofen and Schrobenhausen alone. Not that the problem was confined to Bavaria. In Baden, travelers on the highways had been terrorized ever since 1576 by troops of mounted highwaymen, some of whom "wore red buttons on their hats" as a badge of identification. During the same period there was word from Württemberg of "organized gangs of murderers and arsonists," who launched their nocturnal attacks "suddenly, swiftly, and without warning" on villages and castles, plundering them and putting them to the torch. In 1590 there were reports from Hesse complaining of "unemployed vagabonds" of all kinds who laid fires and robbed and murdered wayfarers. We hear much the same from Saxony: men and women were struck down and robbed on the public thoroughfares; criminals and arsonists started fires here, there, and everywhere. "Often these masterless fellows roam, twenty or thirty strong, across the countryside, seizing people's belongings by force." We hear of even larger robber bands in the Harz, where in 1586 whole areas were laid waste, the municipalities of Heringen and Suhl being reduced to ashes. In the same year gangs of "bushrangers, thieves, robbers, and beggars" made their way through the province of Upper Lusatia. It was the same in Brandenburg: "They go about in gangs of anything up to sixty, lay the people under tribute as they please, smash down their doors and break into their houses, take by force what they cannot get otherwise, attack passersby in the street, rob them and even do them to death, besides causing all kinds of mischief, murder, and mayhem in our cities." According to a reliable report from Mecklenburg, many individuals "from noble and wellborn families" were numbered among the bandits.

Which is hardly surprising. The activities of robber bands in those years preceding the Thirty Years' War still had a certain

134

amount in common with the institutionalized robbery of the Middle Ages, which was based on the principle of the feud. In most cases the feud was no more than a threadbare disguise for pure greed. On the most trivial pretext, and often with a dash of sarcasm, a knight would declare a feud against an individual he proposed to despoil—some prosperous, portly citizen, for example, who had offended his aristocratic sensibilities by not fastening the clasp of his belt properly. At an earlier stage, it is true, high-sounding slogans were put about: people took up arms against towns and villages on account of wrongs allegedly done to some artisan or goodwife, disguising a totally unchivalrous lust for plunder beneath the righteous indignation that could thus be generated. The merest trace of social injustice always makes the use of force particularly ominous. The robber baron was wont to gallop off eagerly as the avenger of injured innocence, the pristine mantle of magnanimity thrown over his black bandit's attire; this salved his conscience and assuaged any sense of shame he might have felt regarding a possible loss of moral stature. For the weapons employed in such feuds were anything but chivalrous: they included robbery, arson, and manslaughter. These were not inflicted on the adversary in person, however, but on his tenants, the peasants. Villages and farmsteads went up in flames, fields were laid waste, cattle slaughtered or stolen, men and women maimed and murdered. In medieval times knights used to sing of the peasants:

> We'll hunt them from the plow
> And roast them like a sow,
> Until we've grabbed our loot—
> And strung 'em up, to boot:

Or:

> Just grab him by the scruff
> And let your hearts be gay!
> Take all his finest stuff,
> His horses lead away!
> Undaunted be, and bold,
> and if he's got a groat,
> Then slit his scraggy throat!

The scourge represented by these bandits was already a long tradition by the end of the sixteenth century. Even the robber barons used to recruit their forces from all kinds of riffraff, a practice described thus in Johannes Rothe's "Mirror of Chivalry": "They know neither troth nor loyalty, they have thieves and cutthroats in their service, with whom they share their booty." From the end of the fifteenth century onward, the authorities, backed by public order legislation, had contrived to root out the robber barons themselves. But arson and murder continued. The ancient appeal of the just feud was not forgotten, nor was that contempt for the peasantry. From Pommern-Stettin we hear that in 1560 "a horde of villains" had overrun towns, villages, and hamlets, murdering, setting fires, and slaughtering livestock. As justification or pretext for these atrocities they alleged "insults and injuries they had suffered ten, twenty, or thirty years previously, which had long since lapsed with the passage of time . . . or else the constraints or chastisement inflicted on them by their lords and masters during the years of their service or apprenticeship." What was good enough for the barons was good enough for the robbers: they preferred to masquerade as high-spirited avengers rather than figure as common criminals. For this reason Gumpprecht's claim that in the country around Straubing there were "thieves and highwaymen in as fine array as any nobleman" is entirely credible. Why should not a saying current among the nobles of Westphalia apply equally well to Bavaria?

> Riding and robbing is no sort of shame,
> The best of us do it without any blame.

With such bandits on horseback, arrogant and prosperous as they were, the Pappenheimers naturally had no dealings. Highwaymen were not interested in a family of shabby tramps; they were after rich farmers and traveling merchants. They used informers in the market place of Straubing to find out when the next convoy of merchants was due to travel through a sparsely populated stretch of country. Plans for attack were laid accordingly. The ringleader had the convoy of vehicles watched by spies. The convoy usually consisted of twenty or thirty wagons, traveling in a column so as to be able to assist each other on bad roads or in case of attack. Since there were not enough inns of any size, merchants not infrequently had to spend nights in the open. In that case they parked their wagons in a large circle so as to form a stockade, led the horses into the center, gave them their fodder, and lit a fire to cook supper. When they wanted to sleep, most of them crawled into their wagons, some stayed by the embers of the fire, and a few stood guard. They were all armed, and knew that they had every

136

reason to be. All of a sudden, mounted bandits would make their appearance, creeping up to the stockade in groups of twenty or thirty, venturing a night attack on the encampment. Woe to the travelers who were not roused and called to arms by some alert watchman. The following day they would be found lying dead among their charred and looted wagons.

The peasants were even more defenseless than wagoners or traders. The Pappenheimers tell us the story of a night attack on a farm in the neighborhood of Mattenkofen, near Passau, which luridly illustrates this defenselessness. The robbers chose their victim with care: he was the wealthy tenant of the most isolated farmstead. The farmer from Mattenkofen often used to take horses and large quantities of grain to market, returning home befuddled by drink but with a bulging purse. The gang followed him secretly, familiarizing themselves with the locality, the layout of the farm, and the habits of the family. One summer night, between ten and eleven o'clock, when the farmhands were all away and the household fast asleep, dark figures approached stealthily, forced the lock on the door with a piece of wire, and entered the house. The farmer's family were dragged from their sleep, blinking aghast at the torches held above them, the brutal faces, the glittering daggers. Where was the chest with the money? the intruders barked at their terrified victims, dragging them from their beds and bundling them into the kitchen. The farmer remained silent; only his wife uttered cries of lamentation. Their wrists were then bound with cords that cut cruelly into the flesh. Was he going to tell them without further ado where the cash was hidden? one of the robbers asked the frightened man. He shook his head vigorously. They broke both his arms, cut off his ears and his wife's ears. He remained silent, she screamed. The two of them were then kicked and dragged by their hair all around the kitchen, but they still refused to reveal where their savings were hidden. Then the robbers heated lard, brought it seething from the hearth, and put it down in front of their victims. They seized the woman and plunged her hand into the boiling fat. The screams of the scalded victim were dreadful to hear. Have mercy, have mercy, she screamed as they forced her other hand toward the pot of boiling liquid. It was all of no avail. Not a word did the farmer utter; he simply groaned terribly when they went on to smash his shins and turn him into a shapeless mass of bleeding flesh with savage thrusts of their knives. Infuriated by such stubbornness, one of the robbers finally slit their throats. After this murderous climax,

137

the gang ransacked the house; by the flickering light of a torch they wrenched drawers from the dressers, smashed open chests and cupboards, burst into triumphant shouts as they found the hiding place with the money and took everything they might be able to sell. Then back into the kitchen, the scene of that gruesome murder, smeared with their victims' blood; they dragged the farmer's corpse into the yard by the legs, hurled the torch into the hay loft, and made off with their booty. From a safe distance they watched the flames leap up and light up the surrounding countryside. Then the robbers vanished into the forest—unseen, unrecognized, unscathed.

This kind of barbaric behavior had precedents, not only in the chivalrous practice of the feud but also in the military operations of the time. In their forays in search of plunder in enemy territory, soldiers used identical methods. This is how a contemporary describes a raid on a farm by mercenaries:[62] "bedsteads, tables, chairs, and benches they burned . . . Our servant girl was so abused in the stable that she could not leave it again . . . They bound our farmhand and threw him to the ground, forced his mouth open with a wooden chock, and poured a milk churn full of vile muck into him . . . Then they really set to, took the flints from their pistols and screwed the peasants' thumbs in their place, and tortured the poor wretches as though they were eager to burn witches, seeing as how they also thrust one of the captive peasants into the oven and lit a fire at his back, though he'd confessed to nothing. They put a rope around another one's head and twisted it so tight with a wooden billet that the blood leaped from his mouth and nose and ears. Every manjack of them had his own notion of torturing the peasants, and so every peasant had his own special torment." The only difference between pillage and armed robbery was that the former was legal and the latter prohibited. "I thirst for booty" was inscribed on regimental banners that portrayed a wolf with bared fangs. In keeping with sound military practice, it was customary to provision troops by allowing them to batten on any territory on which they had inflicted their presence. In this way the burden on the war chest was diminished and the enemy injured at the same time.

What was an approved practice for mercenary soldiers may not have seemed so very reprehensible to those same men when they were discharged and roaming the country between wars. No way of supporting themselves other than by plundering was likely to occur to them; they formed themselves into troops with particular aims and functions as they had learned to do during their military service, and elected their own leaders. In this way military units turned into bands of marauders; mercenaries became bushrangers. Other vagrants joined them and copied their violent methods. The operations of these robbers became so inhuman precisely because warfare had made such barbaric practices the norm. Women were flogged almost to the point of death, men tortured with red-hot pincers, old men hanged, children maimed in front of their parents' eyes—and all this for the sake of money. That these practices were regarded as legitimate in certain cases (that is, in the foraging expeditions of the armies) was as disastrous for the crime rate as was the emotional appeal of the robber barons. Worst of all, however, was the impression conveyed to the populace that the authorities were powerless to protect them from this menace. Sometimes people even tried to come to an understanding with the murderous gangs, which they feared far more than the empty phrases of the innumerable princely decrees aimed at the unsavory rabble and their "accomplices." One of the most eminent criminal lawyers of the time, the Dutchman Jodocus Damhouder, was struck by the positively hostile attitude of the rural population toward the representatives of the law. The peasants would generally refuse to help them, leaning idly on their sticks, as it were, and waiting to see who would win. Instead of assisting the authorities to hunt down robbers and thieves, they offered refuge to the criminals for fear of incurring their wrath. The link between the administration of criminal justice and the sale of public offices was, of course, a further factor in bringing about this state of affairs. There was no point in prosecuting penniless vagrants; indeed, such prosecutions simply gave rise to undesirable expense. An association of imperial cities in Franconia dedicated to the eradication of the brigands operated on the principle of St. Florian, according to which each man wishes a possible conflagration onto his neighbor's property on condition that his own is spared: vagrants who had been apprehended and were then discovered to have no assets were simply pushed across the nearest frontier.

"Whereas the sovereign authorities of the Empire and in our various realms and cities have been quite bereft of all their power, and princes and commoners alike, from the highest to the meanest, are sunk into depravity, none of the decrees and judgments so lavishly launched against beggars, vagrants, tramps, bushrangers, the criminal fraternity of whatever kind, thieves, robbers, and murderers can have the slightest effect, as we daily witness." This is how a preacher summed up the situation in 1571. And the Nuremberg versifier Hans Sachs sighed in 1559: "Might God but send us a German Hercules who would rid the land of robbery, murder, and tribulation, for no one is any longer safe from thieves and murderers."

A new Hercules—that is precisely what Duke Maximilian aimed to be. On the occasion of his accession to power in 1595, a pamphlet showed him clad in a lion's skin and bearing a club on his shoulder. Friedrich Sustris, the author of this allegory on the prince's youthful prowess, was probably not thinking of Hans Sachs's words. But the ambition to rid the country of its worthless riffraff was certainly part of the plans laid by the monarch thus depicted. And that is why the vagrant Pappenheimer family had been lying in custody in Munich's Falcon Tower since April 1600.

MICHEL CONFESSES

All morning long, the torture chamber in the Falcon Tower had resounded with sobs, screams, howls of agony, and desperate pleas for mercy. The grisly arts of Master Georg had, in a matter of hours, reduced the eighteen-year-old Michel Pappenheimer from a robust, self-assured young man to a pitiful human wreck. His youthful physique had withstood the torture for an abnormally long time. He had been hoisted up no less than twelve times by his arms, which were bound behind his back. Each time, Dr. Wangereck's question: What had he and his people done with the children's hands that had been found in Tettenwang? And each time, the victim's reply: He had not had any children's hands, he had seen none, he was innocent. Then they tied a heavy stone to his legs, so that next time he was hauled up, his arms were dislocated. That was no use either, nor did doubling the weight have any effect. So Master Georg was ordered by the commissioners to light a torch and hold it to the armpits of his screaming victim. All in vain: Michel persisted in denying any knowledge of the hands, though when lowered to the ground, he was unable to stand and could do nothing but groan.

At that point Wangereck had discontinued the interrogation and, accompanied by the treasurer and Dr. Hainmüller, had made his escape from the dismal chamber, out into the fresh air under the blue sky of spring, away from the groans to the twittering of birds. How the councillors spent this interval is not recorded in

140

our sources. Possibly they made their way to an inn and discussed the morning's doleful proceedings over three different meat courses and two kinds of wine; we can almost hear Wangereck asserting that the witness's prolonged resistance to torture confirmed only too plainly his own view that the Pappenheimers were indeed in league with the Devil. Master Georg was obviously pitting himself against forces that were not merely natural. Whereupon the others may have nodded approvingly and applied themselves once more to the needs of the inner man before returning, in good spirits and engaged in animated conversation, to the Falcon Tower, where they once more passed through the oaken door and descended the musty stone stairs to the vaults.

There the youth still lay bound and trembling on the floor; his entire body was bruised blue and green; ugly blisters under the armpits marked his burns; his joints were swollen. The slightest movement sent almost unbearable pain shooting through his body. He emitted blood-curdling howls of agony when Master Georg dragged him up from the floor and pushed him against the wall.

Wangereck addressed the pain-racked youth: Now he had had time to think about his situation, perhaps he was ready to tell the truth. There were no children's hands, the young man whimpered. Very well, said the councillor, we'll have to hoist you up again. Michel then implored them tearfully not to continue, he would confess to anything they required of him. Yes, his father and Gumpp had buried the hands in Schölz's vegetable patch. Wangereck: Why had they eaten some of the hands? Michel: So that they would not have to confess. Wangereck: Where had he scattered the powder they made from the children's hands with the object of injuring cattle and people? Michel: When they had been in Pfatter the previous autumn, lodging with a woman who shared her home with her only son and lived next door to the magistrate, his mother had scattered powder on the meadow in his presence. As a result, nearly all the cattle in the village had died. Outside Cham, in a straggling village where the great sickness had then been, they had spent the night once with a farmer whose name he did not know but who had two gates to his yard. There too, powder had been scattered by his mother, and a great many cattle had died of it. Two years before, in spring, he had put powder under the byre door at the almshouse in Irlbach because they would not take him and his people in, and forty head of cattle had died. And a year ago, in the fall, when the dean of Altenbuch refused to pay them for their labor, they had scattered powder by the hencoop in his farmyard. They had also injured a farmer who refused to put them up on his farm although he generally offered shelter to all kinds of vagrants. In Pfatter they had scattered powder by the cherry trees in the garden of a man who lived there with his mother: the man then left home, fell ill, and turned hunchback. That had happened because Michel's father had slaughtered and drawn a cow belonging to this man that had fallen into the cellar, and he hadn't been paid for the job. And he had scattered powder at Raunecker's place in Mündriching because Raunecker had beaten him. But the sickness he caused had passed off harmlessly because his father, old Pappenheimer, had treated Raunecker with herbs and cured him. It all depended whether the powder was meant simply to cause sickness or to kill outright. It you meant to kill a man, you had to treat the powder beforehand with salt, put it into a pan, cover it with a cloth, and then add salt on top of that. Anyone who walked over powder treated in this way was beyond human aid. If the spell was meant only to cause sickness, untreated powder was used. His father and mother knew how to undo the effects of the powder. How they did it he couldn't say, but his mother had always had teazles and other roots in her possession. She had tried to cure Hütlin's daughter from Eglesheim with them, but had not succeeded. Who had put the powder down in that case, he didn't know.

The councillor doubtless interrupted this torrent of words from time to time, so that his clerk could catch up. Then, still seeking concrete evidence, he asked where the suspect had hidden the magic powder before his arrest. The answer: He had his supply in a bag in the pannier[63] he used for carrying his glazing implements, but he didn't know whether it was still there. His mother had kept hers in a leather pouch.—Question: How had he prepared the powder: Answer: They had dried the hands in a pot in the oven, then ground them to a powder, using herbs, which was different from normal witchcraft practice. Question: Who had taught him the art? Answer: His mother, when he was about four years old. He didn't know who she had learned it from. There had been talk of her being an ogress, just as folk suspected the Lipp woman in Altmannstein of witchcraft, but he'd never seen any signs of it, either with Lipp or with his mother.

Wangereck then dropped the subject of witchcraft. Once Michel had admitted to making powder from children's hands, he could hardly deny the charge of murder, because, after all, the hands could only have been procured through murder. It was a confession of murder that the councillor was now aiming at, having already decided to conduct a separate investigation into the charges of witchcraft. And, in fact, the victim, rather than risk a resumption of the torture, readily admitted having murdered numerous pregnant women. He also corroborated confessions made by his father and brothers relating to other murders and robberies when he was confronted with their statements. He became reluctant to talk only when the commissioner, after a glance at his list of questions, asked him how many houses and villages the traveling people had set on fire.

Wangereck gave the dreaded signal, and Master Georg began to bind his suffering charge to the strappado once more, in spite of the young man's frenzied pleas for mercy. He would tell them everything, whimpered Michel. The commissioner ordered the executioner to desist. The victim: In Oberwinkling, near Welchenburg, he and Trooper Jack, a young tinker, had set fire to the farm of a peasant they called Pfeifmichel. Last year, about the time of the solstice, he had used a file to kindle fire in a hank of flax, which Trooper Jack pushed into the thatched roof at the back of the house. But that was the only dwelling that had been burned down on that occasion. Another time, two years earlier, his whole family had been living with a farmer in Unterwinkling and working for him. They had crept into the kitchen by night, taken a lighted dip, and set fire to some straw in the barn. Their plan had been to steal what they could from the house while the peasants were busy trying to rescue the cattle. They had not succeeded, however, because the farmer had posted a couple of old women to guard the things they had dragged out of the buildings. Here, and in the case of other fire-raising exploits, suspicion had never fallen on them. If they had been seen handling burning coals, it was assumed they needed fire in their work. In Neunhausen, the other side of Metten, he and Trooper Jack had lodged two summers ago with a farmer called the Widebauer, and they had been joined there by his parents and little Hänsel. One night, after the others were already bedded down in the barn, he had sat up with the farmer and Trooper Jack in the kitchen. They had played cards and lost money to the farmer. When they went out to join the others in the barn, they had taken a lighted dip with them to find their way through the house and across the yard. They had then set fire to the thatched roof of the stable and run off as fast as they could. But his father and mother, who had known nothing of this trick, had been as much taken by surprise as the farmer and had helped him to save the buildings and gear and put out the fire.

Wangereck was not satisfied with this. He wanted to hear of more cases of arson, prompted the lad, and steered his answers in the desired direction. He threatened renewed torture and put specific questions about "the fire in Eggenfeld" and "the fire in Gänkhofen," and did not give up until he had a confession that satisfied him. Then, changing the subject, he asked what they had stolen from churches—monstrances, vestments, and so on.

Any amount, said the youth eagerly. Two years ago, in summer, for instance, he, together with Meindl and the two tinker lads, had forced open the door of a chapel that stood on a hill at Steinkirchen, near Deggendorf, using an oak staff, and had then broken open the offertory box and stolen two gulden. In Schambach, he, Gumpp, Jack the Cooper, and Georgl from Landshut had broken into the church vestry by night and stolen a gilded chalice, which they had sold to a goldsmith in Straubing. Three years ago, he, his brother, and the two tinker lads had gone into a church in Oberaltach in broad daylight, as if to pray. Behind a grating at the back of the altar they spotted a monstrance covered with a cloth. They forced the lock with a jemmy and stole the valuable piece. There were ten wafers inside. They ate these, then buried the cloth, and sold the monstrance to the same goldsmith in Straubing.

Who had taught little Hänsel to steal from offertory boxes, using strips of wood smeared with glue? Michel: His father or mother must have taught the boy that. He himself wouldn't go in for prigging. It wasn't worth the trouble, a few pfennig, dreier, or batzen. Wangereck: Prigging? What sort of word was that? Michel: Prigging was thieves' slang, it meant stealing. His father, mother, and he himself had trained the boy. Whenever they went to a market, or a fair, or any place where there were crowds of people, he was supposed to fish purses out of people's pockets. The little lad had been pretty smart at that. Wangereck: What had Michel himself stolen? Answer: He hadn't gone in much for stealing; he'd always been afraid he would be caught too easily. About six years ago, when he and the two tinker lads were mending pots and pans for the magistrate in Natternberg, they had stolen a cap, a sword, and a hat from his room during the night and sold them to a young farmer in Wischelburg for half a gulden. From there they made for Staufendorf on the Danube. They lodged with the Widenbauer, and mended pans, but he gave them nothing but half a loaf, so they crept into his house one night and stole a woman's skirt, a man's cap, and a scarlet waistcoat. After that, when he went down by himself to Plädling and spent the night with a farmer called Schwänzl, he was joined by Sugar Bun and Georgl from Landshut,

144

and they stole ten gulden and a woman's skirt from a chest in Schwänzl's back room.

The councillors no doubt nodded their heads as they listened to these and other admissions. Wangereck, who seemed at last to have heard his fill of such exploits, now wanted to know who, in fact, had led Michel Pappenheimer to commit such criminal acts. He replied that his father and mother had trained him to steal, but it was the Lamprey who had made a killer of him. His father had been well aware of that: he had often said to Michel that they would go too far one of these days and get themselves arrested. He was glad now that he had fallen into the hands of the law. Now he could repent of his sins and settle his account with God, because he would not have given up his villainy of his own accord but would have relapsed into his old ways as soon as times were bad.

That was not what Wangereck wanted to hear, however. Wasn't it rather the case, he suggested, that his mother was a witch and that he himself was a limb of Satan? Michel: He had, of course, heard the common talk concerning his mother, but it wasn't true that she dabbled in sorcery. He had never seen her cast any spell, except that she had made a powder from the children's hands and had scattered it on the ground. She had once had a red ointment, but he couldn't say what she had used it for. Wangereck: But they had observed very clearly here in the vault that the Devil was giving him succor. He should try to recall, for the sake of his eternal salvation, whether he had given himself to the Evil Spirit, or whether the Evil One had ever promised him anything. Michel: No, no, God forbid! The reason he had endured the torture for such a long time was just his determination, his pigheadedness.

An answer the councillor may well have greeted with an incredulous smile. He had long been convinced that the imprisoned family, every one of them, were disciples of the Devil. If he refrained from having his witness hoisted up once more on the strappado, it was only because it was now late in the evening and he did not believe that a separate interrogation on the subject of witchcraft was necessary. For the moment he had heard all he wanted to hear from Michel Pappenheimer.

TRUTH AND FALSEHOOD

The reader will no doubt be anxious to know whether the members of our vagrant family really were murderers, robbers, and arsonists, or simply harmless, poverty-stricken tramps. To this crucial question the available sources give no answer. After all, confessions extracted by torture prove nothing. Anyone who forgets that fact is bound to see in the Pappenheimer family the very incarnation of all the villainy and crime of the age.

They confessed to hundreds of larcenies of every kind. Even Hänsel confessed: "His mother had trained him to steal and cut purses and said to him he should sneak up to gaming tables and other places where people gathered at fairs and markets and filch purses from their breeches, or else cut them loose with a little knife she gave him." The adults described other thefts, particularly from peasants' homes. For instance: in Vohburg they had stayed with Hänsel of Eichstätt before the market, and had stolen a purse with seven gulden from his living room. Or else: they had purloined a purse with two gulden in it from the farmer at Holzen, an isolated farmstead near Abensberg. Or, again: four years previously, during the winter, they had made free with a chest belonging to old Widmann in Altmannstein when the key had been left in the lock, and had stolen five gulden. Generally the booty was less impressive: "a couple of bed sheets," "two loaves," "some pieces of meat," "an old pair of trousers," "a pillow," or "a few yards of cloth." Anna and the boy also admitted to "prigging from offertory boxes in churches," fishing coins out of the locked caskets. Hänsel claimed to have extracted as much as ten gulden, and never less than five, from offertory boxes in "St. Salvator's," "in Niederaltach," in Deggendorf, Abensberg, Bogenberg, and Donaustauf. "If you make the sticks fairly wide at the end, and if the slot in the box is rather wide, you can pull out four, five, or six dreier, halbbatzen, and pfennig at one go." This seems a slight exaggeration. Anna, at any rate, swore "by her hope of salvation that she had not stolen more than nine gulden in all from offertory boxes."

In the Pappenheimers' time, thefts from churches constituted a very common crime, and were by no means confined to "prigging" by this method. Not only were churches generally accessible, they also contained much coveted valuables, such as gilded chalices, monstrances, and crucifixes. Apart from these sacred objects, the vestries of many churches acted as depositories for valuable private property. It was the custom of the time to deposit treasured objects in churches, rather in the manner in which they are now placed in the safe deposits of our banks.

"Prigging" was hard work, but there were, of course, other ways of getting at the money in offertory boxes. During his interrogation, Gumpprecht told how he and Jack the Cooper had gone into

146

the church at Mossheim, near Straubing, just when the verger was ringing the Angelus. They hid in the building and had themselves locked in. They then broke open the offertory box during the night, Jack the Cooper forcing the two locks with a jemmy. There were ten gulden in the box, which they shared between them. Then, when the verger came to ring matins next morning, they crept stealthily out of the church. The cooper restored the locks and the boxes in such a way that the theft would not be noticed. That was an essential condition for the success of the operation, for otherwise the verger would have raised the alarm as soon as he discovered the damage, and the thieves would hardly have escaped unnoticed and unscathed from the church and the village.

This method was appropriate, therefore, only when all traces of the crime could be erased. If we are to believe the Pappenheimers, it was much commoner for thieves to smash a church window and to get in and out by means of a ladder. Sometimes one of them would break in like this and then unbar the main door and let his accomplices in. "Almost all vagrants and beggars," said little Hänsel in his statement, "go in for this kind of theft."

Paulus also confessed to having "broken into a church . . . at night through a window," generally in the company of other vagrants, one of whom, the Lamprey, "could open almost any lock with his jemmy." It was he who had "forced open the door of the sanctuary, where they had stolen a chalice from a cupboard." On another occasion a monstrance "along with a silver cross" had fallen into their hands. They had broken up the stolen objects and "sold them to a goldsmith in Straubing that lived down by the market."

Theft was particularly easy whenever fire had broken out—and there were any number of fires in those days. Helpers quickly turned up, some invited, and others uninvited, and they carried everything of value out of the burning premises—not always to rescue it but to make off with it. No wonder there were people who preferred to ban such eager rescuers from their burning property, refusing their offers of help in evacuating their goods and putting out the fire—especially since they never quite knew whether these keen volunteers might not have contrived the pretext for their assistance by starting the fire themselves. Judging by the description of such incidents provided by the Pappenheimers, this sort of dubious altruism was a very prevalent source of crime. Gumpprecht alone reported a dozen cases of arson involving farmhouses, which all conformed to the same pattern. "He and his people" had "gotten into the farmhouse," to do some glazing, to mend pots and pans, or to seek a lodging for the night. Then they had "taken a burning brand" or struck fire from a file and flint, and "set light to hay or straw in the barn or in the stable." As soon as the fire had "caught hold," they had all helped salvage the contents and carry them outside, at the same time keeping an eye open for the chance to steal "whatever they could lay their hands on."

In those days the farmhouses of Lower Bavaria almost all had thatched roofs and were built entirely of wood. Fighting fires by passing buckets from hand to hand was such a pointless undertaking that for the most part people did not even try, but employed all the available hands to rescue cattle and goods, so that a fire was likely to spread very rapidly indeed. If there was a wind to carry sparks onto the roofs of neighboring houses, a whole village, even a small town, might go up in flames in no time at all. Then the fire alarm would ring out from the church steeple in a futile effort to warn of the danger, and especially to rouse sleepers during the night.

The Pappenheimers were accused of destroying the townships of Eggenfelden and Geltofling by fire. The Lower Bavarian market town of Eggenfelden, at that time the seat of a prefecture and a district court, lies on a hill on the left bank of the River Rott. It is renowned for its Gothic parish church, which has survived not only the arson of which the Pappenheimers were accused but other, presumably more devastating disasters. The little town was almost totally destroyed by fire as early as 1552, and then again in 1648. Between 1632 and 1634, Eggenfeld was twice laid waste by the Swedes. Forty years earlier, at least according to the records, our Pappenheimer family achieved the same result. Paulus, Anna, and Michel allegedly arrived in Eggenfelden in company with Sugar Bun and Jack the Cooper. They had "found lodgings with Georg Messerschmied," and had later been joined by Ninefingers, so Paulus said. They had then "resolved to start a fire in the market. So his wife and one of the others, he no longer knew which, had made their way secretly at nightfall into a brewery on the fringes of the market." Anna had "started fires at five different places in the barn, while two of them kept a lookout. The fire had then broken out at ten o'clock in the evening." A great many houses and barns had been burned down. In the general confusion they had stolen clothing, linen, and other things they could easily carry, and taken the whole lot to Messerschmied. He had bought some items from them, and they had disposed of others to Farmer Michl in Rettenbach. If we are to believe the Pappenheimers' statement, they started another fire in Eggenfelden four years later. Michel, "his father, and the whole gang of them, along with the two tinker lads, Georgl and Beindl," had spent a week in the town, "staying with a man they called Jack the Watchman, who lived in a little house on the city wall. They peddled their wares, going in and out of his house. In the meantime they had prepared a mixture of gunpowder one night, ignited it with the aid of a file and flint, and set fire to a little goat stall."

All this may or may not be true. There are contradictions in the various statements, particularly in the second case. Paulus dated the fire as being in the autumn or winter of 1598/99 and gave a completely different account of the event from that given by Michel. According to Hänsel, the arson took place in the summer of 1599, and involved the theft of a monstrance and a chalice. His mother, on the other hand, claimed that she had "come by a certain amount of clothing," but "had not been present when the fire was started." The second "conflagration," whenever it took place, cannot have been of much consequence since it is not noted in the history of fires in Eggenfelden. On the other hand, the chronicle for 1594 does mention a substantial fire in the vicinity of the Gropp market, although there is no suggestion that it was started by vagrant incendiaries.

Under the pressure of torture the victims' actual experience was combined wih pure invention and hearsay to form an indissoluble amalgam of falsehood and truth. A good example is provided by the Pappenheimers' statements about the fire in Geltolfing, a small village in the vicinity of Straubing. This conflagration was reckoned to be the work of a local woman, who was arrested and then went mad in prison. When he was interrogated on 26 and 27 April, Michel obviously knew nothing of this, for he described the sequence of events as follows: Four or five years earlier he, his father, Gumpp, Jack the Cooper, and Abraham the Peddler lodged overnight with a cottager and day laborer in Geltolfing—he and Gumpp in the kitchen and the others in the barn. They set fire to a child's hand in the kitchen, placed it on the table, and then went out into the barn. There they set light to a twist of hemp or flax and scattered powder in the name of all the infernal host. As a result, such a fierce fire was started that not only were a number of farmhouses burned down, but the castle as well, and the church very nearly so. He and Abraham the Peddler stole four gulden from a house. Following that, they all ran into the church and took a chalice, two altar cloths, and some money from the offertory box.

During his interrogation on 3 and 4 July, however, Michel gave a totally different account of the incident. Five years earlier he, his father, Gumpp, Jack the Cooper, Ninefingers, and the tailor from Prunn had been staying on the Durnhof, a farm in the vicinity of Straubing. One day they set off for Geltolfing. There they stayed with a cottager's wife called Gredl, entering the house through the backyard so that no one should see them. Since the cottager and his wife knew them well, they welcomed their visit and ate and drank with them. During the meal they decided to set fire to the neighbor's house with an eye to theft. So Gumpp and the cottager's wife, who was a witch, lit a candle prepared with the aid of witchcraft, and the two of them then went to the farmer next door and pushed the flaming candle into his barn through the shaft hole at the back of the building. In due course a fire broke out, which destroyed a great many houses and the castle as well. On that occasion they stole a small amount of clothing. When the cottager's wife was subsequently accused, she pretended to be crazy. In the prison at Straubing she admitted her guilt and claimed that a black man had come to her and had demanded that she should either kill her child or set fire to her neighbor's house.

Between these two statements Michel had obviously learned that a woman had been arrested as the culprit and that she was reckoned to be crazy. Possibly he was confronted with this story by the court in order to prove the falsity of his initial confession.

His father, Paulus, at any rate, knew the facts when he gave his own account of the fire in Geltolfing on 7 and 8 July. Four years earlier when he, his two sons, the tailor from Prunn, Jack the Cooper, and Ninefingers had been lodging at the Durnhof in the vicinity of Straubing, they went to Geltolfing one day and stayed with a day laborer whose wife, Margreth, was a witch and had been imprisoned in Straubing. There they played cards for a while. While they were doing that, the woman and Gumpp went out, with the agreement of all of them, and pushed a burning candle through the shaft hole into the straw in the barn. He followed the couple and watched. Not long afterwards, fire broke out in broad daylight and spread into a general conflagration. The castle and many houses burned down. Then, pretending to help, they stole some clothing, nothing else, and hid it behind a hedge until nightfall, when they went back to the barn on the Durnhof with their booty. They sold the clothing to Simon the Beggar, blind Pfliegl, and Georg Zauter, who had been sharing their quarters in the barn. The woman went crazy in prison in Straubing, or pretended to be crazy. But that was only her mischief. And the turnkey in Straubing had given her a big belly while she was in prison there.

Of course, the statements of father and son may agree simply because that was how things actually happened, but the whole story smacks very much of rumors current in the Straubing area at the time. It is no longer possible to establish the truth, and that goes for all the statements. Certainly the village of Geltolfing, as well as the castle described in the statements, is still to be found more or less in its original state in the picturesque valley of the Alterach, not far from Straubing. The hamlet and the manor house with its moat have survived the centuries like some sleeping beauty. It is historic ground, at least as far as our family of vagrants is concerned.

The Pappenheimers confessed also to almost a hundred murders, mainly in the course of assaults on isolated wayfarers. All of the assaults allegedly followed the same pattern: two or three lie in wait for the traveler in a wood—rarely in open country or in a barn—take him by surprise, knock him down, kill him, rob him of his possessions, and conceal the body. A few examples: in the spring of 1597, between Geiselhöring and Muttenhofen, Paulus, Gumpprecht, and Michel had been "in a field by a small clump of trees when a farmer they did not know came toward them, in broad daylight." They "believed they would probably find money on him, so they attacked him." The father rushed up to the wayfarer and knocked him down with his long staff. They took the murdered man's money, about three gulden, "and dragged him behind a hedge, where they left him fully dressed, his clothes not being good." On another occasion the three of them had encountered an itinerant craftsman "the other side of Pförring, by the bridge." They "attacked him without warning," knocked him down with the same staff, stabbed him with their knives, "and so murdered him"; then they stole "two gulden in cash, a coat, and a bundle with two shirts." Following the deed, the body had been dragged "into a clump of bushes." Paulus wore the shirts until they were worn out, and had a vest made from the coat. Michel confessed that he, together with the Lamprey and Beindl from Lenzendorf, had attacked a peasant in a wood not far from Regensburg. The victim was armed, and Michel snatched his "weapon" from behind, "at the same time as Beindl hit him with a pointed hammer and murdered him." Then the victim was robbed; they "found five gulden in cash, two pounds of meat, and a loaf of bread that he had been carrying in a bag alongside his weapon." On another occasion, "about a quarter of a mile from Dinzling, a peasant from Rendt had approached him, his brother, the Lamprey, and Jack the Cooper, in a wood. They "attacked and murdered him" and robbed him of three gulden, which they divided among themselves, "and then dragged the corpse behind a bush." "In Tettenwang, in Schölz's stable, where they had all been lodging" four years ago he and his father, his brother, his mother, and a certain "Little John" murdered a horse dealer called Bärtel when the latter was spending the night with them in the barn, "along with two horses." His father "struck the victim on the head with a glazier's mallet, and they all joined in and did him to death." There were seven gulden in the murdered man's purse. They divided up the money "and then buried the dead man by night in the barn."

The interrogators heard the same sort of thing from Gump- precht. A year before, on St. Bartholomew's day, he and the two "tinker lads from the forest called Georgl and Beindl" had met "a stranger, a Bavarian," on the road from Straubing to Michelsberg. They attacked him, "first hitting him on the chest with a heavy club and knocking him to the ground, where they finished him off with their pointed hammers." The booty, amounting to four gulden, was divided up on the spot. Afterwards they dragged the dead man into a ditch at the edge of a field. In 1593 "another man, also a Bavarian, had come toward them on a slope leading up to a wood between Nideraltach and Denkendorf." The Lamprey "struck the same with the long-handled pointed hammer he carried with him, first on the chest, and then from behind with the pointed end, so that the man fell to the ground and died straight away." Then they searched the corpse, found three gulden, "and left the dead man, fully clothed, behind a bush, along with the hatchet he had with him that was used for splitting logs."

Anna gave an account of a murder her husband confessed to having committed "at Pförring, above the bridge." It scarcely differs from his own description of the crime. It had happened three years earlier, the victim "a journeyman with a Swabian accent and wearing leather breeches and a leather doublet." The whole family had been accomplices in the killing, "stabbing him in the body with a knife." The booty consisted of the journeyman's coat and his bundle of belongings.

152

If we can credit their confessions, our family of vagrants committed at least ten such murders annually. That is hardly plausible, however. If the Pappenheimers' route had been lined with the corpses of their victims, suspicion would certainly have fallen on them at some point or other. Only in the case last mentioned here do we find such a hint. Anna related how, after the murder of the Swabian journeyman, "it had been rumored in Pförring that someone had been killed down by the bridge. That was why Schnäckhlhauser warned her and said that they should see what they had to do, and clear off. Which they did. Later on, she was at the market in Grosshausen and met Schnäckhlhauser's wife, who told her that they had found the murdered man and that her people were suspected." On the other hand, this very suspicion may have been the reason Anna's and Paul's statements agree. It is perfectly possible that the stress of torture prompted them to claim as an actual deed something of which they had merely been accused at the time.

Such explanations may readily be found for every one of the crimes admitted by the Pappenheimer family. I do not wish to anticipate the course of the investigation, but I have to say here and now that the court was never to find a single convincing proof of these alleged crimes, in spite of an intensive search for evidence—not even in terms of the legal theory current at the time, which, we may recall, required that a confession of guilt should be supported by some circumstance that could be known only to the criminal. For example, the discovery of the body of a person hitherto missing, in a location stated by the author of the confession, or the discovery of a stolen object in a hiding place named by the thief. Such proofs were totally lacking in the case brought against our vagrants. Everything they confessed to could have been a matter of common knowledge: that someone had been murdered, that someone else had been robbed, that a church had been plundered here, a farm set on fire there.

All the sensational tales of crime that had been circulating for the past twenty years seem to have been incorporated into the Pappenheimers' confessions. They would say anything that came into their heads because they were spared the application of torture as long as they kept on talking. The reservoir that supplied their imagination, consisting of the horror stories picked up on their travels, was emptied to the last drop. And even beyond, for the vagrants obviously recounted the same crime more than once, altering the place and time. A certain amount of truth may have been mixed in with what was mere invention, but it is impossible to say how much. It would be a mistake to make deductions about the crime rate in the duchy from the confessions of the Pappenheimers. If the entire vagabond population had been capable of crimes on this scale, the roads would have been lined with corpses and burned-down ruins. Unsafe as the country was, it was not as bad as that. Reports of robbery and murder attract more attention in every age than they deserve in relation to the general level of security in a country as a whole. If our gutter press, with its tales of sex and crime, were to serve future historians as their principal source, they would receive a distorted impression of our age. This is more or less the case with the Pappenheimers' confessions, which assemble rumors and reports from two decades and place them, as it were, under a magnifying glass. This was in keeping with the nature of the case: our vagrants were to be punished as representatives and as a warning to all the antisocial elements in the country. The case was meant to set an example and to serve as an allegory. As many as possible of the unsolved crimes of the past few years were to be put down to the account of the accused, and to be disposed of and atoned for in this one great cleansing conflagration.

Not that the duke or his councillors were aware of this thought. For reasons that will be discussed later, it never occurred to them that the use of torture makes it harder, rather than easier, to find out the truth. None of them was at all inclined to cold, cynical calculation. In a case of this kind involving their policy toward crime, as in all the other business of the state, they were able to dispense with the kind of objective and rational judgments designed to meet the case in point—for example, the need to "sacrifice" a family like the Pappenheimers in the interests of the state. For they did not view reality as it was; for them, reality was their vision of it. Actuality and wishful thinking combined to form reality, as far as they were concerned. In the eyes of their judges, our family of vagrants became precisely what they were destined to be. In an almost mystic fashion, the shadowy criminal world of the highway was personified in this one family: the more crimes they admitted, the more certain was the court that, by convicting them, it would strike at the very root of the evil. No wonder the judges allowed themselves no doubts but looked rather for explanations of inconsistencies in their preconceived image.

Such was the case when, for example, in spite of so many alleged murders, not a single corpse could be found. Confronted with this fact, the accused claimed that "they had not buried their victims, and that was why none had been found; they had thrown them into a pitch furnace and burned them, which they had learned from the pitch burners. For when pitch was being extracted, the fire burned continuously. They had always carried the dead out at night, and hacked them to pieces on a great oak stump by the furnace, and then thrown the quarters into the fire." This they had done in the vicinity of Tettenwang. This last claim robs the entire story, which is in any case highly fanciful, of any credibility whatsoever, since most of the murders confessed to had allegedly been committed near Straubing and Regensburg. The court was nevertheless satisfied with the explanation. It could think of nothing better, given that it had, from the outset, excluded the possibility that the prisoners might be innocent.

JEWS

What did the Pappenheimers do with their alleged booty? The money, they declared to the court, they had "eaten and drunk away"; stolen clothing and other effects they had sold for small sums to the unlicensed landlords who provided their lodgings. The chalices and monstrances purloined from churches they had taken to goldsmiths. The commissioners wanted to know more details of these transactions; for one thing, they would wish to take action against such receivers of stolen property, and, for another, they might track down some item of loot which could be used as evidence. Their persistent inquiries, however, simply burst the bubble of the relevant confessions.

Paulus first claimed that he and his companions had sold a chalice acquired in a church burglary "to the goldsmith in Straubing by the name of Georg Praun, who lived by the marketplace, for twenty-four gulden, and had shared out the money." Although they had broken up their loot before offering it for sale, the receiver would have known perfectly well what the situation was. He asked them "where they got such things." "We just steal them," was their reply. "And then he told them that if they got any more, they should bring it to him." They did so on several occasions. Another of their customers for precious objects stolen from churches was "a goldsmith in Ingolstadt by the name of Georg Niedermair."

The court wrote to the prince's administration in Straubing and was forthwith informed that there was no goldsmith by the name of Praun, and never had been. When this was put to Paulus in the torture chamber, he rapidly declared that he had made an unfortunate mistake. "The goldsmith in Straubing was not called Praun but Georg Niedermair. He lived in a fine, large house on the marketplace, not far from the church and near the well where they had painted the statue last year." This Niedermair was "a stately gentleman with a long, brown beard, and he generally had three journeymen in his workshop . . . And there was a wineshop keeper that lived near the goldsmith," and he had once been mayor of the city. The goldsmith in Ingolstadt was called Leonhard Niedermair, and was a brother of the man in Straubing. They had sold the loot from churches to both of these men, and a goldsmith in Kelheim by the name of Leonhard Huber.

Thereupon the councillor had sent another official letter to Straubing, requesting inquiries to be made concerning the receiver of stolen property with whom the Pappenheimers had dealt. The authorities there reported to Munich "that there was no goldsmith by the name of Georg Niedermair in Straubing." Paulus, now obviously convicted of lying, was challenged once more. His third version ran as follows: He and his like had sold the sacred objects they stole "to some Jews." In some cases they had been sold through the "innkeeper Schindlmair" in Straubing, whom they knew well, and "who knew all about their doings," and had first-class contacts with Jewish sharpers; in other cases, they had sold direct to Jews. "He, Paulus, for example, had taken some, in fact most, of the stolen monstrances and chalices to three Jews in Deging, in the bishopric of Eichstätt, who went by the names of Essel, Leb, and Moos . . . which Jews could be found at almost every weekly market in Dietfurt and Altmannstein. They were wealthy fellows, particularly Leb, who had a fortune amounting to two thousand gulden, which was well known to everyone."

Surprisingly enough, the court did not follow up this line of inquiry. Indeed, not only was it satisfied with this version, but it insisted on it from that point onward. When Michel, for instance, was questioned on the issue of receivers of stolen property, he too began by citing the names of a number of goldsmiths. Only under torture, and in response to direct questions, did he "finally . . . accuse these three Jews." Although it was quickly established that "Essel the Jew" had long since died, it was toward this man that Wangereck steered the vagrants' statements. In the later interrogations only Essel is mentioned in connection with the whereabouts of stolen chalices and monstrances. "Old Essel the Jew in

Deging" was also alleged to have purchased another sort of merchandise: Christian children. Paulus claimed that when he was negotiating over the first sale of a monstrance, "the Jews had spoken to him about bringing them young children; they would pay him well." Twelve years previously he had accordingly abducted "a boy of about five, old enough to go with him, from a traveling woman in Peisting." He had "taken the boy to old Essel the Jew and had been given twenty gulden for him." Two years ago, he had gone to the "tall Jew they called Moos in Deging" with a four-year-old boy, the son of "a poor beggar woman," whom he had abducted from "behind a garden in Dietfurt." He had sold the child to Moos for thirty-eight gulden. The Lamprey and Sugar Bun would also take children to sell to the Jews.

This confession was essentially in keeping with stories told about Jews all over the country, so that the court obviously saw no reason to question its truth. Jews were suspected of nailing Christian children to the cross and reenacting the scene on Golgotha, with the aim of mocking Jesus.[64] A woodcut in Schedel's Chronicle represents the blessed child Simon being slain in this gruesome manner. A church was built over the grave of the victim, who showed his gratitude by signs and miracles. A similar tale was heard in Zürich, where a child, allegedly tortured to death by the Jews, was buried in the minster and worshiped like a saint. Such stories were invented and spread by zealous preachers like the Dominican Johannes Herold, who exhorted his flock in Basel around 1425 not to eat or bathe in the company of Jews, not to offer them shelter, not to do business with them. More than half a millennium before Hitler introduced the Jewish star into Germany, this divine was demanding that Jews should be obliged to wear different clothes from Christians and that at certain times they should not be permitted to appear in the streets and squares of the city. Jews should be barred from public office, and Christians who were employed by Jews, or even went so far as to marry Jews, should be severely punished.

In keeping with the anti-Semitism propagated by the Church, it was imagined that the Jews desecrated everything that was sacrosanct to Christians. This was consistent with the Pappenheimers' confession that the sacred objects allegedly stolen by them had been sold to Jews. The record of the interrogation states that they had often handed over to the Jews the consecrated wafers contained in the stolen monstrances. It was known from relevant sermons and ecclesiastical treatises how the Jews treated this holy of holies: they stamped on the consecrated wafers, crushed them in mortars, or pierced them with needles until blood flowed from them.

Tales of this kind are the invention of blind hatred. Such hatred usually has deep and complex roots, of which one of the strongest is envy. This was the case here: "If the Jews had been poor, and their sovereign lords had not been in debt," wrote a late medieval chronicler,[65] "they would not have been burned." Charging interest was prohibited for Christians throughout the Middle Ages. On the other hand, Jews were not admitted to the guilds, so that they were virtually forced to become financiers. The Jewish usurer was privileged to a degree, being unaffected by the prohibition on taking interest on his money. During the Middle Ages his debtors included the emperor and the electors, the nobility and the Church, townsfolk and farmers. In accordance with a pernicious practice already mentioned, both temporal and spiritual rulers pawned their sources of income in exchange for ready cash: taxes, public appointments, tolls, and customs dues. In this way they could get the money they needed at the right time and without undue trouble. The bothersome business of collecting the debts was left to their Jewish creditor, who, of course, incurred a good deal of abuse when he and his representatives put pressure on the principality to recover his loan with interest and, if possible, rather more. Letters patent issued by the princes to protect credit transactions strengthened the position of the hated money lenders. The minor aristocracy, the prelates, the abbots, and the patrician families observed with jealous disapproval how many Jews grew more and more wealthy while their own incomes declined. Evil thoughts engender evil rumors. One of the older and more innocuous of these related to the Jewish pawnbroker. Emperor Henry IV had granted the Jews the right to take pledges, and expressly stipulated that they need not inquire about the provenance of objects pledged with them. This provision was tantamount to a "fence's charter." From then on, any thief could count on cash "from the Jew" by pawning his loot. Soon a restriction on this privilege was deemed necessary, and sacred objects in particular were exempted. But the idea of the shady Jewish pawnbroker, modeled on particular individuals, survived even when persecution and prohibitions during the Middle Ages had driven the Jews from large areas of the Roman Empire of the German Nation.

In Bavaria, repeated pogroms had occurred since the thirteenth century;[66] in 1349, there had been a general expulsion of the Jews from the principality. If Jews went on living in the country after that, it was only because they were needed. Neither the aristocracy nor the townsfolk could dispense with Jewish credit. And the Bavarian duke, who had been entitled since the thirteenth century to confer privileges on the Jews in place of the emperor, did not care to forfeit the special tax paid by his Jewish subjects as a form of protection money that frequently turned out to be pretty ineffectual. Thus, hatred and self-interest were constantly in conflict. It was not until the middle of the fifteenth century that a clear victor emerged: Albrecht III and Ludwig the Wealthy, the two dukes who had divided Bavaria at that time, both banished the Jews from the country and pursued a policy of active persecution. In 1551, Albrecht V renewed the decree. His son, the devout William, and his grandson Maximilian continued the policy of anti-Semitism. "Whereas our respected predecessors and sovereign princes, with the gracious consent of His Majesty the Roman Emperor, and on the advice of our Council, have removed the Jews, their wives, and children . . . from our Principalities," declared Maximilian I, "so We herewith desire and ordain most solemnly that no Jew or Jewess may enter our Principality to have their residence nor to pursue any trade or profession, nor may they be tolerated by anyone whatsoever, or be given shelter."[67] In order to travel through Bavaria, Jews required a so-called "conduct," a visa which had to be paid for afresh at each customs station. They were not permitted to stop on the way and had to take the shortest possible route. Jews in transit were naturally prohibited from conducting any kind of business in the country. This would have been difficult in any case, because debts contracted by Bavarian subjects in any such dealings could not be collected. The courts were not permitted to assist Jewish creditors in claiming their rights, and were required, in fact, to collect the outstanding sum, by way of a fine, for the benefit of the treasury.

We may be surprised to learn from our vagrants that there were Jews in Straubing and Deging between the years 1580 and 1600, "who could be found at just about any weekly market in Dietfurt and Altmannstein." After a hundred and fifty years of persecution and expulsions, were there still Jews in Bavaria pursuing their business as moneylenders quite openly? Improbable and incongruous. But that is the case with many things in those days. Possibly the expulsion order was not strictly observed; possibly the ducal decrees were designed simply to deprive the Jews of their rights and not actually to drive them out; perhaps the ducal prohibition fell on deaf ears, like so many other edicts issued by the authorities. The town of Deging was in the see of Eichstätt, which owed its allegiance directly to the emperor, and it is possible that a Jewish settlement still existed there, from which dealers and pawnbrokers made illegal excursions to markets in the principality. Controls at frontiers and on public thoroughfares, and hence the enforcement of entry and residence regulations, were barely practicable. All the same, it is strange that three of the Jews named by the Pappenheimers featured regularly in weekly markets and were said to be "well known" to everyone.

THE BLACK DEATH[68]

An important reason for the expulsion of the Jews from Bavaria was fear of the plague. It was rumored that the dread disease was caused by Jewish well poisoners. On the orders of secret chief rabbis in Toledo they would contaminate drinking water with spells, the secretions of spiders, and oriental essences. These horror stories, like the belief in witchcraft, were hatched in the sunny south of France, presumably in the incense-fuddled heads of those same fanatical priests and inquisitors who preached crusades against the Cathars, Albigensians, and devil worshipers. The obfuscation of the senses by this kind of suspicion spread no less rapidly than the plague itself. In May 1348, nearly all the Jewish inhabitants of Provence were butchered. A few weeks later, almost fifty thousand Jews were burned in Burgundy. In September the first fires were kindled in Switzerland; in the autumn the disease and the pogrom atmosphere reached Strasbourg; in the winter of 1348/49 it affected Bavaria and the lower Rhine. Jews were arrested en masse everywhere, many of them subjected to torture. The confessions forced from them confirmed the dread presumption: in secret assemblies everywhere the Jews had decided to exterminate Christendom, little bags of poison had been given out, and the members of the race had been assigned their lethal task. Fear of the terrible disease turned quickly to implacable hatred of those responsible for the calamity. The scapegoat had been found. It must be said to the credit of the Curia that the pope, in two bulls of 4 July and 26 September 1348, protested against the indiscriminate murder of Jews, but his protest did nothing to check the lynch atmosphere in those areas affected by the plague.

160

Since 1348, Bavaria had been afflicted again and again by the lethal disease, with a particularly bad epidemic in 1429. It is thus not entirely coincidental that the final expulsion of the Jews took place in the last third of the fifteenth century. Many chroniclers reckon the autumn and spring of 1633/34 to be "the real plague year," and not a few customs still remind us of this—the Oberammergau Passion Play, for example, which was initiated as a mark of gratitude for deliverance from the plague. But the nameless sickness was also rampant in the Pappenheimers' time, and on their beat. According to the statements of the traveling folk, Tettenwang succumbed to the plague in 1599. They all agreed that "almost the whole village had died of the evil sickness" the previous year.

"The evil sickness" was one of the common euphemisms used to denote the unspeakable. Others were "the infection," "the great dying," "the black death," "the headache that's going around," "the common mortality," "the bubonic fever," or just "the pestilence." In short, the plague. Superstitious fear forced people to use these various terms: the illness could not be given its proper name because that was bound to summon it up. For the same reason it was best not to talk about it at all. This in itself, of course, did not prove to be an effective measure against the generally fatal disease. One of the reasons for its epidemic spread was the lack of hygiene, as a government decree of the time rightly recognized: [69] "In most of our towns there is such indolence and disorder in the collection of all kinds of garbage that it would be no wonder if the whole country were infected and poisoned by the evil odors thereof. So it happens that, particularly in outlying rural areas, there dwell in almost every cottage two, three, or even four householders, with ten, twelve, or even more children, and all in the greatest squalor, crammed on top of each other like cattle. It may easily be supposed that we may expect in consequence naught but certain pollution and all manner of dangerous diseases."

The terrors of the plague were seldom approached in such a rational fashion. It is true that the horror stories of well poisoning by Jews lost their credibility when the plague affected Bavaria, which had expelled its Jews. It was now assumed that pollution of the air was the cause of the disease, but the reasons for this pollution were the subject of the most bizarre theories. Some people, relying on the customary explanation of blight and catastrophe of all kinds, claimed that witchcraft was responsible: individuals seduced by the Devil conjured up the germs of the disease by means of spells. Others made the opposite assumption: it was not Satan who was responsible for all these deaths but the Lord God, who was chastising men for their sins. This second explanation was the official one, adopted by the duke. That is why the prince's decrees relating to the plague recommended confession and penance, along with better hygiene, as effective remedies. As soon as the disease made its appearance, a priest as well as a doctor should be fetched. On occasion Maximilian also ordained, as a preventive measure, "that our pastors should warn their flocks from the pulpit that during this time of grave mortality they should go to confession and communion each week, or at least every fortnight, while they are in good health and still have time to do so."

When it was observed that piety alone was not an effective remedy, a number of other measures were taken: communication with places where the disease was rife was strictly prohibited. In 1613 the duke imposed a ban on Regensburg, and in 1614 and 1625 he had the trade routes to Bohemia and Austria blockaded. Foreigners coming from infected areas were obliged to swear an "infection oath" before they were permitted to enter the country. Within Bavaria, anyone who moved from an infected place to one that was free of the disease ran the risk of being summarily hanged by the duke's magistrates. "Immoderate drinking of brandy" was forbidden, as was the consumption of small beer, hazelnuts, plums, unripe fruit, and certain varieties of mushroom. It was supposed that comestibles of this kind contained, if not the agents causing the disease, at least substances which fostered it, just as doctors nowadays suppose that there are carcinogenic agents in various foodstuffs and beverages. The bed linen and clothes of the dead were to be burned, the sick isolated. Pigeons, pigs, rabbits, and geese, suspected of being carriers of the disease, were no longer tolerated in the cities.

The true nature of the plague became known only in the twentieth century; consequently, the disease has lost its sinister reputation.[70] It involves a disease of rodents, particularly rats, which is transmitted to human beings only under certain conditions. It is initiated by a low-grade bacterium, the coccus, and transmitted by the rat flea. The source of infection was therefore the black house-rat, which was then prevalent throughout Europe and lived in the lofts and attics of houses, consequently in close proximity to the inhabitants. This species has since been driven out by the brown sewer-rat. When rats first succumbed to the disease, they lost all their fear of man and emerged from their holes and crannies to perish everywhere in the open. The fleas harbored by the plague-stricken rats were replete with infected blood. If a flea left the body of a dead rat and bit a human being, the bacillus found its way rapidly into the bloodstream and attacked the lymph glands, which swelled up into large "plague sores." The pathogenic agent secreted, as a metabolic product, a highly toxic substance, which fortunately numbed and intoxicated the victim. His speech became indistinct, his gait uncertain, and he died in a deep coma, often within a matter of hours but generally after three days. Reports that plague victims suffered unspeakable agony are therefore somewhat implausible. The "violent headache" that contemporary observers speak of was probably a hysterical reaction to the first signs of the illness rather than a genuine symptom. The plague was horrifying, not so much because of the suffering it entailed, but because it was so infectious, apparently irresistible, and terminal in nature.

The disease was never transmitted from one human being to another; the flea was invariably involved, and the house-rat was generally the intermediary. Hence, the course of epidemics was markedly dependent on the living conditions of the rats and the prevalence of the fleas. The claim by contemporary chroniclers that famine and natural catastrophes would set off epidemics was based on accurate observation. The belief that the air was contaminated also has a germ of truth in it insofar as the infected fleas made their way through the air. In recommending open fires and fumigation by burning juniper branches, the authorities were probably inhibiting the agents of the disease. This was less true of other common precautions: people put slices of lemon in their mouths, chewed candied roots, submitted to blood-letting, or rubbed their bodies with aromatic oil. Those who could afford it smoked tobacco. It is possible that this novel indulgence owed its rapid spread throughout Europe to fear of the plague.

In a village like Tettenwang the black death presented very different features from those it displayed in the cites and market towns of Bavaria. In the latter there were plague doctors—in Munich seventeen physicians were appointed in this capacity—as well as nurses and gravediggers. The plague carts passed through the streets by night, their wheels muffled with rags, their platforms loaded with corpses. The sick were to some extent isolated in "quarantine houses" outside the residential area and virtually kept prisoner, although they were provided with food, which was thrust in through the window or placed on a table in front of the entrance, where the inmates could fetch it for themselves. The situation was different in the villages, where a bundle of straw mounted on a pole signaled an outbreak of plague. Here there would be no sign of life on the streets: many of the inhabitants had fled to the woods to avoid the pestilential miasma, others had bolted their doors and windows, literally barricading their homes against the plague. The dying and the dead lay in the church, over-taken by the grisly specter they had been seeking succor from. Corpses rotted in cottages and farmhouses, often mourned by helpless orphans who were likely to starve to death. Their neigh-bor may well have heard them crying, but his fear of infection was stronger than his compassion. Fear of death destroyed even the closest of family ties: children abandoned their parents, mothers their sons and daughters, husbands their wives. Everyone had to look after himself. Priests refused to administer the last rites to those infected with the disease, doctors declined to visit them, gravediggers would not bury their corpses. There are tales of vic-tims who were fully aware of this impending isolation and who awaited death in graves they had dug themselves, or who sewed themselves into a shroud while they still could.

The plague of 1599, which according to our vagrants' state-ments afflicted Tettenwang, had been predicted by Johannes Kep-ler. He derived this knowledge not only from the stars but also from a particular phenomenon: "When, not long ago in Hungary, marks like blood made their appearance here and there on the doors and walls of houses and on benches," he wrote to a friend, "I was, as far as I know, the first man in town to observe on his left foot a small cross, the color of which merged from blood-red to a yellowish shade . . . I am inclined to believe that the nail was driven into Christ's foot at this very spot. In the case of some people, so I hear, a drop of blood appeared on the palm of the hand; and, indeed, the hand of Christ was also pierced. But no one here has anything like what I have." Fear and superstition are sister and brother.

The story of the plague virgin was widely prevalent. She was a specter who flew through the air in the form of a bluish flame, alighting at a place of her choice, where, now in human form, she went from house to house, anointing doors and windows with the fiendish poison. Sometimes she was caught in the act, and her blood-red scarf was seen fluttering in the wind. Anyone who caught hold of it would die, but he would preserve the town from the plague. It was not only simple people who believed this. A man like Martin Luther was also of the opinion that the plague was spread by evil spirits who "poisoned the air or in some other manner afflicted their poor victims with their evil breath and thus injected the lethal poison into their flesh." If a biblical authority thought on these lines, we can hardly blame the uneducated for reverting in their panic to heathen ideas. People saw black dogs roaming about at night, with burning eyes and mangy coats. Three virgins, one of them dressed in white but wearing a black veil, the others in mourning garb but with white bridal veils, also spread the disease at the witching hour. Accompanied by a fearsome dog, they passed through the streets, touching with their plague arrow those houses where the black death was to enter. Many who believed all this went on pilgrimages to Lake Kochel in Bavaria, where they joined in nocturnal candlelit processions, descending into subterranean passages on the "peninsula of the Three Virgins" and praying that they might be spared. Einbett, Wollbet, and Vilbett—as the terrible virgins were called—were represented as statues in the cathedral of Worms and given the title of saint, despite their heathen origins. In this way it was hoped to placate them.

Hardly more Christian was the fervent adoration of authentic saints, St. Ainpet and St. Sebastian, who were beseeched for protection against the three unholy saints. Pictures and statues of these patron saints bore the symbol of an arrow, which, in the form of the plague arrow, was part of the heathen belief in the three virgins. The adoration of St. Sebastian, who had been slain by arrows, as a protector against plague was thus based on a less than pious misunderstanding. In Ebersberg the people were given wine to drink from a skull that was allegedly Sebastian's. The sustaining draught was supposed to give protection from the black death. Small "Sebastian arrows" were snapped up by eager purchasers: if touched by Sebastian's skull, they offered the bearer protection from infection. Other auxiliary saints giving protection against the plague were St. Roch and St. Christopher. The latter saved from death by the plague those who merely looked at his picture. This is why he was depicted in Bavarian villages at that time on churches, mills, and farmhouses, and large enough to be seen from a great distance.

Signs and wonders were rife in that age.[71] Many people encountered death in person. He used to ride a black horse across the countryside and drift down the Danube in a somber barge. At times he would make his appearance in a village, suddenly place his hand on a young bride's shoulder, stroke her hair as she stood aghast, and promise to spare her. Peasants saw him as a reaper standing in a field of grain, harvesting the oats before their time. The scythe hissed as it flashed through the air, the stalks rustled as they fell. But the apparition vanished without a trace if it was approached. Such visions boded no good.

Fiery signs in the night sky heralded the impending end of the world. Comets with tails that scattered ruin abroad appeared at ever shorter intervals, flaunting their menace over the heads of despairing mankind. Each of these celestial scourges visited hunger, hatred, locusts, fires, suffering, and pestilence on the land to which its tail pointed. In 1618, when one of these terrible messengers of misfortune plunged the whole of Western Europe into terror, Pope Urban VII issued a call for public prayer to avert the expected calamity. Reports of pillars of fire, burning orbs, and huge flaming beams that were observed in the firmament from time to time also tended to provoke panic. There were witnesses who claimed that in certain districts the skies had rained down serpents, blood, and repulsive vermin. Poisonous vapors and foul miasmas rose from crevices in the earth. In the air, especially in the vicinity of cemeteries, dismal wailing was sometimes heard. Solitary wayfarers saw ghosts dancing over the meadows at dusk. The inhabitants of an entire village swore that they had witnessed the following scene in broad daylight: thirty coffins in a neat line, covered with black palls; on each stood a dark figure holding a gleaming white cross in its hand. Elsewhere, blood oozed from freshly baked bread. Black horsemen would thunder across the sky, or unseen hearses would creak and rumble through the alleyways.

Such fiery or repellant signs from the heavens were generally regarded as expressions of displeasure on the part of the Almighty, because the Revelation of St. John had ascribed these warning signals to a wrathful God. Other visions, especially those of a minor kind, were specters conjured up or pranks played by wicked demons. It was believed that such demons were everywhere present, unseen but hovering menacingly around men. The more innocuous of them played irritating tricks on the living, others tormented respectable Christians and led them astray. Often the only protection was a prayer that summoned a guardian angel. The battle between light and darkness raged interminably. It was supposed that good or evil spirits governed every unforeseen event, every misfortune, but also every unexpected stroke of good luck. This attitude is not so very different from our own. The moment a man feels he is no longer master of his fate, his fear of such vulnerability cries out for irrational explanations. Man cannot stand the thought of unpredictable chaos. He gazes into a "black hole" in his understanding, into the churning void, and recoils from it. He prefers to place his trust in benign gods or attach his fears to sinister forces rather than face the unplumbed darkness. Alternatively, he builds bridges of "scientific" truths that seem to explain everything, and brings up his children to believe in these truths so that they may be free of fear. Thanks to education of this kind, we "moderns" are better off in a number of respects. Nevertheless, our reaction scarcely differs from that of our forebears when we observe from time to time that the scaffolding of analytical thought, on which we cheerfully stride across the abyss, is a pretty rickety structure, shaky as a framework of steel girders erected at a dizzy height. It is then that we look round for a sure grip, some certainty, however terrifying it may be.

The sudden onset of serious illness often prompts this vision of vertiginous depths, and awakens in men that elemental fear which was the typical emotion of the age in which our vagrants lived. All at once, medical explanations are no more than empty words, for they cannot answer those frightening questions, "Why me, of all people?" "Why now, of all times?" We feel we have been "afflicted," "struck down," or "assailed," by the disease; we "fight" it and try to "conquer" it. In spite of all our superior knowledge concerning the nature of our misfortune as a functional disorder of the body, the illness still seems to us to be something alien, hostile—something demonic. This applies also to other people: their face has the "mark of death," we can "see the sickness in their eyes." We speak as we think.

In those days, such personification of misfortune had not yet been obliterated by enlightened methods of education. Demons stood around the sickbed, demons guided the woodsman's axe into his leg, demons slew the newborn child, demons grinned from every corner, lurked behind every tree. At night, the evil spirits rumbled about the house, bumped on the roof, creaked in the beams; during the day, they howled in the wind, drove the storm and the hail before them, struck down cattle in the meadow, and caused the river to burst its banks. Wicked men used the power of the invisible for all sorts of magic. Some had the evil eye that could kill children and young beasts and that could only be diverted by tucking in a thumb. Another vicious spell involved drawing an old nail from a rotting coffin and driving it secretly into a bench: whoever first sat on the bench contracted the disease from which the corpse in the coffin had died. Injury could also be done to an enemy by fashioning a wax effigy of him, giving it his name, and transfixing it with a hot needle. This procedure inevitably brought about the death of the effigy's living counterpart. Often a mere oath, or a curse spoken in the course of a quarrel, was sufficient to plunge its object into dire distress, for words thus spoken in anger attracted many evil spirits.

How could a man defend himself against this multitude of menaces from every side? Above all, by prayer and self-denial, invocation of the saints, the sign of the cross, and holy water. These things were more highly regarded than medicines. In 1532 Luther wrote to the margrave of Ansbach: "That doctors alleviate such things [illnesses] by means of physic comes to pass only because they know not what power and potency is given unto the devils. There can be no manner of doubt that pestilence and fever and other grave diseases are naught but the work of devils."

According to the findings of modern psychology, fear is manifested when an individual feels unequal to his situation.[72] Every evolution of humanity, every advance in maturity, is accompanied by fear. Such fear is particularly strong in transitional periods in our development; in Fritz Riemann's words, "wherever old and familiar paths have to be abandoned, where new tasks have to be mastered, or where changes are overdue." That obviously applies not only to the individual. Superstition and the fear of demons were so widespread between the fourteenth and the seventeenth centuries, so much part of the spirit of the times, that it might be said that the entire population of Europe was in a state of collective fear. The terrors of the plague may have triggered that fear, but they were certainly not the only cause. What scared people was the glimpse of the abyss. The stable structure of the medieval world was beginning to give way; ancient bonds of a social, legal, and moral kind were breaking down; the supreme authorities—emperor and pope—were losing their aura of divinity. Everywhere, walls were collapsing that had hitherto been regarded as indestructible and everlasting. From the shelter of blind faith and an unquestioned cosmic order, man emerged blinking into the dawn of the age of reason—and shuddered.

Many symptoms of a collective anxiety may be observed. We have already offered evidence of the most important symptom: the chronic anxiety of everyone in that age, the constant expectation of impending disaster. To use one of Sigmund Freud's images, it is as if a considerable "quantum of fear were freely dissipated in the atmosphere" and liable to combine with any suitable imaginative content: a hostile glance became a mortal threat, a bright star turned into a harbinger of doom, a nocturnal noise became a ghostly apparition. Another sign of this pervasive fear was the hallucinations we have already mentioned, such as the parade of thirty coffins bearing black figures holding white crosses. Such visions were experienced as real in those days, although many of the stories were doubtless invention or florid elaborations of something less fanciful. But we may well believe such a man as Johannes Kepler and his tale of the cross of blood. For other phenomena of this kind there are too many credible witnesses for us to suppose that they were merely legend or rumor. The general state of mind was evidently such as to prompt phenomena like those described, given certain situations.

We mention all this because the records of the vagrants' trial are full of reports of ghosts and apparitions. These were not just bizarre fancies or products of delirium induced by torture. Like their confessions of murder and arson, they were derived from the subjective experiences of the Pappenheimers and their friends. Their world was populated not just by pillaging soldiery, cowardly footpads, and a dubious riffraff of beggars but also by good and evil spirits of all kinds. They were more afraid of these disembodied foes than of those they could see; demons were everywhere, and it was hardly possible to escape their malicious attentions. Demons were a terrifying reality to our vagrants and their contemporaries. In order to appreciate this, we have to abandon our justified doubts concerning the existence of evil spirits. Whether demonic spirits, the offspring of the fear that then prevailed, really existed in any scientifically demonstrable sense or whether they only existed in the imagination of their victims is totally irrelevant. What matters is that men felt the threat and saw themselves surrounded by specters. Lock a group of people into a maze and persuade them that there are man-eating tigers in the system. We can describe and explain the behavior of these fearful individuals without having to answer the question whether the tigers really were in the system or only in our experimental subjects' imaginations. The imagined danger threatens them no less than a real danger. Their fear is always real.

It was by no means only simple people like the Pappenheimers who subscribed to the belief in demons. Hardly anyone doubted their existence. Duke Maximilian's "Ordinance prohibiting superstition and sorcery" of 1611 was not directed, as one might suppose from its title, against such illusions; on the contrary, it assumed they were indisputable facts, and forbade the conjuring up of evil spirits, on pain of punishment.

WANTONNESS

Fear manifests itself, according to the temperament of the person affected, in a schizoid, depressive, obsessive, or hysterical fashion. All these reactions may be found in a pathologically exaggerated form in the era we are discussing. We have already spoken of the compulsive conscientious scruples and the zealous piety that affected William V and Maximilian I. In disconcerting contrast to these features, yet stemming from the same root, is that tendency to frenzied dissipation, which can only be termed hysterical, that was peculiar to so many of the Pappenheimers' contemporaries. It relates mainly to the "bestial gluttony and boozing" that was customary in the case of all those who could afford it, rather than to the alleged immorality of the time, the prevalence of which may well be doubted.

There are, it is true, any number of anecdotes in those coyly pornographic histories of culture and morals which used to appear in luxury editions until a few decades ago for the delectation of the "enlightened" and cultivated middle class. From them we learn all sorts of astonishing things about the seventeenth and eighteenth centuries. The convents seem to have been for the most part brothels, princely residences the scene of obscene frolics, bawdy houses the customary resort of the citizens. Such tales, invariably recounted with an undertone of sanctimonious indignation, are mainly based on Zimmer's Chronicle and the "Memorabilia" of Hans von Schweinichen. Even if we assume these stories to be true, we still cannot draw general conclusions about the moral circumstances of the time from this erotic literature. Certainly, there must have been pregnant nuns on occasion, and sexually dissipated courtiers; and such sensational stories would

170

then go the rounds, discreetly murmured from person to person. But this would be precisely because they were the exception. Similarly, the lifestyle of the Pappenheimers and their like was neither "chaste" nor "lewd." There was a relatively natural attitude toward sex. As the family used to spend their nights in the confined space of some barn or other, it was nothing unusual for the children to watch their parents engaging in sexual intercourse. But that is just about the sum total of what we learn on this topic from the trial records. Our vagrants tell of a "verger in Gänacker" who "rollicked with his own daughter," in terms suggesting that it was an extraordinary event and much talked of. We also hear of a "wench in Plädling who had thrown a child into a well; they didn't execute her but just sent her out of the country once she had done her time in jail at Natternberg."

This seems to be at odds with decrees on public morality promulgated at the time.[73] Maximilian announced, for instance: "Having for some considerable space of time observed with most particular disapprobation the degree to which the execrable vice of wantonness, together with illegitimate pregnancies, has grown rife and come to abound, particularly in the rural parts of Our realm among unwedded farmservants and such common folk, and, above all the most reprehensible vice of adultery among young and old of both sexes, it becomes Us, from Our sovereign and paternal concern, to ordain such measures as may henceforth curb such rampant foulness." The duke disapproved of "the common rabble, both men and women, that forever seek out some hiding place or other where they may go secretly in their leisure to practice their culpable lewdness." He required that "the farmhands and the maids should have their sleeping places in separate, locked chambers," forbade "secret assignations and entrance by night into a woman's bedchamber" as well as "prowling by night," and increased the penalties for "the vice of lewdness and unlawful pregnancies that moves the Almighty to great and justified wrath." Elsewhere it is stated that "the authorities are well aware that great occasion for wantonness is given to young peasant folk at those dances held for all and sundry on holidays in the country." A prohibition was imposed on "those jocose assemblies commonly held in spinning rooms and known as distaff romps, to which young country folk and laborers come from afar to indulge in lewdness and wantonness, leading to seduction of youth, violation of virgins, furtive marriages, uproar, and all manner of other evils." Joint excursions into the woods by boys and girls were also banned on pain of punishment, while those "dances which feature offensive gestures" were forbidden, "specifically, hugging and pressing, senseless jostling together, lifting up, clutching, and swinging round of partners."

The moral indignation may have been sincere, but it also had a practical purpose. Here, too, government policy and the Catholic conscience most happily coincided. The duke was pursuing two aims with his campaign against "wantonness."[74] He wished to counteract a decline in the agricultural labor force and also to prevent the development of a rural proletariat below the peasant subsistence level. Both these aims had more to do with Bavarian economic policy than with religiously based moral standards.

The population was noticeably increasing during the sixteenth century, which caused concern. There was still little trust in industry and commerce as sources of national income; in the typical peasant manner, land alone was regarded as the foundation and the essential factor in economic security. The monarch saw himself in the position of the owner of a hereditary estate who is obliged to provide for more sons than his land has hitherto supported. Apart from the attempt to curb future population growth, he attempted to avoid a general rise in prices by artificially holding down food prices, which were otherwise being stimulated by increasing demand; this was done by officially limiting the maximum wage of the agricultural labor force. One might think this measure bound to succeed: in this way, the income of farm workers would have fallen in real terms, and the loaf would have been cut into more, if thinner, slices. But that was an economic fallacy. It did not work, because Bavaria was not, in fact, an isolated farm cut off from the rest of the world. Population pressure led to the growth of towns, the beginnings of industrial production, the spread of small craft enterprises in the countryside, emigration— but not to any increased supply of agricultural labor. So the low wages prescribed by the wage regulations could not be maintained: the farmers' labor force decamped unless it was surreptitiously paid more than the permitted scale. Even then, extra day laborers had to be recruited for seasonal work—for sowing and harvesting, for instance. They were well paid by farmers, who were profiting from rising farm prices. From the economic point of view, farmers favored this kind of employment according to need, rather than a permanent association with their farmhands that would entail all kinds of obligations. Farmers would ask themselves: Why should I feed more people through the winter than I need for the work that has to be done then? The farmservants and the maids, for their part, the so-called "retainers," saw their chance to live more freely as day laborers and casual workers, and no doubt quite rightly hoped to gain from the increasing prosperity of the farmers by going in for all kinds of minor trades and crafts. Hence, more and more casual laborers and fewer and fewer retainers were employed in agriculture.

That did not suit the duke at all. When farm workers left the shelter of individual farms, their high degree of social security was terminated. A farmhand who accidentally injured his leg with an axe, a servant too old to work, had to be supported by their master. The day laborer or the casual female worker who suffered a similar fate were a burden on public services, found their way into hostels and almshouses, ended up as beggars and criminals. To prevent this displacement of risk as between employer and community, the authorities limited the permitted number of cottagers in each village, and prohibited, or created obstacles to, the marriage of farmhands and servants. There was not to be an indigent class of married persons; a rural proletariat was not to be allowed to come into existence. Official regulations do not attempt to conceal the economic background to these measures. Maximilian's "Public Order Regulations for the Realm" offer as justification for the ban on the marriage of rural workers the fact that "at this time such retainers marry young . . . so that they may hereafter go to live in illegal lodging houses." That was the reason, in fact, why "retainers had grown so dear, and scarcely to be had for any fair wage." Apart from this, "poor day laborers," long settled in the district, "and perhaps burdened with many children, were deprived of their employment and hence of their sustenance by such recklessly wedded young folk."

The duke exhorted his prefects not to grant marriage permits to "impecunious folk," and instructed the clergy not to solemnize such "wanton" marriages without express written permission. If, however, "such impecunious persons had nevertheless entered into matrimony, either publicly or in secret, without the aforementioned permission, then they should not be taken in or lodged in any dwelling." These couples were to be expelled from the country. In the report of a chancellor submitted in 1606, the proliferation of beggars and other rabble was attributed exclusively to the fact that "people were allowed to marry too young, and irrespective of whether they had any means of support or not."

Following the ban on the marriage of retainers, of course,

the number of irregular associations and illegitimate births rose steeply. The duke's decrees against "wantonness," seen against this background, are to some extent "supportive measures." A similar explanation may be given for the fact that extramarital relations between servants were punished more severely than those between middle-class townsfolk or prosperous farmers.

This ducal policy did scarcely anything to impede the course of affairs. In some ways the ban on marriage even accelerated the flight of labor from the farms, for the young are the very class of people who, faced with a choice, decide in favor of freedom rather than security. Soon the farmers could not recruit enough labor: wages were too low, conditions too hard. And so the regulations were quietly evaded: pay was secretly raised, quasi-marital relationships were tolerated. The farmers neither would nor could vouch for the "morality" of their retainers. Farmhands and maids generally slept in open cubicles in the loft, often in a communal dormitory. It was seldom the case that all the children who played in the farmyard and helped in the work of the farm from an early age belonged to the farmer himself. A great many practices stigmatized by the authorities as "vicious" and "wanton" were merely illegitimate. Had all the duke's decrees been observed "with proper seriousness and assiduity," there would have been still more families like the Pappenheimers: flotsam of the highways that dared not stay in any one place for any length of time.

THE PETITION

During those early days of May 1600, a poor old tailor from Prunn on the Altmühl was wending his way to Munich. It was that same Georg Schmälzl who had turned up with his friends, Bastl Baumann and Georg Reiter, at the Abensberg town hall to seek the release of the prisoners Schölz, Stumpf, and Augustin Baumann. We may recall that their request had been refused. The local authorities had no power in this matter, the petitioners were told; the accused in question were being held on the orders of the duke and were entirely subject to the jurisdiction of the council of state in Munich. All the same, the three friends were allowed access to Augustin Baumann in prison. He threw himself on his visitors, imploring them not to abandon him, not to be discouraged by their initial rebuff, and not to be put off by the rigors of the journey to Munich. His lamentations and his pleading softened the heart of our little tailor, who, instead of seeking excuses like his two friends, promised his continued assistance. After the dungeon door had closed between them and the desperate prisoner and they had made their way up the steps out of the dank, musty atmosphere of the prison into the bright spring daylight, they no doubt adjourned to an inn to discuss the situation. The tailor, invited by Bastl and Georg to partake of food and drink, reaffirmed his resolve to undertake the arduous journey on foot. He would make representations to the authorities on behalf of Baumann, Schölz, and Stumpf; it was simply a matter of deciding how it should be done. They agreed to draw up a petition in the name of all three. Perhaps they summoned someone to their table who knew how to write, or called on a teacher or a clerk, in order to put their plan into practice. At any rate, a "Petition" was forthwith drafted, in which they asserted their friends' innocence and requested their release. Georg Schmälzl pushed this document into his doublet, took something in the way of rations for the road, and set off for the duke's capital.

Two days later he was approaching the city. Like the Pappenheimers barely a month before, he came from the north by the road from Nuremberg, but on foot and encumbered neither by fetters nor by premonitions of evil. And so he was probably untroubled by dismal reflections as he gazed in astonishment at the ochre brown city in its luminously verdant plain. At the Schwabing Gate he was stopped by the sentries and asked where he came from and what the purpose of his visit was. The petitioner was allowed to pass; he may have been directed to a public hostelry or even told where he could submit his petition.

On the following day, Georg Schmälzl made his way to the Old Palace in good spirits and fully confident that his mission would be successful. His path took him past the house of Dr. Wangereck, whose importance for his own fate the tailor did not then suspect, along the lofty crenellated wall of the west bailey, through the palace moat, then to the right, across the little square by the Gothic court chapel of St. Lawrence, and finally to the main palace gate. Here, the petitioner explained the purpose of his visit to the gatekeepers. After a suspicious glance at the document he presented, they admitted him, and he was sent across the great inner courtyard of the castle to the rooms occupied by the council's clerical staff. Here we may see him standing early in the morning in front of a clerk, hat in one hand, petition in the other, nervously stammering the sentences he had been pondering and composing for so long. Something like this, perhaps: He had come all the way from Prunn, in the district of Abensberg, to submit a most humble petition; namely, three of his friends, cottagers from Tettenwang, Ulrich Schölz, Hans Stumpf, and Augustin Baumann, had fallen under suspicion and been arrested, although they were entirely innocent. For what reason the three had been apprehended he did not know, although he supposed the vagrant family, the Pappenheimers, may have told lies about them. However that might be, the authorities were mistaken if they thought his good-natured friends were evildoers. He, the tailor from Prunn, could vouch for their honesty, and he wished to ask for a review of their case and their release from custody.

While he spoke more or less to this effect, Georg Schmälzl no doubt handed the official his document and, once he had finished his explanation, watched the man's expression as he studied the petition.

To the clerk, the petitioner seemed highly suspicious. The Pappenheimer case was no trifling affair but the major criminal prosecution of the year. In the council offices they had naturally heard the results of the initial interrogations. The vast range of crimes admitted by the Pappenheimers was known, and it was well known that a search for further accomplices was underway. Anyone who had had any contact with the Pappenheimers and their associates must be regarded with the greatest mistrust at this stage of the investigation. We cannot, of course, know what was passing through the mind of that official who was holding the tailor's petition in his hand at that moment. Probably he told the petitioner to wait, while he went to consult a colleague or his superior. At any rate, armed members of the palace guard entered the office almost immediately, seized the petitioner, and bound his hands. The astounded victim no doubt protested, at a loss to understand what was going on: he was innocent and merely a humble petitioner. As far as the officials were concerned, that was reason enough for his arrest. An old man who undertook a three-day journey to Munich to plead the cause of a set of vicious tramps was bound to be a close friend and no doubt hand-in-glove with them. They had seen through his little game, they told him as they seized him; they could well imagine why he had come: to spy and find out whether the authorities were on the track of the truth. Now they would have a few questions to ask the spy. They would soon loosen his tongue in the Falcon Tower.

Denials, protestations of innocence, entreaties were of no avail. The petitioner was thrust out of the office by rough hands, dragged across the courtyard. The gate by which he had entered moments before as a free man, he now passed through as a prisoner.

And so Georg Schmälzl landed up in the Falcon Tower—sooner, in fact, that Augustin Baumann and Hans Stumpf, whom he had wished to save from similar treatment. Seldom was the loyalty of a friend more ill-rewarded. The court records leave us in no doubt whatsoever that the tailor from Prunn would have escaped suspicion and persecution had he not, of his own accord, set out on his arduous journey to Munich to submit his petition. The poor tailor had in any case trodden only the humbler paths of life, but now he had fallen into a pit from which there was no escape.

CHAPTER · 5

Interrogatoria.

·1·

·2·

·3·

·4·

·5·

·6·

·7·

·8·

·9·

·10·

·11·

·12·

·13·

The list of questions drawn up for the preliminary interrogation of ten-year-old Hänsel. The commissioners invoked divine assistance by inscribing the monogram J.H.S., the Greek abbreviation for Jesus, at the head of the list.

· The Abyss

INFANTS' HANDS

From the very beginning, the commissioners appointed by the Munich council of state suspected that there was something uncanny about the Pappenheimers' crimes. We may remember that first interrogation in the Falcon Tower, when Wangereck had caused the rod to be used in order to elicit an answer from little Hänsel. The question was whether he had ever seen children's hands in his brothers' possession. At that time the commissioners had stubbornly insisted on obtaining the information they expected. In the end the "confession" had been forthcoming. Yes, the boy said, his brothers had cut the hands off beggar children and had also murdered pregnant women so as to get at the hands of their unborn children. It is easy to account for this answer; it had been forced out by the rod. But what was the point of the question?

The reason for it was vaguely sinister, cryptic, superstitious. At that time it was universally supposed that thieves and burglars saved themselves from detection by means of magic, in particular by lighting a thieve's candle. This was no ordinary candle but part of a corpse, generally the finger or the hand of a dead child, preferably a child that had not been baptized. This practice strikes us as a kind of cannibalism, or at least as archaic, and yet it is barely more than a hundred years since it died out. Its origins, on the other hand, go back an immense distance. Even in pagan times it was thought that the souls of unborn children, those who had never been suckled on their mothers' milk, floated through the spheres as part of an erratic fiery element—as will-o'-the-wisps, who were liable to alarm nocturnal wayfarers. That is the source of the idea that children's hands would serve as illumination for thieves.

They could do more than that, indeed. Many people believed that the magic power of the soul was retained in all those bodies that had suffered a premature and unnatural death—in the corpses of the unborn or of those who had been executed or murdered. For while death, in the case of the aged and the sick, came about precisely because the soul departed from a spent and exhausted body, that soul was somehow robbed of its proper function by any untimely and violent destruction. After all, it had not lived out its life in its proper integument, and was still—if such an expression may be applied to the ethereal and unseen essence of our being— hale and hearty, so that it clung obstinately to the decaying remains and sometimes survived as a haunting presence after their total dissolution. Anyone who could subjugate such a soul acquired magic powers.

Thieves believed that the hands of unborn children were a particularly effective means to this end, first because children's souls were obviously young, fresh, and robust; second because they were innocent and free from sin; and finally because they were unbaptized and hence of a magic nature. It was believed that the seat of immortality was in the fingers, and that is why the hands were so sought after. Those who had been hanged and were left dangling on the gallows before the city gates were also liable to have their fingers, and particularly their thunbs, cut off, to be used for all kind of magic purposes.

These grisly "thieves' candles" were useful to anyone who possessed them. The souls were obviously not resentful, for they helped the very person who had deprived them of their bodies and was now pursuing his nefarious business with parts of those bodies. Paulus Pappenheimer explained their use as follows: "You put a burning candle on the fingers, and if the people in a house are asleep, they can't wake up until you put out the candle. But if the candle won't burn, it's a sign that everybody's not asleep. And it must be the right hand of an unbaptized child." The old vagabond was not revealing any secrets to the court; he was merely repeating a fairly recent superstition.[75] It was said that the thieves' candles would indicate, on the one hand, whether all the people living in a house were asleep and, on the other, plunge them into an even deeper, and unnatural, slumber. There were variations of this belief, and other particulars that Paulus did not know or failed to mention. The thieves' candles were said to make the

bearer invisible and to cause locks to fly open. Paulus's view that ⟵
candles had to be placed on the fingers was also based on a misunderstanding of the common legend, which claimed that the fingers would be ignited simply on the wish of their owner and could
not be extinguished against his will, except with milk. As the sustenance of infants, milk was able to deprive the unborn child of a
part of its prenatal innocence.

Little Hänsel apparently had no idea that infant hands were an
aid to thieves. When pressed by the commissioners, he mentioned
other uses. "First of all, they sometimes used to cut a little bit off
a finger and put it in bread to help people that had all sorts of ill-
nesses; sometimes they used to boil a hand and give people a broth
to cure the jaundice." His parents and brothers had eaten the
hands, and that was what had really turned them into murderers.
"If you wrap a finger in a cloth and hang it round your neck, they
say it helps against all kinds of illness. Sometimes his brothers
had shown the hands to people and said that anyone who looked
at them, no matter how sick he was, he'd get better." On the other
hand, "If a finger or something was cut off a hand, hacked up and
put down on the ground, all the people that walked over it would
fall ill."

But Hänsel claimed, above all, that the children's hands were
the cause of the crimes his brothers were accused of. For Geindl,
the man who had led them astray and denounced them to the authorities, had secretly given them a powder "in a fresh-baked
roll," that "probably came from a child's hand that was dried and
crushed." That was why his brothers had become murderers, bewitched against their will by that fatal piece of bread. They themselves had told him, their little brother, what had happened to
them, and how, under the power of the spell, they could not help
killing people. The powder made from children's hands, which
had been so treacherously administered and which they had swallowed unsuspectingly, was to blame for everything.

How the commissioners reacted to this fairytale is not entirely
clear from the record. They presumably believed it, judging by
what was to follow. It was beyond doubt, and confirmed by all
the accused, that children's hands were used for all kinds of evil
spells. "When they had started a fire," Gumpprecht explained, the
flames could not be put out if the vagrants "had thrown a little bit
of a hand into the fire." And "if the hands were dried, then crushed
to a powder, and scattered in a man's path or in a meadow where
cattle were grazing, then men and animals would be crippled, suf-

fer great pains, or even die." Paulus had a similar tale to tell: "They had made the hands into a powder, and scattered it in the path of those who had done them an injury, so that they should fall sick if they walked over it."

The superstition concerning infants' hands, in the case of the Pappenheimers, involved more than just theft. Paulus revealed where he had gotten these ideas: "Nine years ago he had witnessed the burning of witches in Ellingen and Wiesensteig and had heard in their shrift that they had worked evil with a powder made of children's hands." He had "noted this at the time . . . and done the same." Remarkable. It can hardly have been a very popular belief in magic if a much-traveled and sociable man such as old Pappenheimer only heard of it through the public reading of a court judgment.

Certainly the roots of the superstition went deep, reaching back into an age of cannibalism before the Christian era. Although it seemed to have withered away, or to have been repressed or forgotten, from about 1450 onward this apparently dead tree began to sprout new foliage and bear new fruit. A song from the fifteenth century provides the earliest evidence of the superstitious belief. It tells of a murderer who took a child from the womb of a pregnant woman in order to cut off its hands. In 1568 we hear of criminals in Swabia who carried with them "the arms of an embryo." A ballad, probably written at the time of our trial, tells of the murder of a "miller's pregnant wife who was bartered." There is evidence of even earlier cases.

This dating suggests a close connection between the superstition involving children's hands and those involving witches. It was primarily witches, as we shall hear later, who stole unbaptized children, performed abortions, and dug up the unbaptized at dead of night. Soon they were also reckoned to be the people who supplied thieves with these hands. But they too had a use for them; for the preparation of the Devil's ointment, as we read in act 4 of Shakespeare's *Macbeth*, required, among other things, "finger of birth-strangled babe ditch-deliver'd by a drab."

As far as the commissioners investigating the Pappenheimer case were concerned, the magic involving infants' hands to which the accused confessed appeared to be evidence of witchcraft. Consequently, the proceedings turned into a witch trial following the very first interrogation. There was now more at issue than simply robbery, arson, and murder.

They had "killed the women," according to Gumpprecht, "not for money but because of the children." For instance: "in a little thicket" near Straubing one day, "a big-bellied woman" had approached him, Geindl, and Jack the Cooper on a path through the fields. She was "a day laborer from Schneiding and was on her way to the village of Pining." They stopped her and surrounded her. Jack the Cooper was carrying his pickaxe over his shoulder and he took it in both hands and struck the woman on the breast as she screamed in vain for help. She collapsed, and they went on hitting her until there was no sign of life. One of them drew his knife, another tore off the dead woman's clothes; they slit open her belly and pulled from amid the blood and guts "a child, a girl it was, and dead." While the child was still half in the womb they chopped off its hands; Jack the Cooper kept the left hand and gave the other to Gumpprecht. Then he ransacked the bloodstained clothing and found ten kreuzer, which he pocketed. Together they dragged "the dead woman" off the path and left her lying on the verge, "just where they killed her . . . covered over with some brushwood." This was Gumpprecht's account, repeated on four occasions—and specifying a different place and time on each occasion. Could it really have been something he had experienced himself?

His father's statement suggests that it was not: Paulus claimed that the hands of unbaptized female infants were of no value, only male hands being suitable for the purposes of magic. He himself had murdered pregnant women on a number of occasions, only to find that the killing had been pointless since the unborn children had been female and hence useless. This qualification was a part of the superstition that was obviously unknown to Gumpprecht.

According to their statements, the Pappenheimers ground most of these infants' hands into powder. The magic portions of the bodies were allegedly put "into a pot" and dried in an oven before being "ground to a powder." The fact that this treatment would, at best, have produced a small pile of ashes does not seem to have raised any doubts in the commissioners' minds concerning the "confessions." On the contrary, they inquired about the appearance of the "powder from children's hands" obtained in this way. The answer: if it was prepared "from the bones alone, it looked fairly white, but if flesh also was ground in, it was more brownish in color." But if it was to be really potent, "it must be mixed with a small quantity of ash that has been burned between Christmas and the Feast of the Epiphany."

CONCERNING THE UNSEEN

The Pappenheimers' world was peopled by demonic beings. We have already mentioned the fear that gave birth to them and the terror they inspired, as well as the assistance they gave to thieves and sorcerers. What was the nature of these unseen contemporaries and fellow travelers of our vagrant family? Not all of them could be pressed into service as easily as the souls of innocent children. The spirits of the dead hovered around graves, dwellings, and places of ill omen. They terrified harmless wayfarers by appearing in grotesque guises. Restless souls roamed through the night as werewolves or transformed themselves into bloodsucking vampires. The man who had been done to death on the highway and hastily dragged into the undergrowth was liable to confront the robbers all of a sudden, to remind them of their ghastly crime by showing his bleeding wounds, and to claim the right to Christian burial.

Such ghosts, human albeit deceased, formed only a small proportion of the omnipresent demons. The largest group consisted of spirits of the air and of light, who were generally good-natured and pursued their allotted tasks with unobtrusive diligence: goblins and elves, dwarves, gnomes, and imps, fairies and white ladies, banshees, pixies, and all the rest. There were brownies, too, and other familiar or tutelary spirits, who were helpful and vigilant and took offense only if people alarmed them or tried to drive them away. Mountain spirits and giants guarded the earth's treasures up in the hills, and from time to time led erring wayfarers out of the gloomy forest back into the light of day. Other demons helped the farmer, day in, day out: tiny creatures lodged in the seeds and roots of the crops, in blades of grass, in ears of grain, in twigs and fruits. If benign, they nurtured the crops and fostered their growth. On the other hand, they were capable of avenging any offense by cutting off the nourishment of the plants in fields and meadows. In all these matters they cooperated with those kindred spirits who were responsible for clouds and rain, frost and hail. It was as well for farmers to show their gratitude to such powers, not to begrudge them their due or fail to paint propitious signs on boundary stones and the stable doorposts so that they might be spared from blight and tempest. Even more dangerous, however, were the demons of disease, a further regiment in the unseen host. Anyone who neglected to protect himself from them by means of holy water, pentagram, and signs of the zodiac might be cast down by these pernicious beings and condemned to some dire disease.

The farmers and cottagers of the district through which our vagrants made their way used to tell countless tales of the exploits of these various spirits. On those evenings when men and women gathered to gossip in the farm kitchens, old stories were handed on, new stories luridly elaborated, astounding events exaggerated even further. In the years before their arrest we may suppose that our vagrants were present at such gatherings around the wooden table of some low tavern, or lying in the straw in a barn—half terrified, half fascinated by what they heard.

They heard, for instance, of two peasants who had but recently been led a dance by a fiery manikin.[76] It was like this: the two were wending their way home through a wood, after an evening's drinking. All at once they saw a will-of-the-wisp leap from a bush and dart on in front of them, keeping a distance of ten paces. The flickering light distracted them and led them off their path. But they hoped in vain to catch a glimpse of the starry sky above; they stumbled through the wood, which now seemed endless although it was really no great size and could be traversed in half an hour. It was not until dawn was breaking and they could hear the Ave Maria sounding from the nearest village that they were released from the spell and reached the edge of the wood; at that point, too, the fiery manikin vanished. But to their astonishment they found themselves at the very same spot where they had first entered the wood. The spirit of the forest had played a wicked trick on them and led them round and round in a circle.

A story that was going the rounds in the Regensburg area sounded even more eerie. Not long before, a little woman dressed all in red had been seen in a meadow near the village of Wissing; she was mowing the grass in broad daylight and occasionally pausing to hone her sickle, which gave out a clear, resonant sound. Those who had seen the ghost crossed themselves and made off as fast as their legs would carry them. The owner of the meadow was a wealthy young farmer, who was only too pleased to have the woman in red mowing his meadow, for the grass grew twice as thick and lush where the spirit had mowed it. The woman who lived next door to the owner of the meadow kept urging him to go out and speak to the little woman in red, which the young farmer prudently refused to do. For his overinsistent neighbor fell gravely ill and was soon at death's door. In defiance of her own wishes, the priest was sent for. He had rarely seen the proud woman in his church, for she was indeed godless and arrogant. When the pious man came to bring her extreme unction, she was lying in bed with her face turned away, and when he touched her and turned her over, she was already cold and dead. But how startled he was to find that this proud mortal had assumed the form and appearance of the woman in red. And ever since then the cows that grazed in that meadow had yielded blood instead of milk!

In Nuremberg the Pappenheimers heard tell of a goldsmith's wife who had a familiar spirit in constant attendance on her. It appeared to her from time to time in the form of a young boy clad in white and bearing an hourglass in his right hand. When danger threatened, he warned her and provided all sorts of other useful prophecies. From Nuremberg, too, came a certain Paul Cruz, who one day set a miniature table for two, with all sorts of delicacies, out in the open air. He had lain in wait nearby until two goblins emerged from the ground, took their places at the table, and set to with a will. In the meantime their host approached cautiously, made his presence known, talked kindly to the spirits, and thus won their confidence. In his way the shrewd Nuremberger one day made the acquaintance of the king of the Underworld, who appeared in a scarlet cloak and permitted Paul Cruz to read his book of mysteries.

Such were the tales of demonic exploits that Paulus and his family found familiar, and yet uncanny. For him and his contemporaries, these were not just old wives' tales or amusing fictions but evidences of a real world encountered every day. Why should such stories be any less true than tales of murder and highway robbery? As we shall see, a man need not be particularly naive to believe that spirits were everywhere present. One had to be cautious and understand the signs.[77] That applied to farmers, craftsmen, and cottagers, but it appled even more to a homeless nomad like Paulus Pappenheimer.

When he and his family packed up their belongings and set out at first light, it was important to note who first met them on the road. A clergyman, an old woman—that boded no good. It was better to turn back and put up with their old quarters for a further night. If a pig or a hare crossed their path, that was also an evil omen, and the same was true of lizards, weasels, or black cats. Sheep, ravens, crows, swallows, and storks, on the other hand, promised the wayfarers good fortune. Again, magpies, the gallows birds, boded no good, nor did the call of the screech owl, which heralded the approach of death. Paulus took account of such

188

things. Fortunately, he and his contemporaries knew that the demons themselves were at cross-purposes, that they foiled each other's plans and warned men against each other. However dangerous these evil spirits might be, there were ways and means of evading their assaults. They were all somewhat naive, a contemptible rabble that could be mastered with cunning and deceit, prudence and magic.

Old Pappenheimer and his wife were experts, as far as that went. In particular, they knew of many herbs with magic power to expel the evildoers from the afflicted body: speedwell and wormwood, mugwort, pimpernel and valerian, liverwort and lungwort, chicory and Solomon's seal. Plucked at the right time, and in the prescribed manner, distilled, dried, or ground to the accompaniment of traditional incantations, they could work wonders, either because the demon could not stomach their smell or taste, or because they attracted another, more potent spirit that drove out the malignant demon. Pimpernel, for example, was repugnant to the demon that caused epidemics; so people carried a piece of the herb in their mouths at the first sign of infection, and also added it to the cattle's fodder. The word then went round the affected district:

> Oh, hearken, folks!
> But give the cattle pimpernel,
> The scamp, the shelty trots full well!
> Give the beasts the herb each day,
> And send the scamp upon his way.

If the peasants wanted to cure cattle of maggots, they plucked a stinging nettle before sunrise, held it in both hands, and recited a verse on these lines:

> Nettle, nettle, hear forsooth,
> Our cow's got maggots in her hoof;
> If you don't drive the maggots out,
> I'll twist your collar round about.

The stem of the nettle was twisted until it broke, and the two parts were thrown backwards over one's head. The spell only worked, however, if the process was repeated on three successive days.

Herbs were a remedy for malevolent spirits of the weather and the soil, as well as for illness. On Midsummer's Day (24 June) the roots of the mysterious fern, which were said to confer invisibility, had to be dug up and dried in the open air, but in such a way that they were not exposed to the sun. If this so-called "St. John's herb" was placed in the window nook in the form of a cross on the day of the solstice, it drove off those spirits that brought bad weather. Twigs from a variety of Juniper tree (*Juniperus sabina* L.) had a similar deterrent effect, for evil spirits could not stand their aroma. They were woven into fences or nailed to stable doors, and the water that cattle were to drink was poured over them.

Everyone knew that the demons could not stand loud noises. Shouts and the cracking of whips drove them off, even the whistling of shepherds upset them, they positively detested the sound of bells, and they could not stand fire or running water. Certain stubborn spirits had to yield if exorcised. It was essential to know their names, however, for only those who knew how to address the demons by their true names showed that they were the stronger. Exorcism of that sort was an extremely hazardous art, and the Pappenheimers had no knowledge of it.

They tried to come to terms with the unseen beings, took note of premonitory signs, avoided direct confrontations with them, enlisted help against some of them by currying favor with others. They were either too awestruck or too astute to join the ranks of the soothsayers and magicians, of whom there were many among the traveling people.

FALLEN ANGELS

Even an erudite and widely read individual like the white-haired councillor Johann Baptist Fickler believed in the presence of demons everywhere. Unlike the traveling folk, however, he did not see in these invisible beings a wild and disorderly horde, the members of which could not be identified as to their origins or aims. As an educated man, he was informed about the origins, the functions, and the hierarchy of the spirit kingdom. Medieval scholars, Church fathers, Doctores Ecclesiae, and the scholastics had evolved a veritable demonology, a science dealing with the activities of the spirits. In Fickler's time this science had become the common property of theologians and lawyers.

Consequently, no doubts were entertained about the existence of demons, for this was stated in Holy Scripture: "When men began to multiply upon the earth, and daughters were born unto them, then the Sons of God looked upon the daughters of men and saw that they were fair, and they took wives from all those that pleased them. At the same time, there were giants upon the earth;

190

and after the Sons of God had dwelt with their daughters, they bore unto them children who became heroes and great men." Biblical scholars agreed that "Sons of God" meant angels who had mingled with men and who had been expelled from heaven for that reason.

Demons were these fallen angels and their bastards, according to the biblical experts.[78] They added, although this was not in Holy Scripture, that the Devil had provoked all kinds of monstrous happenings so as to create a great following of these lascivious angels and their descendants, a veritable host of demons.

This amplification of scripture was not as arbitrary as it might seem. What the Bible says about the "Sons of God," soberly, bluntly, and without comment, was in fact a major scandal, an episode embarrassing to the Creator. His devout and pious spirit-beings, seduced by lusts of the flesh, seeking the ephemeral dust of earth rather than the enduring gold of eternity—that suggested an imperfection totally out of keeping with the idea of an angel, and a rebellious discontent that made a mockery of the idea of heavenly bliss. For theologians there could be only one explanation: God Himself must have willed it so. This idea led inexorably to the idea of the Devil. He too had been willed by God. But if the Devil belonged to the cosmos, then it was quite possible that he had been given, for God's sake, a number of assistants and accomplices. That would have rendered the dramatic fall of the angels unnecessary. But, as the Holy Scriptures demonstrate, God loves moving and heart-rending stories. Apart from their immediate purpose, such stories serve to instruct and edify Christian souls.

This was more or less the argument used by the Church Fathers. It was, with all due respect, not quite honest. In fact, it was popular belief that first confronted Christian theologians with the fact that there were demons; it was only then that the latter began looking for an explanation—and lighted on one in the form of the biblical quotation given above. The grand idea of a single God had conquered the West and dethroned the innumerable heathen deities. But it could not annihilate them; it could only banish them to the forests, the air, and the mountains. From there, they continued to intervene in the lives of the peasants, townsfolk, and beggars who had in the meantime become Christians.

The transformation of the deposed heathen gods into demons represented a shrewd ploy on the part of the Christian Church. It was devised by the man who was indubitably the greatest theoretician of Christianity in the period preceding the Middle

Ages—Aurelius Augustinus (c. 430), bishop of Hippo-Regius. Augustine taught that there had existed since before the beginning of the world a kingdom of good, *civitas Dei,* and a kingdom of evil, *civitas Diaboli.*[79] All good men, and the angels, belonged to the kingdom of God; all evil men, infidels, and demons belonged to the kingdom of the Devil. Christ had achieved the final victory over the diabolical principle, but had not destroyed it. The demons, accomplices of the Devil and his cause, had been regarded by the heathens, with some justification, as gods. They had astonishing powers. Their ethereal bodies (*corpus aerium*) were infinitely superior to the human body, for they were invisible and incredibly agile (*celeritas motus*). They possessed an almost unimaginable acuteness of the senses (*acrimonia sensus*) and, because of their immortality, a greater store of knowledge and experience than any human being. No wonder, then, that they could predict the future and induce or prevent diseases, storms, and bad harvests. They would also attempt to take possession of men, infiltrate their minds, and dominate their thoughts, although they would never succeed in the case of good, God-fearing Christians.

It was a brilliant idea: Augustine acknowledged the existence of the heathen gods because belief in them was evidently so deeply rooted in evey nation that it could not be eradicated. At the same time, however, he reduced the defeated deities to the rank of mere servants of the Devil. Thus embodied in the Church's doctrine of salvation, the miracles and phenomena attributed to the ancient gods could no longer shake the Christian faith; on the contrary, they reinforced it. Augustine relativized in this way all the heathen gods known to him: the demon Venus keeps the eternal light burning in the temple of Venus, so as to distract men from the true Christian 'God; the demon Circe turns men into beasts in order to undermine Christians' faith by such tricks; the demon Diomedes sends out birds to attack foreigners and to flatter the Greeks, so that paganism may be preserved in Greece. Magic and prophecy were doubtless possible, declared the great teacher of the Church, but only with the help of demons. It was they who inspired the godless with a knowledge of things to come, and performed all sorts of utterly impossible feats for their benefit. Christians should on no account allow themselves to be impressed by such pranks; these were nothing but a patently obvious ploy on the part of false gods who had been defeated and unmasked but who would not acknowledge that defeat. "The greater the power over this world that we see vouchsafed to the demons, the more firmly should we cling to the Savior through whom we may raise ourselves up from the depths."

Augustine's method was to assimilate and isolate those things that could not be eliminated. He was prompted not by any tactical considerations but by philosophical wisdom of a worldly kind—something many of his successors lacked. The great Church teacher was concerned above all to show that all these pagan unseen beings, even those that were amiable and useful, served the principle of evil. Later, the emphasis changed: the dogmatists of the Church increasingly condemned doubts concerning the existence of demons. Suddenly it was no longer a sin to believe in the deposed pagan gods; on the contrary, it was heresy to question the existence and the power of demons.

The medieval monk Caesarius of Heisterbach (ca. 1180–1240) conveyed the church's demonology of his time in edifying anecdotes.[80] Here we encounter a knight who did not believe in demons but who suddenly found himself faced with the most terrifying figures. We are told of a wicked priest whose deathbed was surrounded by more demons than there are straws on a thatched roof. Interestingly enough, there is also the tale of a melancholy youth who faithfully serves a knight, and even saves his life, only to reveal himself in the end as a demon. The knight is astonished: "If you are by nature a demon, how can it be that you have served a human being so loyally?" The spirit replies: "It is a great comfort to me to be among the sons of men . . . You may be sure, if you keep me with you, no harm will ever come to you through me." The only reward the worthy demon requests is that his master should purchase a bell and hang it in the belfry of the old ruined church in the village, "so that at least on Sundays the faithful might be summoned to the service."

This is one of the last testimonials of its kind. In Johann Baptist Fickler's time, it seems, educated people could imagine demons only as evil. They all began to be called devils, and Lucifer was henceforth termed the supreme devil. It is only the ignorant who see the jumble of iron filings in a magnetic field as purely random; anyone familiar with lines of force sees them as ordered. In the same way, the learned observer of the spirit realm was able to detect the hierarchical structure of satanic power in the milling crowd. Unlike the common folk, he knew where he stood with these unseen creatures, and what might be expected of them.

The basis of the demonology that was then current was the volume of aphorisms by Petrus Lombardus and the *Summa Theo-*

logica of Thomas Aquinus (d. 1274). According to these writings, angels and demons were disembodied but could assume any form they wished in order to achieve their aims in the world and enter into communication with men. They formed their bodies from earth, vapor, and air, the good angels using the higher elements, the wicked spirits using the lower sort. Even in their corporeal state they were capable of flying with lightning speed from one place to another. They could eat but not digest, since their ethereal bodies lacked the necessary organs. As the Bible witnessed, they were in a position to have sexual intercourse with human beings and were constantly inclined to such perversion. They positively pestered men with their lecherous attentions. Thomas Aquinus examined in detail the problem of sexual intercourse between demons and human beings, for it was indeed a problem: since these ethereal creatures had no functioning organs, they were unable to produce semen. The great thinker found a solution to the problem. The demon, as a *succubus*, first assumed female form and seduced a man. Following ejaculation, the spirit instantaneously took male form (*incubus*) and flew to a woman, whom it impregnated with the warm semen. The "diabolical offspring" of such a union were not bastards of the demon but human children conceived with diabolical cooperation.

Following on these observations, the question of the diabolical paramour became an integral part of learned discussions about the nature of demons. Thomas Aquinas was skeptical, however, concerning another standard problem: it was impossible, he declared, for spirits to turn men into beasts, since this kind of magic ran counter to the divine laws of nature. The master also relegated to the realm of fairytales the theme of "human flight," which was hotly debated during the thirteenth century. Those individuals who were allegedly carried through the air by demons were simply victims of a diabolical illusion. People knew better in Fickler's time. They pointed to the Gospel according to Matthew (4:5), where it was stated that the Devil had borne Jesus up to the summit of the temple. If Satan could carry Jesus Himself through the air, then it would be a simple matter for him to do the same with sinful men.

It was beyond any doubt that demons afflicted men with foul weather, diseases, and other misfortunes. The evil angels would stir the air and occasion storms and thunder, wrote Thomas Aquinas, while Bonaventura regarded regulation of the weather as one of the principal functions of the spirits. Catholic dogmatics still adheres in the twentieth century to the theory "that Satan and his angels, being part of the Creation, have their place in the total scheme of the cosmos, and are capable of exerting a pernicious influence on nonhuman creatures, insofar as God permits."[81]

The demons did not embark on these strenuous activities from sheer malice. They were acting on orders from higher up, which were sanctioned by the highest authority of all. The target of the demons' activities was man, who was to be seduced by them into sin. And this tells us who was pulling the strings: the fallen "Sons of God" were servants of the Devil, who held tyrannical sway in the kingdom of demons. It was he, the king of the Underworld, who hurled his disciplined infantry against the bastions of Christendom.

SATAN—WITHOUT PREJUDICE

Lucifer, the supreme ruler of the Kingdom of Evil, is one of the principal characters in our story. This is not only because it was he who had devised and evolved the crime of witchcraft, which was one of the charges, indeed the main charge, brought against our vagrants; it is also because the Pappenheimers were prompted by him, and him alone, to commit their crimes, and were helped by him to carry them out. At least, this is what we read in the record of their interrogation. From the record it appears that the "Evil One," with his cloven hoof and the stink of brimstone, was also standing in the dock alongside the accused—and this is to be taken quite literally. Certain happenings, to which we shall turn later on, confirmed in the minds of the commissioners a suspicion they had had from the outset: their adversary was intervening personally in the proceedings against the vagrants. He and his henchmen were also in the habit of visiting the prisoners in their cells in the Falcon Tower from time to time in order to influence the course of the trial.

Who was this unseen meddler? The story of his life is ambiguous and has no proper beginning. If we plunge into the deep well of human history, into those regions where darkness and decay prevail, we shall encounter him. As far as we can make out, he is already full-grown, sturdy, and self-confident. He bears a variety of names, is fond of dividing himself into several deities, and loves to terrorize individuals and entire nations. In the Land of the Two Rivers, Mesopotamia, he haunts the Sumerians under the name of Dug; as Lamaštu and Lilīta, he inflicts disease and death on

Babylon; he spreads terror through the land as Pazazu, a cross between man and bird. To the Egyptians he reveals himself in many grisly forms, perhaps because the Pharaoh's children refuse to give evil a name. In Phoenicia, Arabia, and Israel, he was present everywhere from the very beginning. His origins must lie even deeper.

Fortunately, scattered passages in the Bible tell us something about Lucifer's early life. He was, it seems, an angel of God, but he made himself conspicuous by the acuteness of his mind and the sharpness of his tongue, if we may speak in such terms of a spiritual being. He was a member of the heavenly establishment, but from the outset he seems to have introduced a discordant note into the angelic hallelujahs by his habit of contradicting and quibbling. God was patient, and assigned to his recalcitrant angel a function that seemed well suited to his carping spirit: He appointed him as a kind of celestial public prosecutor. As to what happened next, the documentary evidence is obscure. Only one thing is certain: Lucifer, not fully occupied with the duties of his new appointment and still essentially a killjoy and grumbler, began to intrigue against the King of Heaven. In secret and in public he talked in an inflammatory manner, inciting others to treason. Unfortunately, there can be little doubt that a considerable part of the heavenly host, possibly even a majority, succumbed to his rabble-rousing speeches and supported him in his challenge to the Lord. The actual nature of Lucifer's rebellion is a matter of pure speculation. Some authorities suggest an attempt at a putsch, saying that the megalomaniac angel sought to depose God or at least demanded an equal share in the government of the world. Others claim that a clash had come about on account of the planned incarnation of Christ. Lucifer had placed himself at the head of his supporters and vehemently protested the unprecedented elevation of a human being above the heavenly hosts: it was a question of the honor of the angels, who would never be prepared to submit to a god who was merely human. Such were the unworthy statements attributed to him. Earlier theologians are agreed, at any rate, that a heated and unedifying argument developed, a crazy trial of strength between the domineering angel Satan and his Creator. The latter had no choice but to expel the rebel and his supporters from Heaven.

These events, it might be said, show the character of Lucifer in the worst possible light. That would be an overhasty judgment. After all, it was the Creator Himself who endowed Lucifer with a carping and insubordinate spirit, because, in His wisdom and omnipotence, He had planned and foreseen the rebellion in Heaven. God did not wish it to be otherwise, which is why there is something factitious about His rage, and something theatrical about His purge of Heaven. We have already mentioned that the Creator loved such scenes for their edifying effect. They are meant to be recounted with a sly wink. For Lucifer was by no means contrite after his fall from Heaven but at once set about the task allocated to him by God, inciting the demons to seduce and torment mankind, constantly doing what mischief he could himself, and tempting men to sin—in short, practicing evil. There was, indeed, no reason to be contrite. On the contrary: God had allotted him a leading part in the *theatrum mundi*, appointing him His counterpart and adversary. Alone among the angels, Satan was granted a kingdom of his own. True, it was gloomy and inhospitable, filled with wailing and gnashing of teeth, but it was his own sovereign territory, which the fallen angel could govern in relative independence. Satan's power, of course, never approached the glory of God: the Creator only had to raise His finger in order to destroy the Kingdom of Darkness forever. But Satan was at least permitted to act the part of God's adversary and trust that God would keep to the rules of this strange duel, which He Himself had laid down.

But if it was God that planned all this and made it come about, what were His motives, one might well ask, for the creation of a kingdom of devils? Since nothing has, or had, any validity outside God, these motives must lie in God Himself. They have something to do with that predisposition toward the Good which, given the time scale of eternity, He had adopted relatively recently. The biblical God who revealed Himself to Israel was originally neither good nor evil. He claimed the right to be wrathful or gentle, vindictive today, merciful tomorrow, just or unjust. Later, however, He took pity on His human creation and decided on the work of salvation. He became the "Good Lord" who wanted to save mankind through His Son. This decision led to disconcerting consequences, for there is no "Good" without a matching "Bad," just as there is no "Up" without a "Down." Who would recognize the goodness of God if hatred and evil did not exist? God's turning toward the light could only be understood by men if they were familiar with darkness; His "salvation" was comprehensible only if there was also a "damnation." Here lies the symbolic core of the legend concerning Lucifer's protest against the creation of a God-man. The great division between good and evil did not become necessary until God deigned to become good. For that purpose he needed the Devil. The latter was henceforth destined to be everything the Creator no longer was. God was Truth, the Devil was Lies; God was Love, the Devil was Hate; God was Becoming, the Devil was Annihilation; God was Life, the Devil was Death.

At the time he eavesdropped on the interrogation of the Pappenheimers in the vault of Munich's Falcon Tower, this hour of the Devil's birth already lay many thousands of years back in the past. He had not always remained the same throughout his career of evil, which was short enough in celestial terms, but long in terms of human fate. On the contrary, he had always adapted himself to match those changes in culture which men had undergone throughout the ages. This assimilation on the part of the Devil had always taken place—in conformity with his notoriously negative inner nature—through the adoption of the qualities most detested by the current generation. When he encountered the Pappenheimers, his most prominent feature was a perverse kind of lecherousness. He manifested himself symbolically from time to time in the form of a billy goat, although for purposes of seduction he was shrewd enough to slip into the semblance of a Spanish cavalier or a buxom wench. He carried on in a manner calculated to bring a blush to the cheek of the most hardened camp follower, and was capable of intercourse with any creature under the sun. His gestures and words were obscene jests.

Again, this unpleasing disposition should not be held against him personally. As a spiritual being he gained no satisfaction from lewdness and obscenity. There were two reasons for his disgusting behavior, one divine, and the other human. The human reason derived from the fact that those whose words carried weight in the Pappenheimers' time condemned every form of sexuality as the work of the Devil. Since carnal desire, sexual intercourse, and lewdness were decried as diabolical from throne, pulpit and lectern, the Devil had no choice but to be lecherous. For, after all, he was the representative of evil and had to come to terms with the fact that it was certain influential individuals who determined what was to be considered evil. The more rigorous the prohibitions, the more extravagant became the fantasies concerning what was prohibited. And who was to live out these fantasies, if not Satan! So much for the human reason for Lucifer's wicked behavior.

The divine reason was the commission he had been given to lead men into sin and to undo them in body and soul. Theologians and scholars of the age shared Lucifer's opinion that lechery was the best means of achieving that aim. "From the moment of his fall, the Devil has been seeking to destroy the unity of the Church, to injure love, to mar the sweetness of the saints' holy works with the gall of his envy, and to extirpate and destroy mankind in every way. His strength is in the loins and in the navel, because they hold sway over man through the lusts of the flesh. For the seat of lust in men is in the loins, for it is here that the semen is secreted, as it is in the navel in the case of women . . . The reason . . . [that the Devil behaves in an obscene fashion] is not lust . . . but the fact that the vice of lust . . . makes men the readier to indulge in other vices." This is the view of the Dominican Father Heinrich Institoris, author of the *Hammer of Witches*, of which we shall hear more in due course. This book played an important part in our trial.

We might mention other features of the Devil as he sojourned on earth in the time of our vagrants. He preferred to wear black, stank of dung and brimstone, had a preference for the left side, was an uncouth boor and a boozer with filthy habits; he had no equal as a liar and deceiver, loved crude jokes, and never kept his promises. He seems to have had little in common with the Pappenheimers. The commissioners appointed by the Munich council of state, and Johann Simon Wangereck in particular, were, however, of a different opinion.

A SUSPICION IS CONFIRMED

Since little Hänsel's interrogation there had scarcely been a doubt in the minds of the commissioners: the vagrants confined in the Falcon Tower had had dealings with the Evil One. The "magic with children's hands" that the boy had admitted simply reeked of witchcraft. Old Pappenheimer's statements, as well as those by Michel, were of such a kind as to confirm the suspicion. So far, however, all the witnesses had denied that Anna Pämb was a witch.

On 28 April 1600, the court believed that the time had come to fetch the old woman herself into the vault of the Falcon Tower and to persuade her to speak, with the aid of Master Georg's arts. It was a Sunday morning, an unusual time for torture. Presumably Councillor Wangereck hoped for assistance from Him to whom the day was dedicated. For the Devil—and this interrogation was concerned especially with him—would be on the side of the accused.

The sole question: How had she come to take up witchcraft?

199

The record says nothing of her obstinate denials or of the merciless torture. It records only the answer given by the terrified and tormented woman. According to her, this is what happened:

About nine years earlier our family of traveling folk was spending the winter in the almshouse at Kelheim, where they had met others who lacked hearth and home. Among them was an old peasant woman called Ziegler, who was rumored to be a witch. They got to know each other, cracked jokes, talked of this and that. Then suddenly the witch said she would soon be off on her pitchfork again. Would Anna care to come with her?

Anna declined. She wanted nothing to do with that sort of thing. Whereupon Ziegler assured her there was nothing to it; she would take care of everything and make all the preparations; the enterprise wasn't in the least dangerous. And what was more, they might help themselves to a few things. Anna began to waver and think about it—not because she expected to gain all that much by a flight on the pitchfork or because she meant to betray God to Satan. No, she said she would join in the adventure from sheer curiosity, from "pure inquisitiveness and mischief." The following night, about half past ten, Anna waited behind the almshouse for her seductress, who arrived with two fire irons and "a powder made from the crushed hand of an unbaptized child." When the ends of the fire irons had been smeared with this preparation, the women mounted and sat astride them. Ziegler whispered to Anna the spell that each of them had to say aloud in order to start the flight: "In all the devils' names—up, up, away, and nowhere stay!" And, whoosh! they were flying through the chilly night air over the sleeping town, their hair streaming out behind them. The old peasant told the irons that their destination was the wine cellar of a wealthy farmer from Kelheim called Simon. In a moment the night riders were heading for a fine farmstead, hurtling toward the cellar door, which flew open without a sound. Straight on, into the darkness. Then there was a jolt, and Anna crashed to the ground with a scream of pain, bruising all her limbs. The Ziegler woman chuckled and passed some remark on her mishap, then devoted herself to a barrel of wine, drinking it in great gulps. When she had drunk her fill, she told Anna to mount once more. Now we'll fly to Silbernagel's farm, she whispered to her companion, and "enthral" his hired man; he's a fine, strapping lad. In a moment they were out of the cellar again and whizzing through the air in the direction of Silbernagel's farm. The hired man's bedroom window was open, and the two riders flew right through. They dismounted, and Ziegler bent cautiously over the sleeping man. She pulled a little pot from the folds of her dress and smeared her unwitting victim's temples wth an ointment while muttering some words that Anna could not understand. She did this so that the man could not wake up or cry out. Then the old peasant woman flung herself on the young man and told Anna to do the same and lie down with them. The two women then raped the man, who was to wake up the following day feeling feeble and ill, believing it was all a bad dream. After this shameless assault, the two of them mounted their fire irons once more and were whisked back to the almshouse in Kelheim, where their nocturnal escapade had passed entirely unnoticed.

Nine days later, Anna was making her way from Abensberg to Schwaighausen with a milk can in her hand, all alone on a broad meadow. She was still thinking about her fantastic ride on the fire iron, but it seemed to her now no more than a nightmare and best forgotten. Just as well that the whole business had passed off without serious consequences, she was thinking. At least the Devil had not made an appearance that night. She meant to have no more to do with the Ziegler woman; let her seduce others with her black arts. And so she thought that the whole affair was over and done with. But as she was making her way across country, a peasant came toward her on the narrow path, dressed all in black and carrying a gnarled stick in his left hand. He looked at her with a subtle smile on his thin lips, and a shudder ran through her. The stranger stopped in front of her, doffed his hat, and greeted the wretched woman with exquisite courtesy. Where was she bound? he asked her, and what a fine day it was, he remarked; it will soon be spring now, the squirrels have grown quite large already. And when she did not reply, the man in black went on: You were looking for me, Anna; well, here I am. Come along with me, and let us do the business properly. And then the scales fell from Anna Pappenheimer's eyes. But she still could not bring herself to believe what she had long known to be true. Trembling, she cried: God preserve me—I do not know you! What have I to do with you? The stranger's answer was as smooth as velvet, his voice only slightly raised in surprise: You don't know me? But I have known you for so long! You might well say we've been on really intimate terms since a certain night. That was when I carried you through the air. Now I want my reward. In for a penny, in for a pound. You see, I am none other than Lucifer, whom you human beings call the "Evil One." And yet I can be a good friend to those who trust me. Who will look after you better than I will? Aren't you suffering hunger and poverty, aren't you clad in rags, in spite of all your God-fearing ways? Your Christ doesn't seem to be of much help to you, for your loyalty is poorly rewarded. I am more grateful, as you will see. Follow me, and believe in me. I will be your god and give you abundant honor, possessions, or whatever your heart desires, and I will carry you wherever you want, as I did on a certain night.

As he spoke these words he was caressing Anna, fumbling with her bodice, pressing her to him, so that she scarcely knew where she was. The milk can slipped from her grasp, fell to the ground with a clatter, rolled a little way along the stony path, then lay there. In the arms of the supreme seducer, the vagrant woman ceased to struggle, allowed herself to sink into the grass by the path, and sighed in ecstasy as he had his way of her. She felt the Devil's member enter her, and shuddered—it was "as cold as a piece of ice"—and then she abandoned herself in a paroxysm of lust.

When she came to her senses, she heard the oily voice of the man in black: That's the way. You submitted to my will just now, and so it will always be. What we still have to do is pure formality. You must renounce Almighty God, the Virgin Mary, all the saints, and the whole world, acknowledge me as your one and only lord, and deny the Christian religion. I will give you money enough so that you will know poverty no more, and you will serve me. What I order you to do henceforth, you will do, even if it should harm your fellow men and be repugnant to you. Let us take a solemn oath.

And as he required her to take the blasphemous oath, he took her left hand in his left hand. Then he ripped the skin beneath her left shoulder, dipped his finger in the blood that oozed out, and smeared her lips three times with it, inside and out. From his doublet he drew a sheet of paper and a quill, which he dipped into the wound and pressed into her fingers. Anna could not write, so the Devil guided her hand as it recorded the pact in clumsy letters of blood: She, Anna Pämb, otherwise called Pappenheimer, would henceforth be a disciple of the Devil, be loyal to Lucifer evermore, do nothing good, but only evil. Satisfied, the man in black pocketed pen and paper and surveyed his new disciple, who was crouching naked on her clothes and shivering, not simply on account of the chilly morning air. You have black hair, at any rate, he remarked, and you'll do very well for a devil.

As a sign of the inviolability of their pact, Lucifer demanded a scrap of skin from her left breast and from her genitals, a piece of nail from her big toe, hair from each part of her body, taken from the left side in every case. He also made her return what was left of the powder of children's hands that Ziegler had given her on their excursion. From this, together with other ingredients he had with him, he concocted before Anna's very eyes "a slimy, whitish stuff" that looked like an ointment but wasn't. He wrapped this magic preparation in a piece of black parchment and gave it to her "along with a broad gold piece," telling her: With this medicine you can do men or cattle harm if you desire or if you have orders from me to do so. You need only smear it on your victim, and he will fall ill or go lame. Following these words, the peasant in black seemed to be swallowed up by the earth, and Anna was once more alone. She dressed hastily, put her hair in order, concealed the black package in her dress, dragged herself to her feet, retraced her steps, picked up her milk can, and went on her way.

Such was the course of events during Anna Pappenheimer's first encounter with the Devil, as it was conjured up before the eyes of the commissioners listening to the accused on that 28 April. They believed every word. They checked at once whether there was still any trace beneath her left shoulder of the wound inflicted by the Devil, and, sure enough, they found a scar. When the old woman had been released from the terrifying vault, she recanted, but only to give an equally fanciful account of her seduction during a further interrogation. The torture left her no choice.

WITCHCRAFT

From this stage of the trial onward, Wangereck shifted the main emphasis of his investigation to the charge of witchcraft. This was in keeping with a personal interest of this exciseman's son from Lower Bavaria. We may remember that sometimes he had harsh words in meetings of the council of state for those who were inclined to be lenient toward sorcerers and witches. Which does not mean, however, that our ducal commissioner was ultimately responsible for the turn now taken by the case against the Pappenheimers. Wangereck the zealot was also a careerist—it would hardly have occurred to him to apply his zeal to ends the authorities distrusted. As a loyal servant of his monarch, he was simply carrying out what the duke had ordered.

On 24 September 1590, during the reign of William V, a ducal instruction had been issued concerning the manner "in which a judge was to proceed as regards the identification, apprehension, and interrogation of sorcerers and persons rumored to be guilty of witchcraft." This "internal directive," as we would call it nowadays, formed one of the legal guidelines for the commissioners acting in the Pappenheimer case. A single manuscript copy of the "Witchcraft Instruction" has survived the centuries in the archives of the town of Amberg.

In the preamble, "the attorneys and councillors of our Most Gracious Sovereign, Duke William of Bavaria," complain that there are reports throughout the Bavarian principalities of "the dreadful, abhorrent, and most pernicious vice of sorcery and witchcraft, which runs most counter to the honor of God, and which everywhere grows rife." The background to their alarm was as follows.[82]

In Bavaria there had been occasional trials of suspected witches since the 1570s. Regular persecution of witches only began under Duke William V, when, in 1587, a farmer's wife from Steingaden by the name of Geiger fell under suspicion of having caused harm to cattle by means of magic. Contrary to the wishes of the Steingaden priest, who wanted to ignore an accusation reeking of slander and rumor, the municipal magistrate Lidl, in Schongau, forwarded the record of the investigation to the duke's council of state in Munich. The council ordered torture to be used on the accused. Thus, the same authority which was to sit in judgment on our vagrants thirteen years later initiated an epidemic of witchhunting. For this case was succeeded in the Schongau area by a series of frenzied attacks on suspected "ogres" that lasted for years. In the course of a systematic witch hunt, which was ordered by the authorities, hundreds of women fell into the clutches of the law. Thirty-six of them were executed after they had "confessed" to being in league with the Devil, to having harmed men and cattle by the use of magic ointment, to having conjured up storms, and to having ridden on pitchforks to take part in satanic revels. Since names of further accomplices were extorted in the course of every confession, each case led to a host of fresh arrests. With an avalanche of prosecutions in prospect, a certain Doctor Lagus proposed a general amnesty in the Munich council of state, claiming (falsely) that a series of such cases had led to the burning of three thousand witches in Upper Germany, and citing this as a warning. His reasonable voice was smothered in the council. The councillors, well informed through excerpts from the trial records sent from Schongau, gave instructions that torture was to be used on a large scale wherever witchcraft was suspected. They also opposed those compassionate father confessors who encouraged witches to retract their confessions. It was to make every judge in the land familiar with these and other principles of procedure in cases of witchcraft that William V issued the instruction referred to. The intention was also to intensify the search for suspects and to provide the lower judicial authorities with rules of procedure. The burnings in Schongau were to be only the beginning of a purge of such vermin throughout the whole of Bavaria. The duke felt obliged to do this "to save the honor of God, of His beloved saints, and the most venerable sacraments, as well as to avert all manner of temporal hurt and mischief that was visited by this accursed vice, not only upon the bodily well-being of men, but also upon the cherished fruits of our fields."

The instructions regarding witchcraft were sent to magistrates and "our beloved prefects" by special messenger, for the danger was thought to be imminent. The council instructed the recipients, "on pain of fine or corporal punishment, to apply themselves to these matters in such a manner that there might be no omission nor partiality, much less any negligence." Each of them was to begin by announcing publicly in his parish that every subject was duty-bound, on pain of grave punishment, to denounce any person suspected of witchcraft and sorcery. The informer must be honest, respectable, and reliable, but he could base his suspicions on mere hearsay, and his name would not be disclosed to the accused person.

According to these instructions, anyone who practiced soothsaying or offered to find stolen property was liable to be suspected of witchcraft. Anyone who inflicted disease on men or beasts was acutely suspicious—the councillors left it to the judge to establish a causal connection—but suspicion would also fall on anyone who cured a patient whom doctors had failed to restore to health. Witches were also capable of conjuring up "strange and spurious diabolical apparitions and curious specters"; they could turn themselves into "all manner of fearful animal shapes" and could bring about "gales, rain, thunder, hail, and the like." Consequently, anyone who boasted of such exploits was likely to be arrested. Anyone who called on the Devil when he was angry was highly suspicious, as was anyone who wished another person evil, if that person subsequently suffered some misfortune.

When searching a suspect or a suspect's lodging, the duke's officers should watch out for poison, communion wafers, toads, human limbs, "wax figures . . . pierced with needles," and above all for any "handwritten document . . . in which the suspected person has contracted himself to the Devil, denying God, all his beloved saints and the venerable sacraments, or otherwise any mark upon the body, which the Evil One may have imparted to those people in confirmation of their union."

According to the opinion of the duke's councillors, there was invariably a contractual relationship between the witch and the Devil, although this might have been entered into tacitly. This close bond did not have to be proved directly, however; it was sufficient to convict the suspect of sorcery. Sorcery, as defined in the instructions, was nothing other than an attempt to bring about effects that could not occur in the course of nature. It was for this reason that sorcerers "deserted God and put their faith in creatures [i.e. in demons]. Thence it follows that those things which they seek to perform may not be done otherwise than with the help, collaboration, and deception practiced by the Devil, with whom they have either an express understanding or a hidden and secret association to which they have consented following their desertion of God."

Taken in a strict sense, this idea, formulated in William V's instructions on witchcraft, was tantamount to the condemnation of an entire nation. Peasantry, craftsmen, and traveling folk were full of superstitions; their daily customs had implications of magic, although this magic was designed to ward off misfortune rather than to bring it about. Thus any attempt to alter the natural course of things by means involving supernatural forces was stigmatized as witchcraft and hence as diabolical. Hanging up St. John's herb, for instance, or chewing pimpernel, or driving out maggots by means of stinging nettles. Were the authorities really claiming that all these harmless customs were to be "considered devilish sorcery and witchcraft"?

If any doubt on this score remained after the promulgation of the instructions on witchcraft, Duke Maximilian I made it clear in his "Decree against Superstition" of 1611 that his father's definition of witchcraft was to be taken in a literal sense. "*Superstitiones* and false beliefs," he wrote in the preamble to the decree, "are not such . . . trivial sins . . . as is generally supposed . . . because all *superstitiones* and *vanae observationes*, or false beliefs, were devised by the adversary of all mankind, the accursed Devil (against whom may God in His goodness defend us)." He had had reliable reports, declared the duke in that same decree, that widespread superstition had grown apace among the common folk in his principality, "along with the equivocal blessing of beasts and people on account of sickness, and *in summa,* the trickery of soothsaying and the purported revelation of things hidden and yet to come." All this took place, if not with "the express invocation of the evil spirit," at least in the secret confidence that the Devil would lend his assistance. This in itself, however, implied the conclusion of a tacit pact with the Devil. It was to be feared accordingly that the spread of superstition in the country would lead to the "suborning and seduction of some individuals by degrees into the forbidden and damnable vice of witchcraft and sorcery, and to the denial of God the Almighty, His most venerable Mother, the Blessed Virgin Mary, and all the saints." After this introduction, the duke proceeded, on pain of the most severe punishment, to ban among other things the gathering of fern seeds, the digging up of mandrake, the charming of snakes, "the banishing of mice, rats, worms, and other vermin . . . by conjuration and incantations." The use of Christian formulas, names, and symbols did not make superstition any the less diabolical, since "the irksome Devil not infrequently presents himself in the guise of an angel of light," that is, entangles men in his net under the appearance of piety. The decree against superstition cited examples: "To give only one instance among many, we have often heard that a common blessing for sick beasts is used with the following verses: — If it be that the Holy Virgin Mary did bear the child Jesus, then let the pox leave this beast, in the name of God the Father, Son, and Holy Ghost. — Here we have not merely the vanity and conceit that the most sacred incarnation of Christ, which is dedicated alone to the redemption of mankind, should be applied to the healing of a brute beast, but also the doubt expressed in such a senseless blessing, whether the Holy Virgin Mary did bear the child Jesus, etc. And, again, it has come about that the following blessing was used to treat wounds: — Christ was born / Christ was forlorn / Christ was found / May He bless this wound. In the name of God the Father, Son, and Holy Ghost. For, although the invocation of God and the Holy Trinity is good, useful, and proper for a Christian in all his concerns, no certain hope may be reposed in such a rhyme, as if the invocation of God otherwise had no effect, but that God were constrained, as it were, to heal a wound, as often as the same might be blessed with this rhyme. [That is] naught but a most culpable tempting of God the Almighty, in contravention of the first commandment, and devised by the Evil Spirit and his accursed followers."

The ludicrous feature of Maximilian's frontal attack on popular superstition is the incongruity of weapon and adversary, the Quixotic battle with the windmill. He was utterly in earnest about his Decree against Superstition and was prompted by a sense of responsibility for "the land and the people entrusted to Us by God." Was he so ill acquainted with his own people that he believed he could eradicate their deeply rooted magic practices by administrative decrees?

It is more likely that he was seeing himself once more in his favorite role as Hercules. But the elimination of superstition in his realm could no more easily be achieved by threats than could safety on the highways of Bavaria or chastity and sobriety among his rakish subjects. What other means were there? Principally, the exemplary punishment of a few scapegoats. These had been found in the persons of the Pappenheimers.

GOG AND MAGOG

Duke Maximilian was neither a Don Quixote nor a Hercules. Keeping a tight grip on himself, and perpetually dissatisfied with all those around him, he was tormented with apocalyptic fears that forced him to tackle insoluble problems. Ultimately, when the time came, he would have to answer to his Creator for every one of his subjects, while the wrath of the Supreme Being might soon be vented on his principality. In his view, there was every reason to fear that the Almighty, "moved to righteous wrath against us men" on account of his subjects' superstitious customs, "might assail and punish our land and our people with famine, war, pestilence, and many other kinds of affliction." As we may observe once more from this argument, Maximilian's piety had a great deal to do with his fear of punishment. It was not a joyful, confident declaration of faith in a benign and protective father; on the contrary, it plodded on with downcast eyes and a permanent bad conscience. How could the love of God be more than a phrase for him, since he, a moral cripple deformed by his education, had never known the love of a father?

Maximilian's personal fear of God matched the general fear and insecurity of his contemporaries. In the preamble to his Decree of 1611, the duke implied that the war between the kingdom of God and that of the Devil continued to rage unseen, and that it was even now in its final stages. It was true that "the kingdom of the Evil Spirit" was doomed to destruction "by virtue of the bitter sufferings and death of our beloved Lord Jesus Christ," but many men, deluded and ungrateful, would desert to the forces of the Evil One. To counter this desertion and "to appease Almighty God," there was no surer remedy than draconian punishment for the "idolatry" of the sorcerers.

Such a view of things assigned to the battlefield of the ultimate eschatalogical conflict not only Anna Pämb, the wretched, ragged vagabond, but all the other accused in the trial, who were also soon revealed as adherents of the Devil. The Pappenheimers might have been less brutally treated if their crime had not been considered such an important matter of principle. Once unmasked as accomplices of the "enemy of mankind," the Pappenheimers and their friends, in the eyes of the commissioners, grew into monsters who stood on the side of the enemy in the struggle between Good and Evil.

The people of that age were very much aware of the struggle.[83] Fear of the demons which constantly surrounded them made sure of that. In addition, there was a sense of insecurity in a world that had been jolted out of its medieval joints. "The astrologers tell us of dreadful things," the Lutheran Michel Stiefel laments in 1522. "They say the order of the heavens will soon stand as it stood in the days of Noah . . . Item, do we not also see the words of Christ: *Audituri estis etc.*, Ye shall hear tell of strife and war. . . ? The Turk is pitted against the Christian. Among the Christians, the Frenchman is against the Emperor. Under the Emperor, the League is against the Duke of Württemberg. In his land, one house is set against another. One man says yes, another says no. In one and same house, under one roof, there is war." In Maximilian's time the clash of interests within the empire had grown even more acute. Already the shadows of the Thirty Years' War were creeping across Germany. The Turks stood no more than a few days' march from Vienna. The pope was busy forming an alliance with the king of France against the emperor. Did it not look very much as if the end of the Holy Roman Empire had arrived? According to the doctrine of the cosmic eras, familiar to every educated person, this meant disaster. "For when the Holy Roman Empire ceases to be, then the world must come to an end" (Johannes Lichtenberger). The "final battle" between Good and Evil was therefore already in full swing, or was about to begin.

The awareness of this final, decisive passage of arms between spiritual forces was deeply rooted in myth.[84] In early Germanic legends it takes place in the visible world still, and is fought out to the bitter end. Women, children, and old men join in the battle; on the battlefield the men are up to their knees in blood. Prophecies of the sixteenth century project the vision into the immediate future. The warring parties are "the good," "our people," against the "evil ones." Not infrequently, they are actually named: the incarnation of the diabolical host is the Turks! The menace is immediate, perceptible, beyond all doubt. In 1453 the enemies of Christianity conquer Constantinople, in 1456 they march into Athens; by 1526 they have already conquered central Hungary and thus have their foot in the door to the empire. Troops of Ottoman cavalry make repeated incursions into Carniola, Croatia, Bosnia, and Styria, and harry Poland from the south. There are fearful tales of murder and arson committed by these fiends in human form. They fall upon women like wild beasts, their hearts are cold and pitiless.

The Turks are believed to be Gog and Magog,[85] those mythical tribes of which it is written in the Apocalypse: "And when the thousand years are expired, Satan shall be loosed out of his prison, And shall go out to deceive the nations which are in the four quarters of the earth, Gog and Magog, to gather them together to battle: the number of whom is as the sand of the sea. And they went up on the breadth of the earth, and compassed the camp of the saints about, and the beloved city" (Revelation of St. John, 20:7–9). All the ancient ideas about the final battle found a vessel in this eschatological vision and flowed into it. The somber, eerie names of Gog and Magog resounded like the dull clang of a passing bell through an age that anxiously awaited its imminent doom. These ancient syllables may sound alien to our ears, but the myth is still remembered. Our own age too has its bogey: anti-Bolshevism has certainly assumed mythical dimensions.

Gog and Magog have encompassed the camp of the saints—that's how serious things have become. Open conflict is not far off; the enemy is seeking a favorable starting point for his attack by means of guile, intrigue, and treachery. While the Turks are preparing their assault, Satan, their ally and clandestine leader, is sending his invisible demons into the "beloved city." Their task is to find, through lies and deceit, accomplices and spies in the Christian ranks, since the "forces of good" cannot be overcome by honest means. This is the true background to the crime of witchcraft: those who make common cause with the Devil are traitors.

In a sermon delivered in August 1562,[86] Stuttgart's leading preacher made the issue clear: "The laws of God and of the empire declare sorcerers and witches liable to punishment and condemn them to death, not with the idea that these people are capable at their own whim and pleasure of confusing, confounding, and disordering elements and creatures, but because they deny God and the Christian faith, deliver themselves body and soul to the Devil, and are so possessed and engrossed of him, that, in the manner of their master, the Devil, they seek no other end but all manner of injury and discomfiture to men, believing, because they are deluded by the Devil, that they do but those things which God has ordained to be the Devil's work . . . On account of this infidel, wicked, reckless, diabolical volition, intention, and delusion, these unnatural creatures are justly to be regarded as the sworn enemies of God and of all men, and may be punished, as a traitor and arsonist may be punished, even though he has not in fact betrayed the city, nor set fire to it, but because he nevertheless has the determinate will and intention of same." It is the Devil who acts through these monsters and carries out his plans through those human beings who are devoted to him; the intentions of the witches themselves are irrelevant. "If . . . a demon performs some act with the aid of a witch, he does so as with an instrument," declares the *Hammer of Witches* (1484). The battle against witches was a battle against the Devil.

This does not explain the horrors of the epidemic persecution of witches, but it does make more comprehensible the delusions of those who were responsible for them. As far as our trial is concerned, the transcript of the interrogations provide evidence that behind the accused there stood invisible demons. The commission appointed by the council of state, and Doctor Wangereck in particular, were convinced that, in pursuing the Pappenheimer case, they were in their own way making a contribution to the defense against evil, to victory over devils, demons and Turks, to the battle against Gog and Magog.

THE NOCTURNAL RAINBOW

There were very detailed reports of the exploits of the "rampant, rabid, diabolical host of the crazily furious witches and sorcerers"—such was the German title of an influential work by Jean Bodin. It will be seen that the confessions of the Pappenheimers and those accused along with them conform entirely to these reports. This may be because the accused were familiar with the "learned fallacy" in all its details—we know from the vagrants themselves that they had heard in Ellingen and Wiesensteig what charges were laid against the witches who had been burned there. But it may also be a consequence of the methods used to induce the accused to talk. In the transcript of the interrogations there are innumerable examples of suggestive questioning. The erudite commissioners were aiming to elicit particular statements because they thought they knew the loathsome nature of witchcraft.

Such knowledge they derived for the most part from the *Hammer of Witches*, or *Malleus maleficarum*, a description of witchcraft and the means of combating it that has already been mentioned several times.[87] Two Dominicans who had been judges in the Inquisition, Heinrich Institoris and Jakob Sprenger, were largely responsible for this sorry product. Both were appointed by the pope to investigate heresy in Germany during the last quarter of the fifteenth century. It was at that time that the hunt for heretics clearly turned into a search for witches. The clerical gentlemen encountered a certain amount of opposition, however, to the measures they proposed. Either witches were not denounced, or else their conviction was thwarted. Enraged by this, the two Dominicans requested the pope to exert his authority, because it was in his name, after all, that they were carrying out their investigation. The pope obliged—in the form of the bull "Summis desiderantes" of 5 December 1484. In this solemn communication, Innocent VIII confirmed the appointment of his "beloved sons, Heinrich Institoris . . . and Jakob Sprenger . . . as inquisitors regarding the scandal of heresy." Characteristically, the only heresy mentioned in the bull as the object of their campaign was alleged witchcraft, which consisted in "the apostasy of many persons of both sexes from the Catholic faith, who have evil communications with devils" and who "would wreak all manner of injury with their spells."

At first the bull was of little assistance to the two German inquisitors. In the Tyrol, Institoris and his methods provoked so much popular anger that the bishop of Brixen suggested he should leave the country. To this ecclesiastical dignitary, the inquisitor seemed to have turned "quite childish—propter senium." This remark dates from 1486, and at that time even the Church seemed to classify the fear of witches as a senile persecution complex. Barely a year after this humiliating dismissal, Institoris, in no way discouraged, published his *Malleus maleficarum*. His fellow editor, Sprenger, in a so-called "apologia," a kind of preface, wrote "that this work was at once new and old, both brief and expansive. Old it is, certainly, in regard to its contents and its appearance. New, however, in regard to the compilation of its arts and the connection between them. Brief, because it summarizes a great many different authors, and yet long, because of the infinite abundance of its matter. Very little, indeed almost nothing," had been added by the authors. "So that it may not be considered our work, but the work of those from whose words it is almost entirely compiled."

This claim is both correct and false. It is correct that the authors of the *Hammer of Witches* were not the first to invent ideas about the doings of witches—those ideas were very ancient. Sprenger's modesty is false, however, in so far as *Malleus* imparted a new dimension, a legal dimension, to the superstitious fallacies concerning witches. This was because the book combined a summary of known theories with practical suggestions for combating witchcraft. Superstitious belief turned into a crime.

The book was composed in the scholastic style, which may well have made it much easier to use in practice; the division of the whole treatise into individual questions, to which answers were given, made it very easy to follow. These questions were mostly subdivided and clearly arranged in paragraphs which embodied a great variety of quotations backing up the answer given under that particular heading. This structure enabled the courts to consult the *Hammer of Witches* as a modern court consults legal authorities, and to pass judgment on all the detailed issues arising in a witch trial.

Division into three main sections also contributed to the clarity of the book's layout. The first part was designed to refute any existing doubts concerning the reality of the evil practice of witchcraft. The second part was concerned with the exploits of witches. The third and final part contained a "code of criminal law: on the manner of eradicating (witches), or at least punishing them by due process of law before the spiritual or secular courts." As far as its contents went, the book added very little that was new to the existing theories of scholasticism, except for the special suspicion it imputed to women and the extension of jurisdiction to the secular courts.

The *Hammer of Witches* proceeded from the assumption "that the proposition that there are witches, who are able to perform acts of sorcery with the help of demons and by virtue of a pact concluded with them, is truly Catholic and most true." Anyone who contumaciously maintained the opposite was a heretic. The essential feature of the crime consisted in a pact with the Devil, by which the witch truly and literally submitted to him, not only in her fancy or imagination, but with "body and soul." In a celebrated sermon delivered by David Meder during the early years of the seventeenth century, it was explained as follows:[88] The witches first of all "had to renounce the Holy Trinity, Christ, the Christian faith, and holy baptism, abjuring and forswearing them . . . and thus declaring themselves enemies of God. For as long as they persist in the Christian faith, the Devil cannot use them as instruments to do his will. . . . Second, they must also declare that they are opposed to all God's Saints and to all creatures that do benefit the children of God, and that they will harm and confound the same as best they can. Third, they must declare that they acknowledge the Devil as their god, lord, and king, whom they worship and obey in all things."

"As far as the explicit agreement with Satan is concerned," states a contemporary tract, "it should be said that the same is sometimes concluded in words alone, not in writing. Sometimes, however, if Satan wishes to have a more secure bond, he demands a sealed written contract of those who can write, especially before granting them any special request. Sometimes they must also sign their declaration with their own blood."

The pact might, however, be simply a tacit understanding, as a "pactum si non expressum, tamen tacitum et implicitum cum Daemone," as Maximilian's "Decree against Superstition" observed, with due "reference to eminent theologians and lawyers." Indeed, the view prevailed that even the invocation of the Devil was in a sense tantamount to proposing a pact, the acceptance of which need not be expressly stated. How easily, then, could a man become a partner of Satan, and hence his helpless instrument, simply through a thoughtless expletive! It is understandable that the duke imposed draconian penalties on cursing and blasphemy. The witch mark that the Devil placed on his creatures served as proof of the pact.[89] Here, too, as in all things, he aped the Creator, who, according to the prophet Ezekiel (9 : 4), and the Revelation of St. John (7 : 3), also conferred a sign on His chosen people. The witch received *stigma diabolicum* by being touched by the Devil with his finger at some point on her body, or by his grazing her skin. Generally the mark was found in some hidden place after the suspect has been stripped naked and shaved of all her body hair. If the jailor thrust a needle into the place where the mark was found, and the woman did not bleed, this was conclusive evidence of her guilt. Of course, a woman who was found to have no such mark was all the more suspicious. No less a person than Jean Bodin gave as the reason for this the fact that the Devil needed to mark only those of his accomplices of whose loyalty he could not be entirely sure. So the lack of a witch mark was no proof of a woman's innocence; on the contrary, it was evidence that she enjoyed a position of special trust in the kingdom of evil.

Apart from repudiating the Catholic faith and swearing an oath of loyalty, the Devil also required, as confirmation of the pact— according to the *Hammer of Witches*—that his human vassals "should indulge in obscene carnal intercourse with the incubi and succubi."[90] It is characteristic that this theme occupies most space in the "scholarly" discussions of the time. Thomas Aquinas's theory concerning sexual intercourse between demons and human beings was held to be so incontrovertible that Sprenger denounced as heretics all those who relegated it to the realm of fable. Sexual intercourse with the Devil was not a unique incident, so the theory ran, but was constantly repeated in a kind of illegitimate wedlock. "Any such person who has been incorporated into the kingdom of the Devil is forthwith allotted her own special devilish concubine or paramour, with whom she is joined in marriage and sexual congress."

The body, and in particular the sexual organ, of the demon lover should be imagined as ice-cold, since the ethereal creature lacked a warm circulatory system.

The witch remains allocated to her demonic paramour throughout her shameful career. He provides her with the ointment she needs for her spells. Apart from this, "her devil conveys her to covens and back again, fornicates with her, and also orders her to perform this or that evil act, in company with others who have similar instructions." He encourages her when she begins to fear the vigilance of the authorities, keeps her happy with occasional gifts of money and other small presents, and "gives her the grand promise, not only to take care of her, but also to free her from prison, supposing she should be arrested on account of her sorcery, on condition that she remain steadfast, confess nothing, or, if she has confessed, retract her confession. But the promise is a pack of lies, for God Himself assists the authorities in the performance of their duty, so that witches who have been arrested cannot be liberated by the Devil, although he consoles them with the promise to do this until the very moment when the fire is kindled beneath them."

We may be surprised that scholars and educated people in that age fully believed these and many other details concerning witches and witchcraft. It was not, after all the "benighted" Middle Ages, but the age of Galileo, Tycho Brahe, and Giordano Bruno. The golden dawn of the Renaissance and humanism lay more than three generations back in the past; Copernicus, Erasmus, Conrad Celtis, and Leonardo had lived, thought their thoughts, and triumphed, after their fashion. To quote only one example, how could a Jean Bodin, one of the great intellects of the time, not merely subscribe to this sorry superstition but even devote a learned tome to the subject?

The French lawyer and scholar himself gives the answer in the preface to his book.[91] By way of introduction he concedes that "this matter of witchcraft . . . nowadays seems so wondrously strange to everyone, and finds no credence at all with many people." The reason for this incredulity, in his view, lay in the modern age, in which many simply "deny the possibility of something that is impossible in nature." Those who called in question anything that "could not be treated or dealt with according to laws of physics or physical matter" were blinded by arrogance and "insufferable presumptuousness." Craving for knowledge led to blasphemy, "since any man that could explain the reason for all things would be the equal of God, who alone has knowledge of all things." Thinkers needed to be humble; their trust in reason led them to false conclusions. Among other examples, Bodin mentions "Aristotle's error concerning the rainbow." The Greek had maintained that "the rainbow did not occur by night." One could observe to what impossible deductions blind reason might lead us. For the reason given by the Greek for his proposition was a "manifest unreason" and total nonsense: if a rainbow could not appear by night, "then it must follow by the same reason, that all clouds were of the same color. Not to mention many thousands of wonders of Nature, of which the reason has not yet been discovered." Bodin does mention another, however, the "saltiness of the sea," which was to be attributed solely to the "providence or prevision of God," something Aristotle had not realized. And the latter's claim that the origin of "springs and wells" was to be traced to the humidity of the air was "even more senseless . . . considering the great and inexhaustible springs, fountains, and rivers that do ceaselessly flow, since all the air in the world, even

216

supposing it should putrify entirely, could not in a hundred years generate as much water as emerged in a single day from such water-logged localities." Given the fact of the Creation, to seek natural explanations was a false approach. Does not Nature on occasion contradict herself? For instance, the cold snow warms the earth and protects the crops from frost; and hoarfrost burns the vines like fire. All this should teach men to acknowledge the dullness of their own reason; they should not try to be cleverer than the sum of all human experience.

For the "mysteries of sorcerers and witches are not so secret that they have not been investigated and discovered throughout the world during the last three thousand years." The infallible law of God was expressly directed against witches and sorcerers, which was the best proof of their existence. Throughout the centuries, however, thousands of witches had confessed to their dreadful exploits and had "confirmed . . . these confessions by their deaths." The reality of witchcraft was as clear as day; only "know-alls and equivocators" would cast idle doubts on its existence, people "who balance everything on the point of a needle, and doubt whether the sun is bright, ice cold, or fire hot; and if you finally ask them whether they really know their own names, they may well reply that they will have to think about it. And yet they should know that it is no less a form of atheism to doubt the existence of sorcerers and witches than to doubt the existence of God, who has certified and assured us through His Word and Law that one is as true as the other." Doubt, against which Bodin is here inveighing, is the principle of the new age. It had been spreading since the fourteenth century, having originated in Italy in the studies of natural scientists, philosophers, and writers. Blind faith in authority is repudiated; it is becoming fashionable to analyze the world. It is no longer regarded as self-evident that the world is a disc. The ecclesiastical doctrine that the angels move the constellations of heaven is no longer undisputed. The monk wishes to understand what he believes; the merchant wants to make a profit without regard to traditional values; the craftsman wants to escape the tyranny of the guild; the peasant is no longer willing to acknowledge the old system of land tenure; the prince no longer regards himself as bound by feudal oaths. Doubt has worked its way like a woodworm into thousand-year-old beams, and is breeding fast. At first there was no more than a creaking in the ancient joints, but already the first sections of timber have crashed down, and worse is to be feared. Chaos looms: famine, in spite of good harvests, lawlessness, in spite of ancient laws.

There were many scholars like Bodin: sorcerer's apprentices who could not dismiss the spirit they had conjured up. Certainly they had accepted doubt as a principle of knowledge, but, on the other hand, they had not wanted so much doubt that it would give rise to disorder and insurrection in the world. Science was seized by fear of its own radicalism; panic-stricken, scholars sought to stop halfway. Certain areas of knowledge, above all "metaphysics," should be closed to doubt. Understandably, for anyone who dares to rip the ultimate veil asunder, will find himself gazing into an abyss. The *horror vacui*, fear of the void, caused those who knew to recoil in horror. They almost wished themselves back in the sanctuary of medieval faith, in the security of those who asked no questions.

Many of them may have felt that the scales had fallen from their eyes: this new principle will doom us all. Doubt is corrosion, corrosion is decay and death. Was it not doubt, carping criticism, that made Lucifer the adversary of God? Was it not the fruit of the tree of knowledge that robbed man of his paradise?

Bodin does not hesitate to claim that all those who doubt and analyze, "who dare, and almost seek deliberately, by means of printed books, to excuse and to redeem witches in all manner of means . . . are themselves led by Satan's halter, and are prompted by his inspiration to write such offensive books to further the continuation of his hellish kingdom." The Devil has "his own specially appointed people, who write and teach . . . that all that is said of witches is but fairytales and fancy, and that no trust may be put in it." Those who "purported to be wise men" are nothing but "godless, depraved folk." In short: we should not, for God's sake, call in question that which we do not understand, simply because we do not understand it. That would inevitably lead, in Bodin's view, to doubt concerning God.

Not all were affected by this intellectual reaction. Rational arguments against witch trials were put forward by contemporaries like Friedrich von Spee and Johann Weyer. But this crisis in sciences that were still in their infancy was widespread and affected many of the best minds. Given the mountains of learned nonsense published by the most eminent legal and theological authorities of their age, we can hardly hold the ducal commissioners' purblindness against them. They were not men given to doubt.

It soon transpired that all the Pappenheimers were creatures of the Devil. On 3 May 1600, Paulus, Michel, and Gumpprecht were taken one after the other into the vault of the Falcon Tower, and each of them was savagely racked until he confessed, as Anna had done previously, that he had "fallen into witchcraft."

After being hoisted up a number of times, Paulus made the following statement: "About ten years previously, in Niederaltach, when his wife had taught him to make the powder of children's hands and other things with which to injure people and cattle, he was fishing one evening, about six months later, in a brook near Irlbach in Dunckhen, the water belonging to the squire of Fraunberg. There he was approached by a beautiful woman in a tall hat, who asked him what he was doing, sat down beside him, and spoke all kinds of winsome words. Among other things, she asked him to go with her, or to do her shameful will in some other manner." This obscene suggestion, put to him so unexpectedly while he was fishing in some one else's water, struck the vagabond as suspicious from the outset. He demurred. But the fair stranger offered him more than simply her seductive body. She said "she would give him a better living, and money enough. And although he at first refused to go with her and to fornicate with her, having a wife of his own, he finally allowed himself to be persuaded, on account of a wealth of grand promises, and fornicated with her. Whereupon she revealed herself to be the Devil, Erlin by name, although he was already aware of that because of her cold nature. Then he had to promise that he would be her lover constantly."

Two weeks later, while he was "crossing a field alone," between Posching and Wischlburg, "the Devil had appeared to him once again, this time in the form of a man, and finely attired in green" —a description in which there are manifestly traces of the popular image of the Devil as a "wild huntsman." This time the Devil had "called himself Gresl, had spoken to him, and reminded him of what they had done together two weeks earlier." He then demanded that Paulus "should pledge himself body and soul, denounce and forswear God and all the saints in Heaven, as well as all men on earth, which, alas, he did. Thereupon, to seal the bond, the Devil scratched him on his left side, drawing blood, then dipped a pen, or some such thing, in the blood, put it into his left hand, and guided his hand until he had bound himself to the Devil. He also had to give the Devil his left hand and the following symbols: hair from his head, from his private parts, and from his armpit, all from his left side, the Devil tearing it out along with the skin. And also a piece of nail from his left big toe, and powder from children's hands. From this the Devil made an ointment, gave it to him in a little box, and told him that if he smeared it on people or on cattle, they would be disfigured or even die. At that time the Devil gave him about five gulden in all sorts of coins as earnest money." Such "earnest money" used to be given by a master to a newly engaged servant on the conclusion of their agreement.

The resemblance to Anna's description of her pact with the Devil is complete. Shortly after his interrogation, Paulus retracted his confesson, as she had done. And, as in her case, he earned himself nothing but a new session of torture, which led to a very similar account of the course of events.

With the constant assistance of Master Georg, Michel, who was interrogated immediately after his father, made the following confession: "When, about eight years ago, in Tettenwang by the shrine where they were then lodging, his mother had taught him in the kitchen how to make powder from children's hands, an unknown woman had also been present, who, his mother told him afterwards, was the Devil.

"After that, when he sprinkled the powder in the Devil's name in order to injure people or cattle, a man in a red coat and boots came up to him each time and said he was doing quite right, and should persist; he assumed it was the Devil.

"And about a year after his mother had taught him to make the powder, that is, about seven years ago, he was once going by night from Abensberg toward Tann, and the Devil approached him between these two villages in the form of a woman. She talked to him for a while, and asked him to fornicate with her, which he did. The Devil was called Bedin.

"Thereupon she asked him to be hers, and to follow her, to renounce God and all the saints and to believe only in the Devil, which was more than serving God. The Devil would reward him well, look after him, and never desert him. Which he promised, and offered the Devil his right hand. But the Devil would not take it, saying it didn't count; he wanted his left hand, which he gave, along with the following symbols: hair from his head, from his armpit, and his private parts—from the left side, in every case. Also a piece of nail from the big toe of his left foot, and powder of children's hands. Then the Devil scratched him on his left side, drawing blood, which he collected in a little box; took out a sheet of paper, which he placed on his knee; and put a pen into Michel's hand, so that he could sign the pact. But because he could not write, the Devil guided his hand until he had signed as the Devil desired. Then he wrapped up in the paper all the things that Michel had given him, and took them with him.

"In return he gave Michel money amounting to half a taler, together with a strange bluish ointment in a box, telling him that anyone he smeared with the ointment would be bound to fall sick."

During the evening hours of that same 3 May, Michel's elder brother made a statement to the following effect: About seven years earlier his mother had taught him to "make the baleful powder from children's hands." Three years later, in open country near Deckbetten, in the vicinity of Regensburg, "the evil spirit had appeared to him in the form of a woman," at a crossroads. The demon "called herself Masch," and "asked him to be her lover and to fornicate with her. And although he refused at first, she persuaded him in the end by promising him money and anything else he might desire. Then, placing his left hand in the Devil's hand, he abjured, forswore, and renounced Almighty God and all the saints in Heaven, together with all men on earth, promising to do them evil: as a sign of his determination he gave hair from his head, from his armpit, and from his private parts, together with a piece of nail from his big toe, all from the left side; and he also had to sign the pact with his own blood, which was taken from his left side. And although he could not write himself, the Devil guided his hand, until he signed as the Devil desired. In return the Devil gave him an ointment. Whenever he wished to roam abroad, he should smear the fork with it." He should also "anoint people with it, so that they would fall sick and die, and conjure up storms and other mischief."

The confessions are uniform, almost stereotyped in certain details, similar in others, surprisingly different in a few respects. At the beginning there is the trafficking with the magic powder, in some way an open invitation to the Devil, which he accepts either in a matter of days or only after a number of years have elapsed. The actual pact with the Devil is initiated in every case by the subject's succumbing to sexual seduction. Then follows the formal renunciation of God and commitment to the Devil, confirmed in every case by an identical ritual. It is possible that all this was dictated to the accused, which would explain the coincidences quite naturally. It is more probable that the Pappenheimers all had very concrete and detailed notions about how people lapsed into witchcraft. Certainly the subject was much discussed in the circles in which they moved; after all, ever since the 1580s there had repeatedly been talk of sensational witch trials on their "beat." It may have been the report of a single case that was reproduced in these confessions, with minor individual variations, as if it were personal experience.

The small farmer from Tettenwang and the tailor from Prunn were imprisoned in the Falcon Tower along with the vagrants, and were questioned a few days later on the subject of witchcraft. It is interesting to note that they described their seduction in slightly different terms. Ulrich Schölz, 8 May 1600: about five years earlier he had been standing in his field, at his wits' end on account of his poverty, not knowing "how he was to feed his children." While he was "plunged in such gloomy thoughts, the Evil One appeared to him by night, in the shape of a woman, and said to him: Why are you so afraid? I will teach you to earn your bread without all this labor and drudgery. Follow me! When he replied, may God preserve him, he sought no dealings with him, the Evil One departed from him." He had thus resisted the first temptation, claimed Ulrich Schölz. Relieved, "he lay down in a shed on his field, and began to sleep." Then the Devil appeared again "making a rustling noise like a game beast outside his shed," so that he awoke with a start. In his "former shape as a woman," the Devil himself entered the shed and demanded "that they fornicate together. And although he had not previously harbored any devilish or wicked thoughts, he forgot himself when he was given grand promises that the Devil would endow him with goods and money, and thus fornicated with the Devil, whose nature he felt to be very cold." The subsequent description given by the man from Tettenwang refers to the actual ritual of the pact, and it corresponds exactly to the statements made by the vagrants.

But the individual features of the narrative are plain enough. Although his land no longer feeds him, the farmer meets the Devil on his own plot of ground. He does not conclude the pact with him in broad daylight and in the open air, but by night in a shed. The image of the game beast embodied the peasant's fear of marauding game, which is first cursed, then consigned to the Devil, and finally transformed into the Devil himself. Another aspect of the villager's environment is expressed in the Devil's words, "Follow me": thus Jesus had spoken to Peter, and Ulrich

Schölz would have heard the phrase in many a sermon on Sundays. These personal details of his confession seem too subtle to have been suggested by the court.

That is equally true of the statement made by Georg Schmälzl, the little tailor from Prunn, on 16 May 1600. It opens with a remorseful preface: "Having been during his lifetime somewhat loose and reckless, having eaten, drunk, and gambled so that he had in some degree fallen into debt, and not knowing how he might see his way to pay his creditors, who were pressing him pretty hard, he had . . . from time to time thought, that if the Devil would give him money, then he would serve him." And, sure enough, the Devil had one day taken him at his word. What follows coincides almost exactly with the account given by Ulrich Schölz.

There seems, then, to have been a popular notion of such agreements with the Devil. In the Danube region of Lower Bavaria it ran more or less on the following lines: anyone who revealed his thoughts to the Devil was seduced by "promises" of money and by sexual intercourse. Then the Devil required his victim "to abjure God and all the saints, together with the human race," and to swear allegiance to him, the Devil, doing only evil henceforth. The bond had to be signed in blood, with the Devil guiding the hand of anyone who could not write. Hair, skin, and nails from his new vassal's left side were then concocted by the Devil into an ointment designed to inflict injury. This betrayal of Christianity was rewarded, like the betrayal by Judas, with a handful of coins.

CHAPTER · 6

*W*itches brewing a thunderstorm
(early sixteenth-century woodcut)

· The Mill

Today the highway from Tettenwang to Hexenagger still leads, as it always did, through the valley of the Schambach, which has barely changed since the Pappenheimers' time. A little stream, glittering black and silver, winds its way through lush meadows. Hazel, elder, hornbeam, a few poplars and elms grow on its bulging green banks. In early summer the tender green turf of the valley is illuminated by a swaying kaleidoscope of flowers: the glowing yellow of dandelion, hawkweed, lupins, buttercup, crowsfoot, and ranunculus, mingled with the bright reds and pinks of carnations, docks, clover, wild orchids, and valerian, as well as the blue of snapdragon, cornflower, and campanula, and the white of wild garlic, plantain, and pimpernel. Wild irises stand in tender blue and yolk-yellow groups by the water's edge; marsh violets, goat's beard, and flax sway in the breeze. The background is formed by mixed woods in shades of blue and green, covering the hills on both sides of the valley.

The Schambach winds its intricate way steadily down the valley in curves that sweep across the valley floor or thrust it close to the hills on either side. To this day its course takes it past a number of mills, whose wheels have long since ceased to turn and hence no longer disturb the sluggish calm of the brook, harnessing its casual passage to useful ends. Broken grindstones standing by the walls of the houses tell of earlier times. In front of one of these mills, tourists' cars are parked at weekends. From that point there is a particularly fine view of the castle of Hexenagger, which still stands, as it did four hundred years ago, at the top of a steep hill, ocher yellow, with pointed towers and crenellated walls. An inn that now occupies the old Leist mill profits from this romantic setting. One may sit there with a glass of wine, looking across the mottled green of the valley toward the castle, and thinking of the people who dwelled on this spot at the time of our story.

Even then there was a mill here, not large and built of stone like the walls that are still preserved, but a small, gray, wooden building. A field path ran by it, with stony ruts in the grass. Now and then, travelers passed by on foot, occasionally a peasant cart drawn by oxen creaked past, but rarely did anyone stop. The miller who pursued his trade here had little enough to do, for the farmers of Tettenwang used to drive their sacks of grain down to another mill in the valley. They boycotted the mill not by choice but on the orders of their landlord. The Muggenthalers had no share in the profits of this mill, on which they could look down from their fairytale castle. The owner was the convent of St. Anne in Riedenburg.

The convent miller had rented his business, then, from the nuns of Riedenburg, and it was to them, not to the lords of the nearby castle, that he owed his dues. The profit such a small mill produced was extremely modest; it was reckoned at twelve gulden annually per wheel,[92] more or less equivalent to the annual earnings of a servant-girl. As a rule, the miller did not have to pay for his lease in cash, but in kind. For he in turn was not paid in cash. The farmers allowed him the so-called "miller's peck," i.e. about 10 percent of the grist. The miller could also fatten pigs on the waste produced during milling. The lease was to be paid for, therefore, in grain and pork, insofar as the mill produced any profit at all.

The Muggenthalers, who had a mill of their own in the Schambach valley, secured their income very simply: they prohibited their tenants in Tettenwang from having their grain ground anywhere else. The convent mill was thus deprived of its obvious customers in the immediate neighborhood, and had to depend on farmers who were not "tied" in this way. The tenant farmers of the convent in Riedenburg, obliged for their part to drive their heavily laden carts up into the Schambach valley, generally did not care to face the laborious journey.

So most of the ox carts that rumbled along the stony ruts of the track from time to time passed the convent mill without stopping. We can imagine the miller standing by his fence and gazing after the carts with a sigh. The clatter of the slack millwheel must have sounded mocking; the riot of color in the meadow can have given him little pleasure; the view of the castle can hardly have stirred thoughts of romantic fairytales in his mind. Perhaps he was full of confidence when he first took up the lease and moved into this lovely valley with his wife and children. In the early summer of 1599, the time of this flashback, we have to visualize the convent miller as a haggard old man, barely more than sixty but prematurely aged and embittered by his hard life. There had been times in the convent mill when its inhabitants avoided starvation only by scratching the bran from the cracks in the pigsty that had long stood empty. Anna, the miller's old wife, gray and gaunt like her husband, had often foreseen an end to their lives such as she knew from her own parents. They had died in utter poverty. It was a wonder that she had succeeded in keeping two daughters alive of the eleven children she had borne. One of them, from her first marriage, had long since left home and was safe and well provided for as servant to a good master. But Agnes, the convent miller's daughter, was still living with her parents, a girl of marriageable age, buxom and comely. It was on her that the hopes of the miller and his wife rested. With the help of a stalwart husband she might yet manage to rise from penury and obscurity and achieve moderate prosperity and modest standing.

At that time the miller's trade was considered not quite respectable, though not exactly "dishonorable."[93] Like linen weavers, who, according to the peasants' wives who did the spinning, did not weave all the yarn delivered to them, millers were suspected of all sorts of dishonest practices. In a regulation from the sixteenth century we read that the "crimes that millers can commit in the course of their business . . . are so numerous that they can scarcely be counted." Special mention is made of customers being cheated by the mixing of good-quality grain with grain of an inferior grade, by the use of false weights and measures, by illegitimate increases in the charges for milling. No doubt such things happened—there are black sheep in every profession. But the true reason for this suspicion was to be found, no doubt, not so much in these proven irregularities as in general disappointment at the yield of the milling process. Several sacks of grain emerged as a single sack of flour—could that really be right? Even if a man stood there and watched, he still felt he had been cheated. Nothing could be proved against the miller, but gnawing doubts were expressed in conversation among the farmers. The men in the white aprons were decried and vilified, called worthless rogues and swindlers. As far as their standing was concerned, millers were relegated to that group of people that no one wished to have dealings with: tailors, weavers, gravediggers, barbers, musicians—and tramps.

The Pappenheimers went past the mill quite often. They were scowled at, because the miller did not regard them as being on the same social level as himself. Like all the inhabitants of Tettenwang, the convent miller and his wife knew our vagrants, knew about their friendship with Schölz, Augustin, and Jack the Glazier, and did not trust the "gypsies" any farther than they could see them. The dislike was mutual. Paulus and Anna envied the old miller and his wife, who were so much like themselves in years and appearance; they spoke of them, in all seriousness, as "wealthy." Obviously they knew nothing of each other, did not realize that one couple was just as badly off as the other. The entire "wealth" of the convent miller consisted in the fact that he had a roof over his head, although it was a roof of which he might be deprived when his lease ran out. Like the Pappenheimers, he was an outsider; but, unlike them, he had no friends among the inhabitants of the village. That, too, he probably resented: the fact that the vagrant had intimate friends, while he, who had his home there as a tradesman, was denied such friendship. All this was reason enough for there being no love lost between them.

On one of his rare visits to the village, the miller had encountered Paulus in front of Ulrich Schölz's house. The mutual hatred dammed up within them had suddenly found an outlet. It is not certain exactly what happened. Presumably some trivial pretext had given rise to an argument. The tramp, surrounded by his village friends, no doubt teased the outsider from the valley as he passed by and thus provoked a biting reply. Jokes turned into insults, and some expression or other must have stung the convent miller into action. The bitterness accumulated through years of neglect and contempt burst through. He had not yet sunk so low that he need be insulted by a tramp without defending himself. In a flash he had his sneering adversary by the collar, and the latter had seized the miller's shock of white hair. A moment later the two old men were wrestling in the dusty road like a couple of uncouth yokels, surrounded and egged on by the cottagers of Tettenwang, until at last someone who had kept a cool head—possibly it was Anna Pappenheimer—dragged the two elderly fighting cocks apart with a firm hand. They got to their feet, wiped the blood from their faces, brushed the dust from their jackets. Furious glances, derisive sneers. The miller bent down to pick up his hat, and went on his way, with pursed lips and narrowed eyes.

Fortunately, not all the villagers were so ill-disposed toward the miller's family. Some of the passersby making their way through the Schambach valley were not disinclined to stop at the convent mill. They might look over the fence and watch Agnes watering the flowers in the garden or scrubbing the washing in the brook. They might call out a jocular greeting or fall into conversation with her. A number of the young farmhands from Tettenwang certainly made their way up to Hexenagger more often than was strictly necessary. For even if the convent miller's daughter was poor, she seemed attractive to many; indeed, she was the object of jealous quarrels among the young men of the village.

An ardent admirer had once provoked a sensational incident. "With a naked weapon," a dagger, in his hand, he had burst into the convent mill, shouting furiously about Agnes's relations with another farm lad and calling her to account. The girl only just managed to escape her crazily jealous suitor, and did the only right thing: she sent him about his business and reported him to the authorities, who fined him eight taler for his violent behavior. We may imagine the glee with which this tale went the rounds in the village. It was not calculated, of course, to reduce the distrust with which the locals regarded the miller and his family.

THE COMMON CRY

The women of the village met regularly in a farm kitchen to spin, knit, and embroider—but above all to gossip. And sometimes the talk was of the convent mill, with vague allusions and sinister hints.

There were several reasons for this. For one thing, the miller's wife did not take part in these meetings, and people are more likely to speak ill of the absent than of those who are present. The mill was too far away, the walk to the village through the dark forest too arduous and dangerous for the old woman. She was not reckoned to be a member of the village community simply because she was so seldom seen there. And the fact that the mill had no function, as far as the village was concerned, because the peasants were not permitted to use it, had the subconscious effect of intensifying the contempt in which the miller's family was already held. There was a legitimate mill in the valley and a prohibited one, one that was familiar and one that was alien, a good one and a bad one.

In the opinion of many of the people of Tettenwang, there was something uncanny about the lonely convent mill. Villagers returning late from Hexenagger in the pallid moonlight used to make a detour round the wooden house by the stream, which seemed eerie and haunted, wreathed in mist. As they spun, the women would tell each other ghost stories about the mill. For instance, a journeyman miller had come to Tettenwang many years ago. He had learned the black arts down there in the south, and knew how to deal with the Devil. He had asked the convent for the lease of the mill, although he was bound to know that it could never make a profit. But very soon prosperity prevailed in the convent mill. That could only be due to magic. The stranger had made a pact with the Devil, who was obliged to bring him customers. In return, the miller had to let the Devil grind horse droppings and human skulls during the night. When it was used for this purpose, the mill made an intolerable clatter; anyone who heard it would cross himself and make off as fast as he could. But the miller kept his head. He let the Devil do as he wished, until one day some traveling folk with a dancing bear were passing by. He invited them in and entertained them to a meal. There was a good reason for his hospitality: it is well known that the Devil does not like bears; he is afraid of them, as he fears cats. And sure enough, scarcely was the bear under the roof of the mill than the Devil made himself scarce. But when he knocked on the window a few days later and asked anxiously whether the bear people with their monster had moved on, the miller pointed to a piece of fur that he had provided himself with for this purpose. His terrified business partner vanished and was never seen again.

According to another story, the convent mill changed its tenants so often because it was inhabited by witches in the form of cats. After a short time they used to attack the miller, drive him away, or kill him. Fortunately, a miller's lad came along one day who knew how to defend himself. At night, he used to draw round himself a chalk circle that protected him from the phantoms. When the cat-witches appeared snarling in front of him, he cut off one of their paws in a flash. From that time onward the beasts never appeared again.

But other specters were said still to haunt the mill. When the wheel was not working, eerie women used to sit on the sacks. In times of plague, two strange youngsters used to grind the plague each night, with the words: The death of the wealthy we grind, so that the poor their bread will find. Water-sprites climbed over the wheel into the mill, so that it had to be burned down from time to time, preferably every seven years, at Christmas.

232

Legends such as these grew up around every mill. Even if they were not actually believed, no one cared to exclude the possibility that such things happened. Some of the women spinning and gossiping claimed that the miller's wife was an "ogress." Others doubted it; it was possible, however, that the old woman was in league with the Devil. It was said of millers in general, that they knew a good deal about magic and spells.[94] Even the creaking of the mill wheel was likely to summon the Devil, if the right words were spoken. Mills were the seat of magic forces. If you wanted to scare someone like a runaway servant or a faithless lover, you had to obtain a garment the person in question had worn, lay a scrap of it in the pan of the mill, and race the mill wheel. In this way, the deserter, wherever he might be, would be plunged into fear and remorse, and would be irresistibly forced to return. If you wished to recover stolen money, you had to place three pfennig and three poppy heads in the mill pan. Mill water had healing properties. The patient merely had to buy a new pot without haggling about the price, rise before dawn on the next day, put on a clean shirt, go to the mill, and carry mill water home in his pot. If he had not spoken a word on the way, and had not been observed by anyone, he needed only wash himself all over with the magic water, and he would be cured. If such forces issued from a mill, then its inhabitants were capable of pretty well anything. What was more, the miller's wife was old and ugly. That was just how people imagined witches to be.

Some of the Tettenwang peasant women saw their suspicions confirmed when their adolescent sons fell madly in love with the miller's daughter, went out of their way to see her, and were mixed up in fights on her account. Either the "plump creature" who turned the lads' heads was herself in league with the Devil, or else her mother was casting such love spells, for motives that were sufficiently obvious. At any rate, the general infatuation of the young men of Tettenwang fitted very well into the image that people had formed of the miller's family. Deep in the villagers' minds, more of an intuition than a clear idea, was the ancient notion of the mill as a symbol of eroticism and the lusts of the flesh—and a mill to which they were forbidden access must be even more so. The roots of this idea are deep and unfathomable. Even in the language of the Greeks and Romans, the word for milling also means procreation. Many heroes are said to have been born in a mill, which is probably meant to suggest divine procreation. In legends and fairytales, the mill appears as a favorite locality for love affairs. In the Pappenheimer's time, when children asked where babies came from, they were told that they were pulled out from under a great stone in the mill-race. The last image demonstrates that the ancient myth of Mother Earth as a womb had been embodied in the idea of the mill. The fear of the bottomless maw, the primeval cavern, the womb of the Great Mother, which still persisted in the subconscious, found rudimentary expression in all the superstitions relating to the mill.

This is how it was that "the common cry"—the term used in those days for a prevalent rumor—spread throughout Tettenwang that the miller's whole family, or at any rate the old woman, was engaged in witchcraft. It would never have gone beyond this vague whispering campaign, had the Pappenheimers, Schölz, and Schmälzl not been arrested, convicted of witchcraft, and questioned under torture about their "cronies." They had all, of course, heard of the suspicions concerning the miller's family that circulated surreptitiously in the village, and when they were asked about other witches and sorcerers known to them, it was generally the miller's family that was first to be named. This measure of agreement led the commissioners to suppose that the accusations corresponded to the truth.

"The convent miller . . . and his wife," claimed Paulus during an interrogation on 9 June 1600, "have gone in for witchery these thirty years and more—they'll whistle you a fine tune, if you take them in. It's time the wealthy were picked on, otherwise it's only the poor that gets done." On 1 July, Anna Pappenheimer confirmed this: she "had often seen the convent miller from Tettenwang and his wife at witches' revels—but not the daughter. But she'd once seen the daughter going into her father's house with milk (which she'd stolen by sorcery from other people's cattle). It was Schölz that had once shown her how to do that. She was notorious in the neighborhood in any case, and had once been stopped from marrying on that account." Gumpprecht said, he had seen "the convent miller from Tettenwang, his wife, and daughter" at revels and meetings of witches; the miller was "a leader." He would stake his life that the fair Agnes had been present at the Devil's dances, "but he knew no other evil of her." Michel and Hänsel made statements much to the same effect. Ulrich Schölz also declared that the miller's family had a prominent place among the witches: "The convent miller was the . . . master of ceremonies, and the miller's wife was chief among the women." George Schmälzl, the little tailor from Prunn, even claimed to have been present "when the convent miller's wife had brewed up a storm in her house."

The court collected these incriminating statements, and no doubt also made inquiries about the denounced persons. It took a long time to decide on the arrest of the convent miller's family. Within the council there were conflicting views on whether accusations made by criminals, even if they tallied, represented sufficient grounds for the arrest of those accused. While these discussions were still going on, summer came around. In the Schambach valley the meadows burst into flower; the wheel of the convent mill clattered on—although still to little profitable purpose; fair Agnes entered into conversation with passing farm lads, while her parents went on hoping that their daughter would one day be better off than they were. The clouds that had begun to gather over this idyll were still a long way off.

WANGERECK LOSES AN ARGUMENT

There are no records of the discussions which took place at that time in the Munich council of state concerning criminal cases like that of the Pappenheimers. But the following reconstruction of the argument about the fate of the Tettenwang miller's family might be somewhere near the mark. My chief source is an anonymous manuscript from the 1620s, preserved in the Munich State Archives, which describes an argument analogous to our own case.[95] Apart from this, arguments about the issue of denunciation crop up in numerous expert reports commissioned by the Munich council of state following the trial of our vagrants.

Some time at the end of May or the beginning of June, when Doctor Wangereck, as the appointed commissioner in the Pappenheimer case, reported on the progress of the interrogations and the results so far, the convent miller was also mentioned. A number of denunciations had been laid against him and his family, all of them in similar terms. The miller's family must accordingly be regarded as witches and sorcerers. Knowing Wangereck, we may assume that he recommended their arrest.

There was opposition to this proposal, particularly among the young lawyers but also from the representatives of the aristocracy. No weight should be attached to the accusations of such evil individuals. They would assert all sorts of things, from envy, spite, or fear of torture. No credence could be given to such gossip.

To which the commissioner may have replied more or less on

these lines: only someone who had not studied witch trials and the relevant literature could speak like that. Given that witchcraft was not only the most heinous of all crimes but also the most secret and furtive, there was no way the authorities could learn of its existence other than through accomplices and cronies. It stood to reason that such informants could never be of good reputation. On the other hand, those monsters who occupied leading positions were precisely those who were so adept at camouflaging their activities that there was generally no evidence at all, apart from denunciations. For that reason it was always permissible, in the opinion of lawyers, to arrest and submit to torture any person who had been denounced and named by several associates. For although a single statement would not suffice, identical accusations by two or three witnesses must be considered adequate. Everyday experience showed that statements by several accomplices were hardly ever erroneous. Those who had been denounced in this way almost always confirmed the charges against them when they were examined under torture. The arrest of the convent miller from Tettenwang, his wife, and daughter was therefore to be recommended. Otherwise, no progress could be made in the case; for if *testes infames*, disreputable witnesses, were to be rejected, how could a judge obtain evidence from an honest and God-fearing person? A God-fearing person would not be in a position to give evidence about witches' revels.

The doubters were not silenced by this argument. One of them asked, for instance, whether Wangereck himself would have to be regarded as an evildoer if three of the accused were to denounce him? The penal code of Emperor Charles required the report of a crime in good faith as a condition of arrest. Such an offense had to be proved by two or three sound and credible witnesses speaking from their own true knowledge. In this context the word "witnesses" meant that the informer had to be put on oath—otherwise, he was not to be considered as a witness. Now every lawyer knew that the present trial had not yet even reached the stage of a judicial hearing, so that there could not yet be any properly sworn witnesses.[96] The case was so far only an inquiry; it was being officially investigated. But was there any reason why anyone should be arrested on the basis of unsworn and dubious accusations, which, moreover, had been elicited under duress? Could such a marked distinction be drawn between the official investigation and the due process of indictment? After all, it was now becoming a matter of everyday routine for the authorities to conduct inquiries into all manner of crimes and offenses, arresting persons who might or might not turn out to be guilty. It would be as well if they did not push matters too far, simply on the basis of information received. In the present case, the common features of the various statements were based on no more than the common cry in Tettenwang that the convent miller and his family were engaged in witchcraft. These were no more than rumors whispered in dark corners, and as such they proved nothing at all. If the wretches in the Falcon Tower repeated those rumors, that did not in any way alter the legal situation. It was a matter of grave concern, and legally indefensible, that the miller's family should be taken into custody and even tortured. All the circumstances must be more thoroughly investigated before the arrest, before irreparable damage was done to the miller's hitherto unblemished character. The inquisition was no more than an inquiry, and was not competent to establish irrevocable facts.

After all that has gone before, we may be surprised to hear such sentiments expressed in the Munich council of state at that time. To all appearances, the conduct of our case, with the perverse logic of its interrogation under torture, suggests all too strongly an unmitigated obscurantism on the part of those responsible. But this impression is misleading. Even twenty years later, when the epidemic of witch trials in Bavaria had reached its climax, we learn that there was a powerful minority in the council which opposed this lunacy. At that time a certain Dr. Dennich declared during a discussion on witchcraft in the city council of Ingolstadt that "he had been . . . with the chancellor in Munich the previous day. He (the chancellor) also thought very ill of these denunciations. If that were indeed so, then there would be others among the elector's councillors, particularly the younger gentlemen, who were likely to share his opinion." That was tantamount to saying that there should be no fresh arrests on the basis of accusations made by convicted witches. The source quoted is no doubt quite right in suggesting that the councillors in question simply had no desire to persecute and to burn witches. Not a few of them acknowledged openly that the witches' alleged exploits were not real crimes at all but diabolical nightmares.

The answer given by "prevailing opinion" to these objections was on lines laid down by the celebrated Bodin: anyone who spoke like that showed himself to be a protector of ogres and witches, and was probably directly or indirectly prompted by the Devil to trivialize the danger. No honest man, however, had to

237

enter into discussion with instruments of the Devil. If it were true that denunciations by convicted witches were legally inadmissible as evidence, then the prosecution of witches would have to be abandoned altogether. But that was a monstrous idea, since everyone knew that witchcraft was the most abominable of all imaginable crimes. To call its reality in question was blatant heresy, for the many thousands of convicted witches would provide eloquent testimony of the reality of their activities. Or would the doubters be so bold as to claim that the burning of these witches was unjustified? It could not be altogether denied, of course, that the monsters occasionally conspired maliciously to accuse a totally innocent person of complicity in their crimes. But in such cases "Almighty God" had invariably "revealed the innocence of such persons in a miraculous manner." One could rely on this, and would have to go on relying on it. We might have heard Wangereck putting his view more or less in these terms in the Munich council of state.

To put this view in context, we must know what the legal situation was. According to the principles governing trial procedure at the time, statements by an *infamis,* that is, any disreputable person, were not admissible.[97] The evidence of persons who had been convicted, or who were on the point of being convicted, carried no weight either. Only those who could vouch for the correctness of their statements could be witnesses. But these legal principles, like so many others, were not to apply to the offense of witchcraft. This was the doctrine of the *Hammer of Witches:* the witches' crime was so abominable that "in order to deal with it, the evidence of servants against their masters, and of disreputable persons against others, must be admissible." Quite apart from that, there was also argument among lawyers whether the criteria applied by the law to witnesses were to be observed at all in investigatory proceedings. The fiction was still maintained that only a criminal trial initiated by private prosecution could properly be regarded as such. The official investigation was simply the preparation of court proceedings, so that many authorities claimed that the strict legal requirements of a "regular" trial did not apply to these preliminary investigations. In spite of the arrest and the torture of the accused, the fiction was still maintained that their fate would not be decided until there was a public hearing in open court, that is, on the day of execution, when the judge pretended to give a judgment that had long since been prepared in the dossier: it was during this performance that "the staff was broken," i.e. the irrevocable sentence pronounced. The regulations quoted were to apply only to this pitiful remnant of what had once been a public hearing. They were, in fact, superfluous for this purpose, for they could no longer have any effect at that stage.

The opposition with which our commissioner had to cope in the council of state was not, then, as progressive as it might seem at first sight. Indeed, it was putting forward a conservative view by not closing its eyes to the fact that the fate of the accused had already been decided at the investigatory stage. Bearing this in mind, it was seeking for the accused the same protection he had enjoyed as a matter of course under the so-called accusatory procedure in force exclusively only a century or so earlier. What was being sought was only a formal extension of the old procedural guarantees; the substantive issue was their preservation.

This explains why the aristocratic representatives joined forces with the "young doctors of the law." The vote in the Munich council of state ended with a defeat for Johann Simon Wangereck and his friends, the group that revolved around the duke's secretary, Gewold. The commissioner was refused the council's consent to the arrest of the miller's family. He was to conduct even more searching inquiries, to mount a thorough investigation in order to verify whether there was any substance in the accusations. Arrest, however, was not justified. Wangereck was obliged to respect this decision. I imagine he did so with a sour expression and inner reservations, more determined than ever to involve the victims of these denunciations in the case.

LAW AND RELIGION

It is merely probable, by no means certain, that the aged councillor Fickler was present during the debate about the arrest of the miller and his family. He would no doubt have followed the pros and cons of the argument, weighing one against the other, taking sides. Perhaps he even rose himself to take part in the discussion. After all, he had had the chance to study witchcraft and its punishment during his years in Salzburg.

His vote, we may say straight away, would be cast for Wangereck and his friends. Nevertheless, he did not feel himself closely allied to this group. Like everyone else, he knew that the group's secret leader was the duke's secretary, Gewold, and that Gewold, an inveterate schemer and a man who had the duke's ear, had played some part in Fickler's demotion. If the old councillor took Wangereck's side in spite of this, it was because he regarded law and religion as indivisible. For this was the central issue in the debate: was human reason more to be trusted than Providence? Should a man follow his own understanding or the example of the Church?

Fickler was no fool. It must have been clear to him that the miller's family from Tettenwang might be innocent. But it was precisely the function of the investigatory commission to test that assumption. If the objection had been put to him that torture would force even the most innocent person to confess, and that the commission was therefore not equal to its task, the old councillor would probably have lost his temper. As far as he was concerned, this was exactly the objection that marked the heretic. With God's help, judicial torture would always reveal the truth. The Lord never permitted innocence to perish. Only someone with no religion in his heart, who measured the inquisition's methods with the human scale of reason, could conceive such a monstrous suspicion. Law without religion was incomprehensible and, indeed, ruthless.

The inquisitorial procedure in all its details had been conceived in the womb of the Holy Church; only later, barely a generation before Fickler's time, had it been adopted by secular governments.[98] Its blameless origins were to be found in the spiritual shepherd's concern for poor souls. When they visited their congregations, the black sheep must be segregated from the flock, washed clean, and led back into the community. In those days the identification of sinners depended on anonymous informers. The Church saw nothing evil in this, for the blemished soul was simply to be cleansed. The secret informer was, then, doing this soul a favor; he was in the same position as someone who fetches help for a sick man. In the early Middle Ages, punishment and penance imposed on the accused had always been kept within the confines of what was honorable and tolerable.

This did not change until another type of sinner came into prominence. Instead of dealing with individual lost sheep, many shepherds now found themselves faced with a refractory crowd of rebels, who had left the prescribed path not by chance or ineptitude but on purpose and in an organized fashion. It was not a matter of healing minor ailments in individual souls but of combating a pestilence. This came about for the first time during the crusade against the Albigensians in the South of France (1209–29). Pope Innocent III instructed his bishops to appoint special inquisitors, who would uphold order in the parishes, in keeping with tradition, but using more stringent methods and penalties. Innocent's successor to the throne of St. Peter, Gregory IX, already found it necessary to organize the Inquisition as a permanent authority (1232). Its officers were independent of the bishops, its powers were extended, and its activities restricted to fighting heresy. The Emperor Frederick II passed laws to protect the Inquisition and lent the pope his "secular arm" to punish those who were convicted.

From then on, the papal Inquisition acted as a kind of ecclesiastical fire brigade. Wherever the spark of rebellion alighted, inquisitors instantly appeared to smother the fire before it could catch hold. Confronted with the papal officers, every adult was obliged under oath to denounce heretics. At the same time, witnesses were guaranteed discretion. In contravention of Roman law, even persons of ill repute were admitted as witnesses: this, we may observe, was the tradition on which Wangereck's view was based. The next step was the summoning of the individual thus denounced; if necessary, he would be brought by force to face the Inquisition. The guilty person was required to confess to the inquisitor, to show remorse, and to recant his heresy. But what if he were to maintain his innocence? Such contumaciousness placed the inquisitor in a difficult position. His task was to wrest the sinful soul from the Devil's clutches, but he could not acquit the accused until the latter had confessed with due contrition. If the suspect refused to do this, then either he really was innocent, an assumption that ran counter to the evidence and prevailing prejudice, or else the Devil was trying to prevent the loss of a soul which belonged to him. In this case, the confession had to be obtained by force—not least in the interest of the sinner. Methods of torture used on slaves since ancient time suggested themselves as a means of coercion. Their employment secured the most gratifying results. Within a short time, therefore, torture became an essential component of inquisitorial procedure.

At first there was a certain amount of opposition to the new practice. In the early 1230s, the German inquisitor general, Konrad von Marburg, provoked revulsion and horror throughout the country by the brutality of his heresy hunts. The archbishop of Mainz felt constrained to address a letter of complaint to the pope: the inquisitor was forcing the most innocent of people to make untrue confessions by the use of torture. The accused were intimidated, and induced to denounce respectable people by the promise that their lives would be spared. Before Gregory IX could reply to this complaint, some stout-hearted knights took the law into their own hands. In 1233 they slew the dreaded torturer as he was traveling from Mainz to Paderborn. It ought perhaps to be mentioned, however, that the deed was prompted less by love of justice than by concern for their worldly goods. If Konrad von Marburg had not been seduced by greed into choosing his heretics mainly from the ranks of the affluent, so as to confiscate their possessions in the course of the trial—who knows whether he would have been so promptly dispatched by a gang of armored thugs?

Intimidation, blackmail, torture—these were the means employed by the Inquisition. Instead of repudiating them, the pope sanctioned them. In the bull, "Ad exstirpanda" (1252), Innocent IV officially permitted the use of torture—explicitly in order to extort confessions from heretics ("teneatur rector omnes haereticos . . . cogere . . . errores fateri"), and to force them to betray their accomplices ("accusare suos complices"). The end justifies the means. The Church believed that it was entitled to be cruel in its attempt to stamp out heresy. Was not the surgeon also cruel when he cauterized a festering wound?

A man like Fickler was very receptive to such justifications. The prosecution of such vermin as witches was no more nor less than an inquisition in the medieval canonical sense. The witches were also heretics, the most wicked heretics of all: not false believers but actual devotees of the Devil. Since their misdeeds were directed not only against the honor of God and the stability of the Church, but also against the whole of mankind, the state, and the community, it was perfectly in order for a secular commissioner to conduct the proceedings rather than an ecclesiastical inquisitor. Nevertheless, the crime was still a religious crime, so that religion could not simply be overlooked in assessing the procedure to be adopted.

This would be more or less Fickler's point of view. He was first and foremost a Catholic, and only then a lawyer. For centuries, the ecclesiastical authorities had considered denunciation and torture appropriate methods in their fight against evil. How could he have the audacity to make a stand against them by quoting legal principles or common sense? There were instances of such impropriety in his time, and it even found expression in the council of state debate, in which Fickler felt obliged to take sides. He no doubt sensed that people everywhere were beginning to defy the supreme authority—with no justification other than their failure to understand the significance of tradition. They placed their understanding above faith, which, in order to be valid, had to be absolute. The day was not too far distant, when lawyers, instead of accepting the law as God-given, would shape it according to their own understanding. Such aspirations were quite beyond Fickler. There were good reasons why he had his favorite son, Johann Christoph, instructed "in moribus et doctrina" by Munich Jesuits, as well as having him study civil and canon law in Ingolstadt and Bologna.

If the white-haired councillor and devotee of the midnight oil raised his hand to vote for Wangereck's proposal, then, he did not do so from stupidity or obscurantism. Fickler was fully aware of the dangers of an unjustified arrest and the ensuing interrogation and torture. But he was too unassuming to rate his misgivings higher than his respect for the Catholic Church, which had devised and perfected the procedure in question. In his time, however, such an attitude could no longer be considered a matter of course. The secure network of established authority had developed more and more gaps. Many were aspiring to a questionable liberty: a man who thought for himself also had to accept responsibility himself. He could no longer enjoy the untroubled slumber of the obedient servant.

Fickler had a Protestant brother living in Stuttgart. The councillor looked after the latter's two sons with touching solicitude, although only with the aim, admittedly, of leading them back into the fold of the Catholic Church. He succeeded, although one of his nephews had intended to become an evangelical pastor and had even made his debut as a preacher. Their father was incensed by his brother's missionary activities: it was unchristian and anything but brotherly to try to turn his own sons against him and to seduce them into denying their inherited faith. Such reproaches caused Fickler no qualms of conscience whatsoever. For him there was only one authority in questions of morality, as in questions of law: the true religion. Anything approved by that religion could not be false, as far as he was concerned.

THE HEARTH

One summer morning three horsemen were trotting along the road from Altmannstein to Hexenagger, through the green valley of the Schambach with its brilliant array of flowers. The clatter of the horses' hooves, echoing from the hills, was no doubt heard in

243

the convent mill. We may imagine the miller emerging from the doorway and gazing toward the group of riders, who soon appeared from beyond the leafy wood and reached the stretch of road that could be seen from the mill if one looked up the valley: three of the prefect's officers, well known by sight and by name to the miller. They approached with grave faces, reined in their horses in front of the mill, and dismounted, answering the old man's greeting curtly. They were here on official business, one of them probably explained, they had orders from the highest authorities to carry out certain investigations. He should not conceal anything or hold it back, but should give the authorities all the help he could in the inquiries they thought necessary and tell them everything he knew; then the business would soon be over, and no one any the worse.

We can well imagine what a commotion this unexpected visitation caused in the mill. The miller's wife, drawn to the scene by the halting of the hoof beats and by the sound of an official voice, probably swamped the officials with a flood of questions. What had happened, then, did they think the family would shelter evil folk, or conceal stolen property? They could search as long as they pleased. From her window the fair Agnes may have watched the group by the door, anxiously wondering whether she had once more been the innocent occasion of some affray or other breach of the rural peace.

Presumably the officers told the family plainly enough what had brought them here. Those ruffians, the Pappenheimers, had made certain statements in Munich that had to be checked. Amongst other things, they had reason to search the mill for suspicious objects. So they should stand back and make no last-minute attempt to clear anything away.

More or less on those lines. Two of the deputies will have pushed the baffled couple aside and entered the house, while the third stayed with the horses. Loud protestations of innocence, tearing of hair, gesticulations, finally a resigned shrug of the shoulders. So the Pappenheimers had slandered them; they might have guessed that that bunch of tramps would speak ill of them to the authorities as soon as they were arrested. The tramps hated their guts and had done nothing but spread wicked lies about them in the village. Surely those gentlemen in Munich, the councillors, wouldn't believe a word that rabble said?

The convent mill had only one living room on the ground floor, namely the kitchen. We can picture this as a large, rectangular room with a floor of hard-packed clay, a masonry hearth in the middle, but no chimney, walls blackened with soot, with two small windows fitted with pig's bladders on the side of the house farthest away from the road, and a low ceiling of rough beams and planks. A crude staircase, probably to the left of the doorway, led steeply up to the house's two bedrooms. The furniture was sparse enough: a wooden table beneath the windows, a few stools scattered round the room, a chest containing linen or drapes, hooks on the walls with various garments hanging on them, a little dresser to hold provisions, a few shelves, on which stood pots and other crockery. All that was quickly searched, without anything suspicious being discovered.

The space below the staircase was separated from the rest of the kitchen by a partition of wooden planks. One of the deputies opened the door to this closet, which had been ajar. By the light of a pine spill fetched from the fire he could make out a little stove. Why did she need a second hearth below the stairs? the miller's wife was asked. For warming milk, she replied. The cats kept on knocking over the pots on the main hearth, so her husband had built her a second hearth under the stairs and made a little closet she could shut to keep the cats out.

This explanation seemed very flimsy to the officers. No doubt meaningful glances were exchanged, and they nodded portentously. So there was something in the "common cry," and in the Pappenheimers' statements, after all.

What was so suspicious about the little kitchen under the stairs? We, who see in a stove nothing but an object of everyday use, may find this difficult to understand. At that time, however, the primeval mystery that surrounded the fireplace in all cultures was still a vivid reality.[99] The hearth was the focal point of life, and children learned at an early age that it was the abode of fire demons, of ancestral and familiar spirits. To feed them and appease them, dishes with milk, bread, or gruel were placed before the hearth in every farm kitchen. The food was eaten by cats, mice, or weasels, which were thought to be "beasts with souls." The cricket on the hearth must never be killed, otherwise the home would be threatened by some dire catastrophe. Beneath the hearth was the entrance to the subterranean realm of dwarves and goblins, and the crackling and popping of the fire was often the sign of their greeting to the occupants of the home. Poor souls often sat unseen by the hearth, warming themselves and crooning dolefully. Magic emanated from the hearth, which is not surprising in view of all this. If the hearth was not properly furbished, the first person who happened to pass by got a resounding box on the ear from the familiar spirit. Water taken from the hearth had magical properties; if sprinkled on the roof and walls at the right time, it protected the whole house from harm.

The hearth was inhabited, then, predominantly by benevolent spirits. But when witches were brewing their witches' ointment, they could use only evil spirits. So, wherever they could, they built a special witches' hearth that attracted the demons. This is exactly what the officers thought they had in front of them, when they looked into the closet. On the cold hearth there stood a pot containing a stiff paste, a congealed liquid, or something of the kind. That was no doubt witches' ointment. They put a sample into a container they had brought with them. They also looked closely at the firewood piled up beside the hearth. It consisted of dry hazel branches—that, too, was highly suspicious, for hazelwood was used for all kinds of magic. They pocketed a few of the twigs.

After that, they searched the bedrooms, which yielded no further results. They packed the tin containing the mysterious greasy substance, along with the confiscated firewood, in a leather pouch, walked out of the dim house into the sunny summer morning, without a word of explanation, mounted their horses, and rode off up the valley. We can see the convent miller's family standing at the fence with ashen faces, gazing anxiously after the unexpected visitors as far as the bend in the road. Would they return and drag the entire family off to jail?

No such thing happened. After a few weeks, the shock of that summer morning had almost been forgotten. The first peasants' carts with freshly harvested grain were already making their way past the mill. Agnes was once more prepared to banter with passersby, the miller's wife was once more entertaining all sorts of matrimonial fancies, her husband had hopes of a tolerable autumn, in view of the good harvest. The dark clouds over the mill had apparently passed by, without hurling down the threatened thunderbolt.

But only apparently. As early as June, Wangereck had already received a report from Altmannstein describing the search of the mill, and forwarding the evidence that had been found. The letter also contained a record of statements by some Tettenwang farmers and their wives, in which the miller's family were suspected of witchcraft. There were also notes of an interrogation of Anna's

246

daughter by her first marriage, who was employed as a maid by a Doctor Freymann in Randeck. In spite of this fresh evidence, the commissioner did not repeat his request for the arrest of the miller's family until the beginning of August. Obviously he did not wish to risk being voted down a second time. He waited until the informers had been executed without withdrawing their accusations. A witness, however disreputable, who maintained his accusation in the face of death, was, according to imperial statute, of such importance that not only arrest but the application of torture were justified. On this occasion, therefore, Wangereck could offer more grounds for the arrest than were strictly necessary. Without further discussion the council of state resolved that the convent miller of Tettenwang, his wife Anna, and his daughter Agnes were to be arrested forthwith and conveyed to the Falcon Tower. A few days later, the prisoners arrived in Munich.

THE CONVENT MILLER REFUSES TO TALK

This was not the end of Wangereck's frustration: the case was a tough one. In the first place, the old miller turned out to be unusually obstinate when the commissioner had him taken down into the vault of the Falcon Tower at the beginning of August. He had deliberately picked the old man as the first to be submitted to questioning under torture because he was, to all appearances, of a feeble constitution. In any case, Wangereck knew from experience that men can be made to talk more easily than women, who usually withstood the pain of torture longer. In the case of the convent miller, however, our commissioner was to encounter an exception.

The miller gave the necessary information about his antecedents, career, and personal circumstances readily enough, but he denied indignantly that he had ever dabbled in sorcery. As usual, Master Georg showed the obstinate prisoner the instruments of torture. In vain. Would he not admit that they were the object of rumors, that is, people of evil repute, and that, in particular, his wife was regarded as a witch? Well, yes, people had wicked tongues, but it was all lies. His wife was virtue itself, devout and God-fearing. They bound the stalwart prisoner's hands behind his back, pulled on the rope, left him writhing in midair, whimpering, with bones fit to crack. Once more—in vain. Wangereck ordered the procedure to be repeated. In vain. Stones were attached to the victim as he was hoisted up, a ten-pounder, a twenty-pounder,

247

a fifty-pounder. In vain. So they went on all morning, without being able to extort from the miller anything other than protestations of innocence, groans, and moans. Furious, Wangereck gave orders for the old man to be taken back to his cell.

Experience suggested that even the most hard-boiled and stubborn characters were liable to break down and confess if they were hoisted up once more with swollen and inflamed limbs a couple of hours after their first major session of torture. The initial onslaught of pain encountered a sound body and a powerfully determined will to survive. If the offender's limbs had been racked and he had been deprived of any hope of escaping in one piece, he would simply want to get the whole business over and done with as quickly as possible. Faced with death as a blessed relief, he would confess everything without more ado, provided he was not subjected again to the appalling agonies of torture. But here, too, our commissioner was to come across an exception to the rule, for when he had the pain-racked prisoner dragged into the vault again on the same afternoon, the man certainly screamed for mercy, but still insisted that neither he nor his wife, and certainly not his daughter, had ever had anything to do with sorcery.

Did it not perhaps occur to Wangereck, or to one or other of his colleagues, that the miller might after all be innocent? Perhaps. But they had already gone too far to take this possibility into account. Wangereck, in particular, was bound to fear that he would lose face with his colleagues on the council if, having insisted so vehemently on the arrest of the miller's family, he had to explain that his suspicions had proved groundless.

There was no let-up for the miller. Once more he was bound and hoisted off the floor, ever heavier stone weights pulling his joints apart. He went on maintaining his innocence, however. Wangereck instructed Master Georg to light the torch and to burn the intransigent victim's armpits if he still refused to speak. He did refuse and so had to endure this barbaric aggravation of the torture, after which the commissioner was forced to realize that nothing more could be extorted from the prisoner on this occasion. The maimed victim was taken back to his cell: let his physical and mental agony throughout the night prepare him for a resumption of the interrogation on the following morning. It was not the first time that Wangereck had needed more than a single day to loosen a suspect's tongue. This phenomenal power of resistance in the case of the frail old man was, in fact, some kind of confirmation that the suspicion of witchcraft was justified. It appeared that the Devil was giving the tortured man strength, and

248

paralyzing his tongue. But that did nothing to discourage the commissioner. He had elicited a confession in every case to date, and, so he may have thought, he would get the convent miller to talk as well.

But that was another mistake. When Master Georg opened the door of the prisoner's cell next morning to fetch the wretched man for renewed interrogation, he was too late. The convent miller was lying curled up on the straw, his eyes wide open, his mouth gaping. He could speak no more; he had fallen silent for ever. We see the ironmaster bending over him to close his eyes, making the sign of the cross, and we hear him calling for his wife. Then he strode quickly down into the vault to report this dreadful news to the councillors: the Devil had paid the convent miller a visit during the night and had broken his neck.

This was the customary explanation in such cases, and it seemed obvious to everyone. We need not imagine that Wangereck now reproached himself and wondered whether he had not applied the torture too severely. Quite the contrary. The miller's death was, as far as he was concerned, simply confirmation that the Devil was determined at all costs to prevent the miller from confessing. Obviously the confession he had thus foiled would have been an embarrassment to the Devil and harmful to the vile tribe of witches! So the miller had in fact been a sorcerer. It was, of course, a nuisance that the Devil had forestalled them and that they had not obtained the confession necessary for legal conviction. Wangereck's thoughts would have run more or less on these lines when he learned of the prisoner's death.

Wangereck, with Councillors von Roming and Vagh, probably left the gloomy vault and followed the ironmaster up the dank stone steps and the creaking wooden stair to the miller's cell in the tower, where the ironmaster's wife was keeping watch by the corpse. They examined the maimed body, which was now rigid and bereft of sensation. They looked at the pallid face, with the unnaturally gaping mouth, took hold of the chin and moved the head to and fro. This could be done without any great effort. The case was clear: the Devil had wrung the poor wretch's neck. The clerk was standing by the cell door, and Wangereck gave him instructions as to how the incident should be recorded. As far as he was concerned, the case was closed. Such things happened.

One of the few contemporary opponents of witch trials, the Jesuit father Friedrich von Spee (1591–1635), recounts an episode involving a similar case.[100] It shows how prevalent the view then was that anyone who died while in custody on suspicion of witchcraft had been killed by the Devil. "I was sitting at table with the local mayor, a good friend of mine. It so happened that there was also present a physician, who was uncommonly well versed in mathematics, as well as in his own science. For some reason or other, we fell into a protracted discussion with him concerning witches, and were altogether of the same opinion. During our conversation, the jailor entered the prison to take the prisoners their midday meal. Suddenly he burst into the room and reported to the mayor that one of the prisoners, who had been arrested on suspicion of sorcery, had died during the night, and that he had in fact been strangled by the Devil. The doctor and I looked at each other, but the mayor shook his head angrily and said, 'What crazy notions folk have! The poor wretch has been so cruelly racked and flogged during the last few days that people were quite horrified. Yesterday he was lying utterly spent and worn out in his cell, half-dead already. Nothing is more natural than that he should die of his fearful sufferings, and nothing is more credible. And yet nobody will believe it, nobody will say so; they will all declare that he was strangled by the Devil, and spread it abroad as though it were a pronouncement of the Delphic oracle. Odd! How many people have died in jails throughout this entire German Empire of ours, and yet not one of them perished of torture, or the squalor of our prisons. Whoever heard of such a thing? They were all fetched by the Devil, he broke the neck of every last one. And how is it proved? Who was present? Who saw it happen? The hangman says so. He, of course, just happens to be the one man who doesn't wish it to be said of him that he went too far in applying the torture. He is a dishonorable and in most cases an evil man. He is the only one who can give evidence because he is the only one to deal with the corpse and to examine it. The entire belief is based on the evidence of this one man. And no matter how many questions you ask, you will get nothing in reply but repetitions of the hangman's report as the sole and ultimate proof. And yet it is truly remarkable that you will scarcely find in any other matter anyone who has such authority that there is no room whatsoever for doubt. Only the hangman possesses such exclusive authority in this important matter that there is no question of doubt, and everything he says must be regarded as absolute truth, as if Jupiter himself had spoken.' Since this was very much to my own way of thinking, and as I would very much have liked to pursue the matter, I turned to the mayor and said, 'In order to learn more of these matters that we have been discussing here in such an amicable fashion, I would suggest that we send witnesses from among our company, who will see for themselves how matters stand and report the indubitable truth to us. And if the hangman is at hand, so that the corpse may be examined straight away, then let them go along with him and inspect it most carefully. In this way shall we discover with more certainty how matters stand.' This suggestion pleased the mayor so much that he expressed the wish to participate in the excursion. They went off, then, and returned after a short time with the explanation: 'It is indeed so. The Devil has broken his neck; it is quite shattered, loose and flaccid, so that his head lolls from side to side. His other limbs are unharmed and rigid. The hangman showed us all this, and we were standing so close by that he could not have cheated us in any way.' The mayor said, 'That's what I saw with my own eyes; I am myself a witness that this opinion is not based simply on the hangman's report.' All the others spoke to the same effect, and since all doubts had now been removed, everyone addressed himself once more to his lunch. I held back for a moment, took a sip from my glass, then asked, 'Sharing a glass of wine with friends, as I am, may I speak rather more frankly?' 'By all means,' replied the mayor, and I went on, 'If we must draw the conclusions that we have just drawn, then I very much fear that our parents, whom we thought had died honorably in their beds, also had their necks broken by an evil spirit. Is it not the case that, while every human corpse is cold and rigid, the head is slack and can move in all directions? Has none of us ever had to deal with a corpse, then? Have we not watched others handling a corpse, dressing it, and laying it in a coffin, and yet not observed something as obvious as that? Capital! What a brilliant and convincing proof that his neck was broken. If that hangman has regularly availed himself of this proof, as others have done all over the country (as we may assume, indeed I am convinced of it), and if simple-minded confessors believe it—then how many individuals, I would like to know, have been, in all innocence, exposed to public disgrace over the last few years.' With these words, I rose and left the company. I subsequently heard that the corpse had been unceremoniously buried under the gallows a few days later."

GREAT DISTRESS

It looked as if Wangereck would have his work cut out with the miller's wife as well. When she was led into the dank vault early on the morning of 22 August 1600 and was enjoined by the iron-master to show respect to the noble gentlemen sitting on the bench, she burst out sobbing and wailing. Amidst her tears she stammered out that it was a downright disgrace that "the guilty were let off scot-free, while the innocent were called to account." In reply to the question, "How had she come to be involved in witchcraft," she swore that she had been unjustly suspected. The Pappenheimers had denounced her from pure spite and malice, because "she had not wanted to give her daughter to their son." And the special hearth? That had been built in the closet only on account of the cats. And the ointment that had been found in her house? She knew nothing of any ointment, other than what she used to rub on her fingers after heavy manual work.

Wangereck realized that he would make no headway like this, and he had the old woman bound and hoisted off the floor. After she had withstood the procedure no less than five times, howling in agony, she groaned that "she would confess, if only she knew what she should say that would not imperil her soul." Hoisted up once more, she suddenly cried, yes, yes, she was a witch. And: hunger had forced her to consort with the Evil One, for the poor suffered great distress. This last sentence she repeated three times, in precisely the same words.

After that, she "confessed." About three years previously, when there had been neither money nor bread in the house, the Devil had met her in the Schambach valley, in the guise of a farmer. He offered her "money enough," if she would be his, but was given the answer, "If I have suffered distress so long, then I can suffer still." The next day, however, the unsuccessful suitor appeared before her once more and repeated his offer, giving her "six or seven half batzen," even although she was reluctant to take them. Thereupon she lay down with him in the grass and fornicated, the Devil's "nature not being like her husband's, but cold." Following this disgraceful act, she surrendered to the Devil body and soul, receiving from him a ring as confirmation of their pact. Eight days later she traveled abroad for the first time. For this purpose the Devil brought her a pitchfork and gave her an ointment, telling her how she must sit and teaching her how to lubricate the fork properly, and what words to speak: "Now I fly hence in the Devil's name." From then on, she flew on such expeditions frequently, especially on visits to wine and mead cellars in the neighborhood, so as to indulge herself. "Some ten pounds of eggs and lard" had also fallen into her hands. She stole milk from cows in byres belonging to various farmers in Tettenwang, and once, by mistake, milked a cow to death. Moreover, she smeared both men and beasts with the diabolical ointment, "especially the wealthy," whereupon they fell ill or died. "During the time of her sorcery" she also took part in witches' revels on three occasions: "near Mering, below Ingolstadt; near Dolling; and near Tettenwang, on the Stony Hump."

To begin with, the commissioner refrained from asking the woman for details. He now knew he could extract any statement he wanted from the miller's wife. There was time enough to get the details. He was more concerned now with obtaining incriminating evidence against her husband and daughter.

But this the old woman was not prepared by any means to offer. She did not do so during this first interrogation or during the next questioning, which began on 14 September and lasted for several days. Such an incriminating statement was apparently so important to Wangereck that he would not arrange a further interrogation of the daughter until he had it. He knew very well that torture would sooner or later overcome the resistance of the miller's wife. When the two days of the initial hearing did not achieve this result satisfactorily, he wore the old woman down by severe torture on three successive days in the middle of September. Then he introduced a respite of two days, during which the tormented woman could reflect, but not recover. On 19 September he had her brought before him once more. When her limbs were racked again, the woman fell into a state which the notes of the interrogation actually describe as "despair." "At this point," the record states, "when she refused to speak out and tell the truth, she was reminded that she must turn to God, otherwise she could not be saved but would be bound to go to the Devil." This exhortation was reinforced by a hefty tug on the rope. Then the miller's wife replied, "They should only desist, she would gladly be the Devil's prey, for she well knew that she must be his, since he had given her his spirit to eat in something like a dough, and he had come to her when she was going up Stag's Heath. And in any case, she couldn't tell the right truth, the Devil wouldn't suffer it, and had given her a magic potion, as agreed, to prevent her speaking." The commissioners then urged the half-crazed woman not to blame her obstinacy on the Devil but to think of the holy, bitter sufferings of our dear Lord Jesus Christ, and see that it was not in vain, as far as she was concerned.—That was all of no avail, said the woman. "The Devil was in her very heart and would not be so easily removed from her."

The convent miller's wife admitted her exploits down to the

last detail; she offered various versions of the pact she had concluded with the Devil, declared whose cattle she had slain with her ointment or whom she had deprived of health and life. She revealed how milk could be stolen from cows—with a rope that must be pierced at one end with a nail made of hazelwood. "And when she had wanted to take milk from the cows in a byre, she had . . . named the place and said the words: Run, oh milk, in the Devil's name. As soon as she drew out the nail—also in the Devil's name—the milk had run out until there was none left in the cows, which she would know because it turned reddish." The old woman also told how and where she had killed unbaptized infants, and had secretly dug their bodies up after they had been buried. She revealed the name of her demon lover ("he was called Wolfl," Little Wolf) and accused herself of defiling consecrated wafers in the most obscene manner. She did, however, constantly deny ever having dabbled in love potions, and suchlike— evidently she thought the question was aimed at her beautiful daughter. On the other hand, she did admit turning herself into various animals, and pecking the seed from fields belonging to a number of farmers, whom she named. She even disclosed to the commissioners the method used to summon up hoar-frost and thunderstorms. "If she desired to concoct a weather spell, the Devil would give her certain ingredients or substances, but she did not know exactly what; then she would take ointments, and powder from infants, item toad's eyes that she gouged out, and adders' tails that she chopped off; she would put it all together in a pot, add water, set it on a fire made of hazelwood, let it boil a quarter or half an hour, stirring it with a child's hand or a rod of hazelwood until it thickened to a paste. The ingredients she boiled at home in her house, in the special little kitchen on the hearth made for that purpose. On each occasion she cooked about a half-measure, or at most three half-cans full. She prepared the little hearth for the purpose, because she feared it might be knocked over on the big hearth. . . . And, then, when she wanted to brew up a storm, she took about half a salt-cellar full of the substance, put it into an earthenware pot, and carried it out into a field, placing it on a stone, or something, and saying: Look, Devil, make a tempest from this. At once the substance began to bubble, seethe, and hiss, rising up into the air in a cloud, causing thunder and lightning . . ."

All this and more the miller's wife admitted, but she refused to reveal the names of other witches, and certainly would not admit that her husband and her daughter had also engaged in witchcraft. The torture did not achieve its aim until 22 September.

To begin with, the record reports, she would name none of her "accomplices." She had agreed with the other witches that she would betray none of them. Then, as the torture became more than she could stand, she began hesitantly by naming three other women, who had all already been executed for witchcraft. It was not until the commissioners refused to be satisfied with this that she named a number of individuals from among the Pappenheimers' acquaintances as her accomplices.

Then, at last, her resistance broke down. Yes, her husband and her daughter had also been present at the witches' revels. Her husband had accompanied her frequently on her expeditions to various cellars. And Agnes had become involved in witchcraft when she was no more than two years old. She had never been baptized, in fact. When she had given birth to Agnes twenty years ago, "the woman they called Häpflmair in Tettenwang" had also been delivered of a daughter. The midwife at that time, who was a witch too, exchanged the children and took Häpflmair's child to be baptized instead of the child born to the miller's wife, so that the former "had been baptized twice, and the other not at all." When Agnes was two years old and was "lying with her in bed," she "promised the child to the Evil One, and sacrificed her to him." The girl accompanied her mother to witches' dances at the age of "ten or twelve," and was "assigned to a lover" there. That was the terrible thing about the process of torture: it deformed the personality and robbed the individual of his dignity. This is the only way in which this statement can be understood. To say of one's own child at that time that she had not been baptized was to place her outside the community. To say that she had been contracted to the Devil at a time that she herself could not remember, was tantamount, in the given situation, to condemning her to the stake. No doubt the old woman was adrift in an ocean of agony and yearning for death when she complied with her tormentors' demands. It was all the same to her, nothing mattered any more.

REPORT TO THE COUNCIL

Even before he first interrogated the miller's wife, Wangereck had tried his luck with her daughter, Agnes, on 11 August, to be precise. He then concentrated all his efforts on interrogating the mother, having come up against the same determined resistance he had encountered with the young woman's father. Right at the beginning of the interrogation Agnes declared: Although people, and the Pappenheimers in particular, claimed that her parents were ogres, that was unjust. And, underestimating the commissioner's abilities, she added confidently, "It would never be shown to be true of her, either."

Nevertheless, Wangereck first of all attempted a more amicable approach. Who had first led her into witchcraft? he inquired. Nobody, was the curt answer, for she had nothing to do with witchcraft. It was no good her denying it, they barked at her; the witches' hearth in the kitchen of her parents' house revealed the truth. We hear the girl laughing. The witches' hearth? "On the little hearth in the side-kitchen they had heated the milk for making cheese." That was all. She'd laugh on the other side of her face, answered Wangereck, and had the girl bound. Suddenly she was afraid and began to tremble. It had only just become clear to her that the instruments of torture hanging on the walls were intended for her. Bravely she repeated that she was entirely innocent.

Wangereck had been put on his guard by the old miller's death. The Devil would try once again to prevent a statement being made. To drive him off, he first made the sign of the cross over the girl and spoke "some Latin psalms or verses." The name of Jesus occurred a number of times, whereupon the trembling girl said "she did not care" for the Jesus that Wangereck spoke of "but wanted the Jesus that had created her, and died for her on the holy cross." After these words she fell silent for the remainder of the morning. It was no good Master Georg hoisting her up to the ceiling again and again, "once without weights, and ten times with a fifty-pound stone." The record notes baldly that "nothing could be gotten out of her except that she repeatedly protested her innocence." And so it went on, until noon, when the torture and the questioning had to be discontinued. The reason for this was a superstition that is very old, but nowadays forgotten: that midday, even more than midnight, was a haunted, eerie time.[101] Agnes was taken back to her cell, since Wangereck feared that the prisoner might be prematurely rendered incapable of making a statement if he protracted the torture or increased its severity. For this reason he tried another method during the afternoon.

This time, he and his companions sat down at the table in the ironmaster's living quarters. When Agnes was brought from her cell, she was not led down into the gloomy vault with its instruments of terror but taken into the bright sunlight that flooded the jailor's room. There the young woman stood, on legs that barely supported her, with downcast eyes and her arms folded on her chest. Before she was questioned she had been shaved of all her hair and was attired in nothing but a coarse linen shift. It was humiliating for her to be thus stared at, bald and scantily clad, by the noble gentlemen. Wangereck addressed her in the manner of a preacher, spoke of the goodness of God and the sufferings of His Son, mentioned the parable of the lost sheep, and fiercely lashed the mortal sin of those who, in their wickedness and obstinacy, ungratefully rejected God's grace. After this pious introduction, he reminded the girl of the terrors of the torture chamber and of what she had endured that morning. That was nothing but a foretaste of the sufferings that awaited her if she did not come to her senses and admit without further ado that she had been in league with the Devil and had perpetrated all manner of sorcery.

She replied in a feeble and toneless voice. She had nothing to admit, for she was innocent of the charges brought against her. Were God to make a mirror of her heart for no more than half an hour, the gentlemen would see nothing in it but her innocence. Anyone who accused her of sorcery was doing her a great wrong. But since it had come to the point where they had racked her limbs, she would glady forgive her detractors and return to them a fairer measure than they had granted her.

Wangereck broke off the interrogation at that point. Agnes was to be spared any further questioning for more than two months. Instead, her mother was forced to make more and more comprehensive and detailed statements, and finally compelled to incriminate her daughter. It was by no means our commissioner's usual practice to discontinue the questioning of a suspect after a single attempt. Why did he do so in the case of the miller's daughter?

Possibly he really had doubts about her guilt. He was bound to have, one might think. But we proceed from the premise that witchcraft is not a real crime. For Wangereck there was no question that it was. From his point of view, the evidence against the young woman was substantial enough to justify her arrest. It is extremely unlikely that he now took a different view. In the case of the mother, who was incriminated by precisely the same evidence, he clearly had no doubts about her guilt. Her initial protestations of innocence had done nothing whatsoever to induce the commissioner to use torture more sparingly.

There was, however, a very obvious difference between the two cases. The court succeeded in breaking the resistance of the miller's wife by the use of torture at the very first interrogation. On the other hand, Agnes, like her father before her, continued to protest her innocence stubbornly. In fact, her behavior faced Wangereck with a legal problem. According to the principles of trial procedure, an accused who had been submitted once to examination under torture and had not confessed his guilt could not be tortured again on grounds of the same suspicion. The evidence which justified torture was, as it were, expended after the first interrogation and could not be cited again to warrant a repetition of torture. There had to be fresh grounds for suspicion.

This was the principle. Knowing Wangereck, we can imagine that he was in a position to interpret legal regulations of that sort in such a way that they provided no obstacle. The *Hammer of Witches* advised judges confronted with a suspect who obstinately denied the charges simply to prolong the initial interrogation until a confession was elicited. Of course, the resumption of torture on the second or third day could not be termed a repetition—"since repetition is not permitted," as the author quite rightly remarks—but would have to be called a "continuation." In his book on witch trials, the Munich Jesuit Paul Laymann (1575–1635) suggested a more elegant interpretation: a repetition of the examination under torture was always possible on the grounds that "the judge had not pursued the first application of torture to its conclusion, either because the accused had fallen ill or because the judge had realized that he meant to persist in his contumacious attitude, and would not confess."[102]

Wangereck may have had misgivings about resorting to such legal tricks. We would be surprised if he had, however. More probably he thought it expedient to take some account of opposition in the council of state. One of the commissioner's prisoners in the Falcon Tower had already died without making a confession. As the episode quoted by Friedrich von Spee shows, not all of Wangereck's contemporaries were prepared to blame all such deaths on the Devil. That is why Wangereck may have thought it appropriate to cover himself in the girl's case. He did this in two ways. First of all, he wore down the mother through protracted interrogation until she incriminated her daughter. With this trump card in his hand, he brought the case up for discussion at the next meeting of the council.

In his brief address to the assembled councillors, Wangereck used as an aide-mémoire a slip of paper which has survived over the centuries, so that we can reproduce his argument fairly exactly. The miller's daughter had certainly maintained her protestations of innocence throughout a session of severe torture, reported Wangereck, but in the given circumstances no credence could be given to her claims. There was too much evidence against the miller's family. The gentlemen of the council were aware that there had been statements made by numerous persons, all of which tallied. Then there was the "common cry" that seemed all the more plausible in that the daughter of the miller's wife, who was in service with Doctor Freyman, had little good to say of her parents. Third, the court had in its possession a strange ointment, which had been kept in the suspects' home. Even more weight must be attached to another discovery that had been made in the mill: a strange hearth with hazelwood beside it, which was known to be much prized by sorcerers and was used by them to charm snakes. Fifth, the miller, who had been abducted from the court's jurisdiction by the Devil, had shed no tears under torture, which, as was also well known, was a characteristic of witches. Finally, it should be borne in mind that the Pappenheimers had stood by their accusation right up to the time of their death. As far as the daughter and her denials were concerned, there was, in addition to all these reasons, the mother's plausible statement that she had surrendered the child to the Devil eighteen years before, and had later taken her to witches' revels. In order to bring the case to a conclusion, it was essential to submit the miller's daughter Agnes to renewed and stringent examination under torture.

The majority of the council of state shared this opinion. To cover himself, Wangereck insisted on being given a written confirmation, a kind of memorandum: "Dr. Wangereck having duly submitted his report," the council "had resolved that the miller's daughter should be further examined under torture, at the commissioners' discretion."

AN UNREGENERATE CHILD

This resolution of the council was passed on 16 October 1600, a Monday. Early in the morning of the following Friday, Agnes was brought down into the torture chamber in the Falcon Tower for the second time. Councillors Wangereck, Pronner, and Hainmüller, and Steinwandner the clerk, were already sitting there. Wangereck greeted Agnes with the declaration that the council was convinced of her guilt, on the basis of the available evidence. She should not make things difficult for him and for herself, and should finally realize that all her denials were pointless. God in

His goodness would certainly have mercy on her, were she only to unburden her conscience.

To which she replied: "Although they spoke to her a great deal about her soul's salvation, she was not a witch." The commissioner now played his first trump card. Did she wish to suffer the same fate as her father, who had gone to Hell, unrepentant and unshriven? At this time Agnes still had no idea that the convent miller had perished in prison. Wangereck was deliberately trying to shock her: when she did not properly understand the meaning of these words, he informed her in a matter-of-fact manner that "the Evil One had broken her father's neck." The girl was stunned. She did not understand, she said, more to herself than to the commissioners. After all, her father had been "but a young fellow."

The blow hit the mark, but Agnes was able to absorb punishment. When Wangereck again asked her about witchcraft and wanted to know "how she had been seduced into it," she said that all she had done wrong was to be accused by the Pappenheimers. The commissioner: If she did not give up her stubborn ways, they would have to torture her again. The girl: If it must be so, then so be it in the name of the Lord. Jesus Christ had also been tortured.

Then her hands were bound behind her back and fastened to the rope that ran over a pulley fastened to the ceiling. Master Georg pulled on the rope, and the girl was left dangling in midair, racked by pain. They let her hang there whimpering for a while. When she was once more standing on the floor, supported by Master Georg, Wangereck thought the moment had come to play his second trump card. All these denials were quite pointless, he said, for her mother had already confessed anyway and had also revealed to the court that Agnes had been promised to the Devil while still a child and had been a witch since she was twelve years old.

The miller's wife had said that? We can imagine the girl staring aghast at the commissioner. Then she collapsed. The announcement that her own mother had denounced her as a witch had more effect than any torture: Agnes completely lost control of herself. She was shaken by a paroxysm of weeping and could only answer the councillor's insistent questions between convulsive sobs. If her mother said she was a witch, "then she might just as well be one." Who had taught her witchcraft? "I'd as well say, my mother. I'll just have to put up with being a witch . . . Oh, dear mother, go on, make us suffer, both of us!"

Where had she first met the Devil? the commissioner wanted to know. "Thereupon she did loudly sigh," the record states, "and replied, she had never seen a devil in all her born days." Master Georg was then instructed to renew the torture. She had "repented and suffered for all her sins," cried the woman in her agony. And when she was once more asked about the devil, she said resignedly she "had seen him at home."

"In what form did he come to you?"

"I cannot say, I swear; it was at night."

"What did he say, and what did he desire of you?"

"He desired my body. I was to yield it to him. And then I said I would do it."

"What did he give you in return?"

"Nothing. And I had to become a witch."

"In what form did he come to you, and when?"

"At night. He had on a fine black farmer's costume and said he was the Devil. He spoke to me by name and said, Agnes, you are to be a witch. And so I turned into a witch in a twinkling of an eye."

"What did he do with you?"

"At that time he did nothing with me."

"What was the first dance you were present at, and where was it held?"

"Wherever the Devil was, I was there, too."

"I wish to know the place."

"In a wood near Tettenwang, but I don't know what it's called."

"Did you not have to give your soul to the Devil?"

"I can well believe that when a witch dies, her soul belongs to the Devil."

"How did you have to travel?"

"Like the other witches, of course, on a fire iron with a wooden shaft."

"And who guided you?"

"The fire iron."

"What did you use?"

"Lard from a cow that was very thick."

"Who gave you the ointment?"

"The Devil gave it to me when he first came. It was greenish."

"What did you have to say?"

"Fly off, in the Devil's name."

"How many miles did you fly to the revels? How often were you present?"

"No more than two miles. First toward Riedenburg, by the barn in front of the Cabbage Mill, then on a meadow there, later on by the drinking trough."

"What did you do there?"

"I just danced with the others."

"Who danced with you?"

"The men. But I didn't know any of them. The Devil was there, too."

"What did you eat?"

"A broth. But it wasn't me that cooked it."

"What kind of meat?"

"It was pork. We ate it in the broth."

During this entire interrogation, which we have reproduced as literally as possible, the girl was dangling on the end of the rope. Her limbs were cruelly twisted; she was suffering fearful agony and could scarcely breathe. At this point in the questioning she began to lose consciousness because of the unremitting torture. The record notes that she had suddenly begun "to talk in a strange manner," saying, for instance, "My only work is but in prayer," "If I am not pleasing, I wish that I might become so," and, addressing the commissioners, "Sirs, I give you praise and thanks that you have taken care of me," "Spare my mother as little as you spare me," "My father and my mother are also witches." Then: "My soul is all a-tremble . . . how brightly the sun is shining."

They lowered Agnes to the floor, allowed her a respite. Apparently none of those present thought of interrupting the interrogation. She asked for holy water to drink, explaining that she wished to become a child of redemption. Then the poor creature was hoisted up again, and the interrogation was continued.

"What kind of meat did you eat at the revels?"

"What the Devil brought with him. I don't know what sort it was, I'd say it was from a young animal. The Devil brought it."

The girl was already nearly out of her mind with agony, but they jerked her higher still. She screamed aloud. Obviously she had no idea what the commissioner wanted her to say, namely that she had eaten the flesh of young children. She tried pouring out a torrent of words, in the hope of satisfying her tormentors.

"My mother did the cooking, and so did I. My mother rinsed the meat. And we danced round the fire. I danced with the best of them. It was down at the Cabbage Mill, and there were pipers there, too. The Devil quartered the meat, and my father broke it up as well. Oh, I can't bless myself, I have to become a child of redemption first. There was no skin on the meat, my father quartered it, my mother rinsed it clean, and I took it to the fire. Afterward we danced around the fire. The meat had a fine taste. It was good meat. This time the Devil brought it. It was all boiled, we ate no roast meat, it was all boiled . . ."

Finally, with a deep sigh, the victim lost consciousness. The clerk noted at this point that the prisoner "behaved strangely, as if she were feeling unwell," so that the torture had to be stopped and she was taken back to her cell.

The commissioners allowed her precious little time to recover. The interrogation was resumed in the afternoon, but "without recourse to the strappado," as the record states. The girl could be made to say anything her questioners wished, without the slightest difficulty: that children had been eaten at the witches' Sabbath; that the Devil had fornicated with her; how the magic ointment was prepared. She explained her previous persistent denials by saying that the Devil had prevented her speaking out.

On the following Saturday, 21 October 1600, Agnes had to admit to having murdered a number of unbaptized children. She did this without demur, but in an interval between confessions she remarked with a sigh that she might not have come to this pass had it not been for her parents, "but when the pear's ripe, it falls to the ground."

Her confession faltered when she was asked what magic means she had used to kill the children.

"I cast no spells."

She was bound preparatory to torture.

"I used no manner of good things to kill the children." The rope was pulled tight, the swollen joints stretched once more.

"My heart is unrepentant and cannot tell the reason."

The pain became insufferable.

"Today my heart is trembling as much as my legs trembled yesterday. The Devil is still lodged in my head!" And to the commissioners: "May God bless you and keep you!"

Wangereck asked whether the Devil was present with her, whether she could feel him near her.

"The Devil's works are in me. The rogue is still lodged fast in my brain, but help will come to me in time. He must depart from me now."

"In whose name did you have to kill the children?"

"In the Devil's name . . ."

They lowered her, and Master Georg caught the sagging figure and held her up. Wangereck ordered him to seat the girl on the wooden bench by the wall. "I am going to faint," she whispered. "The Devil is lodged in my head. My heart is all a-tremble. Have pity on me, gentlemen, let me lie a while on the bench."

"Were you baptized?"

"I had a godfather at my christening and my confirmation. But my baptismal godfather has died."

Quietly, and with her eyes closed, as if speaking to herself, she said the following words:

"The Devil must go. The Lord God will come." Suddenly she cried out loudly, pointing to her bare feet and stretching her arms into the air: "Look! Look! The rogue's in all my limbs." And again quite softly: "You rogue, you must go. You rogue, you don't want to see me a Christian." Turning abruptly to Master Georg, she continued in a loud and imperious voice: "Do not treat me too gently, Sir Executioner, or something may happen to you too."

Suddenly the girl's body reared up; then she collapsed again. She no longer seemed conscious of what was going on around her; she no longer responded to questions and could not be shaken out of this condition. The commissioners conferred and decided to discontinue the hearing, whereupon the ironmaster carried the girl back to her cell.

On Monday 23 October a Jesuit father entered the Falcon Tower accompanied by two boys in red and white surplices. One was carrying a small silver vessel, the other was swinging a censer. The little procession clattered up the wooden stairs behind Master Georg and stopped in front of Agnes's cell. The ironclad door was unbolted, unlocked, and thrown open. The prisoner was sitting listlessly in a corner; her bare arms and legs were bruised green, blue, and yellow; her joints were misshapen and swollen; her once pretty face was puffy and stained with tears, disfigured by her shaven head. The Jesuit father sprinkled her with holy water and broke into loud and triumphant song in which the children's bright voices joined lustily. A sweet scent of incense filled the room. When the song had come to an end, there was a great murmuring of incomprehensible Latin, on the part of both father and acolytes, who acted as a chorus. The sign of the cross was made a number of times. Then the pious singing was resumed in a mixture of rich bass and high-pitched soprano, which rang through the Falcon Tower. The ceremony was thus concluded. The boys, still swinging their censers, turned about at a sign from the father, while he pronounced a final blessing on the girl and informed her that she had been baptized in the name of Ursula and was now redeemed. Then he too left the cell. The door closed behind him, and was locked and bolted. This is more or less how we might picture the baptism of the miller's daughter, which had been ordered by the commissioners.

Wangereck hoped that the hymns and the murmured Latin phrases had finally deprived the Devil of his power over Agnes, who was now called Ursula. On the Tuesday he had her brought back into the Falcon Tower vault. He could not fail to note, however, that her condition had not improved but had significantly deteriorated. The girl could not even stand up unaided. As soon as she entered the torture chamber, leaning on Master Georg, she seemed to go rigid, or, as the record states, "she behaved as if she had lost the power of speech."

As nearly always, Wangereck began the hearing with a kind of sermon. Now that Almighty God had vouchsafed her so much grace as to rescue her from Satan's vile bonds, she should show herself worthy of such a gift by telling the authorities the truth in all things.

She replied in a barely audible voice: "If I can. I wish to gain my soul's salvation; I no longer want to be the Devil's slave."

The commissioners noticed that the girl was wearing a bandage around her neck, and they asked the ironmaster for an explanation. He reported briefly that he had found the prisoner lying in a pool of blood that morning, with a stab wound in her throat. His wife had applied a rough bandage so that the interrogation could proceed as arranged.

"How did it happen?" Wangereck asked the girl. "I did it myself," she replied in a whisper. "Today at seven o'clock, a little time before the worshipful gentlemen came to the Falcon Tower. That was when the Devil came to my window dressed like a farmhand, and said the rogues—he meant you worshipful gentlemen, the commissioners—the rogues will come back to you now and have you put to the torture again. Look, make away with yourself! That way you'll escape their torture. Otherwise they'll chop your head off and do fearful things to you. You can do it in a flash. In my cell there's a hole in the wall, and I had a knife hidden there. And when the Devil coaxed me like that, all at once it was lying in my lap, and in a flash I stuck it in my throat, and cut myself. But our Lord surely did not want me to kill myself, because when I went to stab myself with my left hand, seeing as how I use my left hand for all my work, I simply pushed the left hand away with my right. After that, I fell down on the floor."

"Where did you get the knife?"

"A week ago, on Friday, I took it from the sheath in which the ironmaster's wife was carrying it, and hid it in the hole I spoke of. After I'd done myself the injury today, I put the knife back in the hole, all bloody as it was, and stuffed an old rag over it."

The ironmaster was instructed to check this statement at once and to send his wife down to the vault. She appeared and, when asked, declared that it was true; she had lost a knife a week ago and didn't know what had become of it. Then Master Georg returned. He searched diligently everywhere, looked in all the crevices and holes in the wall, but couldn't find the knife. The commissioners let the matter rest there for the moment, for they wished to resume the questioning. They had not the slightest intention of allowing the injured girl any respite.

The convent miller's daughter had to suffer the procedure right to the bitter end. She was interrogated seven more times regarding her alleged activities as a witch, sometimes "with clemency," and sometimes "strictly." Interrupted occasionally by fainting fits, she confessed to having maimed both men and cattle, to having conjured up hoarfrost and hail, and to having perpetrated dreadful obscenities with the Evil One. At night, as she lay shivering and feverish, alone in her cell, the Devil used to visit her from time to time, encouraging her, and making cynical remarks about the "Good Lord" in whose name she was being thus tormented. Her parents and the priest had told her lies: mercy was not in Heaven, but in Hell. "In Heaven they chastise the souls, in Hell they have everything they want." Sometimes Agnes was also visited by her aged father. When the moon was high in the heavens outside, and the autumn wind howled through the ancient walls, the miller's poor soul haunted the Falcon Tower. Often he sat by his daughter's side as she lay there, and cried, "Alas! Alas!"

CHAPTER · 7

*M*ercenaries as highwaymen
(contemporary woodcut)

· The Revels

THE DREAM OF FLYING

It is not simply impatience that has prompted us to anticipate events in our story; we have done so in order that matters which belong together should not be separated merely for the sake of chronological sequence. Dates and appointments were significant only for the active participants in the story; the passive participants did not experience time as a series of numerical units governed by the calendar. They watched as it grew dark and grew light again in their cells; they waited for the brisk step of the iron-master's wife bringing them a broth or half a loaf of bread; they started up in terror when they heard Master Georg's heavy tread approaching to summon them to interrogation. Paulus Pappenheimer and his family were not fated to hear the howling of the autumn wind that would frighten the convent miller's daughter. But they too experienced nights of despair, as did Ulrich Schölz and the little tailor from Prunn, Hans Stumpf, and Augustin Baumann. They were not all incarcerated in the Falcon Tower at the same time, but as they saw very little of each other, that is purely incidental. The weeks of suffering that preceded the conclusion of their trial fell into various sections of the calendar; some of them were cold when they first arrived, and waited for their end on sultry July days; others were taken into custody in midsummer, and led out of prison for the last time in November. But the inner course of their sojourn was the same in every case: first, courage and defiance; then pain and misery; later a resurgence of defiance and a final collapse; finally, apathy and mental confusion.

At the beginning of July 1600, Anna Pappenheimer was in this final stage, which began for the miller's daughter Agnes in the first days of November. She willingly told the commissioners of her exploits as a witch, suffered apathetically the torture which was liable to ensue at any point where she was unable to supply the desired answer instantly, and lay in her cell for days on end, shaken by fever. All sorts of ghosts appeared to her. The Devil laughed at her through the window, the children she was alleged to have slain danced round her. Probably she regarded herself as a witch and considered her confession as more real than her actual life, from which she was long separated by oceans of suffering.

She may well have looked through the little window at the sky with its scudding clouds, and wished that she could really fly through the air, away from this cell and a life that had grown unbearable. If her magic powers were not annulled as long as she was caught in the authorities' net, she could realize her dream; she merely had to sit astride a piece of wood or iron, smear some ointment on it, and hurtle off in the Devil's name. She had a very vivid vision of this ride through the air, as if she had indeed "taken flight" in the way described in her confession.

If the old traveling woman had experienced such things, it was only in lurid dreams. Were these merely ordinary nocturnal visions? About a hundred years ago, a retired high school teacher astonished the academic community with a novel theory.[103] The so-called witches were in fact drug addicts, and their sensation of flying was based on unusually vivid hallucinations. The whole business of witchcraft had been caused by a drug, a distillation from the thorn apple (*Datura stramonium* Lin.). It was known, after all, that poor people in particular felt the need at all times— but especially in hard times—of a narcotic that would enable them to forget their hunger and their cares. Women with a knowledge of herbal remedies had very soon discovered the effects of the thorn apple, which had been introduced into Europe by gypsies in the first half of the fifteenth century. That was precisely the time when the belief in witches had arisen. According to the theory, individuals who had seen visions of fornication and worship of the Devil while intoxicated by the thorn apple were so alarmed that they went to confession and revealed in the confessional what they believed to be actual experiences. This promptly caused the Church to issue warnings about the new crime of fornication with the Devil, and to discuss the matter in academic terms. In the meantime, the thorn apple had made its triumphant way through the whole of Europe. "And it is perfectly obvious that the thorn apple and witch trials followed the same path, and it was the thorn apple that invariably made its appearance shortly before the commencement of witch trials in a given area—at least, as far as we can establish this, given the secrecy that at first surrounded the planting of the thorn apple." It was also said to be significant that the delusion of witchcraft invariably reached a climax precisely in times of extreme distress, for instance, before and during the Thirty Years' War. The direr the people's misery, the more widespread was the addiction.

Our present experience rather suggests the contrary, but the theory of narcotic intoxication has recently been revived. Hans Peter Duerr, an ethnologist of the "freak" generation, reverted to it in his book *Dream Time*, adapted it, and put it in context.[104] It was true, Duerr conceded, that not all those suspected of witchcraft had anointed themselves with an ointment liable to promote hallucinations, but there must have been individuals from whose experiences of intoxication the legend of witches' flight and orgiastic Devil's dances had been born. The "flight"—a "trip," perhaps? It was at least an original interpretation of an incomprehensible phenomenon.

As for Anna Pappenheimer, who used to look out from her cell at the blue rectangle of sky and dream of flying, she was hardly likely to be yearning for a "high" inspired by thorn apple or some other drug capable of expanding awareness. The records would have indicated such a wish. The "recipes for ointments" revealed by Anna and those accused along with her referred only to preparations for causing tempests and other mischief. The "flying ointment" they all claimed to have received from the Devil himself. But, quite apart from that, the drug theory breaks down in the case of those involved in our trial, simply because they did not smear the ointment on themselves but on their instruments, the pitchfork or fire iron. If they had been concerned with some kind of intoxication, even if they did not actually eat the paste, they would at least have had to inhale its vapor. Only a single statement in the records indicates that the witches' flight had been prepared by the taking of a herb, that is, the claim by little Hänsel (on 5 May 1600) that "his mother had eaten boar's wort when she wanted to fly abroad." Boar's wort (*Carlina acaulis, Carlina vulgaris*), also known as the silver thistle, is certainly a sudorific and diuretic herb, but it does not bring about intoxication. The child obviously mentioned the plant because it seemed to him to have specially demonic qualities, on account of its blossoms, which respond to changes in the weather.

In Anna Pappenheimer's case, the dream of flying seems not to have been based on any personal experience or state of intoxication. It emerged from the unplumbed depths of the unconscious, from that mythical, primeval abyss of our being, from which most of our dreams come. Anna's vision was so vivid because she was not merely repeating what she had been told: she was reliving certain feelings. Flight through the air on a piece of wood is one of those utterly fundamental legends that cannot just be explained away as a tradition.[105] In the very cradle of our culture, in the fertile land between the Euphrates and the Tigris, it was believed that women versed in magic rode off to nocturnal assembles on staves; the mythologies of the Egyptians, the Persians, the Hebrews, the Greeks, and the Romans also tell of such things, with variations and elaborations of a characteristic kind in each case. It is scarcely probable that this knowledge was simply taken over by the Germanic peoples—it was based on indigenous sybilline murmurings about peoples in the far North, in the land of the Western Goths, for instance, who believed that witches rode on staves to their meeting places and returned before dawn. The old Norse women of the night used a stave from a fence for their flights; for an unseen fence, the boundary dividing the human realm from that of the demons, was the place where, in a sense, they were seen to sit. An old Munich bedtime blessing contains a warning against the *zcûnrite*, the woman riding on the fence, and the word *hagazussa*, from which the modern German *Hexe* is derived, originally meant "fence woman." In the cathedral church in Schleswig there is a medieval fresco in which a *hagazussa* is depicted: she is riding through the air on a broom, her hair streaming out behind her.

Loose, flowing hair, a symbol of liberated sensuality—does it not perhaps reveal the ultimate foundation of this dream of flying? It is after all remarkable that originally only women were believed capable of nocturnal flight. And why were they all riding on a wooden staff? Ethnologists and religious scholars have found quite a number of answers to that question. It was not only the Germanic peoples who worshiped staves and poles as idols, and the magic wand has always been an instrument for conjuring up the power of the demons. Such "explanations" are not really explanations, however, but merely an enumeration of other myths in which the staff plays a role similar to the one it plays in the flight of witches. The experts seem shy about advancing the most obvious interpretation. One does not need to be a depth psychologist in order to recognize the staff as a phallic symbol. A psychiatrist knowing nothing of the ancient legends concerning witches would not hesitate for a moment to explain the dream of flying by this symbolism. It is the correct explanation. All the findings of ethnological investigation into witchcraft superstition support it. Hobbyhorses make their appearance most commonly in fertility dances and ancient initiation rites undergone by young people approaching marriageable age. It is interesting that the record of our trial provides evidence that the alleged flights by witches invariably took place at times of the year when popular custom invokes the concept of fertility: between Christmas and New Year, shrovetide, Easter, May Day, Pentecost, and the early days of summer. According to an old custom in Hesse, girls ride on a broom in front of the stove on New Year's Eve, or ride past the chicken coop on St. Matthew's Eve (21st September), in order to learn whether they will marry during the coming year. The sexual core of the symbolism is particularly obvious in this case.

The dream of flying astride a stick, hair flowing free, was a female sexual fantasy with which even Anna was familiar. Of course, she knew nothing of what this mythological image signified. Did her educated contemporaries think of it? Their subconscious was able to read the language of symbols, but it also prevented them breaking the taboo. It is hardly coincidence that erudite Church scholars took up the subject of flying witches with insatiable zeal precisely at a time when chastity was elevated above all other virtues. Learned treatises on the nature of the witches' flight were a favorite theme of the fifteenth century.[106] Did the celibate scholars sense instinctively the sexual menace of the orgiastic woman on her stick? They certainly did everything they could to ward her off. First of all they agreed on a doctrine which stated that the witch did not fly under her own power but was carried by the Devil. If she herself believed that she was flying under her own power, then that was an illusion stemming from pride. Anna, indoctrinated with the "prevailing theory" of witchcraft, was well aware of this: "The fork does not fly by itself, but it is guided by the Devil." Once the witch had thus been deprived of her power, the dream lost its emancipatory challenge, which is probably what had subconsciously provoked the theological scholars. Riding on the staff was no longer a woman's triumph, she was not capable of achieving gratification herself but was entirely dependent on him who guided the staff. The dream having thus been defused, the scholars set about demolishing it altogether. For this purpose it was dragged from the vague and shadowy realm of mythology into the cold light of reality. The flights were not merely a diabolical sham or excursions of the soul from the sleeping body; Satan actually carried the witch bodily through the air. This image could be linked to the account in the Gospel of St. Matthew (4:5) of how Jesus was carried up to the pinnacle of the temple, and it was comfortingly remote from any suggestion of sensuality. A real event is a self-sufficient fact, while a mythological symbol stands for another order of reality. If the witches' flight was deprived of its symbolic character, there was no need to fear another reality.

For Anna, however, the dream of flying remained no more than a dream. In her interrogations she described it very vividly, but she had never experienced it. This is precisely why, I believe, she sometimes dreamed of flying on a stick when she looked up from her straw litter through the little square window into the blue summer sky. She had to atone for a sin she had never committed, pay for a journey she had never made. It is understandable that she longed to experience at least once the delights that only real witches knew.

THE FEAST

Southwest of Tettenwang there is a hill, overgrown with bushes, stunted conifers, and low shrubs. On the northern slope, up among the flourishing weeds, the weathered ruins of a long forgotten building have survived the passage of time. Even in the Pappenheimers' day there was no longer a building there. But the remains of old foundations that have almost vanished today could still be seen from afar, and they had given the hill its name. It was called Wall Hill, a term long since forgotten and unknown to the present inhabitants of Tettenwang. Nevertheless, it is impossible to miss the hill. Coming from the direction of Laimerstadt, you turn right onto a cart track about eight hundred yards short of the first houses of Tettenwang. This track leads up to the sparsely wooded ridge forming the summit of the hill. Here you leave the track and proceed diagonally through the undergrowth in a westerly direction, at first climbing gently, then descending a slight slope. After a few moments you reach a grassy clearing, the site of the following scene.

A Thursday, half past ten at night. Flames dance in the darkness. The air is filled with rushing and hissing. Witches' sticks and pitchforks arrive from various directions, bearing women with flowing hair, occasionally men, even children. Soon the quiet clearing is thronged with a great variety of figures silhouetted darkly against the light of the fires. But among these silhouettes there are even more somber figures. Devils! They are showing new arrivals to their places, shouting instructions, calling the crowd to order. Two large circles are formed with a fire flaring in the middle of each. Around one of them sit the high-ranking witches, around the other are their "inferiors." The few males in the circle are timid, silent. The women are relaxed and self-confident. There are young, old, ugly females, most of them naked or scantily clad. They know each other, exchange greetings, gossip and giggle.

A roll of thunder interrupts the conversation. Smoke and sulphurous vapors rise from the ground, and suddenly the assembly see their host before them. He lords it over them on a mighty black throne that shines and glitters mysteriously in the light of the fires as though it were studded with innumerable diamonds: Lucifer, the overlord of all the devils, and king of the Underworld. His eyes glow like mirrors reflecting the sun, so that it is not easy to describe his features. It is even possible that he has none. His garb is black; only his regal robe is purple. Servants bow low before him, devils of the lower ranks waiting on their king. They, too, are clad in black, in fact in the manner of "those Walloons that journeyed by water down to Hungary," that is, in the costume of the Low Countries. The moment the Devil appears, the whole company kneels down. With heads bowed and hands clasped, the witches and warlocks pray to their lord. "Our Satan which art in Hell . . ." runs the prayer in chorus, an exact inversion of the Lord's Prayer. A number of women shuffle on their knees toward their dread master's throne, bearing before them the sacrificial offerings they have brought: the rigid corpses of unbaptized infants. With a gracious wave of his hand, the Prince of Shadows accepts the gifts, which his servants snatch from the donors' hands and carry off to the fires, where they are to be boiled and roasted. In the meantime, a number of demon lovers approach the throne, each of them pushing a new member of the company in front of him. One after the other, the novices repeat in the presence of Lucifer the vow they swore when they were first recruited. The figure on the throne dismisses the devout congregation with an obscene gesture, for, in spite of his majestic air of command, this king is the very epitome of vulgarity; indeed, his dignity is marked by an extreme degree of tastelessness, obscenity, and filth. Among the more innocuous features of his particular kind of majesty is his habit of shamelessly breaking wind, with such a thunderous noise and infernal stench that even a tramp like Paulus Pappenheimer was embarrassed.

The two groups form once more, according to rank and standing. Each group crouches round its appointed fire, while auxiliary devils and witches begin to prepare the banquet. Cauldrons are hung over the fires, and the water in them begins to boil instantly by virtue of magic spells. Women pluck poultry and prepare meat for grilling; in no time at all it is turning on the spits. Devils acting as stewards provide illumination for the feast. They pick a number of women from among the subordinate witches and make them take up positions at regular intervals all around the clearing, with their legs wide apart and their backs to the assembly. When the candle devil makes his appearance with a basket full of tallow candles, these candleholder witches bend forward until their heads touch the ground and their naked buttocks stick up in the air. Each has a burning candle inserted into her anus, and has to hold it upright or she is given a good thrashing. One of these living candlesticks happens to be Anna Pappenheimer. "They thought very little of me," she later complained to the authorities, "I was always having to hold a candle, for they stood me on my head and—begging your pardon—stuck a candle in my backside."

While the clearing is being illuminated in this festive fashion, menial devils hand out silver beakers and fetch beer and wine. Others bring the food, which, surprisingly, is already cooked. There are "boiled and roasted infants, without hands and feet, like sucking-pigs," and also horsemeat, hare, and buck; the poultry consists of ravens and crows, served with toads and frogs. Omelettes and bread brought by the witches are handed around, but all this, like the meat, is unsalted, for the Devil hates salt—it is numbered among those good things which have no place in his world of evil. Sometimes a witch brings a pinch of salt in a cloth to give some savor to the banquet, which is not particularly appetizing. But this kind of subterfuge and disobedience does not pass unnoticed: the devilish stewards who constantly circulate among the lip-smacking old hags and sorcerers seem to smell the salt. Scarcely has one of them sprinkled a pinch of salt on her portion than one of the dusky creatures is by her side. He drags the offender from the circle of feasting guests and gives her a good thrashing, to the accompaniment of laughter and catcalls from all those present.

The meal is barely over when devilish pipers appear from nowhere, take up their positions at the edge of the clearing, and on a barely perceptible sign from the chief devil, who is still seated on his throne, begin to play dance music. A veritable infernal symphony bursts out. Shawms wail, flutes warble, trumpets bray and screech. The effect is quite different from any earthly wind band, especially since the ensemble is reinforced by instruments we humans have never seen: flutes and fifes, some like corncobs, others like cowhorns. The din is infernal. Clinking and tinkling, rumbling and screeching fill the air. The gluttons stop chewing, the boozers put their mugs aside, everyone springs to their feet and starts to move. The strange music stirs the senses, arouses the most secret instincts to the point of unbridled lust and insensate gratification. Yelling, the witches and their demon lovers make up a kind of round dance. They form a wide circle, each person placing his hands on the hips of the person in front. Their figures move rhythmically in the light of the fire, performing ritual steps, thrusting out the left foot, moving one pace forward, and two back. The human circle twitches and trembles like the body of a restless serpent, moving backwards in a clockwise direction, for the Devil loves everything that is left-handed and perverse. The music grows ever wilder, the "disk" rotates more and more rapidly, people begin to stumble and fall over each other with wild screams, the order of the dance begins to dissolve, and, as the orchestra works up to an ecstatic *furioso*, it gives way to the pandemonium of a general orgy. Of course, every witch has a demon lover allotted to her, but at this stage of abandonment, she takes her pleasure with others besides. Even the eleven-year-old Hänsel knows that "they tumble all over each other, mother, father, and their children all together." And Augustin Baumann confirms that "the witches have to fornicate with their lovers. After that, it's a free-for-all, and one monster takes on another." All sorts of abominations take place, "sodomy as well as ordinary fornication, between the breasts, under the armpits, from the back, and from the front." According to our informants, the large proportion of the women in the company of witches is accounted for by the fact that women are better adapted to such orgies than men. The Devil accepted only "grand seducers" into his circle, and even these he took reluctantly and with ill-concealed contempt. "They take no account of males . . . and among a hundred women there's scarcely a man to be seen." This suits the witches; after all, there are quite enough demon lovers present to satisfy their carnal appetites. If they are thrown together with a warlock in the abandoned rough-and-tumble, they have to observe the rules of the game and make do with him, but they much prefer the demon lovers, for, according to Augustin Baumann, they can "do as they wish with them."

His Sable Majesty looks down graciously from his throne on the animal antics beneath him. The general petting, pinching, grunting, and gasping in ecstasy are music to his ears, the revolting perversities are a heart-warming sight for him, the obscenities and expletives that are whispered or shouted are his kind of poetry. But when he notes that his guests' activity is abating, the sexual tussle subsiding into a sodden slumber, he gives the signal for the orgy to cease. The stewards drive the intertwined bodies apart with kicks and punches, while the music changes to a fanfare. The fun of the festival is finished; now the mood becomes very solemn.

In the flickering light of the human candlesticks, the depraved company assembles for divine or, rather, diabolical service. Like dogs, they crawl on all fours to the king's glittering black throne and take up their positions in dense rows. They worship their master in chorus, with a member of the king's diabolical entourage acting as precentor. During this performance it pleases the supreme ruler of darkness to transform himself in wondrous fashion. He rises from his throne, shedding his purple mantle; he turns gaunt and hairy, his hands and feet are changed into horny hooves, his glittering eyes move sideways and a muzzle grows out between them, his pointed ears become longer and longer, horns begin to sprout from his forehead. The trunk of this deformed figure then leans forward and skips down the steps of his throne. In the form of a black billy goat Lucifer joins his followers to receive their homage. These tributes take the following form: witches assume the "bridge" position, twisting sideways out of their kneeling posture in such a way that their bellies face upwards and their arms and legs support their arched bodies. Thus, with their "private parts turned toward the heavens," they approach the devilish billy goat from behind and kiss his genitals. If the object of this honor desires to grant a special mark of his favor to one of the witches, he leads her from the circle of devotees and briefly copulates with her.

278

Then Lucifer is once more back on his throne in regal dignity, ready to open the practical part of the assembly. One by one, witches and warlocks have to come forward and give an account of the evil deeds they have performed since the last meeting. A number of them falter and confess that they have done no more than slay a few head of cattle and summon up a middling storm; this time, alas, they have not killed or crippled any human beings. The punishment for such indolence follows literally hot-foot: stewards seize the idle offender and beat her on the soles of her feet. Another has used the Devil's ointment for purposes of healing, which manifestly enrages the monarch on his throne, and she consequently suffers a more severe penalty, i.e. a regular flogging. A third gives protracted illness as an excuse for her inactivity, but the Devil refuses to accept this, since he detests justice. So the woman, who has barely recovered from her sickness, is soundly beaten. Most of the witches and warlocks have done their due, however, and are graciously allowed to depart. Each of them is given a special task by the Devil, which must be performed before the next meeting is due: one of them has to kill a neighbor's cattle, another is required to ruin the harvest in her village, a third has to make the pastor fall ill. Finally, each is allocated her portion of the poisonous ointment, and the black monarch announces the time and place of the next meeting. In his closing remarks, which are larded with abuse, oaths, and vulgar puns, he exhorts them to be more diligent in injuring Christians, and concludes with an invitation: "Drink, you old bags, dance for a space, and depart in the Devil's name." Whereupon Lucifer vanishes with a clap of thunder and a stench of sulphur.

It is already one o'clock in the morning and high time to depart, for the nocturnal travelers must be home by the first cock crow. Once the cock has crowed, the time for flying is past, for the ointment then loses its magic power. A good many who set off home too late have come to grief on the way and have had to limp home on foot. Immediately their master has disappeared, therefore, the men and women mount their pitchforks and make off. The candle devil puts out the candles and releases the old women from their uncomfortable posture; the stewards remove the remains of the fires and all traces of the banquet. In an instant the clearing lies silent and peaceful in the moonlight. Not a blade of grass has been crushed, not a trace of the revels remains.

Not much has changed up on Wall Hill since those days. It is still a lonely spot with a fine view of Tettenwang and of the gently rolling countryside round about. But it is only worth going up there in daylight, for there are no witches' revels there now, and there never were. The scene just described, reconstructed in every detail from the records of the Pappenheimer trial, was one of the collective nightmares of the age.

CONVERSATION BENEATH THE CHESTNUT TREE

The prisoners in the Falcon Tower knew precisely what went on at such witches' Sabbaths and were able to give descriptions of other customs and crimes, which coincided in all particulars. Such knowledge could be acquired effortlessly and without recourse to any secret pact. The exploits of these unnatural creatures were widely discussed in those days. Even children would listen to the sensational stories their elders told each other, and duly noted the constantly recurring characteristics and customs of the mysterious beings. We happen to know by hearsay of such a conversation that little Hänsel may well have listened to, open-mouthed and wide-eyed. I can vouch for what was said, for it is preserved in the records of our trial. Even the place and the participants have not been invented, although we cannot now establish who said what, and how and when it was said. All the same, it could have been very much as described below.

It is August 1597. Paulus and his family had traveled up the Danube from Deggendorf during the preceding weeks. As always, they had moved aimlessly, and at a leisurely pace, offering their services as tinkers and emptiers of privies at farmsteads along the way, inviting the crowds to their gaming table at fairs, and begging for alms at church doors. At the end of June they had left Straubing, had roamed about the district round Regensburg in the middle of July, and had turned their backs during the last few days on the River Danube, which was at a pitifully low ebb at this time of the year, although still fickle and unpredictable. They had been in Abensberg since the previous day, having, as usual, found accommodation with the tenant of the Meadow Mill.

And so we may observe our traveling folk sitting around a table in the open air, beneath a chestnut tree, on a sultry afternoon. With them are the miller and his wife as well as Zuliedl and Black Jack from the nearby village of Aunkhofen, who have come over for a chat. The sun is still high in the sky, covered every now and then by dark clouds that gradually grow denser. The day's work is over, however—we may remember that the working day finished very early then, because it began at first light. There is going to be

280

a thunderstorm; clouds of gnats dance over the damp meadow that lies between the mill and the stream, but no one takes any notice. They are too busy swapping stories. Anna is in the middle of a tale she heard from a farmer's wife in Kelheim only a few days earlier, which she is in the process of embroidering. "The watchman in Kelheim," we can hear her saying in a mysteriously hushed voice, her head bent low, "who's called Hans and lives by the Old Mill Gate, he watched a witches' dance not long ago. He's standing on top of the gateway late at night and keeping a watch on the town and the fields round about, as he's supposed to, and he sees the light of a fire out on the moss, where the road to Affecking runs. That'll be gypsies or some such riffraff, he thinks to himself, and he gets down from his lookout and takes up his pike and goes off into the dark fields, heading for the flickering light of that fire. And as he gets closer, he hears music and people laughing, and he still thinks it's gypsies although he's wondering about a funny sound in the air, like high-pitched fifes. But then he suddenly knows it's witches dancing there because he can see naked white bodies tumbling about among black devils, and a king sitting on a glittering black throne. And he's barely realized what sort of evil company he's stumbled on at their dancing when he's spotted by the devils and witches. They all start screeching and yelling, and they're just about to leap on the watchman, and they'd have killed him, to be sure. But he keeps his head and makes the sign of the cross and shouts out as loud as he can, "Help me, Lord Jesus!" And he spits, "Fie on you, you host of Satan, you'll do me no harm," and flings his pike away and legs it as fast as he can back into the town. And when he notices that it's all gone quiet behind him and there's no one following him, he turns and sees that all the spooks have vanished without a trace. And as soon as it got light next day, he went back to the place where he'd seen the light of the fire, but there wasn't a sign of the dance. There was just one thing he found in the grass: a basket full of eggs. I expect one of the witches dropped it as she was flying off."

"I can well believe it," we hear Black Jack rejoin. "This past year at Martinmas the very same thing happened to some of the farmers in our village as happened to the watchman in Kelheim. They'd had their fill to drink, and they were merry enough when they set off home across the fields from Abensberg late one night. Black as pitch, it was, not a star in the sky, but all at once they see a blinding light in front of them, and it was like there was a ring or circle of fire right there ahead of them. One of the farmers realized straight away what it was all about, and he cursed and said to the others: 'Who's for going on? The field's full of devils.' Not one of them dared go on, and they all raced back to the town gate. There they found some pieces of rotting wood that shone in the dark, and they sat down on them because they shield a man from evil spirits. That was lucky for them, because while they were sitting there waiting, there was an awful rushing in the air; something whizzed around their heads; and one of them felt something plucking at his arm. That was witches. The Devil had sent them out to fetch the farmers. It would have gone badly with that drunken crew if they hadn't been sitting on that rotting wood. It was only the wood that saved their poor souls. And then, once the clock had struck one, they could go home in peace because the witches aren't out and about at that time."

The miller disputes that. "As long as it's night, I'd not advise anybody to go to such eerie places," he says. But others agree with Black Jack. In the early morning and just before daybreak there was nothing more to fear. So the conversation rambles on for a while. Then Zuliedl, a diminutive young man with tangled curly hair, says that he is not afraid of witches. The others fall silent and listen expectantly. "If you see one of them flying past, you just have to be brave and shout at her, and she loses her magic power and crashes to the ground, along with her pitchfork. A year or two ago, Hans, the night watchman from Abensberg, saw the wife of Englmann the cobbler and her mother, the carpenter's wife, flying through the air at eleven o'clock at night. He shouted as loud as he could at the pair of them, and the daughter fell into the lane just in front of his house—along with a bucket of lard she'd just stolen from a farmer. The carpenter's old woman got away with it, because she was already back in the house when the watchman shouted."

"Shouting takes their power away only if it comes from the authorities," claims Gumpprecht. "If one of our sort shouts at witches, it makes no odds. Perhaps it only annoys them; that's why you have to keep quiet if you see one of them, which God forbid."

The miller's wife, who has been silent up till now, turns on little Zuliedl. "All that about the cobbler's wife and her mother is nothing but lies. Everybody was talking about it then, and the authorities looked into it and questioned Hans the night watchman. There was nothing in it, even if the whole town was gabbling about it, and nobody would talk to the pair of them."

282

"So you think they were innocent?" sneers Zuliedl. "I don't believe they're innocent. They found the bucket of lard, and that's proof enough. I heard from Hans the watchman himself that the bailiff took it up to the manorhouse. The town hushed up the whole business, the council wouldn't let it be looked into. All of a sudden, nobody was allowed to say anthing about the cobbler's wife, and people were threatened and told that anybody that said anything about her or did her any mischief would be put inside." The miller joins in the argument. "It was quite right for the council to put a stop to all that scandal and slander. They went on burning all those witches in Abensberg for nearly a year, and some folk said the fires wouldn't go out as long as there was anybody left alive here."

"All right," exclaims Zuliedl indignantly; "you go on being kind to those devilish females. They'll smear their ointment on your doorpost soon enough, and you'll come to a wretched end. They didn't stop the burning on account of them being innocent; it was because some councillors' wives were mixed up in it."

"When our betters get involved," agrees Paulus Pappenheimer, "then they put out the fires. That's the way it is: they've two different standards, those authorities. And still, I reckon there's as many witches among the rich as among the poor."

The sky is overcast with brownish grey clouds. Sharp gusts of wind whip up the dust in the yard behind the mill and toss the foliage of the chestnut tree beneath which the company are sitting round a table on their roughly fashioned wooden benches, growing more and more heated as their discussion proceeds. The miller's wife says they should go inside, the thunderstorm will break any moment. But the others scarcely hear her and wave her away impatiently. It hasn't even begun to thunder yet. Anna has started speaking again. "I heard them reading the confessions in Kelheim, when there was that great burning of witches. They said then that there was lots of grand folk among the witches, just about as many as on a market day in Straubing. Things are no different with the Devil than they are in this world: people that are rich, and grand, and good-looking, they're looked up to and picked out. They have their special places, and at the witches' Sabbath they have their own separate circles. It's a parable, as if they put the grand folk at the front tables."

"It'd be a queer thing," argues the miller, "if there was more justice with the Devil than with men." Then Michel: "The poor have to work like slaves, and all they get for it is to be looked down on, here and there as well." And his brother adds: "The poor are not just passed over, they get beaten into the bargain. In Ellingen I heard them say that the Devil gives his people a good hiding if they're not evil enough or if they're sorry for what they've done. There was one of them sitting on the condemned cart that was all bloody about the head, and they said the Devil had beaten her cruelly with a black knotty cudgel because she wanted no more to do with him. I was just a lad then, but I'll never forget it. But I wondered all the same why so many folk stand by the Devil if he gives them such a rotten time." The miller's wife nods. "It don't pay to be wicked. They do say that the Devil turns witches into toads if they don't obey him, so that they are beaten or trodden on by men."

"That's right," agrees Black Jack, "and that's why it's a bad sign if a woman has bruises and wounds on her body, and can't rightly say where she got them." Zuliedl backs up his friend: "And if she wakes up battered in the morning, when she went to bed in good shape. There's many a husband has no idea that his wife's a witch, because she always puts him into a deep sleep before she flies off. For instance, on the morning after a dance, witches sleep an hour or two longer than usual. It's not a good sign if a farmer's wife sleeps longer than usual in the morning without a good reason."

The rustling in the chestnut boughs over the speakers has grown so loud that Zuliedl has to shout. The first lightning darts from the dark, menacing sky, and great, heavy drops splash in the yard. All the assembled people jump up, throw jackets and shawls over their heads, and hurry into the house, urging each other on with shouts and jokes. The first clap of thunder crashes out. This is how people can be mistaken. The thunderstorm was much nearer than they thought.

THE CRIME

Not even Dr. Wangereck's opponents on the Munich council of state denied that the ponderous, hotheaded Lower Bavarian was a highly competent lawyer. His legal arguments were seldom contradicted at meetings of the council. In his special area, the crime of witchcraft, he was regarded as a leading expert.

The crime of witchcraft? Wasn't that simply a monstrous illusion, which was not amenable to a legal approach even if it was regarded as a reality? A number of legal historians hold this view, arguing that lawyers in those days subdivided the witches' activities into a number of distinct criminal acts, the pact with the Devil, for instance, being ranked as blasphemy, demonic fornication being charged under the heading of sodomy and adultery, and spells administered with the help of magic ointment prosecuted as sorcery and poisoning. This explanation was arrived at so readily because the crime of witchcraft does not figure in the penal codes of the time. It cannot be correct, however. Wangereck called the crime he was prosecuting "witchcraft"—not "blasphemy," "sodomy," "adultery," "poisoning," or "sorcery." He spoke of witchcraft in exactly the same way that a judge nowadays would speak of "robbery-murder" rather than calling it malicious damage, extortion, grievous bodily harm, murder, and theft. Unlike modern judges, Wangereck and his colleagues were not obliged to reduce the set of actual circumstances with which they were faced to a precisely defined set of statutory facts, by the application of strict rules. They were not subject to the principle, "No penalty except in conformity with a relevant statute." They passed sentence intuitively, instinctively, in keeping with current judicial sentiment.

That is why it is incorrect to try to construct retrospectively a formulation for the crime of witchcraft that would have some resemblance to a statutory offense. That was done repeatedly. "The *crimen magiae* in the technical sense," the judicial core of the crime of witchcraft, was "the alliance with the Devil with the aim of doing mischief with his help and through the use of cryptic devices and procedures." So runs the definition in a relevant historical study.[107] I doubt whether a word as fraught with mythology and secret terrors as "witchcraft" can simply be replaced by a definition without leaving much that is inexplicable. This cannot be done even with such basic legal concepts as "duty," or "law." The judicial practice of the age had no need of a concisely defined "set of statutory facts," such as we have been speaking of. We are thinking too much in modern terms, if we take the word "witchcraft" as a kind of abbreviation for a number of precisely definable criminal characteristics. Certainly there were such criteria. But there was also a wide and obscure penumbra of meaning surrounding these main criteria. Light must be shed on this if we wish to understand what lawyers visualized under the term "witchcraft" in those days.

Our best approach is to examine the specifically "legal" use of the word, and its function in the context of indictment, conviction, and sentencing. We should therefore look at the sources from which judges drew their interpretation of the law. At that time it was not only statutes and regulations that served as legal sources, as is the case nowadays, but also the traditional theories of Roman law, along with veritable libraries of commentaries, the Bible itself as *ius divina*, learned literature of all kinds, the usages of the courts, and opinions from academic authorities. The modern lawyer looks in vain for some kind of order in this jumble of sources. Only in the relationship between imperial and territorial statutes was an order of priorities established by means of the so-called saving clause of the Caroline code, or penal code of Charles V.

It is only people like ourselves who miss system and hierarchy in the matter of guidelines. We regard the law as the work of men—a lawyer in the year 1600 did not. The question of priority or subordination would have meant nothing to him. As he understood it, justice and injustice were alike part of the divine creation. As far as their essential substance was concerned, the various sources could not be mutually contradictory; if they were read correctly, they complemented each other. Demonstrating that incidental *contraria* were only apparent, not real, was an important exercise in method for law students in the sixteenth century.

However long we search, we can find nothing about the crime of "witchcraft" in any of the "classical" sources of criminal law of the time. Only in article 109 of the Constitutio Criminalis Carolina do we read, under "Sorcery": "Item, anyone who does harm or injury to others by sorcery shall be punished by death, and such punishment shall be carried out by fire. Where, however, someone has made use of sorcery and has harmed no man, then shall the punishment be otherwise, according to the nature of the case." In their final judgment, the judges in the Pappenheimer case also made reference to this provision, although they did so in a strangely involved and logically contorted manner. It was not the pernicious practice of sorcery that they proposed to punish "with the harshest and most fearful penalties as may be inflicted on man, viz. by burning," but "the heinous, abominable, and dreadful sin of sorcery and witchcraft, *a fortiori*, however, the denial and renunciation of God's Majesty, and that of all His Heavenly Host." The legal argument is by no means drawn solely from article 109 of Constitutio Criminalis Carolina nor, indeed, from any single quoted article. The basis of the judgment is allegedly provided by "the divine Holy Scriptures, the common statutes of

286

the Empire, especially the salutary Penal Code instituted by His Most Worshipful and Most Excellent Majesty, the Emperor Charles V."

The Bible, then, occupies the first place as a legal source. There is nothing surprising about this. Insofar as it was possible to derive legal principles from Scripture, the latter, as divinely inspired, was accorded the highest standing and continuing validity. The Old Testament actually contains nothing about witchcraft but plenty about sorcery and superstition, which are condemned with varying degrees of severity.[108] "There shall not be found among you any one that maketh his son or his daughter to pass through the fire, or that useth divination, or an observer of times, or an enchanter, or a witch, or a charmer, or a consulter with familiar spirits, or a wizard, or a necromancer. For all that do these things are an abomination unto the Lord: and because of these abominations the Lord thy God doth drive them out from before thee" (Deuteronomy 18:10–12). And: "Neither shall ye use enchantment, nor observe times" (Leviticus 19:26). Or else: "Regard not them that have familiar spirits, neither seek after wizards, to be defiled by them" (Leviticus 19:31). Or: "And the soul that turneth after such as have familiar spirits, and after wizards, to go awhoring after them, I will even set my face against that soul, and will cut him off from among his people" (Leviticus 20:6). And, above all: "A man also or woman that hath a familiar spirit, or that is a wizard, shall surely be put to death: they shall stone them with stones: their blood shall be upon them" (Leviticus 20:27). Elsewhere there is specific reference to the female sex: "Thou shalt not suffer a witch to live" (Exodus 22:18).

Evidently our judges also applied to the vagrants the First Commandment given to Moses, which states: "Thou shalt have no other gods before me . . . for I the Lord thy God am a jealous God, visiting the iniquity of the fathers upon the children unto the third and fourth generation of them that hate me" (Exodus 20:3, 5). They stressed that witchcraft was, in the theologically colored legal jargon of the time, *crimen laesae maiestatis divinae:* high treason committed against God's Majesty.

Apart from these sources, the principal argument was founded on the "general Imperial law." This referred to those provisions of the Roman legal tradition quoted in the witchcraft literature of the time—particularly the *Hammer of Witches* mentioned above—which were concerned with witchcraft. These were the penal statutes of the code known as "Corpus Juris Civilis," and summed up under the heading, "De maleficis et mathematicis et ceteris similibus." According to these statutes, poisoning was a more heinous crime than simple murder: since the effect of the poison could not be explained in terms of organic chemistry, it was regarded as murder by means of magic. Sorcerers were to be burned ruthlessly, it is stated, for they confound the elements, destroy innocent lives, and dispose of all their adversaries by means of their evil art. There was no doubt that these were venerable statutes, enacted by emperors who had a totally different notion of the Roman Empire from that of a Bavarian judicial commissioner of 1600; nevertheless, they were imperial in the best and most unambiguous sense. The court might well refer to them. It might have recourse also to the "Treuga Heinrici" of 1224, which, in the tradition of the Emperor Constantine, excluded discretion on the part of the judge in the sentencing of "haeretica, incantatores, malefici." In fact, none of the relevant regulations mentions "witchcraft." As in the penal code of Emperor Charles V (the Caroline code), from which we have quoted article 109, the term used is invariably sorcery. Here, as in the Bavarian territorial legislation of 1516 and 1553, a distinction is drawn between pernicious and harmless sorcerers. This did not refer to witches. Article 109 of Constitutio Criminalis Carolina in no way applied to "sorcerers who enter into a pact with the Devil," wrote the celebrated Saxon lawyer, Benedikt Carpzow. It is true, he was writing thirty-five years after our trial, but with the aim of explaining the former "prevailing opinion." In the other articles of the Caroline code which might apply to the crimes committed by the Pappenheimers there is even less about witchcraft: murder by poisoning (art. 130), simple murder (art. 137), malicious damage (arts. 128, 176), robbery (art. 126), arson (art. 125), theft (art. 157ff.), sacrilege (art. 171ff.), blasphemy (art. 106), sodomy (art. 116), adultery (art. 120), procuring (art. 123), "treason" (art. 124). "Vexatious," "malicious," "against law and propriety": these terms certainly occur, but there is no mention of the "heinous, abominable, and dreadful sin . . . of witchcraft" cited in the judgment. Could it be that this crime is not dealt with, or even mentioned, in these familiar old sources, simply because it was neither familiar nor old?

It is true that the fallacy on which the crime was based was anything but novel. The idea of witches or wise-women reaches back deep into the origins of human culture. Prosecutions against such unnatural creatures had occurred as far back as the thirteenth century—not, indeed, in secular courts but in ecclesiastical courts, where the issue was sin rather than crime. There is no evidence of regular criminal prosecution of witches by the secular authorities before the beginning of the sixteenth century. The first mention of such an unprecedented case before the Imperial Court of Appeal occurred in December 1508. At the time of our trial scarcely a century had passed since then. Schwarzenberg's Bamberg Penal Code, the model for the Caroline code, came into force in 1507; no wonder it makes no mention of witchcraft. It was intended as a set of secular statutes for an ecclesiastical ruler, not as a handbook for the Church's inquisition. And in 1532? Would it not have been possible to extend the Bamberg criminal code in this direction? As a matter of reediting, it certainly would have been; as a political issue, it was not feasible. It was itinerant preachers from Rome—the Dominicans and the judges of the Inquisition, Heinrich Institoris and Jakob Sprenger— who brought news of this novel and unbelievable crime. They castigated the new offense as the most terrible form of heresy—a word that jarred on the ears of the Protestant imperial princes. They had no intention of giving their blessing to it as part of imperial law. That they later embraced this superstition themselves is another matter altogether.

Witchcraft does, however, figure in a publication designed for judicial use: Ulrich Tengler's *Layman's Code*.[109] This work, popular because it was in German and clearly arranged, was the vademecum of every self-respecting, minimally qualified man of law. It is highly probable that it was known to Wangereck, who was very well read. He may on occasion have followed the same line of argument as the author: "That such an evil reprobate should bring about hail, showers, frost, and other such violent weather to the detriment of crops, likewise inflicting on man and beast distempers or painful injury, or else travel from one place to another, and practice lewdness with evil spirits—this is scarcely to be comprehended, fathomed, or believed by human reason. When, therefore, all manner of doubts and disputation did arise among those learned in the law, as to whether such heretical practices of these monsters might be credited, to wit, that they be capable of causing or inflicting such mischief, wherefore the secular judges did from time to time dilate thereon, that such evil had gone unpunished in certain places, so that this heresy had grown rife, and that but recently such tales had been made known from their experience by Papal Inquisitors, and there had been caused to appear some books, particularly in the Latin and the German language, and especially one entitled *Malleus Maleficarum*, this same having been approved by very learned men, and also licensed to appear in printed letters by His Royal Roman Majesty, in the fourteen hundred and eighty-sixth year, reckoning from the birth of our dear Lord Jesus Christ, and having three distinct parts with many questions and arguments therein." In default of other sources, then, the *Layman's Code* had recourse to the *Hammer of Witches* to instruct the "secular authorities" how "such evil and transgressions might be altogether eradicated, and with what statutes the secular and ecclesiastical courts might proceed against, condemn, sentence, and punish the same."

Tengler's *Layman's Code* first appeared in 1509, although at that time it did not contain the passage just quoted. That was added in the new printing of 1511, under the heading "On Heresy, Soothsaying, Black Arts, Sorcery, Witches, etc." Can this date be used to mark the invasion of the secular penal code by the inquisitors' ideas? Only up to a point. More than thirty years later a similar popular manual for judicial use appeared, which exerted as much influence as the *Layman's Code*. Compiled by the Munich magistrate Andreas Perneder, it contained not one word about witchcraft. Sorcery, however, was mentioned. Perneder drew a distinction between evil sorcery and soothsaying on the one hand, and benevolent magic on the other, by which "a patient might be succored, or his vineyards and fields shielded from harm, as also from showers and hail." There was no mention of "the heretical practices of witches and suchlike."

These words, like the entire passage in the *Layman's Code* referring to witchcraft, are redolent of theological doctrine. Why should a lawyer, of all people, quote the *Hammer of Witches* as an authority with the force of law—at the beginning of the sixteenth century, too, a time when resistance on the part of secular judges to witch trials was still perceptible throughout Germany. In an age, in fact, when the prosecution of witches in the secular courts was an extraordinary event. The aroma of incense that floats round the witchcraft paragraph in the *Layman's Code* betrays its author. His name was not Ulrich Tengler but Christoph Tengler. He was a professor of theology at the University of Ingolstadt, and the son of the man who was ostensibly the sole author of the *Layman's Code*.

The clergyman did not admit that he was coauthor, with his father, of this work. It would not be proper for him, as a priest, thus to confuse canon law with secular law. This is the gist of an epistle dated 13 June 1510, which was issued with the revised printing. He claimed he had merely suggested certain additions to his father and had helped him to frame them. His aged father took a different view: his son had "handed his book back to him with a number of additions and extra headings, and had collated the index of literature quoted." This is no doubt what happened; the son's account was merely an elegant evasion. The aged Ulrich Tengler, who died in 1510 or 1511, had asked his son for assistance. The latter had edited the work in radical fashion, insinuating the language of the Inquisition. We do not know whether the original author, with one foot in the grave, even read the proofs of the work. We may well doubt it. It is certain, however, that he gave his blessing and allowed the amended book to appear in print. Seldom has senile infirmity had such fateful consequences. It was partly to blame for the ideas of the *Hammer of Witches* finding their way into the practice of the secular courts. The fact that the *Layman's Code* quoted the *Hammer of Witches* as an authority alongside the Roman codices endowed this trash with standing and influence in legal circles.

Other authors also played their part—in particular, the highly respected imperial legal consultant, Jodocus Damhouder from Bruges. He incorporated into his *Praxis rerum criminalium* entire passages from the *Hammer of Witches.*

At the time when the council of state was sitting in judgment on Paulus Pappenheimer's family, the legal status of the *Hammer of Witches* had long been equivalent to that of statute law. That was one of the factors which sealed the fate of our vagrant family and their fellow accused. For a man like Wangereck to cling to the spirit and the letter of the *Hammer of Witches* proved that, however hot-headed he might be, he was still a very competent lawyer.

A DAY IN THE LIFE OF A JAILOR'S WIFE

Very little has come down to us about the ironmaster's wife, who performed a range of lowly tasks in the Munich Falcon Tower. We do not even know her name. The prisoners, to whom she brought their meals and occasionally fresh straw for their cells, called her "the ironmaster's wife." We have to imagine a woman of about thirty, not ugly but not pretty either, not squeamish but not coarse. What with all the pain and squalor suffered by the inmates of the Falcon Tower, we are liable to forget that the jailor's wife did not have an easy life herself. The reason lay in her nature, which I believe I know something about, in spite of the meager information in our sources.

The ironmaster's wife was neither stupid nor dull nor harsh. She would have had to be all these things not to find life in the Falcon Tower hard. On the ground floor of the prison she acted as a housewife, looked after her husband and her children, cleaned and washed, placed a few flowers beneath the crucifix. On the northeast side of the building she had laid out a little garden in which a few vegetables and some wild flowers transplanted from the meadows struggled to exist, for very little sun found its way into the quadrangle between the high walls. In this way she tried to lead the life of simple, ordinary folk. But she knew that beneath her little domestic kitchen there lay a vault of horrors, while above it prisoners languished, chained to the walls of their evil-smelling hutches. She could hear the footsteps of these poor wretches on the wooden stairs as they were taken to the torture chamber for interrogation. She saw them in their pitiable condition following the torture. And when her scowling husband joined her and the children at their meagerly furnished table and said grace before their midday meal, she knew that the screams of his victims were still ringing in his ears. Was it possible to talk about the weather, the price of beef, or the Sunday picnic with the children that they had planned? Of course it was possible, and they did it, but they never ceased to be aware of the misery that surrounded them; conversation about everyday things always had an undertone of terror. The ironmaster's wife was unable to separate her official life from her private life as may have been possible in later ages, for the two were linked and interwoven. When she went shopping and did the cooking, she was doing it for the prisoners as well as for her family. It was not uncommon for interrogations to take place in her living room. People in the street did not see her simply as a housewife; they avoided her as "dishonorable" on account of her husband's occupation.

He had not assumed office of his own free will. The record suggests often enough that he was no more coarse and violent of disposition than his wife was. He took no pleasure in the prisoners' sufferings, but in all probability he was afraid of the power of the demons, whose presence he believed he could sense often enough as he practiced his cruel trade. What forced him to pursue his vocation? We do not know, we can only suppose that he himself had once been a prisoner and had been pardoned simply because there was need of a jailor. He was not permitted to "give notice," for, had he given up his office, he would once more have been treated as a prisoner, and possibly suffered punishment or death.

Whereas the ironmaster approached the inmates of the Falcon Tower as the henchman of the authorities and as their torturer, his wife was the only person who ever did them any favors. She looked after them. She did not exactly provide them with everything a person needs, but she brought them water, bread, soup; she brought them fresh air by opening the cell window at their request; she brought them cleanliness by changing their straw litter and washing their clothes from time to time. And so she became their confidante: she carried messages from one to the other, told them something of the world outside, and sometimes warned them in advance when the commissioners were coming. She was more intimate than anyone else with the prisoners, who were in her care for weeks and months on end. She talked to them, got to know of their memories and hopes, and certainly knew more of their guilt or innocence than the court did. And she saw, too, what the torture did to them, how they became physically more and more wretched and mentally more and more confused. She bandaged their wounds and tried to console them. More she should not and dared not do. Once her compassion seduced her into giving a woman prisoner a knife so that she could put an end to her misery. It all came out, and very nearly ended badly for the ironmaster's wife.

Among all these wretched creatures, it was the fate of little Hänsel Pappenheimer that most deeply moved her. The eleven-year-old boy, who had been lodged in his mother's cell for the first few weeks following the committal of the vagrants to prison, had been placed in a cell of his own in June, on the orders of the commissioners. It was only thanks to the ironmaster's courteously worded protest that the child was not fettered to the wall. Ever since the boy had been thus isolated, the ironmaster's wife had taken over the role of mother. When she was distributing food or making her customary rounds, she used to stay longer in Hänsel's cell than with the other prisoners. Sometimes she brought him a toy to play with, a doll woven from straw, a few wooden blocks to pass the time in his dungeon.

It was not easy to gain the boy's confidence. At first he behaved in a reserved and aggressive manner, answering back insolently or petulantly, shocking the ironmaster's wife with vulgar curses and expletives. For he claimed, with defiant pride, that he was the child of a witch.

His mother had been forced by torture to make this confession to the commissioners in his presence, on 5 May 1600. She had no choice. On that same day, Hänsel had been interrogated for more than an hour in the vault. The rod had forced from him the confession that his mother had apprenticed him to witchcraft. "His mother often took him with her when she set out on her pitchfork," the child had said, "to the place where the devils came together to enjoy themselves. He had seen the Devil for sure, all loathsome and black . . . sitting on a chair with his servants around him. The place where they went was like a house or a town. Anyone who looked up in the air saw dreadful things. The devils and the women all laughed together, played all sorts of pranks, tugged each other's hair, danced in a ring, then all flew off again. His mother told him he should watch what she did, so that he would be able to do the same when he came to fly abroad himself." After this confession the interrogation was interrupted and his mother was fetched. She vigorously denied that the child had ever had any truck with the Devil, whereupon the commissioner told her to admit that the boy had not been baptized and that he was the child of a witch. When Anna would not admit this, she was bound in front of her child's eyes and hoisted up—and left hanging until she declared through her sobs and tears, "because . . . the Devil said, when a witch was with child, then the child was his, she had promised him Hänsel already in her womb, as well as in life. And although Hanns Scheiflinger was nominally his godfather in the eyes of the world, he had nevertheless not been baptized, but, as the Devil himself had told her, a changeling had been put in his place and baptized instead of Hänsel. She didn't know, however, where he had taken the changeling from. During and after her confinement she had been very ill, and for several days had known nothing of what went on around her. Later, when the boy was five years old, she and the miller's wife from Kelheim, where they had cast a sickness on Rautenbusch's cattle, were once making their way late in the evening towards Regensburg, and sat down by the bridge outside the town. There her demon lover pestered her once more about the boy. She had taken the child with her on the way to Grass, and had him with her in Farmer Widmann's barn, where she was lodged at the time. And because the boy was asleep, she pulled his arm from under the blanket and bared as much of his body as the Devil needed in order to take blood from his side. Otherwise there was little need of promises or written contracts since he was already the Devil's child, promised to him while still in the womb. And although she took the boy with her on her flights for some two years following, it wasn't until later, when he was some weeks above seven years old, that he was made to swear an oath and give other tokens to the aforesaid Devil, at a meeting in the marsh at Mossmüll. But because he did not yet have any hair on his private parts, she gave some hair on his behalf and also had to speak some words instead of him. And it was about three years since that these promises had been given. It was only afterwards that she began taking him regularly to assemblies of witches, but not on every occasion on which she had gone flying. He used to sit at the meetings and behave like any child. He could not fly by himself, and he would not be eleven until next Michaelmas . . . She did not know where the Devil had gotten the other changeling child. And she would say once again, the boy had not been baptized. And for that reason she would ask them to help the child, for God's sake."

There had been a response to this plea: orders had been given that the child was to be separated from his mother, and a priest had been commissioned, who duly christened little Hänsel on 13 May, giving him the name of Cyprianus, with the customary ceremonial of chanting, the muttering of Latin phrases, and the sprinkling of holy water.

In spite of this, the boy had remained withdrawn and defiant. The ironmaster's wife had been able to gain his confidence very gradually. She was familiar with this kind of recalcitrance. Her own boys were not so very different: despised and constantly teased by other children, they too would defend themselves with defiant pride against a world that relegated them to the rank of outsiders on account of their father. It must have been obvious to her that such behavior was not necessarily a mark of diabolical obstinacy, which does not mean that she doubted the tale of the witch-child. It was widely told that witches often carried a stolen child to the christening instead of their own, so as to dedicate the latter to the Devil. Midwives who were also witches made use of this device to doom the newborn children of unsuspecting mothers instead of taking them to be christened. This was why women invariably distrusted midwives. Hänsel might well be Satan's child, but if he had been promised to the Devil even before his birth, he was not to blame for his association with the Evil One. He was destined to squirm at the end of the Devil's rope, like a hooked fish on the line. After all, he had never had a free choice between the Savior and his adversary. Why, then, was he kept in confinement and so brutally treated? Why should he be burned as a sorcerer, as the ironmaster occasionally predicted? Following his christening, one would have thought, the Devil's hold on the child was broken, and the fateful bond dissolved that had made him guilty in all innocence. Such were the questions that may have preoccupied the ironmaster's wife as she closed the door of Hänsel's cell after visiting him, and bolted it behind her.

In spite of his willfulness, he was simply a child of about ten, not a diminutive devil. No one can say whether the boy told his foster mother the truth about himself and his family as she sat there in his cell, stroking his hair and comforting him. Only one thing is certain: State Councillor Wangereck was on a false trail when he forced the child by dint of savage torture to confess that "he had several times fornicated with his fair lover." Since little Hänsel's involvement in witchcraft had been proved, the commissioner thought it appropriate to substitute the regular torture for beatings with the cane that were customary in the case of minors. With *crimina excepta*, as he no doubt explained in learned terms to the reluctant ironmaster, the usual restrictions would not apply.

Following these more stringent interrogations, the boy's battered little body had to be carried back to his cell. There, the ironmaster's wife would take the wretched mite in her arms, bind up his wounds, and comfort him, trying to hide the bitterness that may almost have choked her. Then she left him alone in his cell and went down the two flights of stairs to sit with her husband and her children at the sparsely provided table, talking about the weather, the price of beef, the picnic planned for Sunday.

EVIL SPELLS

Since six o'clock in the morning, Bavaria's young duke had been sitting, pale, gaunt, and solemn, at the desk in his study, ruling his realm. He was alone, with a vast pile of documents and papers, which his private secretary, Dr. Christoph Gewold, had arranged as usual according to urgency and topic, stacking them in piles on the vast desk. Maximilian wished to work by himself, giving his instructions in writing. He rang only rarely for the footman who waited outside his door, handing him a folded note with a few scribbled lines, instructing him to take it to the Chancellery in the Old Palace, to the chamberlain's office, or to a meeting of the council of state. The ruler spent most of his time sitting erect in his armchair, scanning sundry papers, occasionally laying a page down, picking up a pen with his right hand, and writing a brief note in the margin of the report, petition, or recommendation. For instance: "A pity there's so little brain in such thick heads." And: "There's no need to write something twice if it can be done once, at the right time." Or else: "It's a scandal that nothing is kept secret in the council of war or the Chancellery. I wish to warn them and point out that, if I catch one of them again, I'll set up a court-martial and have them cast dice to see who'll pay for the rope." In contrast to the taste of the age, but understandably, in view of the piles of documents on his desk, the duke was so infuriated by the long-winded and stilted style of these submissions that he could not refrain from mordant comments.[110] He detested time-wasting; his people were to spare him circumstantial preambles and labyrinthine clauses, and to state the case succinctly. "Action, not learned twaddle" was what he wanted. Everything proceeded far too slowly, in his view. And that included the trial of the vagrants, of which he happened to be studying a summary.

The document in question was entitled "An extract touching the witchcraft and sorcery of the evildoers detained in the Falcon Tower" and contained a summary of the evil spells to which the accused in the Pappenheimer case had confessed. Its contents were bound to alarm the young duke, who was obsessed by fear of witches. The vagrants and their associates had brought about the illness or death of several hundred people by their spells, doomed about a thousand head of cattle, destroyed the crops of innumerable farmers by means of rainstorms and frost, and "ruined numerous marriages."

Impatient and overworked as he was, the duke no doubt skipped rapidly over the details. Because "he hadn't wished to pay them for their work," Michel and his brother Gumpprecht had scattered a devilish powder in the path of the "Dean in Altenpuech," so that he had fallen ill. "He had treated Ramecker in Mundriching with a powder, because he had once struck him—but not so that he should die." In fact, "his father had bathed him with herbs, and had done him much good, for which he had been given three taler." According to his own account, Michel had killed "over fifty children" and "more than a score of old folk" by means of magic spells. "Every familiar devil made his victim kill children and eat their hearts." In the course of another interrogation he listed eleven persons by name whom he had killed or crippled by applying the diabolical ointment, and, over and above that, claimed to have "killed or crippled some twenty other persons." Nonetheless, "the Devil had beaten him because he had not done more." But there was one comfort: "not every man could be thus afflicted, especially not the clergy, or those who lead a God-fearing life." In general, "the better kind of folk" were hardly vulnerable at all. Gumpprecht Gämp-Pämberl gave it as his opinion that "they were more assiduous in their observance." Old Pappenheimer, too, who himself had slain more than a hundred people by magic spells, was of the opinion that witchcraft would not work on everyone—indeed, "scarcely on one in a thousand, otherwise the whole world would be unsafe."

The duke was quite clear about the reason for this sorcery. It was done from sheer spite, as the council's report confirmed. Michel Pappenheimer had said, for instance: "He had felt no hatred of folk, but he had had to do it on orders from the Devil, who forced him to do it." The "Extract" included interesting details about the methods used to cast these evil spells. Anna, Pappenheimer's elderly wife, who had injured some sixty people, revealed to the court: "Harm could be done to people with powder as well as with ointment, but the ointment was more effective. The effect of the powder could more easily be countered." Apart from that, she said, "if she wanted to apply a spell to someone and kill him, in fact, she had to use Satan's black ointment, but if she merely wanted to make him fall ill or to cripple him, then she had to use the white ointment given her by her demon lover, Salion. This could be applied for a spell of one, two, three, or seven years, so that the victim would be ill for that amount of time, or even die. And she had wrought so much mischief of that kind during the last nine years, that she could not tell it all . . . The words used when the ointment was applied had to run: 'I anoint thee for so many years, in the name of all the devils, and of my familiar, who taught me this art, and I have promised him that thou shalt be crippled or even die.' And it must be done of a Tuesday or a Thursday night, which are his evil nights." Another kind of evil spell was effected in the following manner: "The magic had to be poured into a hole or buried, and was of such a nature that whatever passed over it first was bound to suffer such distress as was wished upon it. The substance was buried as a rule beneath the threshold of a room or chamber, or the doorstep of a house or stable, ointment and powder together, wrapped up in a rag. But it did mischief only to the first creature that passed over it; after that, it might lie as long as you liked, it would do no more harm."

The duke turned over the pages. It was "beyond all measure" what "mischief was inflicted on cattle by anointing with the Devil's unguent or by the sprinkling of powder," he read. Often the vagrants "scattered such things upon a pasture that whole herds of cattle perished of it." "The beasts did not all fall down at once and together," Michel had stated, "but one after another, and the substances that they had buried had often retained their power for anything from one year to fifteen years." The powder could also be "buried beneath the threshold of the byre door, from which many beasts perished when they were driven across it." Many individual cases were listed and briefly noted in passing. Michel Pämb: "Last spring, when the folk in the almshouse in Irlbach refused to take him and his family in, they sprinkled powder under the byre door, beside the gate leading into the lane, and in the lane itself where the cattle were driven through, so that a great many cattle perished—about forty head." Georg Schmälzl: "About a year and half previously, in summer, he spread ointment and powder made from infants' hands under the threshold of Farmer Mair's byre in Eintal. Two of his cows died of it. The substance must be buried in a little earthenware pot in the name of all the devils, and as long as it remained, so long would the cattle die of it. But people soon found remedies. Down on the Danube there were any number of soothsayers and adepts, particularly a man in Mainloch, near Pointen, whom they called Anderl the Wise One, and everyone went to see him." And then there was talk of the conjuring up of storms. The duke read: "Whenever there was a meeting or a banquet in a field, a storm was conjured up afterwards. And for that purpose, each of the women had to give hair from her head and from various parts of her body—her armpit and her private parts, both from the lefthand side. The chief devil then mixed this in a vessel with water or something, she did not rightly know what, and placed it before them. One of the women, whom he chose for the task, had to approach, dip a whisk into the pot, and sprinkle the liquid over herself and the Master in the name of all the devils. Thereupon a gale would spring up, and the chief devil said to them, 'Fly off in the name of all the devils, you still have time.' But he always kept back one woman with him, who had to fire off the tempest." This did not quite tally with another description. According to Gumpprecht Pämb, he had conjured up storms by "mixing devil's ointment, the powder from infants' hands, hair from his body, and a kind of balsam weed that grows by fences, with water, and putting it into a new pot, in which it was boiled . . . And if the stuff in the pot boiled for a long time, the storm would last a long time." A third statement gives another account of such spells: "Out in a field he had put devil's ointment, children's powder, and hair from his body into a new pot, added water, and boiled the mixture. Then he had taken the pot in his left hand and cast it down on the ground in the name of all the devils, so that the stuff ran out on to the ground. The violence of the storm depended on how much of the mixture was used." A storm that had been caused by magic spells could be recognized by the fact that there would be hairs in the hailstones. The ringing of bells, which was the usual practice in the country, was only a partial remedy. While the bells were being rung, it is true, the witches "could not approach too closely, for the sound of the bells sometimes scattered them. But if this kind of exorcism was practiced too zealously, the storm would break with even greater violence and would do even more damage than it otherwise might have done."

The duke turned a few more pages. The Devil had sometimes changed his creatures, now incarcerated in the Falcon Tower, into beasts, he read. "If the Devil wished to transform them, he usually made them into cats, dogs, goats, wolves, magpies, and crows. If they were changed into magpies and crows, they usually had to settle on the fields and peck up the seed that the peasants were sowing. He was unable to change them into sheep or doves, on account of our dear Lord." One of the prisoners "had sometimes been changed into a toad by the Devil, and placed behind a fence, with the intention of poisoning people as they passed by."

"On the ruination of marriages" was the title of the following paragraph, which particularly interested Maximilian. It was claimed that the prisoners had "set a number of married couples against each other." This spell was practiced in the following manner: "When there is a gale in the forest, the trunks of the trees rub and graze each other." The symbolism is unmistakable. "When a trunk is found that has been chafed and rubbed bare, a piece of wood must be carved out from the bare place, in the name of all the devils. It is then burned to a powder and put into people's soup or other food, to last a period of four, six, or more years."

What followed in the remaining pages of the "Extract" was quickly perused. The prisoners had allegedly ruined the farmers' grain by scattering a diabolical powder on it as they flew on their way, "so that the ears wilted and lost their kernels," and the harvest "yielded much less than otherwise." They had also flown to

300

stables and cellars, in order to steal. "When they arrived at a cellar, the Devil had already opened the door for them beforehand." They had then taken all manner of provisions, but had also made merry with the wine they found stored there. "When they set out for a meeting in the fields, they go first to the cellars and drink . . . although the Devil was displeased, if any of them should drink too deep . . . If any of the women should drink more than her fill in a cellar and could not therefore set forth at the appointed hour, she was thoroughly thrashed. . . The poor among them fly abroad so as to bring home eggs, lard, and such things. And they often fly also to scratch up grain and seed from the fields." And then there was mention of "Desecration of the Holy Sacrament and of other spiritual things," "Covens, or witches' assemblies," "On the exhumation of children," and so on and so forth.

We may deduce from our sources that Maximilian found this report fell short in one important respect. Confessions had been submitted to him. But what about the trial? He was probably reflecting irritably that every day the prisoners spent in custody was costing him hard cash. How much more time did the council propose to waste on the case? We can see him reach for his pen and write: "A report to be made on the present stage of the trial. Maximilian." Then the voluminous report found its way to the right-hand side of the desk, where the documents lay that had already been dealt with. The young monarch reached for the next file from the heap marked "Council Business." He had no time to waste. He was busy ruling.

ON THE AFFRONTING OF GOD

If Johann Baptist Fickler had been permitted to watch his former pupil working at his desk, it would have seemed important to him that the duke studied with particular care that part of the "Extract" which dealt with the desecration of the consecrated Host. The old teacher would no doubt have taken occasion to point out that the most heinous feature of that crime was the affront to the honor of God. The bewitching of men and cattle, the conjuring up of tempests, and the mischief done to farmers might well be reprehensible and worthy of the death penalty, but such activities did not threaten to destroy mankind. This was, however, precisely the threat posed by the blasphemous doings of such monstrous creatures. It was the Pappenheimers' disparagement of the most hallowed things that showed them and their accomplices to be so much worse than ordinary footpads, arsonists, and murderers. They were in fact individuals who were likely to involve Bavaria in the most dreadful calamity by incurring the wrath of God.

But leaving that aside—although it was difficult to leave such a fearful peril aside—was it possible to imagine a more abominable crime than the desecration of the body of Christ, our Savior? The prisoners had confessed to committing this atrocity on a number of occasions. "When he, Paulus Pämbs, received the Holy Sacrament at Eastertime," one of the statements read, "he kept it, and afterwards bit it several times so that fair-sized drops of blood were seen to come out of it. And he also stamped on the same, so that it suffered wounds and bruises. He also threw it into the fire, and the flames turned blue. He threw it into the privy on two occasions. After doing such things he felt dizzy and thought he was going to fall down."

Gumpprecht Pappenheimer had confirmed this statement. "His father once cast the Host into the privy. In Wischlburg his father bit the Host, so that it shed blood—especially the part he had in his mouth. But they just laughed at this, and scarcely thought it worth mentioning." He himself had also been guilty of desecrating the Host on a number of occasions. "When he received the holy sacrament . . . he had always taken it out of his mouth again . . . trampled on it, put it into his shoe, and walked on it. Then he threw it into the fire or threw it away. That was what the Devil wanted." And from Pappenheimer's wife they heard that the Devil had made her bury Hosts, or trample on them. Her son Michel made a similar confession. "Because the Devil ordered him to do all manner of evil, he took Hosts, which he stole along with certain monstrances, and also took the Host from Communion on five occasions, spitting it out, trampling on it, kicking it, throwing it away, and defiling it in the basest fashion . . . His feet swelled up so badly . . . that he often could not force them into his shoes."

These confessions showed that it was possible to commit this fearful blasphemy, but that God rarely failed to give a clear indication of His anger—drops of blood oozed from the Host, the fire changed color, the evildoer suffered dizziness or swelling of the feet. This was a miraculous confirmation that it was not simply a wafer of flour and water that had been desecrated but the very body of Christ. As the tools of Satan, the prisoners had declared a feud against the Savior, and had insulted Him. They had never passed by "a crucifix or Station of the Cross" without spitting on

302

the ground, and during the act of Transubstantiation they had been lacking in devotion—they had always "cast down their eyes and carried on with their villainous pranks."

It was not only the religious zealot in Dr. Fickler who saw the essence of witchcraft in these blasphemous practices, it was the lawyer as well. One of the most respected professors of jurisprudence of the age, Jodocus Damhouder of Bruges (whom we have already mentioned), although himself no great churchman, chose not to deal with the crime of witchcraft under the heading "Of pernicious Sorcery" in his manual for criminal courts: it was linked with high treason, as *crimen laesae Maiestatis divinae.*

Lese majesty was the main issue and had been so from the outset. We may remember that the pope's Holy Inquisition had discovered the crime in the first place, and had designated it as the purest and most vicious form of heresy. In prosecutions brought against Albigensians, Waldensians, and Templars, torture had brought astonishing facts to light. The heretics concluded veritable pacts with the Devil, they had physical intercourse with him, they flew to nocturnal Black Masses where stolen children were sacrificed and eaten after the manner of cannibals. Following a wild dance they plunged into an orgy, and before departing they were given an ointment by the Devil with which they were to inflict injury on men and beasts alike. At that time, during the thirteenth century, no one spoke of witchcraft, but the crime was known in all its details. What was it, fundamentally? It was deviation from the only true Catholic Church. Anyone who subscribed to heretical doctrines was guilty of insulting God; but anyone who insulted God would not shrink from the ultimate extreme of evil, and was likely to become a Devil worshiper. Had not Christ himself said, he who is not for me is against me? According to St. Augustine's doctrine of the City of God, there was only an "either-or" in the struggle between God and Evil. Anyone who deviated from the true faith was prey to Satan. In the war between saint and devil, no one could be neutral. A man who refused to accept the discipline of the orthodox army might well talk of conscience and of his own insight, but he was still a traitor serving the enemy cause. Put on the rack, he soon confessed the whole truth: he was disobedient because he was obeying the orders of the enemy commander. The more frequently such confessions were extorted from heretics, the more advisable it seemed to search for traitors in the ranks of those Christians who were to all appearances loyal, for the shrewdest of deserters would not display the signs of their insubordination. Such disciples of the Devil committed all the atrocities that had been admitted by Albigensians, Waldensians, and Templars, but they did not openly voice their opposition in matters of religion. They were nevertheless arch-heretics, more dangerous, indeed, than those who gave themselves away by rebellion. The war that was being waged by the Holy Inquisition concentrated more and more on that group of traitors, who were soon termed witches, wizards, or ogres.

It was the clergy who first detected such criminals and arch-heretics in German lands. Pope Innocent VIII had learned in 1484, "beyond all doubt, and with no little dismay, that in certain parts of Upper Germany, as also in the sees of Mainz, Cologne, Trier, and Salzburg, very many persons of both sexes, forgetful of their own salvation and deserting the Catholic faith, copulate with devils as men or women, practice all manner of mischief, and by means of spells, incantations, conjurations, and other detestable superstitions abort births of women and of animals, blight the fruits of the earth and of trees, the vines, as well as men, women, and beasts . . . also fields, meadows, crops and other produce . . . inflicting cruel pain and suffering on men and animals . . . to the effect that those same men might be barren, and the women not conceive . . . And in addition to this, they break their solemn oath, denying the faith that they adopted on receiving the Holy Baptism." Wherefore the pope "conferred on his beloved sons, Henricus Institoris . . . as well as Jacobus Sprenger," the authors of the *Hammer of Witches*, "the necessary authority as Inquisitors to investigate this heretical mischief," and removed "all obstacles through which the discharge of their duties as Inquisitors might be in any way impeded." God's representative on earth was concerned to stifle the evil at source, to root out the arch-heresy before it had a chance to spread. It was souls that he was concerned about.

These hardly constituted a legal entity, one might feel, that could be protected by means of the criminal code. But Dr. Fickler was of a different opinion—and he was not the only one. The duke felt himself responsible not only for the physical well-being of his subjects but also for their spiritual salvation. He saw himself as the father of a household, an image we may recall, as someone who would one day have to answer before God for the behavior of his subjects. In the "General Instructions for the Prosecution of Witches" issued by Duke William V, it is made quite clear from the outset that it was the affront to God's majesty that made

304

witchcraft such a heinous offense and required that the authorities prosecute it with the utmost rigor of the law. "The monarch ordained by God" must seize the sword in the first place "to restore the honor of God, all His beloved Saints, and the Holy Sacraments"; the "temporal loss" was of secondary importance. The official list of questions, which formed an appendix to the "Instructions" and was consulted during the interrogation of the Pappenheimers, reflects this idea concerning the *crimen magiae* committed by witches. Immediately after questions relating to the identity of the suspect ("Name, age, place of birth, identity of father and mother") and the grounds for suspicion ("For what reason was she reputed . . . by many to be guilty of witchcraft") the judge was to proceed at once to the essential feature of the offense: "Whether she had not surrendered herself to vile Satan, denying God, his Saints, and also the Holy Sacraments." Questions concerning actual sorcery were not put until later, which shows that this issue was of secondary importance in the official view. God will also figure largely in the sentence passed on the Pappenheimers. The infringement of human law is, of course, also condemned, but the main issue remains "the denial and abjuration of the Divine Majesty and all His Heavenly Host." The accused "were lost to all sense of God's honor," and had acted in a "damnable, godless, and unnatural manner," "in contempt of the Holy Commandments, indeed, in contempt of the most holy name of God Himself." In Bavaria in the year 1600, anyone who offended God also offended His temporal representative, the duke. He believed he had been called to office by the grace of God, and he had his own interests to look after. William V was convinced "that Princes and those in authority are ordained by God for the purpose of protecting the true service of God and the pure unadulterated Religion, of governing their subjects without fear or favor, and of maintaining peace and order." The sequence is anything but random: the protection of religion was the first priority. How could it be otherwise, in an age when faith and power moved ever closer together to confront their external foes! Both were equally threatened by new ideas of every kind. The claim put forward in the *Hammer of Witches*, that the world was approaching its end, appealed to particularly responsive souls. "And so the world is now . . . inundated with every manner of wickedness on the part of demons, since the depravity of men ever increaseth and love dwindleth."

Fickler, as a professor of law, could have supplied the young duke with further, purely constitutional reasons why the prosecution of any heresy, and particularly witchcraft, fell within the competence of secular courts. He had taught the young prince that his position in the state corresponded to that of an absolutist Roman emperor of the late period. The latter's powers included sovereignty in matters of religion. The territorial state of Maximilian's day aspired to rule absolutely over its subjects, and that absolute power naturally included above all the control of conscience. To achieve that, as I mentioned earlier, the ruler sought supremacy over the Church, which was rewarded for its subordination by active state sponsorship. Prosecution of heresy on behalf of the state was thus no small indication of that absolute power to which the duke laid claim.

This was, then, by no means the least important reason why the campaign against witches was first and foremost a state prosecution of heresy, and only incidentally a defense against material damage. The heretical nature of the offense was also emphasized by lawyers. Damhouder called sorcerers and witches apostates. They were to the Devil what pious monks were to God. Their deeds he described simply as the consequences of this sin. A celebrated contemporary, the criminal lawyer Benedikt Carpzov, also defined witches as people "who, falling away from the Christian faith, make a pact and common cause with the Devil." As far as their criminal liability was concerned, the actual harm inflicted by these persons was of minor importance. It is significant that apostasy was an essential feature of witchcraft, and this was the reason that "infidels"—unbaptized Jews, for instance, or gypsies— could not be culprits.[111] They could not abjure the true faith, for they had never possessed it. They too were persecuted for many reasons, but never on account of witchcraft. Non-Christians, by definition, could never be witches. Belief in witchcraft was not stupid or blind; after all, it had been trained in dogmatic theology in the South of France.

The element of heresy might be lacking in the case of learned necromancers, who were not infrequently members of the clergy. That was an uncertain issue. In Prague, the emperor had surrounded himself with alchemists, cabbalists, and astrologers. Admittedly, he was thought to be not quite right in the head, but he was a good Catholic Christian. Did these people practice witchcraft? Possibly even the head of the Holy Roman Empire himself? Unthinkable! The abbot Johann Trithemius, author of a standard work attacking the vermin who practiced witchcraft, had himself been a celebrated sorcerer. The highly respected necromancer Dr. Lucas Gauricus had actually become a bishop. And wasn't the whole world agog with the tale of Johann Faust of Knittlin-gen, who boasted with impunity about his pact with the Devil? In none of these cases was an accusation of witchcraft raised. The wise magicians were sorcerers, it is true, but not heretics. Dr. Gauricus, a personal friend of Pope Paul III, occasionally quoted from the Bible: The woman shall crush the serpent's head beneath her heel. From that it might be concluded that man is stronger than the Devil if he has the will to be so. A necromancer of his sort was playing a game with demons. They had to serve him, which vexed them but amused God. Dangerous thoughts, declared Dr. Martin Luther, who was among those who heard such remarks: "He who invites the Devil to be his guest will not easily be rid of him."

Many people shared this view; the dividing line between black and white magic was a gray area. It all depended on whether a particular person could be considered more potent than the Devil. What was regarded as a high-spirited prank in the case of students might have the appearance of a hideous crime in the case of a peasant servant-girl. The issue was: Who was in thrall to whom— the Devil to man, or man to the Devil? It was only when such playing with fire led to apostasy, and the pact with the Devil assumed a heretical character, that witchcraft was mentioned. In Faust's time, the Devil was obviously considered less invincible than was the case later. But even in earlier times, witchcraft would certainly have been imputed to a gang of vagrants like the Pappen-heimers. Sorcery was not an art to be practiced by common folk. If a bishop dabbled in it in order to vex the Devil, the Pappenheim-ers surely practiced it because they were members of the cult.

In the council's "Extract" there was therefore very little about the actual crime of the prisoners confined in the Falcon Tower; it was taken as read. For Fickler's taste there was probably too much about evil spells, which were merely a consequence of the much more dreadful offense of heresy, and too little about the affront to God. If the council had taken more notice of the old gentleman's advice, the "Extract" would have been couched in different terms. But no one bothered to ask his opinion any more.

CONFESSIONS OF A NONE TOO VALIANT TAILOR

The council commissioners were convinced that supernatural powers were trying to influence the course of the prosecution they were conducting. In particular, they believed in the existence of demons who were preventing the prisoners from telling the truth.

But God too seemed to be taking an interest in their battle against the vile tribe of witches. How could the appearance in Munich of Georg Schmälzl, the tailor from Prunn, be explained otherwise than by the intervention of divine providence? We may remember that the good-natured old man had turned up in the council's offices at the beginning of May in order to hand over a petition on behalf of himself and his friends in Tettenwang, Bastl Baumann and Georg Reiter. The petitioner had aroused the suspicions of the officials there, and they had had him arrested on the spot. He was lodged in the Falcon Tower and interrogated on the subject of witchcraft for the first time on 16 May 1600. It required no more than a minimal degree of torture to persuade this none too valiant tailor to talk. Even after the initial session, it was obvious that the apparently harmless petitioner from Prunn was in reality a veritable monster, a wizard, and henchman of the Devil, like all the other accused in the Pappenheimer case. Schmälzl confessed that he had been a sorcerer for the last six years. At that time he had been making his way during the summer from Kelheim to Prunn, and had "drunk his fill at Essing," halfway between the two places. When he resumed his journey, "the evil spirit in the shape of a woman approached him in open country between Essing and Prunn," and "promised him a great deal of money" if he "would be hers" and "do her will." "He allowed himself to be persuaded by her fair words and grand promises, and fornicated with her, and her nature was cold. As soon as that happened, the Devil asked him to be his lover henceforth, to deny Almighty God, to forswear Him, to owe allegiance to the Devil alone, and to do whatever he was ordered. And to seal this pact he not only placed his left hand in the Devil's left hand, which was rather cold and rough, but he also had to sign the pact with his own blood, which the Devil took from his left shoulder. Although he himself could not write, the Devil guided his hand. Apart from this, he had to give the Devil hair from his head, from his eyebrows, from his armpit, and from the left side of his private parts, in order further to seal the bond. In return the Devil gave him about ten gold pieces . . . and a red ointment. For which money he bought drink and some clothing.

"The ointment, however, he had to smear on a fire iron when he wanted to take flight, and he had to mount the fire iron and set off with the words: 'Fly off in the name of all the devils, up, up and away.' If he used the ointment to smear on men and beasts, they would fall sick, become crippled, and wither away.

"And although his familiar devil came to him almost every

308

night following the pact, and also by day when he was alone, it was four weeks before he led him out, mounted on his fire iron, for the first time. They went in the direction of Hagenhill to an open field where three trees stood close together. There was an assembly of men and women, along with the Supreme Devil and other familiar demons. The Supreme Devil was clad in red and was sitting on a black chair that was also trimmed in red. His familiar demon introduced him to the Supreme One in the presence of the other devils and witches. He had to kneel down and swear that he would be the enemy of God and His Heavenly Host, and do whatever he was commanded to do, being promised money enough in return. He was then given fifteen gulden, as well as a reddish ointment, and told he must rub this ointment on people and on cattle and they would fall down and die from it. On that occasion he was not suffered to say anything other than what his familiar demon told him to say."

After that, they partook of a meal of boiled and roasted children's flesh, and drank their fill of wine. Then they danced, and each of them indulged separately in all manner of scandalous obscenities with his demon lover. Then they took counsel together and decided when they should meet again, and what each should do in the meantime. For the most part Schmälzl was commanded to do mischief to people and to cattle, and to kill them. The women were given even more instructions: to lead astray mothers who had but newly given birth, to slay children and bring them to their dances, to conjure up hail and other sorts of foul weather, and otherwise to ruin crops. On that occasion there were four males present at the dance, "to wit, the convent miller from Tettenwang, the late Paulus Weber from Kelheim, Gumpp Pappenheimer, and himself, the tailor. Item, about a score of women, but he had known only two of them, namely the miller's wife, and Paul Weber's wife from Kelheim, who had also died since then." Later on, he was often "at banquets and dances," on Tuesday, Thursday, and Saturday nights, "at the following places: In a field by Hagenhill, toward Grashausen, outside the village, close by three trees. At Laimerstadt, on the outskirts of the village, going toward Hienheim, in a lane there. At Grashausen, on a scrap of meadow beside the chapel. There he commonly saw the convent miller as master of ceremonies, old Pappenheimer, and his two elder sons, Jack the Glazier and Augustin the bread delivery man, also the miller's wife, Pappenheimer's wife, and Paul Weber's wife from Kelheim.

"Since entering upon witchcraft . . . he had received the Holy

Sacrament each Eastertide, but always took it furtively from his mouth in a kerchief, as if he were wiping his lips, carried it off home, then crushed it at the Devil's behest, spitting on it, cursing it, and otherwise fouling it in the most depraved manner. One time he trod on it, threw a fragment of it into the fire, and burned it. Not that anything happened to him on that account, except that the fire turned blue and gave out strange flames. The remaining Hosts he wrapped up in a rag, put into a pewter tankard, and kept in a chest in which his wife used to store linen and yarn in front of the bed at home in Prunn. They might still be found in that same place; he did not believe that his wife had gotten rid of them because he had told her to leave them alone, they were good for all manner of things. In any case, she knew nothing about them, where he had gotten them, or why, or what he used them for."

Wangereck, of course, had a letter dispatched to Abensberg, enclosing a transcript of this statement. Shortly afterwards, deputies searched the tailor's house without finding any trace of the Hosts. Georg Schmälzl was then taken down into the torture chamber once more on 16 June and confronted with this proof that he was lying. Thereupon he declared the truth to be that "he always took the Host from his mouth as soon as he received it in church, and took it out to the field with the three pear-trees near Hagenhill, ready for the next revels. He would take them out the evening before, however, because they could not take them along when they flew at night, and would hide them, in the branch of a tree for instance, until he arrived with his familiar demon to fetch them. Then he and others who had Hosts, took them out and defiled them in the vilest way outside the circle, spitting on them, and trampling them underfoot. When they fornicated with their demon lovers, they did so on top of the Hosts, and wiped their private parts with them. They threw them into a pit dug for that purpose, pissed on them, pranced, and wiped themselves with them, using the pits no differently than as a privy or carrion pit . . . And they also treated crucifixes and other sacred objects, such as rosaries, in the same way, broke them, threw them down, spat on them, trampled on them, and flung them into the pit . . . The pit into which they had thrown the Holy Sacrament and the crucifix was by the hedge, not far from the three trees. And if they were to search there," the tailor hastened to add, with the possibility of renewed torture in mind, "if they were to search there and find the pit, he did not think they would unearth the Hosts, because they would long since have rotted."

310

According to the old tailor's own statement, he had inflicted illness or death on no fewer than twenty-two persons by the use of the diabolical ointment. Among them were those who neglected to pay him, like Georg Mair of Nusshausen, near Prunn, on whom Schmälzl had inflicted a severe attack of lumbago because "he had been unwilling to pay his debt"; or "Zächerl of Baiersdorf, the other side of Prunn, whose hand he had smeared with ointment while they were carousing together. That was some five years since, and the man died within seven weeks. He did it because Zächerl was unwilling to pay him what he owed." The same thing had happened to people who intimidated the little tailor, or beat him. He had also murdered children, dug their corpses up secretly, and taken them to the witches' revels at Hagenhill. "The women gut and roast the children, quarter them and season them with pepper and suchlike. They kept the right hands from the boys and used them for magic spells, such as stirring up storms. The other bones from the skeleton, the head, hands, and feet, that they could not eat, they burned to a powder and used for their spells. The innards and the private parts they buried again."

He had also killed a great number of animals. For instance, "a year since he had smeared his ointment on a black cow grazing in a meadow, so that it fell sick. It belonged to the farmer at Pichelhausen, near Essing, and he had done it from sheer envy." He had "buried ointment and powder beneath the threshold of the stable belonging to a farmer called Wolf in Altenhexenagger. One of his horses had come to grief because of it." "And so he had often entered farmers' cow sheds by night, and taken milk and cream from the cows by milking, although nothing had otherwise befallen them, except that they had yielded no milk the following morning. But if they were milked too hard, or too often, they too were ruined and were sure to die. If a little of the ointment were smeared on a cow, then the milk was of such a kind that it could not be churned. He had been meant to do even more mischief to men and beasts at the Devil's behest, but he had not done so. Because of that, the Devil had often treated him very ill, scratching him and hitting him, and threatening to tear him to pieces."

He also claimed to have raided cellars, for example, "at Farmer Simon's in Kelheim, at Heislinger's, the landlord of the inn at Neustadt, Michel Mair, another landlord in Neustadt, and Georg Seiz, a landlord at Riedenburg." On these expeditions, the "chief fiends . . . went ahead and opened the cellar doors." They drank "from all kinds of vessels they found in the cellars," and he often had so much to drink that he did not know how he had found his way home again. When witches were flying abroad, they "could sometimes be heard or seen, especially those leading the flock. And if they were shouted at, they had to drop something; recently a witch from Abensberg dropped a bucket of lard as she flew off, and then came to earth herself, was caught, and condemned." His wife had never noticed his nocturnal absences on such excursions to cellars. "When he flew out in this manner, he usually laid a broom beside his wife."

As far as the casting of weather spells went, which was a female specialty, he claimed to have been an onlooker only and not to have taken any active part. "At Pentecost two years ago, he was present when the miller's wife in Tettenwang was busy brewing a storm. She took water in which she had washed her feet and left standing overnight, added Devil's ointment and hair from her body, stirred the mixture in a tub by means of an infant's hand. Then she carried it out into the fields in the direction of Hagenhill, sprinkling it on the ground here and there. A storm sprang up as she proceeded from place to place, and it wreaked havoc on the summer crop a mile and half round about in that district." "Just after Easter two years since, the aforementioned miller's wife, assisted by her husband, conjured up three frosts round about St. George's day, and these affected, and in some cases blighted, the grain and the vines for three miles around Prunn, Kelheim, and thereabouts . . . For hoarfrosts of that kind almost the same stuff was used as for conjuring up storms, namely, water in which feet had been washed, Devil's ointment, powder made from children's hands, and hair from the witch's body. That had to be sprinkled in the name of all the devils, wherever it was wished that the frost should strike, but it had to be clearly said that a frost was intended."

Such were the confessions of the tailor from Prunn, whom the Munich court had secured, thanks to the intervention of divine Providence. Admittedly, this fiend continually played down his position within the company of witches, trying to make the commissioners believe that he had been small fry and not one of the dangerous kind. He had "never wrought mischief by means of poison, nor dealt with poisonous beasts, nor sought to sow strife between spouses or other folk. He did not know how to recover stolen goods by spells, nor did he practice such magic, and he had never indulged in unseemly sex." Was that the truth? Well, that simply depended on whether Wangereck resolved to submit this not very brave tailor to further torture.

ON PREVAILING OPINION IN THE LEGAL PROFESSION

About the beginning of July 1600, probably following a meeting of the council of state, Johann Baptist Fickler received a heartwarming piece of news. His favorite son, Johann Christoph, at that time the prince's Bavarian councillor in Straubing, would come to Munich the following year as state councillor and confidential secretary. This promotion was not to be taken simply as a mark of ducal favor toward the prince's former tutor. It was also a mark of recognition in regard to the young man's qualifications, and that filled the elderly councillor with paternal pride. Fickler had had his son educated in conformity with his own notions, sending him to Ingolstadt and Bologna, but also to the papal courts, where he spent a period of practical training. The aim was to make him into a thoroughly sound legal practitioner. After returning to Ingolstadt, the young Fickler had graduated as Doctor of Civil and Canon Law at Pentecost 1597. He was hardworking and obsequious—quite different from his brother Hans, with his dreams of a military career. The very paragon of a successful administrative lawyer.

Even his doctoral dissertation marked him as such: a "Legal Discussion of the so-called Witches and Fiends." No doubt in keeping with his father's advice, he took full account of the basic maxim observed by every successful lawyer: always subscribe to "prevailing opinion." At that time, of course, this phrase, so familiar to every first-year student of law, had not yet been coined, but the principle was the same. One's own ideas might well prove a stumbling block, criticism of leading authorities was a questionable business. One could hardly do more damage to one's career prospects than by dissecting generally accepted views or espousing opposing views that were "untenable." The emergence of prevailing opinions is a political and social issue. It is not difficult to say how they are sustained: by a host of intellectually subservient career laywers, Johann Christoph Fickler and his ilk. If nowadays we find this tale of a witch trial embarrassing, that does not necessarily imply a judgment on the young man's intelligence and moral character. He was simply reiterating what his professor, Andreas Fachineus, had taught him, and the latter was merely repeating what was said in the "recognized" authorities and doctrine.

For the "prevailing opinion" of lawyers at that time reckoned that witchcraft was a real crime. Johann Christoph Fickler concedes in his "Legal Discussion" that there were a few individuals of some standing who claimed that the alleged crime of witchcraft was nothing but an illusion, and that the pact with the Devil, the

313

obscene antics of the witches, and all the rest of it, were merely fantasy and superstition.[112] Such doubters were wont to demand an end to the persecution of witches. But no heed should be paid to these wayward voices; the view to adopt was that of Jean Bodin, who, after all, had actually proved the existence of witchcraft.

This proof ran as follows:[113] statements by witches tended to agree not only with each other, but also with those of other nations, and with investigations carried out by learned men. Those who made these confessions "are for the most part quite simple, untutored folk or old women . . . who have never read Plutarch or Herodotus, nor conversed with witches from France and Italy, drawing comparisons, so that their statements might coincide in substance and in detail. They have never read the fifteenth Book of St. Augustine's *City of God*, where the author states that there can be no possible doubt, and that anyone who denies that evil spirits were wont to have sexual intercourse with women must be an outrageous booby." It was also "strange to hear that these witches declare and state, with one voice, as it were, that the evil spirits who make their appearance in the shape of a man are usually black . . . Now, as we have mentioned, the witches of whom we are speaking have not observed what Valerius Maximus wrote of Cassius of Parma: namely, that a tall, pitch-black man had appeared, who, when asked who he was, had replied . . . , that he was an evil spirit." On the basis of this argument, Bodin would certainly have regarded our vagrants as convicted witches, for their confessions coincide down to the last detail with the account of witches' exploits given in his book *Daemonomania*. Before we deride this ludicrous line of argument, we should, of course, bear in mind that we have the benefit of hindsight in judging its validity. The average lawyer in that age apparently took no exception to Bodin's threadbare logic.

Young Fickler, at any rate, followed Bodin's teachings slavishly. He adopted the latter's definition of witchcraft, and even the sequence of his treatise. From this it may be deduced that the French scholar was rated as a high authority at the University of Ingolstadt, when the *crimen magiae* was discussed. Another pillar of the "prevailing opinion" propagated there was the book, *De confessionibus maleficarum et sagarum*, "On the Confessions of Witches and Magicians," which is also quoted in Fickler's "Discussion." The author of this work was Peter Binsfeld, not a lawyer like Bodin but doctor of theology and suffragan bishop in Trier. There were ignorant men, declared Binsfeld, who objected to

314

Bodin's proof of the real existence of witches, claiming that the identical features of the confessions might easily be explained by the coercive power of torture. That was absurd, because it was precisely the torture that proved the truth of the statements. For this same reason, denunciation on the part of a self-confessed witch was sufficient evidence to warrant the application of torture to any person thus accused. Binsfeld's book, which first appeared in 1589, was published in a German version by the Munich printer Adam Berg in 1591; it aroused so much interest among Bavarian lawyers that it had to be reprinted the following year.[114] A study of witchcraft by the Jesuit Martin Del Rio (*Disquisitionum magicarum libri VI*), which reached Munich in the spring of 1600 in a Louvain print, evoked a similar response. We may assume that the Pappenheimer case, which was then highly topical, had a not inconsiderable influence on the commercial success of these works. Del Rio did not deviate from the traditional prevailing opinion, although he recommended caution in the prosecution of witchcraft.

All these leading authorities thought it indisputable that sorcery could only be practiced with the aid of the Devil. This aid he provided, however, only in virtue of a pact which was entered into either tacitly or in explicit terms. In his doctoral dissertation young Fickler repeated this theory from the *Hammer of Witches*. It was, after all, the prevailing opinion. Apart from that, a young lawyer might well be impressed by the erudite discussions conducted on this subject. The pact with the Devil, he was informed, was an "innominate contract," a contract based on the formula *Do ut facias*—nowadays we would call it "contract of service." The Devil's proposal was: "If you sign a contract with me, I will avenge you, make you wealthy, etc." In return, the human party gave his soul. One legal peculiarity of this form of contract should, however, be pointed out: as far as the human party is concerned, it sets forth a purely unilateral bond, an *obligatio pura*. Only the Devil has a right to enforce its terms. "Even if, as a matter of theoretical calculation, a mutual contract with corresponding obligations exists, the demon cannot be subject to any duty of performance, either according to private or natural law, for he is not a creature consisting of body and soul." On the other hand, this circumstance does not affect the legality of any debt thus incurred. "For anyone who concludes a contract is aware of the other party's nature, or else such knowledge is legally imputed to him." A further legal subtlety of the diabolical pact was the possibility, already mentioned, that the pact might be entered into tacitly. The Devil's proposal is invariable, and a matter of common knowledge. It is a specific offer to an indeterminate number of potential partners. As soon as a person "enters the uncertain area of superstition and seeks to encompass an effect which cannot be brought about by natural forces," then the contract is concluded, for the Devil can assume, first, that his aid is being sought by the very fact of this mode of behavior, and second, that the person in question knows on what conditions he is prepared to furnish this aid. The lawyers proved, in equally erudite fashion, that a pact tacitly concluded in this manner was precisely equivalent to one that had been explicitly entered into.

A resplendent edifice of learning! It no doubt needed a layman to see that it was built on swampy ground. A medical practitioner, Dr. Johann Weyer, personal physician to Duke William of Cleves, published a book in 1563 under the title, *De Praestigiis Daemonum* ("On the Illusions wrought by Demons").[115] In it he wrote: "As far as the pact is concerned, the same is verily . . . a false, deceitful bond, both null and void, which the Devil foists upon a zealous man by means of cunning and all manner of guile and dissimulation. As when he conjures up in slumber or otherwise an apparition or evil spirit . . . Or so moves the relevant humors and spirits *in nervis opticis* that weird phantoms appear to him. That the matter should stand thus we may infer without further ado if we but care to view and judge by the measure of reason and our Christian faith how unequal in nature are the two parties that enter into this bond, together with the form, manner, and measure of the contract. Whence it becomes clear as crystal that such divers feats as have been ascribed to witches, or as have been by themselves confessed when submitted to torture . . . are not the work of witches but the work of Satan himself . . . that needs not one jot or tittle of man's aid or succor. . . . Now, this pact, which is entered into via the fancy or imagination of one party, and in bad faith by the other . . . has no power to bind those two together. For when it is said of the Devil, he stretches out his hands and clasps the hand of the witch to seal the bond, all reasonable people know full well that this is but a vile and stinking lie. For how could that be, when Christ, who is Truth itself, testifies in plain words that a spirit has no manner of flesh about or in him."

Young Fickler did not need to trouble himself with this view and took no account whatever of it in his learned tract. A little later, Benedikt Carpzov was to write: "A good many years since, many a book was put forth stating that witchcraft may be reckoned more as a superstition and a state of melancholy than as a crime, and strongly arguing that the same be not punished by death."[116] But "Weyer's views are of no great substance, being that he is a physician and not a lawyer. There is but slight reason for his view that women are not transported in body to revels and association with evil spirits." The prevailing opinion among lawyers has rarely taken any account of common sense evinced by laymen, and those who epitomize the successful administrative lawyer follow the accepted opinion slavishly. This was the case with young Fickler: had he lived 150 years later, he would have written a tract *against* the persecution of witches. Why? Would he have been a different kind of man? Certainly not; but the prevailing opinion would have changed.

CHAPTER · 8

*S*treet jesters
(contemporary woodcut)

⋆ The Vault

Early one summer morning, two horsemen set out from the capital. They were the first travelers to pass through the Schwabing
gate, which had only just been opened by its drowsy watchmen,
and they rode out into the broad green plain, following the highway that led to Nuremberg. As they rode past the fenced fields and
pens that confined the duke's grazing cattle, they replied only
curtly to the greetings of the peasants with their cartloads of fruit
and vegetables. The country folk doffed their hats respectfully as
they approached, for the riders were official personages, representatives of the authorities, as could be seen from the multicolored
plumes they wore in their broad-brimmed hats, the quasi-military
elegance of their attire, and the trappings of their steeds. The leading horseman was armed in the manner of a trooper: in his right
hand he held a long lance, its bottom end resting in a holster slung
from his saddle. At his left side he carried a broad-bladed dagger in
an ornate scabbard fastened to a broad leather belt between bulky
provision pouches. The martial impression was emphasized by a
chain of crudely forged iron links which was slung across the
man's chest and clinked rhythmically against the greasy leather
doublet he wore over his colorful, wide-sleeved blouse. The chain
was no mere decoration. It identified the rider as a man empowered, in case of need, to carry out arrests in the name of the duke.
He was one of the many representatives of the supreme ducal authority whose name has not been passed down to us by history: a
cog in the machinery of authority, a tool of the central power,
a man who was entitled to no particular identity by virtue of
his office.

The name of the second rider we do know, which shows that he was not one of those cogs in the massive clockwork of the state that could be exchanged at will, but a senior official. He was called Kaspar Steinwandner, and he held the office of clerk to the treasury. He had been involved in our case from the outset, and the reader has long since made his acquaintance although he may have overlooked Steinwandner and underestimated his importance. It was he who sat silently by, with his stack of official paper, his freshly cut quills, and his inkwell, and kept the record of all the interrogations in the Falcon Tower. He now had with him a number of copies and extracts from his transcript; they were safely stowed in a large leather pouch that hung from a broad strap passing over his right shoulder, and bumped gently on his left thigh as he rode. Of the two horsemen, it was easy to see that he had the higher rank. Instead of the rakish trooper's attire worn by his companion, he was clad in a dark blue suit in the Spanish court style, with a close-fitting, long-sleeved doublet, buttoned in front, and breeches reaching to the knee, puffed at the hips and tight at the thighs. The white of the rectangular collar that almost covered both shoulders was matched by the cuffs that covered the ends of the dark blue sleeves of his doublet, and by the hose that terminated in dark-colored, laced leather shoes.

The clerk and his bailiff—for this was the office of the horseman who preceded him—had set out so early in the morning in order to reach Altmannstein in one day's ride. Their purpose was to check forthwith, and on the spot, certain statements made by the prisoners confined in the Falcon Tower.

This was because the written requests for assistance sent by the commissioner, Dr. Wangereck, to the prefect of the Abensberg-Altmannstein district had unfortunately been responded to in a dilatory and negligent manner. Voluminous communications had been dispatched to Alexander von Haslang, informing him in detail of the confessions made by the Pappenheimers and their associates and requesting him to verify these statements. In each case he had accepted the letter from the messenger from Munich, broken the seal, and studied the contents. He was "to make inquiry," he read, for instance, "whether an unbaptized male infant, born to a family called Rothütl in Hiendorf, had died some six months since," or "whether Khuoferl of Hüttenhausen had died of a lumbago some four years ago," or "whether Frühmess-Liendl of Tettenwang" had lost a chestnut mare a year ago." The request was not for ten or twenty such investigations but for several hundred. Even if the prefect had set his entire staff to work, verification of such matters would have taken many months. But he had no intention of doing that. It was all very well for the council to ask for investigations and reports. The expenses arising from the inquiries did not fall on the council but on the official responsible for conducting them, and they would diminish his official emoluments. Of course, the request from Munich had to be dealt with. His officials would be given a list of the relevant matters to take with them when they rode out on their regular visits to the parishes. If one of them happened to have business in Hiendorf, he might call on Rothütl and ask whether a child of his had died lately, but the prefect felt himself incapable of carrying out any more detailed investigation. He replied evasively to the reminders from Munich, sent incidental results of his officers' inquiries, and felt unable to comply with exhortations to deal with the matter "more speedily." He might well have said to himself, with a shrug, that the search for evidence required of him was nothing but bureaucratic harassment, the pettifogging punctiliousness of scribbling jacks-in-office, for whom Alexander von Haslang, swashbuckling man of action as he was, had nothing but contempt. The people in Munich had the culprits and their confessions. What more did they want? They should execute the scum and be done with it.

That was a swashbuckling mode of thought. From a legal point of view, the matter was not quite so straightforward, in spite of Dr. Wangereck's skill in interpreting the law. It is true that the accused's confession was the most significant feature of the inquisitorial procedure. It was the queen of proofs—*regina probationum*. In the absence of a confession, the accused could not be condemned, so the principle stated, and the torture was meant to elicit that confession. But, we may remember, a precondition of that principle was the existence of a *corpus delicti*. The act to which the accused confessed must be proved beyond doubt to have been committed. But that was simply not the case with any of the crimes mentioned in our trial. When the accused were arrested, nothing was known of any actual crimes committed by them; there was nothing but allegations, surmise, and rumors to the effect that the Pappenheimers and their associates might be capable of committing certain crimes. Numerous confessions had been elicited by dint of torture, but they were worthless, lacking anything in the way of supporting evidence. The court found itself in the unusual situation of having identified the culprits before there was any judicial proof that punishable acts had been committed. According to trial procedure laid down in the Carolina, this simply could not happen. But the sixteenth-century criminal code included a provision for cases where an accused, after being arrested, admitted more than was originally charged. In such cases it was permissible to produce the corpus delicti retrospectively, and, if it were indeed found, the prisoner might be found guilty of the crime he himself had disclosed.

That was the provision the court was trying to make use of when it requested assistance from the prefect of Abensberg and Altmannstein in checking the Pappenheimers' statements.[117] It was anything but a matter of pettifogging routine. It was in fact an "investigation and inquiry" into the circumstances described by the criminals, as stipulated in the Caroline code. They could not be found guilty without their confessions being verified in this manner. What had been submitted so far in the way of "investigations" or findings on the part of the local authorities seemed meager in the extreme. Take a few examples from the files: on 20 May 1600, Gumpprecht Pämb had confessed "to having murdered Georg Prexl, a farmer from Harlanden . . . somewhere between Rietenburg and Harlanden, to having taken about nine florins from him, and to having dragged his body into a haystack." A note in the margin reads: "Write to Rietenburg for information." Below that, another hand has added the result of the inquiry: "It was found that Farmer Prexl is still alive. But there may be several Prexls in Harlanden." On 26 April, Michel Pämb had stated that Pappenheimer's wife "had scattered powder on a meadow in Pfatter last autumn, from which almost all the cattle in the village had perished." Marginal note: "It appears that last year, between Pentecost and autumn, almost all the cattle in the village had perished." There is a similar note appended to the statement that "his brother Gumpp" had "scattered powder in Altenpuech, so that the dean and the landlord of the inn had fallen sick." It reads: "It is found that the dean was sick a year ago and is still in a poor way." Concerning an attack on "a butcher coming on horseback from Geisenfeld" that Michel claimed to have carried out with the Lamprey, Sugar Bun, and Gilg the Glazier, the initial note reads: "Nothing reported in extract sent to Pfaffenhoven; hence information to be sought whether a butcher reported missing in Geisenfeldt." And then: "Found that a butcher, Paulus Schuef by name, had departed from Geisenfeldt on account of debts and has not been seen since." Hänsel Pämb claimed to have stolen a purse in Traubling. A note states that "information has been received that a certain Barthlner Wilkhoner of Traubling lost ten and a half florins last year at the fair in Luckhen-Point, his purse having been in the tail of his doublet, containing some eighteen batzen, a taler, the remainder in kreuzer and half-batzen."

The coincidence of confession and investigation was especially vague in the case of alleged witchcraft. In Augustin Baumann's file, for example, we find: "About a year since, smeared ointment on the child belonging to Georg Weber, a tailor in Detenwang, being about a year old, at that time lying in broad daylight in his cradle, so that it died within three days." Information reported: "Some three years since (the tailor) lost a child of six weeks old, which had fallen sick and died within five weeks." Augustin: "Some two years since he had rubbed ointment on a girl some twenty weeks old, the daughter of Farmer Friemess in Detenwang, as she lay in her cradle, whereof she died within three days." Information received: "Five years ago he lost a daughter aged a year." Augustin: "Five years since, he had anointed Piechlhänsl's young boy, aged ten or twelve weeks, in Laimerstat, whereof he had died in a matter of days." Information received: "Four of his children had died." Augustin: "Stegerhänsl's young boy, aged about fifteen weeks smeared with ointment some four years since, and so killed him." Information received: "Nothing found." Augustin: "Last summer he had laid hands on the chest of the miller of Riedt, near Laimerstat, who had once been a trooper, in pretence of good fellowship, but had smeared the Devil's ointment on him so that an ulcer appeared, of which he died in the space of three days." Information received: "Died of the infection." Augustin: "A year since, while he had been delivering bread to Stachel at Hagenhil, he had gripped Stachel's wife by the shoulder as though in sport, but smeared her with the ointment, so that she died a few days later." Information received: "Complained much but still living." Augustin: "Smeared old Stegerhänsl of Hagenhil as he drove home by night, so that he died five days thereafter." Information received: "Still living but suffers great pain on account of swelling of the feet." Augustin: "Some five years since . . . scattered powder in the path of the cobbler in Detenwang, which he passed over, and he grew lame in one foot and still is so." Information received: "Has been swollen and sick some nine months." Such was the available evidence: flimsy.

But, as the reader already knows, it was not merely flimsy, it was inadequate in the eyes of the law. For, in accordance with the penal code, a deed was proved "beyond all shadow of a doubt" only

when, following "the confession of the person questioned . . .
zealous investigation and inquiry is instituted regarding the aforesaid deed, and discloses such facts as an innocent party could not
know or vouch for." But the facts which investigation had elicited
up to that point were not of that nature. Certainly there had been
a burglary in the monastery chapel of Altmühlmünster in 1598,
which Gumpprecht had confessed to. It is true that "some ten
years since, a vintner from Schwelblweyss, U. Riedl, had been reported missing, and was later found in the Danube," which more
or less matched Paulus's confession that nine years earlier "he had
assaulted and done to death . . . (a man) between Degernheim and
Schwalbenweiss, . . . dragged the corpse a little way off the path,
and left it lying fully clothed." And, after all, "the daughter of
a woman called Lippi Seiler in Kehlheimb" really had died, as
claimed by Anna Pämbs, who had allegedly treated her with the
Devil's ointment some four years previously. True, the girl had
died eleven years before, but Anna might have been mistaken
about the date. Yet all these coincidences could derive from the
fact that the events described were already known, in some way or
other, to the persons being questioned. Those who roamed the
countryside like the Pappenheimers were, after all, in a position
to learn all sorts of things. Proof that they had indeed committed
the acts described would have been forthcoming only if they had
mentioned circumstances otherwise unknown, which could not
be known to anyone other than the perpetrator, and if these cir-
cumsances turned out to be true when checked.

The commission entrusted to the two horsemen who were now
setting off early in the morning on the Nuremberg road was to
provide the missing evidence, and to do so with all possible speed.
They were approaching the hamlet of Schwabing, and the intervals between the peasant wains and tradesmen's carts intent on
reaching the Munich market in good time grew shorter and shorter.
Hats were doffed to the eminent official and his military escort,
but the greeting was returned only briefly. Kaspar Steinwandner's
mission was anything but a simple one and little calculated to put
the clerk to the treasury in a jovial frame of mind.

ESTABLISHING THE TRUTH

The vault in the Falcon Tower, that dank cellar dimly lit by the
flickering candlelight, still resounded several times a week with
the sobs, groans, and screams of its victims. The commissioners

sat with impassive, official expressions at their table, while Wangereck, glancing from time to time at his list, fired question after question at the object of the interrogation, giving directions as necessary to Master Georg. In every case the torture elicited the desired answer.

This mode of establishing the truth seems to us barbaric and hence contrary to all legal precept. The impassive expressions on the officials' faces were not, however, a symptom of ruthlessness but an expression of their conscientious zeal. Even nowadays we may detect this expression on the faces of officials who are cruel because they are being correct, harsh because they are carrying out their duty. Our councillors, who had been appointed to sit on the commission, were merely complying with statute law with which hardly anyone found fault. One day, perhaps, people will be equally taken aback by the impassively official demeanor of judges in our time who remand juvenile offenders in custody. In those days it was known that the prisoners were being subjected to a terrifying and humiliating ordeal, but it was done in a sober, official way, in the firm conviction that it served the interests of the law. "Examination under torture is to be employed, according to the degree of suspicion attaching to a person, frequently or more rarely, severely or with restraint, according to the discretion of a sound and reasonable judge." So it was stated in the Caroline code. From this statement the judicial doctrine of the time deduced that the procedure ought to be a gradual one; torture was to be applied only to the degree that was necessary to elicit a confession. Even when this does not appear to be the case, the court was adhering to this maxim. For example, the child, Hänsel, was interrogated first, in keeping with the principle: "If recourse is had to examination under torture, and there is more than one suspected person," then the first person to be examined should be "the most faint-hearted and the most feeble." In the course of each interrogation, the torture was gradually intensified. It began with a *territio verbalis*, which is usually noted in the record as an emphatic "reminder," or a "solemn exhortation." The second stage was *Realterrition:* all the preparations for the infliction of torture were carried out. That was often quite enough to loosen the suspect's tongue, especially in later interrogations, when he was already familiar with the agonies of torture. Actual torture was thus the third stage, which, in its turn, might be intensified by degrees, according to the method used, the duration, and the frequency of repetition.

The commonest form of torture employed in the Pappenheimer case was, we know, the "strappado." The delinquent's arms were bound behind his back, as already described, and a rope fastened to the bonds round his wrists was led up over a pulley fixed to the ceiling. The executioner pulled on this rope, so that the victim's arms were wrenched up painfully behind his back and he ended up swinging in the air. The torture could be made more severe by attaching stones of varying size to the subject. How common this mode of torture was is demonstrated on almost every page of the transcript: "Although first of all he would confess nothing of his own accord, he nevertheless spoke out after stretching." "He said it was no small matter that he confessed from sheer terror and pain, because the executioner had immediately bound him and then stretched him." "Although at first she would confess nothing at all in spite of being stretched a number of times without weights, and in spite of having been solemnly adjured to speak during the course of the morning, she nevertheless spoke of her own free will that same evening." "Is unable to name either the village or the farmer in question, in spite of repeated stretching." "On the morning of 22 August 1600, she was hoisted up without weights eleven times." "This morning drawn up once without weights, and ten times with a fifty-pound stone." "Although this morning he would at first say nothing of his own accord, nor yet after being stretched and tortured twelve times, latterly with double weights, he did after all speak in the afternoon, on threat of renewed torture." Torture that regularly began, as was customary in our case, with the binding of the accused, followed by "stretching," was considered particularly harsh, even in those days. Normally torture began with thumbscrews. It was only when "thumbscrews proved of no avail" that recourse was had to binding, in such a way that "the executioner did not merely bind the subject's wrists, but began to jerk the cords to and fro with a sawing motion, which causes such acute pain that the bound persons are apt to scream and cry and whimper." The actual "stretching" was even more agonizing and became more and more intolerable the longer it lasted. Not infrequently the humerus was dislocated in both arms, and the iron-master had to wrench the victim's arms back into place following the torture, "which was not effected without loud wailing and screaming." After the first application of torture the victim's limbs swelled up; repetition was even more painful.

Our commissioners sat there with their official faces and, by invoking their sense of duty, suppressed any compassion they might have felt. It was their business to establish the truth. They failed to achieve their end, however, for torture forced the victims to lie. "For fear of torture, since his hands were already bound behind his back," Paulus once declared, he had confessed to a murder which had never taken place. On another occasion, when little Hänsel was asked "why he had told so many lies yesterday," he said he had been "so terrified that he did not know what he should say." This was even more obviously the case with the convent miller's wife: "When she was first asked how she had come to practice witchcraft . . . she replied that she was altogether innocent of the charge, and although the Pappenheimers had denounced her, they had done her wrong . . . But when she had been hoisted up four, or half a dozen times, and observed from the questioners' constant exhortation that they would not easily desist, then she began to speak in these terms: She would gladly confess if only she knew what she should say that her son might not be consigned to perdition and might be saved." It didn't take much to see that torture was a totally unsuitable method of establishing the truth.

The gentlemen with the impassive faces were not blind; nor were they stupid, or cynical. What made them so sure that they were serving the law by this cruel expedient was their belief in the power of demons. They saw themselves as acting the part of exorcists. In their view, torture was the most efficacious means of casting out the Devil from the person they were questioning.

As far as we are concerned, the criminal is a person who offends against the norms of society and hence acts against the common good. This is why he has to be punished, whether it be by way of retribution, self-defense, or deterrence. This view was not altogether unfamiliar to our commissioners, but it seemed to them to miss the essential point. Criminality was for them, above all, sin, a turning away from the good, a propensity for evil. St. Augustine's view of the world, to which we have repeatedly referred, furnished their idea of criminal behavior. Men were everywhere, and at all times, beset by demons and spirits of darkness who tempted and seduced them with evil lusts and favorable opportunities, prowling around the Christian flock like a pack of werewolves, hoping to seize and slay the weaklings. The criminal was a sheep who had been attacked in this way; the wolf would eat his way right through the sheep's body, as in the tale of Baron Münchhausen's horse, emerging at the mouth and concealing his fiendish nature under the sheep's skin. The battle against crime was a battle against the Devil.[118] That was understood in a literal sense, as is clear from early medieval sources. The criminal was regarded as a man possessed by the Devil, who had to be liberated by means of exorcism. In Carolingian times, judges admonished the unseen spirit: "I drive thee out, abominable spirit of evil, through God the Almighty." It was especially robbers, murderers, defilers of women, and sorcerers who were considered as possessed, for they had committed "mortal sins" and thus placed themselves beyond the scope of Divine Grace. From the outset, this idea was linked to the conviction that the Devil prevented the criminal from confessing his crimes. For, as the practice of confession demonstrates to this very day, the admission of guilt was regarded as the decisive step on the path back to God. The Devil naturally fought it, for he had no wish to lose his victim. As long as the evil spirit was lodged in a man's bowels, he hardened the victim's heart and paralyzed his tongue (*inimicus, qui totis semper visceribus inhibat*). That was why the criminal, once he had been apprehended, had first of all to be freed from the constraint placed on him by the Devil; before that had been done, he could not be expected to speak a word of the truth. But how could the judge prevail against such a mighty adversary as Lucifer?

The answer was obvious: by appealing for divine assistance. The medieval trial by ordeal was based on this idea. It was considered certain that God would perform a miracle in order to reveal the truth. To overcome the power of the Devil and to frustrate any influence he might exert on the trial, the accused was blessed, made to fast and take Communion, clad in white, and led barefoot into church. For the ordeal itself, the pure elements of fire and water were used, for God had worked wonders with these elements since time immemorial, whereas the Devil had no power over them. The accused was made to walk over red-hot coals, or was bound and thrown into running water: pure fire would burn the guilty man, pure water would cast him out. In this way, God Himself was able to pronounce judgment, rather than the criminal, who was prevented from speaking the truth. Water and fire provided the confession required of the guilty, and acquitted the innocent.

Trial by ordeal was subsequently replaced by the Inquisition. But the demonological interpretation of crime persisted, at least as far as witchcraft was concerned. In Jodocus Damhouder's commentary on the criminal code, a contemporary work to which we have already referred, a woodcut illustration depicts three judges extracting a serpent from a sorcerer's jaws. The *Hammer of Witches*, which plays such an important part in our trial, also describes those who conclude pacts with the Devil as being possessed by him. The second question in part 1 reads: "It is true that demons make use of witches only to bring about their perdition; and if it be objected that they should not be punished, since they are but tools or instruments that do not act of their own free will but in the hand of a master, then the reply must be that they are tools possessed of a soul and acting of their own free will, although under the terms of the pact they have concluded with the demons they no longer have control of themselves." A man who has surrendered to Satan no longer possesses a free will. We may recall what Hänsel Pappenheimer said about his brothers: once they had partaken of the powder made of infants' hands, they "had to do it."

In keeping with ancient tradition, the *Hammer of Witches* ought to have recommended trial by ordeal as a means of circumventing the Devil. It was not in a position to do so, however, for in 1215 the Church had prohibited such recourse to the Deity for purposes of proof. Instead, it recommended another means of discovering the truth and breaking the power of the Devil: torture. Torture, it is true, would be of little avail without divine assistance, for the witch was "rendered so insensible to pain by the Devil (*insensibilis in illis doloribus efficitur*) that she would sooner be torn limb from limb than bring herself to confess anything of the truth . . . It follows that certain witches do confess most readily, whereas others confess not at all: this is because, if the Devil has not been cast out by God, he may of his own accord abandon the former, in order to drive them to distraction by confounding them and confronting them with the prospect of a fearful death . . . It may be seen that many do seek to bring about their own death, taking their lives . . . by means of a noose, the same being plainly the work of the Evil One, so that they may not obtain God's pardon by way of the sacrament of confession" (part 3, question 13). A man who has entered into association with the Devil will be sustained during torture by his master, who will make him resistant to pain and hence prevent him from confessing. A suspect will find it easy to confess only after the evil spirit has departed from him. Given divine assistance, therefore, torture was "a means of setting men free from the demons that possessed them" (Hans Fehr).

This was the reason for the firm assurance and the confident severity practiced by our commissioners. Once the initial obstinacy of their suspects had been overcome, they were sure to hear "the truth" in every case. The longer a man persisted in his denials, the more certain it was that he was possessed by the Devil. But the resistance of the Evil One was broken in every single case. It was not feasible that torture alone could achieve this effect; there was bound to be direct divine intervention through the agency of an angel: *divina coactio per sanctum Angelum*. The officials in the vault of the Falcon Tower knew that God was on their side.

THE FATHER CONFESSOR

Spiritual assistance was required to wrest the prisoners once and for all from the power of the Devil. The prisoners having admitted their guilt, a priest was required to reconcile them with God by means of confession and absolution, and hence to free them entirely from the diabolical coils. This act was not designed simply to restore the penitent's peace of mind; it was also part of the war on evil that was being waged by our commissioners. With God's help, the torture had revealed the truth, but the wolf was still lodged in the sheep. He had to be expelled before the issue of the trial could be regarded as securely settled. The council of state had summoned the dean of St. Peter's to perform this function.

And so, one fine summer afternoon, we may observe the reverend dean in Ulrich Schölz's gloomy cell. He is seated on a stool especially placed there for him, clad in a black cassock, with a large wooden cross resting on his chest. His head is bent slightly to one side, and he has raised one hand to shield his face from the fettered prisoner. He is preparing to hear confession. The stool replaces the confessional, the hand held between ear and face substitutes for the customary grill. Presumably this father confessor felt the task allocated to him by the council to be a nuisance. Could not the job have been given to a more junior, rank-and-file padre from the Jesuit College?

For the dean who was seated in Schölz's cell fastidiously clutching his cassock—Dr. Wolfgang Hannemann by name—was no common or garden priest but a highly educated scholar of superior rank. Although barely over forty, he already headed Munich's oldest parish, a pastor of the modern type, a brilliant preacher and a militant opponent of the Lutheran heresy. He had studied philosophy and theology in Ingolstadt, where he had been personal

332

assistant to Professor Nikolaus Everhard, and had then moved to Bologna with the aim of improving both his knowledge and his status. It was there that he had acquired a doctorate of theology. And the council of state expected a man of his caliber to act as confessor to a bunch of witches!

For good reasons. A contemporary instruction warned that "all manner of subordination and other inconvenience" might be suffered in such cases, were a confessor not chosen with due circumspection.[119] This was also the reason Duke Maximilian later gave orders that "henceforth no Franciscans, Augustinians, or other clergy be permitted access to prisoners; nor should such access be permitted even after promulgation of sentence, on the pretext of visiting and providing spiritual comfort, until the prisoner be released from confinement to be conveyed to the place of execution." It was already known what might happen if such inept pastors were given their head; a number of them had caused a deplorable fuss during the Schongau witch trials when they claimed that the convicted prisoners were, in their view, entirely innocent, that they had admitted guilt only from fear of torture, and that they had nothing to say in the confessional or before God. The authorities had only just been able to prevent a resumption of the trial and postponement of executions which had already been arranged. In some cases they were even forced to nullify, by means of renewed torture, recantations which had been insinuated into the ear of a father confessor. In order to avoid contretemps of this kind, the council of state could not be too careful in its choice of a confessor. Their trust could be placed only in the Jesuits, who were aware that they were more popular with the authorities than with the people.

And yet it was a member of the Society of Jesus, speaking on behalf of many prison chaplains, who was to raise his voice and draw attention to their profound scruples. Father Friedrich von Spee, who himself claimed to have been confessor to witches, launched an attack in his *Cautio Criminalis* of 1631 on the most vulnerable aspect of the Inquisitorial trial procedure.[120] He was prompted to pose the question "whether torture was a proper means of revealing the truth." "Lawyers claim," stated Spee quite correctly, "that torture is employed so that the truth may be revealed." But he continued ironically: "How should the truth thus be revealed? Let the reader take thought and tell me. I, for one, do not know, and although I have long pondered the issue, it has become no clearer to me, unless the lawyers mean to say that there is no truth in this matter other than the proposition that everyone is guilty who is subjected to torture . . . There are two kinds of men: those from whom you may extort the truth, and those from whom you may extort a lie. Supposing you have tortured a man, how do you know to which of these two categories he belongs? Presumably the latter kind is the commoner, since it is easier to suffer death than to endure torture." At another point Spee speaks plainly of the alleged "magic power to remain silent," in which our commissioners clearly believed—as witness the interrogation of Agnes, the convent miller's daughter. "If an individual remains insensible to torture, there is talk of a magic power to remain silent. Thus, when nowadays a witch fails to confess after being subjected two or three times to torture, it is said that she is using magic, that the Devil is sealing her lips so that she is unable to confess; this in itself is then said to be adequate proof that she is guilty and may therefore be exorcised and tortured once again . . . In the first place, I would deny that Titia would not have been able to withstand two or three sessions of torture by natural means. A person is able to withstand a great deal by natural means. How do people know that this 'great deal' does not include the agony of torture? Thus, if the accused endures torture and says nothing, it cannot invariably be said that he does so by means of magic . . . But I am ready to concede that Titia could not in fact have withstood the pain of torture unaided. So be it! That is even more to my advantage, for I would then draw the following conclusion: Titia was able to withstand the torture only through the assistance of the Devil, or of God. Consequently, the torture was so severe that it could not be borne by natural means. If that is the case, then the judges who ordained the infliction of such pain acted in contravention of the law. If that is the case, then the torture itself was in contravention of the law, and hence null and void by any conceivable statute. I will express the same idea in another way. The judges say Titia is still suspected of witchcraft and may be put to the torture once more because they have found new evidence. But what does the new evidence consist of? Of the fact that she employed magic in order to withstand the previous torture. But how do they prove that? By the fact that the torture was of such a nature that it could not have otherwise been borne. I will concede that, and add: the judges have therefore acted in contravention of the law by employing such agonizing torture that it could not be borne naturally, without the use of magic. Consequently the judges have acquired their new evidence by means of

334

an illegal procedure. Supposing Titia really had been able to withstand the torture only with the aid of the Devil, or of God: why do they choose to say that the aid came from the Devil, and not from God? When Titia was so cruelly maltreated, she was either innocent of the crime of which she was accused, or else she was guilty. If she was innocent, what should be more plausible than that God should have succored an innocent person subject to such dreadful torture? If she was guilty, well then, no doubt it was the Devil rather than the Lord our God who stood by her. And yet the judges are not entitled to assume that this is the case and that Titia is in fact guilty, since that is precisely the issue and that is precisely why they were to seek new evidence . . . If they accept as new evidence of Titia's guilt the fact that she would not confess even under the most severe torture, then this fearful suffering was inflicted on her unnecessarily and pointlessly. For what was the purpose supposed to be? That the judges should achieve absolute certainty as to whether Titia is guilty or not? But if they so wished, they could just as easily find her guilty from the outset. For the conclusions they had drawn in retrospect, they might just as well have drawn beforehand. Titia will either confess her guilt under torture, or else she will not. Whichever is the case, she will be found guilty all the same. If she confesses, then she is guilty because she has admitted guilt. If she does not confess, then she is guilty nevertheless, because she did not confess, even when exposed to the fearful agony of torture. So she is guilty, whether she confesses or not."

It is entirely possible that even Dean Hannemann was troubled by such thoughts as he made his way home after a visit to the Falcon Tower. But, unlike his younger colleague Spee, he did not allow them to shake his faith in authority and in the Church. The authorities approved of torture—to argue against it smacked of revolt and rebellion. And Hannemann knew who the instigator of such ideas was: after all, he warned his flock against the seducer and archenemy every Sunday. It was not difficult for someone who had listened to the confession of witches to arrive at the conclusion that torture was a senseless institution; what was difficult was to fight such thoughts, to suppress them as improper. That was why it was necessary to have a highly respected man to perform this office; that was why the duty had devolved upon this distinguished Doctor of Theology and parish priest.

The cell stank. Before the confessor's visit the ironmaster's wife had, of course, changed the straw and opened the window, but it was impossible to expel from the dim chamber the dank, oppressive air, the miasma compounded of excrement and the sweat of terrified inmates. Hannemann muttered the prescribed Latin phrases, relinquished his hold on his cassock for a few seconds in order to make the sign of the cross with his right hand, and then whispered in the customary manner to the fettered prisoner, through the grill formed by his left hand, that he should confess his sins before God the Omniscient, the Almighty, the All-forgiving. Whereupon the prisoner began to speak in a cracked and feeble voice, no doubt hesitantly at first, and then more fluently.

What may Ulrich Schölz have said to his confessor? That he was in fact innocent, and that his greatest sin consisted in his failure to withstand the torture? Above all, that he had falsely accused those peasants and artisans of Tettenwang, whom he had denounced as witches and sorcerers, of taking part in nocturnal flights and revels, he himself never in fact having been present on such occasions? Very probably. For the prisoner knew that his fate was sealed. Frank and honest confession was the last chance he had of appearing pure of heart before God's throne. In the priest's presence he was unable to stand by his statement that he had entered into a pact with the Devil. For this was not merely a lie but an insult to God, who had saved him from that fatal step. So we must assume that what the prisoner said, incoherently at first, and then with increasing clarity, consisted of a denial of everything he had admitted under cruel torture.

No one knows what the confessor's response was. It is possible that he did not believe a word of what the chained prisoner said, barked at him, told him he was incorrigible and ungrateful. Perhaps he was numbered among those prison chaplains whose "sole purpose," as Spee wrote, "was simply to induce the accused to confess. They simply keep on repeating 'Confess, confess' . . . Once the accused have confessed, then everything is well and good, as far as these confessors are concerned. Then they call the accused children of eternal life, then they say that they have gone repentant to their death . . . I know it has happened that a priest has been so sly as to promise an accused a reduction of his sentence, which was never in fact implemented . . . But it is quite unseemly for the clergy, as I have heard tell of some, to make suggestions to the judges as to how the accused may best be tortured." Perhaps Hannemann threatened to inform the commissioners of Schölz's recantation, which would have meant a resumption of torture. Schölz would then certainly have reverted to his previous admission of guilt. Spee maintained in his book "that there are many who even persist in their admission of guilt during the sacrament of confession when they are in fact innocent, either because they are confronted by ruthless priests, to whose zeal they succumb, or because they do not wish to be tortured again."

But perhaps the confessor, given the circumstances, believed what the prisoner said. In that case he was plunged into a profound dilemma. If he were convinced of the innocence of a convicted prisoner, should he not prevent the execution of Schölz? But anything he said to the commissioners would merely have entailed a prolongation of the wretched man's sufferings, for it would have been the pretext for renewed torture, the outcome of which was a foregone conclusion. Should he not protect those who had been falsely denounced? But that too would be the occasion for further torture of the accused man, without changing the ultimate situation. Faced with this hopeless situation, any clergyman who believed what he was told by those who confessed to him was simply exposing himself to the torments of an uneasy conscience. How could one escape such qualms without becoming simply a court bailiff?

Presumably Dr. Hannemann was clever enough to find some recondite way out. He could leave the question of guilt or innocence to God and not allow himself to ponder on the matter. The conversation in the gloomy, noisome cell was subject to the secrecy of the confessional. After listening to the prisoner's hoarsely whispered confession, the dean no doubt closed his eyes and resumed his muttered Latin phrases, concluding with an "Ego te absolvo!" Then he will have risen from his stool to make the sign of the cross over the wretched sinner for the last time.

Only once during our trial did the priest succumb to the terrible conflict in his heart. He revealed to the commissioners that in the course of his confession Gumpprecht had said he had "wronged a number of people" by the statements he had made. This earned the penitent a further morning's torture in the vault, which had certainly not been Hannemann's intention. Otherwise, he no doubt devoted all his intelligence and erudition to repressing the improper, rebellious doubts in his own heart.

A DEBATE IN THE COUNCIL OF STATE

At the daily meeting of the council of state late in the morning of 12 June 1600, Wolf Konrad, Baron von Rechberg, the officiating president of the council, raised the issue of the trial of the criminals confined in the Falcon Tower. His Grace, Duke Maximilian, wished to have a report on the current state of affairs, and this would have to be prepared without delay. The monarch's impatience was understandable: after all, two months had now gone by, rather too much time for the sentencing of such tramps. The commissioners appointed to interrogate the prisoners should explain what progress they had made in their investigations and say whether the duke might not look forward to a speedy execution. The chairman would have spoken more or less in these terms.

Whereupon Dr. Wangereck rose to his feet and began to speak. If the trial had not yet been concluded, he began his report, this was due, for one thing, to the very wide area in which the crimes had been committed and where, in consequence, inquiries had to be made. The prefect of Altmannstein and Abensberg had been requested to follow up certain information provided by the accused. What had been reported back to Munich was encouraging but not yet complete. The commission had therefore dispatched the clerk to the treasury, Steinwandner, to Altmannstein, with instructions to pursue the investigation and to clear up the case as quickly as possible. Although he could thus count on receiving "information" from the Munich treasury shortly, he had still not received from Straubing and Landshut any reply to his request for confirmation of the admissions made by the accused. For the clerk to the treasury to be sent to those districts as well would be impracticable, and a political issue, since they could not very well encroach on the powers of the local treasurer. All the same, they had "not neglected to dispatch their own messengers there and to exhort them," i.e. the local authorities in Straubing and Landshut, "to send the information requested." There had, however, been no response so far.

There may have been signs of unrest among the councillors following this statement. We may hear the president asking whether the confessions and the information so far obtained were not sufficient to justify execution. It was highly desirable that the proceedings be brought to an end one way or another.

Certainly, Wangereck may have replied. In the Munich treasury there was enough evidence available "relating to a small number of murders, cases of burglary of churches, and especially relating to persons slain by witchcraft, to warrant proceeding forthwith to execution on account of these crimes." But proof of the "major offenses" was "expected from Landshut and Straubing."

At this point the treasurer, Ernst von Roming, himself one of

338

the appointed commissioners, put in a word. All those present in the council would recall very well the reasons which had prompted them at the time to proceed with the prosecution. They had thought that this case from Lower Bavaria would provide an obvious and salutary example to stem the wave of robberies, murders, and pillaging throughout the country as a whole. The confessions made by the accused had demonstrated that the case was more than suitable for that purpose; it had even transpired that they were dealing with witches and sorcerers. There was already a vast amount of talk about the trial in the streets and squares of Munich. It was reported by word of mouth, from whatever source, that the people expected a great deal of the trial. Word had gone out throughout the country, which was precisely the intention. A vast crowd could be expected on the occasion of the executions, for "the evildoers were mighty notorious, and many would look forward eagerly to hearing their shrifts read out." If they were to execute the Pappenheimers and their associates merely on account of the crimes that had been proved so far, the whole exercise would have been pointless. The purpose of the enterprise was deterrence. To achieve the aim of an "exemplary execution," the only crimes that mattered were those that the people should be deterred from committing. The council could not be satisfied with the meager results of the investigation so far; they were only half-baked. It was important to "go the whole hog."

This speech met with general approval. One of the councillors, however, still wanted to know why there was so little convincing evidence after two months of interrogation and inquiry. We can hear Wangereck's reply: it looked to him, "judging by the information that had come in, almost as if the Pappenheimers . . . had deliberately made false statements and concealed the true facts so that they might make themselves out to be innocent, or to be lesser criminals than they were alleged to be." If the absence of information from the treasuries of Straubing and Landshut was infuriating, even more so was the invention of murders that had never happened. Four murders had been confirmed as a result of inquiries carried out by the prefect, Alexander von Haslang, in Abensberg. Hardly a great result since the vagrants had admitted "something like three times as many, when taxed with them, or else had accused each other of, when brought face to face." According to the commissioners, there were "three reasons" why these admissions were not confirmed by information from other sources. In the first place, there was the "cunning and malice" of

339

such inveterate villains, which was shown by the very fact that "they had been able to conceal their crimes for so many years." Since they had escaped the attention of the authorities all that time, they no doubt thought "they could weary and mislead the authorities by false statements which were not corroborated by other information." That was a mistake! For "both in the Penal Code and in common law" it was "ordained . . . that such persons might repeatedly be submitted to examination under torture—which would be done forthwith, as soon as all the necessary information was to hand." Another reason for the unsatisfactory results of the inquiries lay in the nature of the crimes to which they had confessed. The Pappenheimers and their associates had "for the most part killed unknown wayfarers they encountered in the countryside, who were not readily missed since they had no fixed abode in the country. Moreover, those they had murdered in dwellings in Tettenwang were, by their own admission, peddlars and tramps, whose bodies they had borne off into the woods by night and buried there." No one could have seen or heard anything of this "unless one of their company were to reveal it, as had now come to pass." Thirdly, and finally, inquiries had not been conducted in a proper manner. Questions had simply been asked in the relevant villages, whether the people there had heard of this or that deed, whereas individual persons ought to have been questioned with no one else present.

This information still did not satisfy one of the learned councillors—was it Dr. Franciscus Soll or Matthaeus Pittelmair? Someone, at any rate, who looked askance at the prevailing Gewold clique. He wanted the commissioners to tell him what the nature of the existing evidence was. Had circumstances been corroborated which could be known only to the perpetrator of the crime in question? Had the remains of corpses or other unmistakable clues been found?

Not exactly, we can hear Wangereck answering irritably. Of the many hundreds of corpses that the Pappenheimers had on their consciences, not a single one had been found; nor had the remains of bones or other evidence been traced. He had not neglected to question the prisoners concerning the whereabouts of their victims. Their reply: they had dismembered the corpses and cremated them in a pitchburner's furnace in the woods near Tettenwang. No trace of the furnace had been found, however. It was obvious that the Devil was implicated in the disappearance of such vital clues. Otherwise, sufficient indications had emerged that the evildoers had committed crimes even worse than appeared from their confessions. There were, for example, innumerable signs of witchcraft, one of them having confessed that he had killed such and such a person at such and such a place some months previously by smearing him with a diabolical ointment. This statement had been corroborated in every detail by information received.

The questioner may have retorted that such evidence was judicially inadequate and would not provide the basis for exemplary punishment. For instance, no lawyer could regard a charge of black magic as proven in the case quoted. Presumably the whole village knew that the alleged victim of the spell had been ailing for several months. Anyone could have made the confession in question and claimed the deed as his. The commissioner had said quite rightly that these evil people were trying to lead the court astray. For that very reason it was necessary to seek truly incontrovertible evidence to secure the victory of justice and to ensure that those murders which had not been invented but had actually been committed were atoned for in the eyes of God. At this point or thereabouts, the president broke off the discussion. They were grateful to the commissioners for the work they had done so far, and were no doubt all of the opinion that it was better to delay the execution of the criminals until corroborative evidence arrived from Straubing and Landshut and the clerk to the treasury returned from Altmannstein. They would inform His Grace to this effect regarding the state of the prosecution. And with that the council's morning session was concluded.

Wirtenberger, the secretary to the council, summed up the discussion that same day in a letter to the duke. "The commissioners appointed from among our number to question the evildoers incarcerated in the Falcon Tower" had made the "necessary and detailed report" to the council on the case. From their report on the present state of affairs it emerged that "there were considerable doubts about proceeding with their execution." It was therefore recommended that execution be delayed until the arrival of further evidence, which had already been sought. Maximilian found this letter on his desk the following day, as he sat there governing his realm. He skimmed over the lines and then scribbled his instructions rapidly on the covering sheet: "To await further information, but same to be sought urgently. Maximilian."

In the meantime the questioning went on in the Falcon Tower. The topic was now almost exclusively witchcraft; the commissioners had almost lost interest in the long list of murders, robberies, arson, and thefts of which the Pappenheimers had originally been accused. It was only when information received from elsewhere did not tally with the relevant admissions in this area that explanations were demanded and the "highway crimes" became the subject of interrogation. The emphasis in later interrogations moved to the issue of "covens." The prisoners were asked "whom they had seen at gatherings and revels of witches."

It must be said to the credit of our "riffraff" that most of them avoided denouncing anyone else for a considerable time. They frequently named people who had died or who were thought to have left the country. But the commissioners were not satisfied. Torture extorted more and more names from the prisoners, so that the list of alleged "cronies" grew longer and longer, and finally included some four hundred names. In the course of a torture session on 1 July 1600, Anna Pämb alone accused no less than ninety-nine persons, among them "the old innkeeper's wife in Affeckhing, who has since moved away from there . . . 7. Gadl Schwarz, midwife, whose husband went off to the war. 8. Widmann, midwife in Niederaltach, a widowed old woman . . . 10. The wife of Hanns Punckhen, clerk in Niederaltach, who used to work in the monastery . . . 16. Hanns Khramer from Leichterwalde, together with his wife, who used to live in the manor house but lives now in the lake house, half a mile from Leichtenwald. 17. The marsh miller of Posching and his wife. 18. The wife of the Straubing cobbler. 19. Hanns Müller's wife, haberdasher and milliner in Straubing . . . 27. A midwife called Schwarzhauser from Thonaustauf . . . 31, 32. Farmer Schwarz from Deissing, prefecture of Altmannstein, and his wife . . . 36. The tailor's wife in Altmannstein, whose husband is on the council and lives down by Lederer's . . . 61. A woman called Jobst, gatekeeper down on the lower Danube gate (in Vohburg) . . . 65. The wife of Pastor Preu in Vohburg, who is also a pastor's daughter . . . 76. Beinds Püzer in Mundraching, where she kept her inn . . . 80. Reigl, midwife in Landshut, a handsome, tall, buxom woman and the most respected midwife, lives in the Pfattengasse. She kills many children at birth. I saw her on the moor by Landshut and at other places round Landau where revels were held . . . 92. The old beadle's wife in Rietenburg, whose husband was slain, was a great witch and ringleader. 93. The Platthaus woman who traveled round the country was a witch, and could mostly be found at all the fairs, but particularly in the almshouse of Deckhendorf. I have a list where some two hundred women that are witches are written down."

More than 80 percent of those denounced were women, in keeping with the Devil's alleged preference for the female sex. Our trial thus reflects the well-known fact that women were more likely than men to be accused of witchcraft.[121] An important reason for this lay no doubt in the scholastic theory of witchcraft, which attributed this crime mainly to women. "The female sex being so frail," claimed the *Hammer of Witches*, "there is to be found among them a great number of witches." For women constituted a sex "in which God had invariably instilled something of grandeur to the undoing of the strong," a sex "that was intemperate in good as well as in evil." The *Hammer of Witches* sought to "prove" by means of a hotchpotch of quotations from patristic and classical authors that women were more stupid, more sly, more lascivious, and more wicked than men. "Women are of slight understanding, almost like boys," we read. And: "A woman that is fair to look upon and loose in her morals is like a golden ring in the snout of a sow; the reason is natural: because she is more prone to lusts of the flesh, as may be seen from her obscene carnal practices. These failings are also suggsted by the manner in which the first woman was created, for she was formed from a curved rib, that is, a rib taken from the breast, which is bent and, as it were, turned against the male creature. This infirmity also explains why the female is always deceitful, for she is but an imperfect creature." Even the derivation of the Latin word for woman, *femina*, was quoted in support of their views by the learned authors of this crude nonsense. "The word *femina* comes from *fe* and *minus* (*fe* = *fides*, i.e. faith; *minus* = less; hence *femina* = one who has less faith) . . . And so woman is wicked by nature, since she doubts the faith more readily, and also denies it more readily, which is the foundation of witchcraft." So it went on in this style. "If we survey history, we shall find that almost all the kingdoms of the earth were destroyed by women." "As woman is deceitful by nature, so is her speech: her throat, that is, her talk, is smoother than oil, but in the end as bitter as gall." "Let us hear more of her manner of walking, her posture, her bearing: it is but vanity of vanities! There is not a man on earth that so endeavors to please our gracious Lord as even a passing fair woman doth strive to please men with her vanities." "Such is the woman of whom it is written in the seventh chapter of Ecclesiastes: 'And I find more bitter than death the woman, whose heart is snares and nets, and her hands as bands: whoso pleaseth God shall escape from her; but the sinner shall be taken by her.' She is bitterer than death, that is, the Devil . . . And yet more bitter still than death, for the death of the body is an overt and fearful foe; but woman is a covert, insidious foe. And hence she is no longer called a perilous snare set by the huntsman, but a snare set by demons, because men are not ensnared simply by carnal lusts . . . since her countenance is a hot wind, and her voice the hissing of a serpent, but also because women do cast spells on countless men and beasts. Her heart is called a net, that is, the fathomless wickedness that prevails in her heart; and her hands are bonds to bind men; if they lay hands on a creature to bewitch it, they accomplish what they set out to do with the aid of the Devil." "Let us conclude: all this comes to pass because of carnal appetite that is insatiable in women . . . And this is why they have dealings with demons, so that their lust may be satisfied . . . Hence it is but logical to speak of witchcraft as a matter of female witches, and not of men, so that we may consider the matter in its principal aspect; and may the Lord be praised, who hath seen fit unto this day to preserve the male sex from such depravity."

The motives behind this erudite stupidity, or stupid erudition, are obvious enough. The scholastic thinker was generally a cleric leading an ascetic and celibate life, and nothing disturbed him more than his own sexual desires. Women were taboo, bad for the welfare of his soul, and hence bad altogether. Nothing was more calculated to inspire sinful thoughts than the sight of a woman. Instead of seeking the blame for this in himself, he began to invest the object of his desires with diabolical features. The fox says of the grapes he cannot reach that they are sour. The more contemptible women are made out to be, the easier it is to endure a life without them. And the more sex was invested with diabolical features, the higher were the barriers erected round one's own sexual instincts.

The real reason for the belief that witchcraft was a female crime must, however, lie deeper than that.[122] The myth of women who fly by night figures in almost all cultures. The Greeks' Artemis roamed the forests with a retinue of dryads, as a "lioness among women," the Romans' Diana and her female retinue hunted their quarry after the manner of men. We have already mentioned

344

that the belief in female magicians who were wont to ride out on poles or staves may be traced back to the primitive peoples of the Chaldean culture. Among many patriarchal peoples, at certain times of the year there were, and still are, wild female festivals during which the "weaker sex" abandons its passive role and all the bonds of propriety, literally letting its hair down, indulging in ecstatic dances, and parading phallic symbols. In Austria, as recently as 150 years ago, so-called *Perchtln* used to parade on the nights between Christmas and New Year: women with flowing hair and bare breasts, their faces blackened with soot. Many of the customs associated with "Women's Carnival" in Cologne are reminiscent of such ancient emancipatory rituals. The witch, or *hagasuzza*, the fence rider, undoubtedly belongs to this tradition. Her orgiastic ride on a staff led into forbidden territory, into the area "beyond the pale," back into the primeval world, into the black recesses of Mother Earth. Woman was closer to the bowels of the earth than man was; she it was who gave birth to new life; she was a part of the great mystery. The witch was probably of the female sex long before she was turned into a devil by ecclesiastical superstition.

However that may be, it was almost exclusively women that our prisoners in the Falcon Tower accused of witchcraft, thus remaining loyal to the generally prevailing superstition. But there are other subgroups that are worth noting. Almost 10 percent of those denounced were midwives by profession. This, too, was in keeping with prevailing belief. The *Hammer of Witches* declared: "No one does more harm to the Catholic faith than do midwives. For if they do not kill the children, they carry them from the chamber as if to perform some necessary task, and, raising the child on high, they dedicate it to the demons." We may remember that the legend of the changeling contributed not a little to the general distrust of the profession. Most witches were allegedly to be found among midwives, for it was easiest for them to get hold of unbaptized infants. But here too the real reason for this apprehension lay deeper. The midwife is associated with birth; she is intimate with the mother giving birth; she is an "initiate" who stands close to the primeval nature of motherhood. That is why people felt there was something uncanny about the midwife. Regina the midwife had been the Devil's favorite witch, claimed Anna during questioning. He had "respected her above all others because she had killed the unbaptized infants she took from their mothers at birth, pressing her thumb into their backs, or the nape of the neck, then digging them up again and bringing them to the Devil." A nightmare that haunted almost every mother in those days.

There was also a disproportionate number of wives of tailors, cobblers, bakers, and millers among the women denounced. The reason we know already: tailors, cobblers, bakers, and millers work with raw materials—cloth, leather, grain, flour—that was usually supplied in those days by the customers themselves. Naturally, the customer often reckoned the amount of raw material needed to be less than the tradesman believed. Such matters were difficult to check, so that disputes were not at all uncommon with these tradesmen, who acquired the reputation of not always being as honest as they might be. Apparently the wife of a dishonest tradesman might all the more readily be thought capable of traffic with the Devil. Even plainer was the reason for the large number of wives of innkeepers, brewers, and wine merchants on the list of those denounced. Such women did not enjoy the best of reputations: anyone who served men with intoxicating liquor had to ward off not only their advances but also the reputation that they failed to resist those advances. A hint that the tavern keeper in question was "a great paramour," or "a depraved woman," was seldom lacking.

Presumably the first people the Pappenheimers named as their "cronies" were those who were rumored throughout the country to be in league with the Devil. From time to time we read in the record that the person in question had "long been notorious as a witch." Personal hostility does not seem to have been a prominent motive. Paulus Pämb even said on one occasion that "the old miller's wife in Kelheim he knew well, she was an enemy of his, but he did not know whether she was a witch, otherwise he would say so." This statement suggests, incidentally, that the commissioners asked specific questions about certain suspect individuals, just as they knew that Anna Pämb was reckoned to be "a witch or weird sister in the district round Abensberg and Kelheim." An "Interrogatoria of the tinker lads' mother, the old Pappenheim woman" includes, besides the question, "Whom had she seen at all these gatherings and revels?" four actual names, which were obviously suggested to the woman. On the other hand, the court worked its way through all the places the Pappenheimers had visited, and asked for the names of members of the witches' sect. In reply they were given the names of people the vagrants happened to know, or general statements to the effect

346

that "in that place there were also many respectable wives of citizens who were witches, but they could not recall who they were, or put a name to them" (Riedenburg), or else, "There were many such witches there, but he could not name them" (Ingolstadt). Gumpprecht declared to the court, "He reckoned there were some thousands of witches in the country, and even if one of them was apprehended and confessed, they had no fear, for the Devil comforted them, and persuaded them that nothing could befall them." And Paulus said he had often "heard at gatherings that there were so many witches in this land that they could scarce be counted." Wealthy and respected townsfolk were also members of the sect. "There had even been women there (at the revels) in gold chains, velvet, and silk, but he had not recognized any of them: the Devil did not suffer them to mix with the common herd."

Quite a number of these "cronies" were entered in the "wanted" list by the court, although there was little inclination out in the rural prefectures to begin a witch hunt on the basis of the Munich lists. The communications from Munich were noted, pushed into a drawer, and the suggestion they contained was quickly forgotten. It was only in the Abensberg and Altmannstein district, which was directly subordinate to the council of state in the latter's capacity as an intermediate authority, that a number of women were temporarily taken into custody. The other people who had been denounced were spared the fate of the Tettenwang miller's family, because not all of Duke Maximilian's officials were as keen, efficient, and expeditious as they might have been.

GHOSTS

From what we know of the turnkey Sebastian Georg, he was a courageous fellow. Nevertheless, a shudder must have run down his spine as he made his final round of the Falcon Tower after darkness had fallen, lantern in hand, checking, as his office required, that the prisoners were secure, their fetters in order, the doors locked and barred. It was quite possible that the Devil was lying in wait for him on the stairs, or standing behind a cell door, ready to blow out his lamp. It was of little avail to tell himself that the Evil One's power could not harm the servants of a legitimate authority. Could he, as jailor, consider himself a representative of that authority when he performed his duties reluctantly and under duress? And would not the Devil's hatred of him, the torturer, be greater than any respect for law and tradition?

Master Georg was accustomed to the presence of the Devil. Whenever he bound a victim in the torture chamber and hoisted him up by the arms, he could feel the Archenemy close at hand. He was lodged in the head of the victim, he bore down on his tongue to prevent him from speaking, he supported him on invisible hands, so that he should not feel too severely the burden of the weights that were tied to his legs as he was hauled aloft. This was what those possessed by him used to say as soon as the demon had departed from them. "The evil spirit had stopped him from speaking," Hänsel revealed after it had taken so many strokes of the rod to make the child confess. And when his father Paulus gave his answers during one interrogation with "a strangely quavering voice," he was questioned the following day in great detail about this suspicious circumstance. The commissioners' premonitions were confirmed. "Three nights earlier, before he was questioned the last time about the Tettenwang folk, the Evil One had come to him in the vault. He bleated like a goat, which startled Gämperl, and when he turned toward him, the Devil spoke to him and told him how they would deal with him, Gämperl or Pappenheimer, and what they would do to him. But he comforted him and persuaded him he should confess nothing, and he would help him through his ordeal. The night before Gämperl was due to be tortured next morning, the Devil came to him once again and addressed him as follows: in Lutheran or other heretical places he would have helped him escape, but he could do nothing for him here on account of the clergy. Gämperl might do no more than consider or bear in mind that he belonged to the Devil in any case; there was nothing to be done, he should not have committed in the first place those crimes and the sins of which he was well aware. Whereupon the Devil flew into Gämperl's mouth in the form of a puny little gnat or fly. Afterwards, during the torture, he sat down at the back of Gämperl's tongue, on the lefthand side, and spoke with a small, quavering voice, as if it came from an empty pot. When they gave Gämperl holy water, the Devil flew out of him again in the shape of a gnat or fly. Thereupon Gämperl confessed, not having been able to do so before, for the Devil had persuaded him he should not give in; he would rescue him from this imprisonment. But that he had not done. When Gämperl had first confessed to witchcraft, upstairs in the living room, the Evil One had stood outside the window in the form of a man, dressed as an artisan, and had beckoned to him, and given him to understand that he should not confess."

348

Down in the vault, the ironmaster was facing not just the evil-doers but the Devil in person. Certainly the prisoners often claimed at first that their resistance to the agonies of torture stemmed from their own will and determination; they denied that it was the Devil who gave them strength, saying "it was his own strength and obstinacy that had stopped him from confessing until the afternoon, when his limbs were cold and swollen." They cried out, "No, God forbid that I should have given myself to the Evil Spirit, or that he should have promised me anything." But in the end they admitted that supernatural forces were at work. They stated then that the Devil had not let them out of his sight ever since their arrest. Old Frau Pappenheimer, for instance: "When she (Anna) was lately asked whether she had not been beset by the evil spirit while in prison, seeing that she had at first refused to confess under the torture to which she was subjected, or whether she had seen the Devil in person, she stated that when she was arrested in Tettenwang and was being taken on a sleigh to Altmannstein, a man in black ran behind the sleigh. And when she had been conveyed from the town hall into the jail, her familiar once came to her by night on such a mighty wind that she feared the prison might fall down; he promised her that he would free her from her bonds and lead her out of captivity. But she would not consent, saying she wished to remain and commend herself to God. And she had holy water brought to save herself from further temptation. Since that time she had seen him no more, and he had not sought to tempt her again."

Augustin Baumann made a statement on similar lines: "He had never seen the Devil here (i.e. in the Falcon Tower), but the Devil had once come to him in prison at Altmannstein to console him, telling him to be of good cheer for he would spare no effort to deliver him from prison." Michel Pämb stated that "One night, he (i.e. the Devil) had looked at him through the window while he had been in prison at Abensberg. Asked him what he was doing there; all would soon be well, he would soon deliver him from custody." Empty promises. The prisoners revealed, indeed, that the Devil would not find it at all easy to liberate them. "When the Devil learned that one of his creatures had been apprehended and executed, he reassured the others that nothing would befall them, and was angry that the prisoners had allowed themselves to be caught and had not made their escape in good time. Sometimes, however, he barely asked after them, remarking that he was sure of their souls anyway, and could procure others in their stead."

"Whenever one of the coven had been put to death, the Devil would announce it to them at the next gathering, and they would consult as to whether those responsible should go scot-free, or whether they should suffer some ill. But they thought that even if they were to kill one of the executioners, another would take his place forthwith. And in any case they could not always get at their intended victims. And if one of the coven were careless enough to be caught and sentenced, no one was much concerned; they simply said, that's the end of her, the idle whore."

Such statements were calculated to reassure the ironmaster, as far as they went. But could they be believed? The accused told all sorts of tales, and a jailor like Sebastian Georg knew that torture did not always bring the pure truth to light. What was a man to make, for instance, of the claim that eating the hearts of infants rendered the prisoners immune to torture? Paulus Pappenheimer declared that the Devil had instructed each of them "to kill twenty-one children within a year and to eat their hearts, so that they would be unable to confess" if they were arrested. We hear the same kind of thing from his wife, Anna: "Should a witch, be it man or woman, not wish to be made to confess, or to be sure that the authorities could not come at them, then they must kill one hundred and one children and eat their hearts. Each and every man and woman must fulfill that number, but the Evil One might give of three hearts to anyone who found favor with him, so that they could not confess." Gumpprecht gave a different account: according to him, it was the hands and not the hearts of murdered children that worked the spell: "If you had one of them, and a pouch to keep it in, you would not be so readily apprehended, nor could the authorities lay hands on you as easily as they otherwise might . . . If you were to eat such a hand and then be taken into custody or put into prison, you would not be so easily able to confess. He and his people had eaten some of them." Agnes, the convent miller's daughter will speak of magic spells that were alleged to prevent arrest and confession: "She had been made to eat three hearts, but only parts of each." The Devil had also presented her with a herb of about a finger's length. "As long as she carried it with her, she could not be arrested. And he had given her a long stick to place in her right shoe, telling her they could not be touched, and even if they were to be taken, he would help them make their escape.—He had given them a heart, so that they would be unable to confess to the authorities."

We might think that Master Georg would listen skeptically to such tales. He was in the best position to know that there was no defense against torture. Everyone had confessed unless, like the convent miller, they had succumbed prematurely to its effects. The Pappenheimers at any rate had not profited from their knowledge of spells that enabled a man to stay silent, that was obvious. The commissioners, however, seemed to regard this implausible superstition as a real danger. Again and again they asked the prisoners quite specifically "how many infants' hearts a man would have to eat to be safe from the clutches of the authorities." Naturally they were given answers like "three," or "a hundred," or "the more a man ate, the less the authorities could prevail against him. They must be from unbaptized children, and a man must have slain the child himself if the spell was to work." What was the point of it all? The Devil never left his own in the lurch in any case, he was present during the interrogations, and turned the ironmaster's task, abhorrent enough as it was, into a grisly, fiendish revel. There was no need of any special spell to achieve that effect. It was the Archfiend who caused the victims' eyes to roll and start in such gruesome fashion; it was he who twisted their features into grimaces that haunted Master Georg in his dreams. They lapsed into unconsciousness, suddenly fell silent, burst into paroxysms of weeping, or screamed dry-eyed—all that was the Devil's doing. That was how he betrayed his presence, and his interest in this trial. Once it had seemed to the ironmaster that one of the witches was extraordinarily heavy, as he hoisted her up. He well knew who it was that had made him sweat. And, sure enough, she admitted a few days later that the Devil had crouched on her back throughout the entire interrogation, "had squeezed the breath from her, preventing her from speaking, and telling her she should say nothing."

To have such an adversary was no joking matter. Had he not already broken prisoners' necks? Oddly enough, the ironmaster felt safe from the Devil only in the dim light of the tallow candles that flickered in the torture chamber. For that was where the commissioners sat. They were representatives of authority beyond all doubt, and so were in a position to defy the unseen presence. And, what was more, the gentlemen, especially Councillor Wangereck, were versed in spiritual methods of casting out evil spirits. Before every interrogation, the sign of the cross was made over the suspect and a prayer was read. "Jesus, Savior, who doth bless us," the commissioner would cry, "give us now Thine aid!" Christ's seven last words on the Cross were inscribed on a scrap of paper which was hung round the prisoner's neck. Then he was given holy water to drink. If it transpired, in spite of everything, that Satan would not give up his victim, Wangereck would pronounce certain religious formulas, such as "And the Word became flesh, and was replete with Grace and Truth," or else he read out psalms and pious verses from a prayer book he had brought with him. Sebastian Georg had also been advised by the commissioners always to keep some salt and some herbs that had been blessed on Palm Sunday, sealed up in wax from a consecrated candle and hanging around his neck. In particularly hazardous cases, or with particularly stubborn prisoners, Dr. Wangereck used to bring along some holy relic in an ornately chased reliquary, borrowed for a few hours from the ducal treasury. The precious object would gleam incongruously in the flickering candle light of the gloomy vault. The most mighty of demons could be driven out by this means. No, the ironmaster was not afraid as long as he was in the presence of the commissioners, but at night as he made his last round by the light of a guttering dip, he sensed something eerie in the atmosphere. The tower was full of creakings and groanings; there were strange rustlings and bumps. The noises might come from the wooden beams, from a restless prisoner, from the rats scuttling hither and thither—but in all probability it was the Devil who caused them. He visited the fettered prisoners. They, too, suffered not a little from these uncanny manifestations. The tailor from Prunn, in particular, used to tell the ironmaster or his wife every morning of ghostly apparitions. He was as white as a sheet as he told them, for instance, that "something had come to the closed window of his prison the previous night, humming like a great bumblebee but otherwise saying nothing. He was terror-stricken and hid under his blanket. He believed it was his familiar demon, whom he had now denied, however, for he wanted to have only God in his heart." Or else, "Says that on two successive nights, when he had the window open to air his cell, a great bumblebee had flown into the prison and buzzed round the cell, so that he was mightily afraid. But as soon as he called on God and the Holy Savior, the bee flew off." This was perfectly credible, given the tailor's markedly timid disposition. The commissioners would nod their heads sagely when they heard of such things: it was well known that the bumblebee was one of the favorite forms assumed by the Devil.

Little Hänsel too was visited by the Devil almost every night. On 6 May, the child admitted that "his familiar demon had appeared at his cell window every night since his arrest (except for last Friday night) and had told him that his folk had already confessed but that he would say nothing. His mother had also heard this herself." When Hänsel was locked in a cell by himself, he often used to scream with terror during the night; so they found it necessary to bring a peasant lad who had been detained for different offenses and put him in the same cell with the boy. But this did not put an end to the weird events. Hänsel's fellow prisoner bore witness "that one Tuesday, at midnight, something entered the prison, but he could not see what it was. It caused an almighty commotion, overturning the bench and throwing down both pillows, which he picked up again for the boy."

How, then, given the presence everywhere of this dreadful adversary, could the ironmaster not experience a thrill of horror as he once more went on his evening round from cell to cell, mounting the creaking wooden stairs? Whenever he heard a sound or felt a draught, a chill ran down his spine. But there was nothing for it but to cross himself and to place his trust in the magic power of the wax that hung around his neck. Perhaps Master Georg also hoped that the Devil would not overlook the fact that he was no more than a subordinate and that the commissioners were his opponents as well. Vain reassurance. How could a man like our jailor fail to know that the great get away scot-free: it is only the small fry that go to the Devil.

THE PROCESSION

In the meantime, the feast of Corpus Christi had come around.[123] In Munich, the route to be taken by the procession had been lined since early morning by almost two thousand soldiers. As in previous years, a specially constituted committee of court clergy, state councillors and chamberlains, civil servants, city councillors, and artisans had made the arrangements for the event. Bavarian processions had long "been reckoned throughout Christendom to be caeteris paribus, by no means the meanest," but the Munich Corpus Christi procession was calculated to put all other spectacles of the kind in the shade. It had been instituted some twenty years previously by Duke Albrecht V on the advice of the Jesuits. He had been determined to offer overwhelming proof that Catholicism in his realm had triumphed over every sort of heretical conspiracy. Glitter and glory, pomp and pageantry, music and massed crowds were designed to sweep the last doubter off his feet and to fill the faithful with pride. Banners, chiming bells, and music, the surging thousands, the hum of voices, and the massed choirs would carry more conviction than any sermon. Tableaux, a riot of flowers, were to overwhelm the eye, which is notoriously more susceptible to persuasion than the ear. The intention to provide a show for the masses could, of course, be most happily combined with the aim of showing honor to God by means of this lavish expenditure of resources.

These festivities, ordained by the highest power in the land, had become during the few years of their existence one of the most brilliant events in Munich. It was only in the early stages that His Grace had had to augment the enthusiasm of his courtiers and civil servants for a popular procession of this kind by threatening grave consequences for anyone who absented himself from it. By this time everyone looked forward to the colorful procession, which generally took place in brilliant sunshine, since the organizing committee never failed to distribute alms in good time, enjoining the recipients to pray for fine weather. It was now rare for the duke's spies to report the absence of senior civil servants or particular citizens. The festival had become so generally popular that they had to be content with accusing certain participants of not being sufficiently devout.

On this occasion, too, everyone had turned out to take part in the procession. Farmers and craftsmen, eager to witness the spectacle, had streamed into the capital from miles around, bringing their families with them. But there was also the inevitable swarm of beggars, jugglers, and players, who, in spite of all the official bans, had high hopes of rich pickings in the festive atmosphere of the city. The streets and squares were still relatively quiet as the last preparations were made for the parade. Young women were still putting the finishing touches to the carpets of flowers that had made their appearance in front of some of the houses, the result of hectic activity during the early hours of the morning. Thousands of summer flowers, picked at the crack of dawn in the meadows surrounding the city, had sacrificed their yellow, pure white, dark blue, red, and violet petals to create these mosaic patterns. They represented a vast diversity of ecclesiastical symbols, framed in intricate borders: a chalice, for instance, with the Holy of Holies, formed from marsh marigolds and marguerites; crosses of every pattern and size, made from lady's smock and clover flowers; a rosary made from the globular flowers of club-moss; the bleeding heart of Christ in crimson rose-petals, effectively contrasting with a background of blue forget-me-nots. From the win-

354

dows hung sheets on which unskilled hands had painted brightly colored holy pictures, a St. Benno with a roguish smile, or a soulful Mary, her eyes cast heavenward. Every two or three hundred yards, altars had been set up in the open air, wooden structures decked out with carpets and curtains, and framed in young birches that had been rammed into the ocher soil of the street for this special occasion. The floral decorations still had to be augmented here and there, poultry had to be chased away from the altars, children had to be stopped from treading on the carpets that had been laid on the dusty street.

Heavenly harmonies poured from the open doorway of the Church of Our Lady into the square outside—a composition for choir and orchestra specially written for the festival by Orlando di Lasso. *Gustate et videte*, rejoiced the voices that streamed from the dim, incense-laden interior of the cathedral, as the procession made its way down the central aisle of the nave and out into the open. In the leading rows of the parade, preceding the priest carrying the monstrance under the shelter of a baldaquin, we may observe some familiar faces. The thin, pallid face of the young duke, darkened by his severely trimmed beard and sweeping mustache: he paces solemnly on his way, rigidly erect, on thin, silk-stockinged legs. His black, gold-embroidered breeches, and the black doublet that tapers down to a point, are in the Spanish style. Spanish, too, is the sword by his side, Spanish his entire bearing. Next to him, his monkish father, sole occupant of a monastic palace. He, too, is clad in black, and in the Spanish fashion. He does not stride proudly erect, however, but walks with a stoop, a pious, pensive pilgrim. They are followed by the grandees: the chief court marshal, Baron Stephan von Gumpenberg in resplendent costume, next to him the president of the council of state and chief chamberlain to the duke, Wolf Konrad von Rechberg, Lord Chancellor Joachim von Donnersberg, the chamberlains Astor Leoncelli and Giuglio Cesare Crivelli, Philip Kurz von Senftenau, and Friedrich von Gaisberg, colonel and commander of the Life Guards. Then come the representatives of the nobility on the council of state, Treasurer Ernst von Roming and the chief justice, Karl von Kulmer, then Chancellor Gailkircher and the learned councillors, among them Dr. Wangereck, the stolid but hot-tempered lawyer from Lower Bavaria; the schemer, Dr. Gewold; and Dr. Fickler, the gray-haired keeper of the archives. We can see them all as they emerge from the dim recesses of the church into the brilliant summer morning, their hands clasped devoutly.

Did any of them spare a thought for the prisoners in the Falcon

355

Tower? Scarcely likely. Even for the appointed commissioners, the case was only one preoccupation among many. If the thoughts of these eminent worshipers ever strayed from their devotions, it was in the direction of political and personal concerns. The topic of the day was the recently announced death of Edward, margrave of Baden, which gave an unexpectedly promising turn to the dispute with Baden. Speculation was rife as to whether Maximilian would pluck up his courage and exploit this favorable opportunity to execute a daring foreign policy coup in the name of Catholicism. Their thoughts may also have strayed toward the Turkish campaigns in Hungary. This dreadful threat to Christendom was a permanent exhortation to fervent prayer and the subject of intercession, even on this high holiday. Otherwise it was the customary problems of career and family that occupied one or other of the eminent participants in the procession: a vacancy for a privy councillor, a petition for a grant toward the building of a house, the impending marriage of a daughter. The Pappenheimer case was mere routine, like drafting legal opinions for the duke or reading the papers in appellate matters. Such tasks were not performed out of any consuming personal interest but simply so that they might be disposed of as quickly as possible. The thought of that dank vault under the Falcon Tower would not in any case have been fitting on this sunny, festive holiday.

The procession that streamed out of the melodious shadow of the church grew longer and longer. The head of it had already reached the Kaufingergasse as the red and gold baldachin borne by acolytes swayed out of the nave. Beneath its shelter, the principal parish priest carried before him Our Lord Jesus Christ in order to show Him the city streets once each year. The body of God's own Son, in the form of a yellowish wafer about the size of a taler, gazed through a window of a monstrance. This miniature castle, with its forest of pinnacles and towers and its infinitely intricate decorative chasing provided a fitting abode for the Holy of Holies. It was followed by the serried ranks of the clergy: monks and nuns from the various monasteries and convents in Munich, the pastors, deans, and canons of the city. Among them was Dr. Hannemann, parish priest of St. Peter's and confessor to the prisoners in the Falcon Tower.

In the meantime, in the shadow of the cathedral on its north side, the tableaux vivants had begun to form under the strict supervision of official marshals. Now, at a given signal, they joined the procession. As they made their appearance on the cathedral square, the groups of mummers were greeted by the crowd with "oh's" and "ah's" and repeated rounds of thunderous applause. The music had come to an end, but all the bells in the two mighty onion towers had started to thunder. In the midst of this clangor there could still be heard the voices of the monks and nuns, who had begun to intone a *Te Deum laudamus*, which was eminently suited to the occasion, for at that moment innumerable figures of a patriarchal God emerged with measured step from behind the cathedral to join the procession. They were all of imposing stature and clad in flowing linen garments. They greeted the crowds majestically, at the same time stroking their long gray beards somewhat nervously. They were followed by ninety angels— hand-picked, handsome youths in long white shifts, complete with paper wings. Thereupon a number of Abrahams made their appearance, powerfully built men with beards, dressed in sackcloth and leaning on knotty shepherd's crooks. A new wave of applause burst out, for now came the high priests, stout and sanctimonious, the corners of their mouths drawn down in condescension, their plump fingers clasped on bellies that were padded out with cushions. There was much applause, too, for the pharaohs, who had made up their eyes with charcoal to give themselves a forbidding appearance. They were wearing sumptuous garments, dressing gowns from the inheritance of Duke Albrecht V which had been lent them for the procession on condition that they tied on table napkins when it came to the inevitable round of drinks. No less than sixteen Mothers of God formed the next group, among them a Virgin mounted on an ass for the flight into Egypt, who attracted much attention on account of her long blond hair. Another, representing "Mary in her suffering," repeatedly squeezed the juice of a pomegranate into her eyes so as to weep the more convincingly. A dungheap had been mounted on an ox-drawn cart; on it sat Job, scratching his festering sores with potsherds. Another cart was got up as a whale, which from time to time swallowed and then regurgitated Jonas, a nimble youth. Lazarus looked pitiful, a skinny, jaundiced individual with red ulcers painted on his naked torso; St. Augustine, played by a white-haired innkeeper, made a venerable impression; the giants, armed with clubs and played by the tallest men to be found in the duchy, were properly terrifying. But in the opinion of the awe-struck onlookers the climax of the procession was provided by the three Magi, who rode past on genuine camels from the duke's menagerie. But that was by no means the end. An aged Noah passed by, pulling goats, sheep, dogs, and donkeys on a long rope; the centurion of Capernaum walked beside a stretcher carried by Samaritans, bearing his servant, sick unto death. The patient, duly healed by Jesus, leapt up at regular intervals and skipped about, only to return to his deathbed at the next street corner. There were any number of such scenes and figures, and no end to the astonishment they evoked. A good half of our Bible history paraded in the wake of the powers-that-be, the Holy of Holies, and the cream of the clergy. The mummers were also joined, of course, by those devout onlookers who had not chosen to take their places in the lanes and squares along the route. Residents along the route were fortunate: they stood, surrounded by friends and neighbors, at open windows, enjoying a privileged view of the spectacle.

So the parade made its way through Munich. Now and then the procession came to a halt, so that Lazarus ended up among the Virgins, the angels were thrown into confusion and landed among the High Priests and the Pharaohs, where they had no business to be. That happened each time the swaying baldaquin at the head of the procession halted at one of the street altars with its decorative carpets and green birchtrees. The body of Christ in its glittering golden pavilion was displayed, while the priest raised his hands and intoned Latin prayers. The voices of the approaching worshipers, eminent and humble alike, were joined in a hymn that had been struck up by the clergy.

All this singing, and the ringing of bells, the shouts of the crowd, the applause and the hum from the streets could be heard in the stuffy cells of the Falcon Tower. There the fettered prisoners lay, listening to the festive sounds. No doubt they were longing to be present, to join the cheerful throng, to gaze in wonder with all the others. Perhaps it occurred to one or the other of them that the next procession to delight the holiday crowds would take place on the judgment day, when his hour had come. The prisoners from the Falcon Tower would certainly take part—not gaping at the spectacle, however, but gaped at, sitting on the unyielding benches of the knacker's cart as it lurched its way through the streets.

PROOFS BASED ON SUPPOSITION

Kaspar Steinwandner and his anonymous military escort returned from their expedition to Altmannstein rather less jauntily than they had set out ten days before. They had collected a great deal

358

of "information"; they had called on farmers in Tettenwang, Hagenhill, Laimerstadt, Buch, and Prunn; they had questioned townsfolk in Riedenburg, Kehlheim, and Affecking; they had visited certain eerie places in the hills and in marshy meadowland. But they were not bringing back any judicially sound evidence. Not a single one of the circumstances connected with the crimes admitted by the prisoners in the Falcon Tower was such that only the criminal himself could have known of it. Insofar as their confessions had contained such evidence, it remained uncorroborated. Old Pappenheimer, for instance, had spoken of the murder of a traveling tradesman and claimed to have dragged the corpse into some bushes on the road between Hagenhill and Tettenwang and to have left it there. The clerk to the treasury and his assistant had been there, had found the spot at once with the help of the description given, but had found no trace of a body in spite of an intensive search, not even the slightest remains. It had been like that everywhere. In spite of its longwinded phrases, the report that Kaspar Steinwandner submitted to the treasurer, Ernst von Roming, on the day following his return contained nothing but this disappointing conclusion.

Von Roming then discussed the legal situation with Wangereck, probably following a meeting of the council of state. The clerk had been told to bring the files, along with the relevant statutes and legal authorities. The case was to be brought to a conclusion at last; the prisoners were not to be permitted to delay a decision any longer. Wangereck and the treasurer did not doubt for a moment that the misleading evidence in the confessions was simply intended to hold up proceedings. It never occurred to them that the prisoners might be totally innocent and had confessed under torture to purely fictitious crimes simply because they had no real crimes to confess. Now, of course, they could be subjected to renewed torture, and that, indeed, had been done repeatedly on the basis of "information received." The result had been that the new confessions extorted from the prisoners also turned out to be for the most part pure invention; in the remaining cases it was not possible to produce a corpus delicti. No progress was being made.

In the strictest interpretation of the law, not one of the many hundreds of crimes to which the Pappenheimers had confessed could be proved. But was it necessary in this case to stick to a strict interpretation of the law? Not in the least. For the proceedings were concerned with *crimina excepta* such as robbery, murder, arson—and above all with witchcraft. These grave and secret offenses, it was generally admitted, could not be detected and solved by the usual methods of proof; on the other hand, it was precisely in the case of such crimes that the need for prosecution was most manifest. In the view of legal authorities, the judge was not bound in these instances by legal restrictions and rules of evidence.

That was the prevailing view, stated as follows by a leading lawyer of the time: "In the case of clandestine crimes, proof that rests on supposition is treated as if it were full proof."[124] Of course, this supposition could not be based purely on the suspect's confession. "In addition to the confession, there must be some other mode of certainty (*alia certitudo*), but in the case of clandestine crimes, or those which are difficult to prove, it is sufficient to have circumstantial evidence that they have been committed. The manner in which certainty of supposition may be deduced in crimes of witchcraft cannot be determined in detail but must be left to the discretion of an intelligent judge. In the opinion of learned scholars there are, in fact, numerous signs from which the existence of witchcraft may be deduced; for instance, the fact that a suspect who has confessed to witchcraft has had frequent association and friendship with other convicted sorcerers. Membership of a particular community, too: birds of a feather flock together. Or the fact that the witch's bed was empty while she was at a witches' Sabbath. Or the fact that a woman has the evil eye and pronounces spells. Or the fact that a woman is incapable of shedding tears."

In the Pappenheimer case there was any amount of such evidence. In the first place, the common factors in many of the confessions pointed to the vagrants' guilt. In the interrogations the commissioners had always placed great importance on seeing that the statements of the various suspects coincided in some particulars at least. Suggestive questions had proved to be a suitable means of achieving this, and the commissioners had refused to accept evasive answers or denials. They "solemnly admonished" the suspects and ordered the ironmaster to make the torture more and more severe until they had the statement they were looking for. "Although at first he would not confess of his own accord, or admit that he knew anything of infants' hands," the record would then read, "he nevertheless did state upon being earnestly admonished, and after being twice stretched, he had seen four or five of the aforesaid hands in the possession of his sons . . . Where they had procured the same, or where they had put them, he could not say." The councillors were not prepared, however, to accept such protestations of ignorance. The suspect was pressed further. "Later he stated that they had buried them in that part of Schölz's barn in Tettenwang where straw or hay was kept." The court was not satisfied with this answer, presumably because the barn where the Pappenheimers were arrested had long since been thoroughly searched, without result. "He denied, however, that this was the hiding place," the record continues, "saying they . . . had buried them in Schölz's pigsty." But the commissioners still shook their heads. "In the end he confessed on solemn oath as the pure truth that they . . . had buried them . . . in the kitchen garden behind Schölz's barn." This, at last, was the answer expected, for it tallied with confessions of the other suspects.

With interrogation methods of this kind, the court was able to elicit the desired statements, even without suggestive questions or direct influence. But these occurred as well. For example, the names of those the suspects were supposed to identify as their accomplices were read out to them. Or else obvious mistakes were eliminated from the confessions: "First of all she spoke of doves . . . (i.e. as a dish served at a witches' Sabbath). But when she was corrected and told that the Devil could in no wise suffer these birds, then she replied that he had rather taken magpies or some such fowl." And, similarly: "Spoke first of the woman called Ziegler, but when she was reminded that the same was dead, she spoke rather of the miller's wife and excused herself on account of her muddled head."

The judges went to great lengths to stop the accused recanting: "Although he at first recanted and would admit nothing, especially concerning witchcraft, on being solemnly admonished by the commissioners and reminded of what he had heretofore admitted, he was disposed once more to confess, saying he had thought thus to preserve his life and come off unscathed."

It was not simply a matter of eliciting a plain answer to all the items on the schedule of questions. There were contradictions that had to be eliminated, supplementary questions that had to be put. Often the confessions were inherently inconsistent. "When it was then put to him, how could it be that he had committed this theft some five years since, making use of an infant's hand, when it was but three or four years past that he had slashed open the two women and had had hands in his possession, he replied that he could not so strictly put a date to the theft." More frequently a statement would contradict the confessions made by the other accused, so that a fresh interrogation was necessary. "This investigation was undertaken because the sons confessed to matters of which their father had said nothing, and in part vice versa." Inconsistencies were occasionally noted in the margin when the record was later checked: "Michel confesses to setting this fire but cannot recall that the tailor was present." "Gumpp claims to know nothing of this." At one point we find, "Better to inquire concerning this fire," or "ask whether it occurred by day or by night." Such "inquiry" was necessary also when "information" was "received," so as to make the confessions consistent.

The accused were also confronted with statements made by others, which they regularly corroborated, although this occasionally led to further confusion: "Albeit they confessed, according to other statements, especially that of Michel, which was put to them, to having stolen a monstrance from St. Salvator's Church, which could not be the case, since they were all so securely kept that it would be well-nigh impossible to steal one." In general, however, the commissioners were successful in getting the confessions to tally.

This was particularly important for the court as far as complicity in a crime was concerned, for these statements were designed to elicit mutual incrimination. In this connection it was often necessary to overcome determined resistance on the part of the accused. Even little Hänsel, as we have mentioned, was reluctant to corroborate the statements by his elder brothers with which he was confronted. "Didn't know—thought his brothers had confessed in response to the torture, but afterwards they had told him, because the jailor often let him go to see them, that it had not been found so after inquiry. If he were to say much, he would be the death of them, and he knew nothing other than what his brothers had told him, namely that they had stolen money and clothing from Farmer Durn near Straubing, but when a letter was sent there, it was found not to be so. Moreover, they had confessed to fourteen murders under torture . . . If asked, they might tell his mother as much." The adults were even less willing to incriminate their friends and parents. The court occasionally took account of this in drawing up the schedule of questions, as the reader may recall. As, for example, in relation to the question whether Pappenheimer's wife really suffered from "the falling sickness, or whether she was merely shamming," where a note of instruction for the ironmaster was added: "May be tortured to the limit, so that he gives evidence against his mother, since, according to the father's statement, he best knows all things relating to

362

her." If incriminating statements were available, but no corresponding confession, the court would stage a so-called "confrontation." Paulus Gämperl, for example, had confessed to more than Gumpprecht accused him of. "When confronted with the son in this matter, the father confessed . . . stating also that he was sure his father might have also taken some money from the murdered horse-dealer." Or the father confessed to the theft of a monstrance, believing his sons had done the same: "The following day, on being confronted with both his sons in this matter, he recanted, weeping, and saying that, because his sons at first had claimed it to be so, he would have let the matter be, but it was indeed not true." Gumpprecht had accused his mother of desecrating the Host at places other than those specified by her, so that a "confrontation with his mother" ensued. She was also confronted, so the record states, by little Hänsel, who had confessed under torture to having flown to witches' Sabbaths with his mother. We may recall that the woman had been forced, in the presence of her child, to declare that he belonged to the Devil. "When the mother was further questioned whether she had taken the child with her to such revels, and whether the boy was baptized, she would not at first confess that she had taken him with her or that he was a child of the Devil, but claimed that the lad was baptized . . . Thereafter, however, and on further admonishment, she said that since she had been compelled to promise the Devil to bring the whole world under his sway (were that possible), and since the Devil claimed, when a witch was with child, that the child was his, she had promised him Hänsel both in her womb and in life." Other confrontations were equally successful; there was a total of twelve in the course of the proceedings. The method was the same throughout: the accused was forced to watch his or her fellow accused being tortured on account of the divergent statements they had made. We can imagine how rapidly this method of interrogation led to consistency between the statements when the partners in the "confrontration" were members of the same family.

Mutually corroborative statements obtained in this manner were supported by other grounds for suspicion. The view that "birds of a feather flock together" tended to incriminate above all those villagers who had been intimately associated with the vagrants. In a number of instances, one or other of the prisoners had shown himself incapable of shedding tears under torture. To make quite certain of this, one of the commissioners had then approached the bound victim, placed his hand on the latter's head and enjoined him solemnly: "For the sake of the bitter tears shed for our salvation by Our Savior, Lord Jesus Christ, on His cross, I urge you, if you should be innocent, to shed tears forthwith. If you should not be innocent, then you cannot." But those thus adjured had striven in vain to shed tears. The reason was obvious. Through this remnant of the trial by ordeal, God proclaimed the truth in place of the criminal, who was prevented from speaking. So the Devil was mortified and mocked, being powerless against such a manifestation of guilt.

But there were still plainer signs that confirmed the commissioners' assumptions. Except for little Hänsel, all the prisoners were found to bear scars on their bodies that were identified as witch marks. When the consecrated needle used for this purpose was inserted at those points of the body, no blood was forthcoming. In the view of all recognized legal authorities, this was tantamount to a regular corpus delicti in the case of witchcraft. There was, in addition, a mass of items of "information," which, although not individually conclusive as evidence, nevertheless served to strengthen the commissioners' conviction that the prisoners were guilty—and quite rightly so, in the light of prevailing opinion. After all, the *Hammer of Witches* had quoted as "evidence of the crime" possible "threats that the witch has uttered, saying 'You shall have no more days of health,' or the like, the effect being seen to ensue forthwith." There was any amount of evidence that people whom the prisoners themselves claimed to have smeared with the Devil's ointment had actually fallen sick or died. It had been proved in numerous cases that fearful storms had raged at places and times named by the Pappenheimers in their description of weather spells they had cast. Farmers who were said by the accused in their confessions to have been their victims had indeed lost cattle and crops. Many of the persons alleged to have been murdered by the Pappenheimers had in fact vanished without trace at the time of the deed, some of their bodies had even been found. The commissioners had asked direct questions concerning a number of these unsolved murders and had elicited confessions that satisfied them. There was an overwhelming body of evidence to justify their suspicions. Wangereck and von Roming noted down the evidence in summary form, compared their transcripts with the information obtained by Steinwandner, leafed through the tomes that lay on the table, and came to the conclusion that, apart from the actual confessions, there was ample evidence against the prisoners to justify substituting their own persuasion of the guilt of the accused for such concrete evidence as might still be lacking.

And so the case came full cycle. Because there was a host of unsolved crimes and inexplicable disasters to cattle and crops throughout Bavaria, the idea had been generated in the council of state, as we have suggested, that the elusive perpetrators should be deterred by a large-scale show trial, as soon as some of them fell into the hands of the law. It was then that news arrived of our vagrant family. There was no evidence against them, of course, except for the accusation made by a convicted thief, since executed, but these homeless travelers were judged capable of any crime. They belonged to that group of persons who were held responsible for the misfortunes of the country and for the widespread lack of security. They were suspect long before anything particular was known of them. Everything that followed stemmed from this suspicion. It was this suspicion that dictated the commissioners' schedule of questions and spurred them on to repeat the torture with ever increasing severity. It was this suspicion that distended the transcripts into voluminous files and ensured that the scope of the trial was enlarged to include people like the convent miller of Tettenwang. And now, when it came to weighing the evidence, it was this initial suspicion that undergirded the judges' persuasion of the prisoners' guilt, shaping the motley collection of facts into a mosaic pattern of which the outlines had been determined long before our vagrants were arrested.

That does not mean that the commissioners, with their endless poring over the transcripts and their learned discussions, were simply acting out a farce. There is no indication that they ever thought of bending the law, even to serve some higher end. A calculation of that sort is unnecessary if the criminal jurisprudence of the time permits prejudices to be translated into legal judgments. So it was in those days. In the case of so-called exceptional crimes, presumption served as proof. From the outset it was suspected that the Pappenheimers were guilty of the most heinous crimes. Their conviction now followed from that suspicion.

Legal logic from the year 1600.

POINTLESS PREPARATIONS

At last they would need his advice after all, Johann Baptist Fickler no doubt thought to himself when he learned in the middle of July that the case against the Pappenheimers was about to be concluded. The judgment was shortly to be discussed in the council. It was very likely that one of the doctors of law or even the president of the council, von Rechberg, would turn to the prince's former tutor, now his archivist, and ask for his suggestion. For, after all, he had written a book on the whole question of the legal punishment of witches and sorcerers. Moreover, he was not short of experience in cases like this, having participated in witch trials during his years in Salzburg. The duke's council could consider itself fortunate that it had such an authority among its number. It would be the first occasion for some time that he had been asked for advice. He would do well to prepare his performance carefully and draft a sound reply.

He would begin, of course, with the Bible, quoting Exodus, Leviticus, and Deuteronomy, according to which sorcerers should not escape with their lives. Attention should also be drawn to the worldwide threat posed by the witches' sect, to news of the havoc wreaked by the diabolical hosts in France and in Italy, so as to make clear that it was not only obedience to God that required the extirpation of these enemies of mankind but also the vital interest of the state. He would then touch briefly on the Pappenheimers' other crimes and point out that however abominable murder, robbery, and arson might be, witchcraft excelled all other felonies in its dangers and its offensive nature. For while the former represented merely an assault on man's possessions, the latter was an affront to God and, indeed, the gravest imaginable affront, involving a pact with the Devil.

After these introductory sentences, he would continue as follows: "According to ancient custom and usage, it is the practice to punish with fire and to burn soothsayers, sorcerers, witches, and suchlike monsters which, by their abominable falling off from God and by their illicit communication with damned spirits of Hell, in contravention of the supreme majesty of God and Christian duty and faith, have cast themselves into atrocious vice and shame, together with others that they led astray or sinned against, leading to their utter ruin and destruction."[125] Even though divine law, as well as Roman law, demanded simply the death penalty without specifying the mode of execution, it had nevertheless always been customary among Christians to burn the offender. "Whereas it has been the case from of old, and in many places until but recently, that sorcerers and ogres were burned and consumed alive by the flames as an awful example and to deter others from hazarding such dreadful penalty, insomuch as doctors of civil and canon law have thus been correctly expounding the laws here in question; and whereas a judge is constrained to observe the statutes with due regard to the opinion and understanding of those authorities that expound the same, except in cases where the sovereign power has reason to mitigate or amend the penalty imposed upon such felonies; nevertheless, in these present times, albeit some few sorcerers and ogres as were exceedingly contumelious, blasphemous, and determined to depart this life in despair both of God and their immortal souls have indeed been cast into the fire or burned alive on account of their unspeakable felonies, it has notwithstanding become the practice of well-nigh all Christian judiciaries so to mitigate the penalty that any sorcerer who abjures the company of evil spirits and his pledge to the same, once again confessing allegiance with all due contrition to the one true God, should not be subjected to the enduring torment of the flames while still alive but should be strangled and suffocated, or else beheaded with the sword, according as the custom of each place may be, and the corpse alone cast into the fire to be burned to ashes as a warning to others and as a token that justice has been done in due form. This in consideration of the fact that such secular authorities as love God and practice Christian charity must needs bear in mind that certain of these delinquents, supposing all should be burned alive, might, by reason of bitter resentment or despondency, fall into even grosser sin or despair and hence merely migrate (which our good Lord forbid) from one fire into another."

Fickler would put forward these considerations, but he would then go on to speak of the outrageous degree of the offenders' guilt in the case now to be decided—a degree of guilt which not merely precluded any mitigation of the sentence but called, indeed, for it to be carried out to the letter and with all imaginable rigor. For the Pappenheimers and their followers had forfeited their lives several times over, not only on account of witchcraft. The thefts which they had admitted were in themselves capital crimes. Did it not state in Charles V's penal code: "If anyone be detected thrice in larceny . . . then he is decried as a habitual thief, and considered on the same footing as a rapist, and is hence to suffer the penalty of death"? If the total value of the stolen property exceeded five gulden, that was an aggravating circumstance. Even graver was "prigging and theft" from churches, theft from offertory boxes by breaking them open with the aid of "prigging sticks." For the law stated: "If anyone break open, unlock, or steal by any ruse from the box in which holy offerings are collected, daring to use any contrivance for this end, then he is to forfeit his life." This applied in all its rigor to the numerous thefts from churches perpetrated by the vagrants. They had, in fact, confessed to having "burgled churches and vestries . . . by night" in order to purloin monstrances and chalices. This was a graver offense than common theft by breaking and entering: "Item, should someone steal a monstrance, containing the Holy Sacrament, from the altar, he is to be sentenced to death by burning. But should someone otherwise steal gold or silver consecrated vessels, with or without the Host, or chalices or patens . . . also such as break into a consecrated church, ciborium, or vestry, or force open locks with dangerous instruments, these thieves are to suffer death in keeping with the circumstances of the case, and at the discretion of those versed in the law."

Fickler would then continue his argument: each single robbery admitted by the vagrants was even more deserving of the death penalty. The criminals had lain in wait for innocent wayfarers, slain them, and robbed them. According to the statutes of the penal code, this was not merely "malicious robbery," to be punished by the sword, but "deliberate, wanton murder," to be punished "by breaking on the wheel," and since they were dealing with particularly grave offenses, "by some manner of corporal punishment, such as tearing the flesh with pincers, or dragging on a hurdle, before the final execution." But that was not all. These people had laid fires, as a result of which "many dwellings and towns had been burned to the ground." For this offense, too, the law laid down death by burning: "Item, malicious arsonists, on conviction, shall be put to death by fire." Above all, however, the "grisly, murderous crime" of the nocturnal attack on the croft in Matikhofen proved the prisoners to be "murderous arsonists" who should themselves be burned alive. They must be seen as "wanton despoilers," who constituted an unlawful, outrageous threat to the community at large, who had deliberately defied the law, and who were therefore, according to imperial statute, persons "of whom might be expected, for causes duly shown, evil and criminal acts," pests who should be executed in the cruellest possible manner, both as a punishment and as a warning to others.

This was how the old councillor would speak. His colleagues were to hear how well he knew the current penal regulations, how precisely he had incorporated in his statement everything reported by the commissioners, how perfect his knowledge of the

368

prevailing doctrine was. A good many of them thought he was nothing but a retired schoolmaster and a decrepit archivist. They had to be shown that he had been appointed tutor in law to the reigning duke for good reason: that he had been selected for his comprehensive scholarship and his astute legal mind. For that reason he was not content simply to enumerate the relevant penal regulations but sought to deploy more profound arguments. The present case, he would say, was characterized by an almost unbelievable accumulation of those "very grave and exceptionally heinous crimes" termed *crimina excepta,* or exceptional crimes, for to that category belonged not only witchcraft but also theft from churches, arson, murder, and highway robbery. But what did all these crimes have in common? The vital interest that the authorities had in their exemplary punishment, for each and every one of them constituted a direct threat to the survival of the community. Probably no case was more calculated than the present one to act as a general deterrent through the exemplary execution of the criminals. But the judgment, and the "shrift" which was read out in public, must state quite clearly that desertion of God in favor of the Devil was not only the most dreadful of the crimes to which the accused confessed but also the origin of all the others. It was by no means sufficient to rely solely on article 109 of the penal code, which stated: "Item, anyone who does harm or injury to others by means of sorcery shall be punished by death, and the punishment shall be carried out by fire." For witchcraft was not simply a matter of sorcery. As a punishable offense, it derived from the law of God, and from the Roman civil law, as already mentioned, and from the proper interpretation of the second clause of article 109, already quoted: "Where, however, someone has used sorcery, and harmed no man, then shall the punishment be otherwise, according to the nature of the case, wherefore the judges should seek counsel." Before the crimes of the witches' sect were fully known, this provision had been interpreted to mean that some lesser penalty should be imposed for innocuous sorcery. But now the clause should be read in the following sense: "Wheresoever a person has made use of sorcery by entering into a pact with the Devil, then, in keeping with the counsel offered by legal authorities, an extraordinary penalty should be imposed, even should the person have inflicted no harm." The counsel of the leading legal experts was unanimous to the effect that it was precisely in such cases that the sentence of burning alive should be imposed.[126]

Following this climax in his legal submission, Fickler would then come to his conclusion. On the one hand, the criminals confined in the Falcon Tower had deserved death by fire on account of their practice of witchcraft; on the other, they had earned it equally on account of their crimes of arson, burglary of churches, and murder in association with arson. Their highway robberies ought to be punished by breaking on the wheel and with red-hot pincers, the other thefts by hanging or drowning. Given the multiplicity of crimes to which the prisoners had confessed, they really ought to suffer many hundreds of deaths. But, alas, even the most abominable criminal had only one life to lose. Therefore, the most severe penalty they had incurred, namely, death by burning alive, ought to be combined with all the severest additional penalties that could be thought of. This was his well considered advice, founded on his knowledge of the relevant learned authorities.

This is how we may imagine the observations Fickler had prepared for that moment when he would be asked to give his opinion on the case in the presence of the assembled council. They were in keeping with current penal jurisprudence, which a man like Dr. Wangereck would know intimately. For this reason the council of state dispensed with any discussion in committee of the penal issue, and simply delegated to the commissioner the task of drafting the sentence. Nobody asked for Dr. Fickler's opinion. It was not thought necessary to have recourse to the keen legal mind of the duke's former tutor, now demoted to the position of archivist.

CHAPTER · 9

*I*mprisonment
(contemporary woodcut)

· The Place of Execution

High on a hill and visible for miles around, some three hours' ride from the capital, lay the castle of Oberneuching, seat of the noble family of Neuchinger. Dense forest surrounded the ancient walls, which, with their crumbling, mossy stones, overgrown with ivy, suggested a ruined medieval keep. The ridge of the much-patched roof sagged under the burden of its age; the rotting castle gate hung loose in its rusty hinges. In spite of its obviously dilapidated state, the building was inhabited. Goats were grazing in the moat, children were playing in front of the castle gate, perpetually open because it could no longer be closed; underpants, sheets, and shirts in a diversity of colors hung on a line stretched across the castle courtyard; a tattered banner fluttered from the balcony. The proud possessor of this poverty-stricken idyll was Christoph Neuchinger of Oberneuching, husband to a hardworking woman with the red, scrubbed hands of a laundrymaid, father of nine children. He makes his entrance into our tale about noon on 20 July 1600. It was at that moment that excited boyish voices announced an arrival, even before the visitor, still hidden by the forest, had made his way up the steep, stony track, heralded by a clatter of hooves and the snorting of his horse. The colored coat-of-arms on the leather pouch the stranger carried slung over his shoulder revealed that it was the duke's commission that brought him hither. He rode into the courtyard, greeted by the children's cries and ignoring the chickens that ran squawking from his horse's hooves. He reined in his mount in front of the lord of the manor, who bustled forward to meet his guest. The rider sprang from the saddle, doffed his broad-brimmed hat with its luxuriant plumes, swept it around in an extravagant gesture while bowing in the courtly Spanish manner with just a hint of genuflection. This salute was offered less to the master of the dilapidated castle than to the office he held. Christoph Neuchinger was the *Bannrichter,* or executive justice of the Munich treasury: a hanging judge, to be precise.[127]

He owed this position to an almost superstitious horror of "judicial bloodshed" that was typical of the time. This led to a curious division of labor. Supreme jurisdiction, which involved the power of life and death over delinquent subjects, represented, as it were, a vital crystallization of political power that was much sought after and jealously guarded by the duke. The prefects and district justices, the treasuries and the council of state exercised this jurisdiction on behalf of the sovereign; the cities and one or two major landowners defended it as an essential part of their autonomy. No one was willing to surrender the power to pronounce capital sentences. But neither were those who wielded this power willing to incur the taint of bloodshed in person. Condemning others to death was a shameful, repulsive duty. Anyone who shed the blood of others, even the blood of convicted criminals, was soon ostracized by those around him and risked forfeiting honor and respect. Everyone wanted to bear the sword, but no one wanted to wield it himself. In order to achieve the former and avoid the latter, those authorities who exercised the power of life and death engaged men of straw. They appointed inferior magistrates who were required to assume the shameful part of their duty: the so-called *Bannrichter.*

The duke did not care for the idea. He visualized a hierarchically graded judiciary, with himself as supreme justice, strictly organized from top to bottom, with officials who were directly responsible to him. His view of his own function implied that the power over life and death was part and parcel of his divine mission. If he were to delegate this power to someone else, then he wished to know to whom he was delegating it. He did not mean to invest a chosen official with such a vital function merely for the latter to delegate it in turn to someone else. He therefore prohibited the practice. The response was a storm of protest. At the Diet of Ingolstadt in 1552 the Bavarian estates demanded official recognition of the office of executive justice, presumably on the same lines as in Austria or Salzburg. They firmly rejected the suggestion that "prefects and district judges of noble standing should sit before the criminal and pronounce a judgment which brought

374

shame on the nobility." The duke, who was then, as almost always, in financial difficulties which could be solved only with the aid of the Diet, seemed to yield. By 1580, the appointment of a substitute to implement capital punishment was already so institutionalized that the prefect of Kelheim protested vigorously at having to "break the staff," i.e. pronounce sentence of death, in person. He knew of "no prefect in Upper and Lower Bavaria," he grumbled, "who was subject to such burdens and impositions." In the collegiate courts too, the horror of pronouncing the death sentence was evident. From the penal code of Charles V we learn that "for some time, and in certain places, a number of the nobility and other persons that have a personal obligation to sit in penal judgment have refused to sit in such courts, being reluctant to do so by reason of their rank." The aristocratic administrator-general of Bavaria had from the outset delegated to district and municipal judges the power of capital punishment, originally conferred on him. They, for their part, wished to appoint an executive justice, just as the patrician chief magistrate of Munich unhesitatingly employed an inferior magistrate for the same purpose. The sovereign fought in vain against the reluctance of his officials to sully themselves with blood. On 14 June 1581 William V wrote to his council of state: "Whereas it has come to Our notice that certain of the Prefects of Our realm are loath to hold the power of criminal justice and hence propose to depute the same to others, (We do most strictly enjoin) the President of Our Council and Our Councillors, together with all that exercise office therein . . . to take most earnest note that all such Prefects as exercise authority on behalf of the Sovereign do embody the power of criminal justice in their own person, and shall pass sentence or, as the usage of each place may be, require the same to be set forth by the Clerk of the Court. . . . Our office here . . . shall communicate this same forthwith to the other administrations of Our realm."

In spite of this instruction, which seems, like so many other ducal decrees, to have been ignored, the office of executive justice was officially recognized and his terms of reference set forth at the Diet of 1584—William V was once more in need of money. Most important, the financial aspect was discussed. There was henceforth to be an executive justice for each treasury, and his "emoluments" were to be provided jointly by the prefects of the relevant district. It was further decided—and this may strike us as odd, after all that has just been said—that the executive justice should be an "honorable member of the nobility." Possibly the aristocracy, in spite of their reluctance to administer criminal justice, nevertheless wished that the newly created office might at least be secured as a source of income for the most indigent members of their class. However that may be, it was by virtue of this decision that Christoph Neuchinger of Oberneuching became executive justice for the Munich treasury in that same year—an office he still held in July 1600.

The bow and the flourish of the plumed hat were addressed, therefore, not to the person of the impoverished knight but to the office he held. After the messenger had thus paid his respects and addressed the knight formally, he drew a thick sealed dispatch from the pouch with the ornate device and handed it to its addressee. Neuchinger, having just come from his labors in stable and garden, no doubt wiped his hands on his shabby doublet before taking the bulky letter. Then, since the official part of the visit had been completed with the handing over of the missive, we can see the pair of them stooping to slip beneath the washing on the line and making their way to the wooden table which stood under the shady pergola, leaving the horse in the care of one of the justice's sons. It was customary to provide the messenger with food and drink before he set out on his return journey. And so, no doubt, the master of this dilapidated but teeming ruin called his wife, who brought their perspiring visitor bread, bacon, and cider. They were generous folk, even if they were poor.

While their guest was partaking of this refreshment, Neuchinger had time to break the seal on the letter and to study the covering note, which ran something like this: "By the Grace of God, We, Maximilian, Count Palatinate on the Rhine, Duke in Upper and Lower Bavaria, etc. To our Well-beloved, Greeting. Whereas Paulus Pämb, otherwise known as Pappenheimer, Anna, his wife, and Gumpprecht and Jacob, formerly Michel, the sons begotten in wedlock of the said Anna, further Ulrich Schölz, farmer, and Georg Schmälzl, tailor, on account of witchcraft and other abominable crimes, have been confined in the prison of the Falcon Tower, what statements they have there made, and what has been concluded concerning them, this and other matters you may learn from the records herewith enclosed. This being so, We have committed both the above-named persons to God and to criminal justice. Accordingly we have sent the said papers to you so that you may pass judgment in pursuance of the criminal law. Should, however, the case too far tax your understanding, then seek counsel in the proper quarter; We trust that you will dispatch a judgment, after due consultation, to Our Council of State in preparation for execution of the same. Dated: Munich, 19 July 1600, Wirtemberger, Secretary."

This was a purely formal letter, and the impoverished lord of the manor was familiar with its invariable phraseology. In his sixteen years of service as executive justice he had received many letters in almost identical terms and had learned to read them aright. The council of state had once more "committed" a number of prisoners "to God and to criminal justice." To put it plainly: it had condemned them to death. The "records herewith enclosed" were flimsy. They consisted mainly of a list of the crimes of which the condemned were accused; this ran to several folio pages. Apart from that, nothing but a draft of the sentence that Neuchinger was supposed to pass if the letter addressed to him was to be taken literally. The recipient was in no way dismayed by this. He was well able to distinguish between his own person and the other person, for whom he was acting as proxy. The instruction "to pass judgment in pursuance of the criminal law" did not concern him personally. His tacit agreement to accept the sentence in his capacity as deputy was taken for granted. The whole thing was make-believe. The council of state, in asking for a sentence to be passed and drafted in terms of the transcript, was in a sense talking to itself, for it was the council, and not its deputy, which had the power to pass sentence of death. What the councillors had delegated was not power and responsibility, but ignominy and disdain.

Christoph Neuchinger would not in any case have been the man to pronounce a judgment in a criminal case which was designed to be of such signal significance.[128] He was no lawyer but simply a loyal servant of his liege lord. For nearly twenty years he had, in his own words, "permitted himself to be used with unsparing diligence, night and day, in coping with each need that arose." From necessity, of course, rather than from inclination. His present master was ultimately responsible for the fact that the manor of Oberneuching conferred no title to land, so that Christoph, unlike many other nobles, could not live on the fat of that land. Nevertheless, he had served the ducal house devotedly all his life. In his youth he had belonged to the sparse entourage of Maximilian's uncle, Ferdinand—for scanty wages, for Ferdinand, warrior and black sheep of the family, had little enough to call his own. The reason for his penury was ducal disfavor. That, in turn, was the result of a delicate love affair with a commoner, which had been legalized by the promise of a civil marriage. A clique of courtiers who had provoked the martial suitor into a defiant rage by their jibes were in part responsible for this outcome. Neuchinger had acted as a kind of chamberlain to Ferdinand, who had been banished from court. He had subsequently become executive justice, not because he was in any way specially qualified, but simply because there had been no other applicants of noble birth. The office seemed too despicable and arduous to his peers. Nothing better had been on offer. The flock of children in his crumbling ruin had to be fed; he himself was reluctant to give up the hereditary seat of his forefathers. So he had assumed the odious burden that reeked of blood, had borne it for fourteen years, had grown old, and had fallen sick from sheer repugnance. He had no knowledge of the law. His office required histrionic rather than legal skills.

When the messenger had arisen from his brief meal and somewhat more prolonged chat in the shady pergola, had put on his plumed hat and mounted his horse the other side of the washing-line, the lord of the manor probably passed on the news to his wife as she came to clear away the bread, the bacon, and the cider jug. He had to go to Munich again and perform his duty; a big affair, it seemed, breaking on the wheel, burning alive. He would set off next day and would not be back for a week. She should get together everything he would need, and see that his justice's robes were in order. Then the justice told one of his elder sons to go to the local farmer and hire a nag at the usual agreed rate. For this impoverished knight had no horse of his own.

PROLOGUE BEHIND THE SCENES

At seven o'clock in the morning, on Friday 26 July 1600, Master Georg once again received distinguished visitors. His wife had swept the living room on the ground floor of the Falcon Tower, scrubbed the table, and placed fresh flowers below the crucifix in the corner. The case against the Pappenheimers was to be brought to a preliminary conclusion today. Treasurer von Roming, Councillors Wangereck and Hainmüller, along with the clerk to the treasury, Kaspar Steinwandner, made their entrance, took their seats on a bench and wooden chairs, and ordered the ironmaster to fetch, in turn, the prisoners Paulus and Anna Pappenheimer, their adult sons Gumpprecht and Michel, then Ulrich Schölz, and the tailor from Prunn. This time the visitors had not come to question the prisoners but to announce the day of judgment.

Soon afterwards we can imagine Paulus Pappenheimer entering the room, the first of the accused, hollow-eyed, pallid, woebegone, dragging his chains and staring apprehensively at the solemn faces of the assembled gentlemen. Von Roming instructed Master Georg to take off the poor prisoner's fetters.

He referred to the prisoner as "poor"; it was the first time the maimed victim had heard a word from his tormentors that had an undertone of pity. But he presumably knew very well that the word implied no regret for the torture and suffering inflicted on him and his companions: it was merely the formal expression of his doom. The adjective did not refer to the man's ruined body but to his soul, which would soon stand before God and hence deserved pity. The word "poor" used by the treasurer meant: you are to be executed within three days. The old vagrant knew that, although he may have had no idea of the judicial significance of his appearance before his judges on this day.

"Should the ultimate penal sanction be determined," the Caroline code declared, "the sentence is to be announced three days beforehand, so that the condemned man may reflect on his sin, deplore it, and make confession of it in good time." Bavarian local law required the same: "Once the judgment has been reached and sentence drafted, the prisoner is to be led into the beadle's or jailor's chamber, his statements and confessions are to be read out to him, and he shall be asked whether he stands by them. And should he thus do, then shall it be proclaimed to him that he shall suffer public execution under the criminal law on the third day thereafter following, in order that he may in the intervening time make his confession, make his peace with God, and partake of the Holy Sacrament." The formal announcement of the forthcoming public trial and execution took place, therefore, in accordance with statute and for the benefit of the poor soul. This was the ostensible justification, a pious tribute to the Almighty. In fact, the object was to deprive the prisoner of any chance to rescind his confession.[129] For although a confession was not in itself sufficient to secure a conviction, it was nevertheless, according to the doctrine of the Inquisition, the keystone of proof, *regina probationum*. An accused who denied his guilt could not be executed. As a rule, of course, torture ensured that the court obtained the necessary confessions, but it could not prevent the accused, once the torture was over, from withdrawing his statements as false and obtained under duress. What then? As we know, a fresh confession of guilt was then extorted from the accused. For, said the lawyers, "whoever has confessed to his offense under interrogation and torture, yet will not stand by his statement but revokes all that which he has hitherto said, the same may once more be put to the torture on the order of his judge, in all due form and law . . . the torture, by common consent of Drs. Bartolus, Baldus, and Marsilius, having been rendered void by reason of such recantation, the case being as if the accused had never been put to the torture, so that such evidence as was laid against him retains its first force."

But, in spite of all this hair-splitting logic, the lawyers were unable to exclude the possibility that, just before sentence was passed, a recalcitrant prisoner might withdraw the confession extorted under torture and hence demolish the principal ground for his execution. The day set for sentencing would then have to be postponed, and a new confession of guilt obtained by force. But who could guarantee that the accused, thus reconvicted, might not recant once more on his way to the place of execution? This had occasionally happened, particularly in cases of witchcraft, because the victims being led to the stake were unwilling to make their appearance before the throne of God with the lie of their guilt, and particularly the false witness borne against innocent people, on their consciences. They would rather submit to renewed torture than endure the everlasting torments of Hell. It was in order to forestall this possibility that William V laid down explicit procedures in his "Instructions concerning Witchcraft": "Such persons as have been found guilty of their offenses on sufficient grounds by reason of their own confession, and have already in law been condemned, shall not be suffered to put forth their case again and to revoke their confessions, notwithstanding that they deny their offense . . . but the statements and evidence that have solemnly been entered during the proceedings shall be deemed established and not subject to withdrawal or amendment. Otherwise, judicial proceedings would be pointless and there would be no end to such matters."

To help bring matters to an end, the lawyers promulgated a final day of judgment. The "shrift," a summary of all the admissions relating to the crimes included in the court's judgment, was read out to the prisoner in the presence of at least three witnesses. This was the prisoner's last chance to dispute or withdraw the statements made. Beyond this point, the admission of guilt was final and the grounds for conviction unshakable.

The old vagrant would scarcely have had any idea of the juridical function of this appearance before his judges. It was not explained to him. The treasurer probably addressed him more or less in these terms:[130] "Paulus Pämb, known as Pappenheimer, you have but recently uttered with your own lips a shrift and confession in the place where you were examined under torture, and it has been so written down. It will now be read to you so that you may hear it." Whereupon the clerk cleared his throat and, picking up a carefully prepared, numbered list, began to read out the numerous confessions made by the prisoner which the court regarded as having been corroborated. At the top of the list came the crime of witchcraft, the pact with the Devil, the nocturnal excursions and revels, the evil spells, desecration of the Host. Then followed a list of murders, robberies, burglaries, thefts from churches, and instances of arson. The summary filled many pages and took nearly half an hour to read. Paulus listened with bowed head. Should he have protested? He knew from bitter experience that even the correction—not to mention the withdrawal—of a statement once made would merely lead to new torture, which he was too feeble to endure. So he simply listened in silence to the endless catalogue of his sins. When the clerk finally fell silent, and the treasurer asked him whether he wished to deny or amend his shrift, as a whole or in detail, he shook his head.

The treasurer instructed the clerk to make a note in the record to the effect that the accused still admitted the deeds and crimes that had been read out to him, the instigation of criminal prosecution not yet having been proclaimed. Then he turned once more to the old tramp: "Your own shrift and confession having been read out to you, which you have once more assented to, by order of His Grace, Maximilian, Count Palatinate of the Rhine, Duke in Upper and Lower Bavaria, as being the proper authority by God set over you, I do hereby proclaim and declare that penal proceedings be instituted against you, Paulus Pämb, or Pappenheimer, on this next coming Monday, the same being the twenty-ninth day of July, and that you are herewith bound over, when the customary bell is rung to signify the hearing of criminal matters, to appear on the morning of that same day in front of the Town Hall of our Prince's capital city of Munich, there to hear the charge against you and to await such verdict and sentence as may be pronounced and handed down."

This was a theatrical set piece, unaltered throughout decades of use, addressed less to Paulus Pappenheimer than to the character he was meant to act from that point onward. Obviously the summons to appear before the Town Hall on the 29 July was not addressed to the old vagrant, who, in spite of the symbolic removal of his fetters, was totally deprived of his freedom of action and was nothing but the object of judicial proceedings. It related in fact to a free individual, who was required, as provided by the ancient procedure for prosecution, to present himself to an independent judiciary. The part of the accused within the terms of this ancestral usage had been allocated to our prisoner. The inquisitorial proceedings had been concluded with the reading of the shrift. Now that it was certain that Pappenheimer could be condemned and executed, it seemed as if the months of questioning, the mountains of paper, and the search for evidence had never been. On Monday a judge would turn up—we already know the impoverished knight who had been chosen to play this part—in order to pass judgment according to ancient custom. Thus, as centuries before, the accused was to appear in open court to answer charges laid against him by the prosecutor at this final hearing. The judgment would be pronounced there and then, and the sentence immediately carried out. That was the gist of the theatrical performance that was to be shown to the public. The treasurer's summons to the prisoner to present himself in front of the Town Hall was a prologue acted out before the curtain was raised for the main performance.

"Following upon this exordium," reads the stage direction in the script I have in front of me, that is, an "Administration of Criminal Justice" of 1575, "the poor prisoner is to be informed that, albeit the written law be strict and severe in punishing evil, as ordained by God and the temporal authority, he should nevertheless take solemn heed, and address himself to God Almighty alone, commit his earthly life and his death humbly to the will of the Almighty, and pray for eternal life with staunch faith, hope, and trust, not despairing of the sacrifice of our dear Lord Jesus Christ." We may assume that the treasurer left this solemn injunction to Dr. Wangereck, who was better versed in Catholic homilies to the condemned. The old tramp listened in silence, with downcast eyes, and when the speech was over, he meekly resumed his fetters. Master Georg took the prisoner back to his cell, and then fetched Anna, who in turn faced the dignitaries in the turnkey's living room. There she heard, like each of the accused in succession, the same formal words, and listened to a shrift that varied only in minor details from case to case.

The procedure took all morning. When it was over, the prisoners had a surprise. Instead of the usual crust of bread and watery broth, the ironmaster's wife brought roast meat and a beaker of wine into their cells. They had been given no such fare since their arrest five months earlier, and they ate and drank greedily. And if they had failed to follow the rambling clauses of the text read to them in the ironmaster's quarters, now they could smell and taste what their fate was to be. They were to die within three days.

PREPARATION AND ANTICIPATION

For a week now they had been digging, hammering, and sawing on the outskirts of the city. The gallows hill looked like a building site. Inquisitive spectators gathered in small groups. Merchants' carts and peasant wains, creaking up the highway to Pasing from the Neuhaus gate, or traversing the leisurely stretch of a mile or so through fields and meadows as they approached from the west, all came to a brief halt by the hill, which lay on their way. Craftsmen, market traders, flunkeys on their way to and from the city, all stopped to watch the progress of the work. There was also a great number of children and idlers, drawn by sheer curiosity.

The preparations were being made outside the city limits on rising ground northwest of what is now the Theresienwiese, and south of the present-day Hacker bridge. They were worth seeing and gave rise to great expectations. Six deep holes had been dug by the knacker and his assistants; in these, large stakes had been planted, to the accompaniment of much cursing and panting. Then the excavated earth was shoveled back and packed firmly around the stripped trunks. The semicircle formed by these poles, each about thirteen feet tall and a foot in diameter, had already attracted the curiosity of passersby on the Wednesday evening. The purpose served by these stark pillars became clear the following day, when bundles of brushwood were piled up round them, making six pyres, each a good six feet high and twelve feet in diameter. At the same time, the executioner was busy building his "griddle"—a grating made of angular timbers, laid flat on the ground. The eager onlookers deduced that the imminent executions involved not only fire but also the wheel. For, so the well-informed spectators explained to the uninitiated, the criminal would have to suffer breaking on the wheel as he lay bound on the grating.

It was long since known for whose benefit these lavish preparations were being undertaken. For some weeks now, the talk in taverns and alehouses had been of the prisoners in the Falcon Tower.

The gory details of their abominable deeds went the rounds. These murderers and arsonists had been in league with the Devil, it was said. It was Old Nick himself who had given them orders to destroy the whole of Bavaria. Then there was talk of a changeling: among the prisoners was a child fathered by the Devil himself, with a hideous face and the legs of a goat. There were some who claimed that the evildoers had merely laughed at the torture they underwent and had insisted that the Evil One would carry them off through the air just before their execution. Others thought that beyond belief, because it was common knowledge that magic spells did not work within the domain of the civil authority. Interest in the case increased day by day, with each new rumor. Who spread these tales? Some people referred to a close acquaintance of the ironmaster of the Falcon Tower, but that was pure fiction. The constantly increasing flow of information had its source in the Old Palace. It was in the duke's offices that the case had first been talked of, and it was here, too, that news first spread that the execution of these scoundrels from Lower Bavaria was going to be a very special event. The state councillors positively encouraged their clerks to pass on what they had learned. For, after all, it was their intention to set an example. A large audience was exactly what was wanted.

They would have no cause to complain of any lack of interest. Once it had become known on the Friday that the case would be heard and execution carried out on the Monday, eager spectators began to arrive in the city from all directions. Many of these visitors were eyed suspiciously by the sentries at the gates, and not a few were turned away. For it was among the traveling folk, the beggars, tramps, jugglers, and charlatans, that the news of the impending spectacle had spread most rapidly. They had been arriving in large and small groups ever since the Saturday morning, from Dachau and Augsburg, from Fürstenfeldbruck and Landsberg, from Burghausen, Landshut, and Freising. Ragged figures, lame, with unshaven faces; emaciated women with straggling, graying hair done up in greasy kerchiefs; bawling infants; yelping dogs; mercenary troopers, bristling with weapons and sporting garish, loose-fitting blouses beneath their much patched leather doublets. A tooth puller with an assistant dragging a little cart with the instruments of his profession. Jugglers, fire eaters, wire walkers, conjurers, ventriloquists, actors, tramps, craftsmen, mendicant friars in greasy, threadbare habits, students, itinerant engravers. It was not a sense of solidarity with our vagrants that had brought

384

them to Munich but the hope of doing business amid the throng of onlookers. Just as the Pappenheimers themselves had once made their way to similar events in order to earn a crust or two with their cries for charity and their gaming table, so now it was their impending execution that attracted their fellows and all the other varieties of traveling folk.

By Saturday all the inns and unlicensed lodgings were crammed. In the tavern gardens, oppressively warm in spite of their shade, the hubbub was even louder than usual as local inhabitants and visitors harangued each other and consumed lavish quantities of beer and wine. Someone was talking about the witch burning of 1590, which he had witnessed as a young man on that self-same spot where the criminals from the Falcon Tower would die on Monday. On that occasion there had been four stakes erected on the gallows hill, and three widows and a young woman had been tied to them. One of the witches had been a seamstress who had consorted with the Devil for thirty years. She used to fly by night to the cemetery outside the Sendling Gate to dig up innocent little children. A similar story was contributed by a visitor from Tölz, where they had burned a number of witches from the manor of Hohenburg last year. An elderly local citizen spoke of a bizarre execution that had taken place not on the gallows hill but right here in the marketplace. That had been in the spring of 1591, when Marco Antonio Bragadino, the gold maker, had been put to death.[131] He had been no common felon but a nobleman from Venice, in minor orders, and an adept in alchemy. He had told the pious Duke William that he could make pure gold from base metal. This seemed like a godsend to a prince chronically short of money. In 1590 he brought the Italian prodigy to Munich and installed him there, where he lived like a lord, surrounded by thirty-six servants, enjoying great respect and high favor, for almost a year. However, he tried the pious duke's patience too far. Instead of freeing the duke from his debts, the Venetian asked for larger and larger sums of money, claiming that he needed it to procure the alchemical ingredients for his gold making. In fact, he spent the money on high living and had not the slightest intention of keeping his promise. In the end, the duke realized he had been duped and had the nobleman arrested. When put to the torture, Bragadino admitted forthwith that he was a swindler and knew nothing of the art of gold making. So in April he was tried and sentenced in the Munich marketplace. A lofty podium was erected for the trial, with a red-painted gallows next to it, complete with gilded rope. Bragadino was bound with gilded cords. His two great black dogs, no doubt fiendish servants in the form of beasts, were also led to the place of execution. They barked wildly when their master was beheaded, and were then shot.

This story was generally applauded by the carousing company, for scarcely anyone doubted that the gold maker's dogs were indeed demons. The Evil One did his best to help evildoers to the very end, someone remarked, and the authorities would do well to take every precaution. Eerie things went on, it was said, in the vicinity of the Falcon Tower. Especially between eleven and twelve at night, the Devil could be heard calling, "Hand them over! Hand them over!" It was nothing but the wind, objected someone. But the wind could have been summoned up by Old Nick, was the reply. It wasn't just the weather that caused the winds round the Church of Our Lady, when it was calm elsewhere. Every inhabitant of Munich knew the reason for that. When the church was being built, the Fiend had flown into a rage at this devout enterprise and had thought up all kinds of ruses to impede the progress of work on the site. In spite of everything, the house of God was completed. But now the Devil sought to destroy it by means of a storm. When he rushed into the church through the rear doorway, he was unable to see a single window on account of the huge projecting pillars. He rejoiced then at the folly and the clumsiness of the pious builders, and gave up his plans for the church's destruction, thinking that a church devoid of light could do him little harm. He departed with his mind at rest, but on the spot where he stood the black imprint of his foot can still be seen. Later, when the Devil noticed that the people of Munich were flocking into their new church, and that it was light enough inside, he was not a little put out. But it was too late for him to enter the building, for it had already been consecrated. That is why he storms around the church and, to this very day, causes winds to blow to prevent people from going to church.

These were the kind of stories told during that last July weekend of 1600 in Munich, in the crowded tavern gardens to the clinking of glasses and mugs, as people whiled away the time until the great spectacle that was to come.

On Sunday, the highway to Pasing was unusually busy. After attending church, families walked out to the gallows hill to inspect the place of execution, where preparations had now been completed. Even without this notable sight the walk was well worth the effort. From the top of the hill one could see the walled city with its moat and its host of towers, lying there on the broad plain, pastel-tinted in the hazy summer air. After gazing at the six stakes with their piles of brushwood and the wooden grating laid on the ground for its fearful purpose, many of the parents may have turned to enjoy the view, while behind their backs the children scampered inquisitively up the wooden gangways on the brushwood piles to the place where the poor sinners would stand next day amid the crackling flames.

SLEIGHRIDE WITHOUT SNOW

Christoph Neuching of Oberneuching had been in Munich for some days now. He had called on the council officials in the Old Palace several times to lodge a complaint. After reading the shrift and the draft sentence, he had realized what the scale and significance of the impending execution implied, and had come to the conclusion that his present emoluments as executive justice did not cover the responsibility of directing this kind of major public spectacle. He had to make several approaches, and it was only through the good offices of the clerk, Kaspar Steinwandner, that he was finally granted an interview with the treasurer when the latter came to attend the meeting of the council of state on Wednesday, 24 July. His complaint was on the following lines: the planned execution, on account of which he had hired a nag and come to Munich, exceeded the limits of what might be expected of him. It was not only that six persons were to be sentenced at once. It appeared from their confessions that all six accused were creatures of the Devil, so that he had reason to fear the wrath of all the spirits of Hell if he handed the scoundrels over to the public executioner. What was more, he was not dealing here with simple executions but with an accumulation of the most severe and horrifying penalties that could be inflicted on human beings. For sixteen years now he had borne his baleful office and sullied himself with blood, although he belonged to an ancient and venerable family. He had never once refused to relieve his lord and prince of the odious task of pronouncing the death sentence, although he had been granted little in return: in spite of his onerous duties he had scarcely been able to feed his tribe of hungry children. There had never been a case such as this, and in spite of the loyalty and humility he had shown throughout his service he was not willing to conduct a trial of this kind without the aid of a second justice.

The treasurer first of all severely admonished this mutinous man of straw, and then no doubt tried to reason with him. In vain, for his words carried no conviction: he was bound to admit that the executive justice was right. And so he promised to raise the complaint in council and to think of ways of solving the problem.

He did speak to the other councillors, who did their best for the man of straw. On the following day they handed him a letter addressed to the deputy magistrate of the city of Munich, instruction this official to participate in the trial and sentencing proceedings scheduled for Monday. The treasurer informed the executive justice that he should call on the city council during its morning session, bearing this instruction from the sovereign, and then discuss all further details with the deputy magistrate appointed to help him. It was as simple as that. The council of state had solved the problem according to a well-tried formula, by simply shifting an unpleasant duty to the city administration. There was no thought of assigning the task to the ducal chief justice, for instance, or even a member of the council of state. The duke's officers wanted nothing to do with the sanguinary business of passing death sentences. They expected the city, as a matter of course, to assume the responsibility for trial and sentence. It was city employees, not the duke's men, who were building the pyres out there on gallows hill. The scene of the trial was to be the marketplace, not the ducal palace. There was no such person as a ducal hangman; the municipal hangman would perform the executions. And now that the executive justice required help, the city's deputy magistrate was instructed to take part in the theatrical spectacle of the judgment and sentence. Was the Munich city council no better than an authority subject to the sovereign's court, with no rights of its own?

That was not exactly the case. Appeal could be made to ancient tradition. Even the oldest municipal statutes, the so-called "Rudolfinum" of 1294, specified that Munich governed itself through its city council. According to its constitutional statute of 1403, the administration of the city was deputed to a kind of patrician parliament, consisting of an inner council of twelve members and an outer council of twenty-four.[132] The election of these city fathers was effected by three electors, who, in turn, were elected by the citizens. Anyone who owned house and land, or paid at least half a pound in tax annually, was entitled to vote. In fact, the duke retained the power to confirm elections to the council, and required the councillors to come to court and swear an oath of loyalty and allegiance. Thus, the city's self-government was clearly subordinate to the duke's will and limited by him. The more powerful the new sense of statehood grew in the Bavarian dukes, the more firmly they pulled on the reins of civic government. Interference in city affairs became more and more provocative: withdrawal of the salt trade, regulation of meat prices, seizure and demolition of entire buildings to facilitate plans for ducal building projects. At the same time, the court insisted more and more on an obsequious attitude on the part of the city fathers. This insistence occasionally took grotesque but very significant forms, as in the following sequence of events. The city council decided on 10 January 1592 to discontinue the traditional festive sleighride on the Sunday following Twelfth Night, which was customarily attended by the lord mayor, the city council, and the patricians with their wives and daughters. The duke, with his entire retinue, usually watched this sleighride from the windows of his residence. It is difficult to say whether the sovereign reckoned that he had simply been deprived of an entertainment he had come to enjoy, or whether he regarded this parade of prominent citizens as a tribute that had become his due by custom. Whatever may have been the case, William V responded at once. On 11 January an order went out to the councillors that the sleighride would indeed take place on the following day.[133] In vain the city council protested that no snow had so far fallen and that several of their wives were pregnant, so that a sleighride without snow would be not only arduous but hazardous. The duke's reply is not known, but we need not assume that he relented. Twelve years later, in 1604, Duke Maximilian issued a decree in which he complained about the cancellation of the sleighride and ordered the city council, on pain of punishment, to arrange it at once, "whether it snows or not." Who would dare to appeal to ancient privileges when dealing with a short-tempered prince who was not even prepared to accept that you needed snow in order to have a sleighride? They came to heel and obeyed—even if they muttered and ground their teeth.

The executive justice's reception was not particularly friendly.[134] On Friday, 26 July, he made his way early in the morning across the marketplace, now the Marienplatz, passed through the high, arched entrance to the Town Hall, and mounted the steep steps. A civic constable stopped him and asked him his business. He was the executive justice, Christoph Neuchinger of Oberneuching, he replied, and he was bringing an important message from His Grace the Duke to the city council in general, and to the deputy magistrate in particular. Whereupon the constable, convinced by the ducal seal on the missive held out to him, conducted the visitor up some more stairs to the council tower and to the great council chamber. He knocked on the door and entered without waiting for an answer, pushing the executive justice in front of him. The councillors turned around irritably to inspect the intruder.

Presumably, one of the patrician councillors was interrupted in the middle of a speech concerning the regulation of milling or the tax on brewing. Turning toward the lord mayor, the constable explained that His Honor, the executive justice, had come on behalf of the duke and had insisted on being admitted at once. With these words the city officer took his leave, leaving the visitor alone with the councillors. What did he, or, rather, the duke, have to impart that was so urgent (we can hear the lord mayor ask), so important, that he should force his way into the assembled council and thus take up the time necessary for their meeting? Neuchinger probably said nothing but made his way uncertainly to the chairman of the council and handed him the treasurer's letter. The lord mayor broke the seal, and his face darkened as he scanned the few lines the letter contained.

Then he read out, approximately as follows: "By the Grace of God, We, Maximilian, Count Palatinate of the Rhine, Duke in Upper and Lower Bavaria, etc., offer to the Council and City of Munich Greetings, and give you to understand that We herewith order and command the Deputy Magistrate of Our beloved capital city to render all assistance unto Our Executive Justice in the trial and sentencing of six offenders at present in custody in Our Ducal prison of the Falcon Tower, the criminal session being ordained for this forthcoming Monday."

A murmur of dissent probably ran through the ranks of the city fathers. Deputy Magistrate Krügel asked permission to speak, and rose to his feet. He was appointed to his post by the city, not by the duke's court. The affairs of the Falcon Tower were no concern of his. His job was to try, and to sentence, such offenders as were subject to municipal jurisdiction. He had nothing at all to do with those in the duke's custody. When he was appointed and sworn in, there had been no mention of any such duty. What he was being asked to do was in fact no part of his duties. Whatever view the assembled council might take of the duke's suggestion, he personally refused to assent to it.

Thus began the customary debate in such cases. Agreement with the deputy magistrate was expressed, strong words were directed against such attempts on the part of the court to usurp the city's authority, the order was described as improper, the view was even put forward that determined opposition must be mounted against the growing number of new obligations that were constantly being foisted on the city. There were warnings, on the other hand, not to provoke the duke's wrath, attempts to soothe ruffled feelings and put the matter in perspective. The case should not be taken as an issue of principle; a quarrel with the monarch might have undesirable consequences for all of them. In short, the proposal was to give way once more and obey the order. The deputy magistrate did not agree, until the lord mayor put forward a compromise proposal. It was proper for them to submit humbly to His Grace on this occasion. But they would do so under protest and, in particular, complain to the court that the duke was using the services of a city official without making any separate payment for them. The matter was then voted on, and a deputation was appointed that would accompany the executive justice back to the Old Palace straight away in order to make the city's view clear to the gentlemen there.

So the executive justice made a second appearance that same morning in the offices of the council of state, accompanied this time by the municipal deputy magistrate, the clerk to the city council, and one of the city councillors. The treasurer was summoned from the council of state meeting to listen to the respectful complaint. The city council had taken note of the duke's order to the deputy magistrate to assist the executive justice in passing judgment and sentence at the forthcoming criminal session. But the deputy magistrate "was not appointed by the court, nor was this activity included in the terms of his appointment, so that it could not be imposed on him against his will. Nevertheless, he had offered most humbly on this occasion, as a favor to His Grace, and in obedience to the worshipful council, to carry out the said task, hoping, however, that on future occasions some emolument would be forthcoming."

That went without saying, the treasurer replied brusquely, and it had not been necessary for them to call on him on that account. So this problem too was solved, and there were now two judges to pass a sentence on our vagrants that had already been decided days in advance.

FINAL VISITS

In the three days between the announcement of the final hearing and the public sentencing itself, the prisoners in the Falcon Tower received a number of visitors. The first to come, and not for the last time, was their father confessor, Dr. Hannemann. Hitching up his cassock, the clergyman made his way to each of the cells for half an hour in turn, to listen to confessions of guilt or protestations of innocence behind an outstretched hand and under the confessional seal of secrecy, to impose penance, and to give absolution.

Spiritual aid was thus provided, but legal aid was lacking. There was no attorney among the visitors during these final days. The assignment of legal advocates to the accused during this last phase of the proceedings was not, in fact, unusual—even if the intention was merely to forestall any claim on the part of the prisoners or their relatives that they had been put at an unfair disadvantage. In the rules of criminal procedure which came into force in Bavaria sixteen years after this case of ours, it was explicitly laid down that legal assistance was to be assigned to every accused person after the drawing up of the shrift and before the final judgment was drafted. But in 1600 it was entirely at the discretion of the court to decide whether this support was called for or not. The "Instructions concerning Witchcraft" promulgated by William V in 1590 merely stated: "Concerning these grave matters, the same procedure is to be followed as in other penal cases of a criminal kind which affect honor, property, blood, life and limb, and they have the same right to the admission of their advocates or procurators." A regulation subject to a wide range of interpretations. No criminal court in Bavaria read into this sentence an obligation to grant the "poor prisoner" legal advice in every case. And a man like Dr. Wangereck would certainly not have seen why he should officially engage attorneys and pay them from treasury funds to act for pernicious vermin like the Pappenheimers. The case was sufficiently involved and expensive as it was. This attitude was undoubtedly in keeping with the councillor's character as a loyal servant of his master, for the duke thought exactly the same. As late as 1692, a memorandum on this issue was to be promulgated by the sovereign: it made no reference to any obligation to provide legal aid, while the freedom to engage legal consultants was rigorously restricted: "Admitting advocates indiscriminately in criminal cases is a dubious practice, and, since provision for the same is already made in the rules of criminal prosecution, it should be left to the discretion of the council of state whether, and when, such legal aid may be granted." In our case, the council of state was not placed in the awkward position of having to make a decision. None of the condemned persons in the Falcon Tower had friends to provide them with an attorney; they could not have afforded to employ one anyway, since they were penniless. Quite apart from that, no lawyer would have been ready to accept the brief, no matter what the fee. It was all too easy to burn one's fingers with cases like this, involving witchcraft. The risk was considerable. The *Hammer of Witches* warned: "For an advocate must first of all inquire into the nature of the case, and if it appears to him to be just, then let him accept it, should he be willing to do so; should he observe, however, that it is unjust, then let him refuse it; he must be careful not to defend a cause which is unjust and hopeless . . . If a disreputable advocate knowingly misleads his client into defending an inauspicious cause, he is answerable for the resulting damage and expense." And since everything had already been decided once the final hearing was announced, and the guilt of the prisoners was already proved, a defending lawyer would have made himself guilty of giving aid and comfort to heretics and would run the risk of excommunication. Even the best of advocates would have had his hands tied. The only chance of changing the judgment so as to favor his clients would have been to procure evidence calculated to exculpate them, and to have their confessions revoked. But it was precisely this course of action that was barred by the law, which stated, "should an advocate maliciously instruct the prisoner to revoke his confession or employ other illegitimate means of prolonging the trial, then he is to be remorselessly punished in accordance with the nature of the impropriety he has committed."[135]

For all these reasons there was no lawyer among the visitors who came to see the prisoners in the Falcon Tower between 26 and 29 July. But one citizen of Munich made his appearance, armed with razors and scissors, in order to prepare the poor victims after his own fashion for their final court appearance. The council of state had commissioned the barber, Kaspar Zechetmair, to cut "the wicked people's" hair. This task, undertaken in the presence and, where necessary, with the assistance of Master Georg, did not merely serve a self-evident function of an aesthetic or hygienic nature. It was not a question of improving the prisoners' appearance for the purposes of a public trial. Indeed, their neglected appearance would most usefully have enhanced the repulsive impression they made on the onlookers. Moreover, the customary service provided by a barber would have been vastly overpaid at the scandalous rate of five gulden and twenty-four kreuzer that Kaspar Zechetmair charged—and got—for his labors. The council of state, otherwise so thrifty, was concerned that the demons' power over the prisoners should finally be broken and undesirable incidents avoided on the day of execution. The barber's scissors complemented the confessor's cross.

For hair was regarded as the seat of life, of the soul, of vital energy.[136] There are hints of this throughout our account of the trial. We may remember that the Devil made our vagrants give him hair from all the hair-covered parts of their body, in order to confirm the pact and to strengthen his hold on the other party to the agreement. Human hair belongs in the same category as Devil's ointment and weather spells. The dream of flying on a staff was linked to the image of a witch with free-flowing hair. Behind all this was an idea we have already mentioned, very prevalent then and still not quite forgotten. There is evidence for it even in Holy Scripture: "And Delilah said to Samson, Tell me, I pray thee, wherein thy great strength lieth?" After a number of evasive answers, Samson replies: "There hath not come a razor upon mine head; for I have been a Nazarite unto God from my mother's womb: if I be shaven, then my strength will go from me, and I shall become weak, and be like any other man." Legends and fairytales too are full of this superstition. "Give me but one little hair from your head," the wild man cries to the boy, "and I shall have you entirely in my power." The boy in Grimm's fairytale has to seize three golden hairs from the Devil in order to overcome him. Charles the Great sends Huon of Bordeaux to the East to pluck hair from the Caliph's beard. At the time of the migration of peoples, the Frankish kings were known by their flowing locks, in which their magic power resided. Their hair must never be cut. Warriors and knights pursuing a feud let their hair grow until they had fulfilled their vow of vengeance. Men taking an oath would touch their beards or the hair of their heads to confirm their vow. Exorcisms regularly began with the shaving of the subject's hair so that the Devil should lose his power over the possessed person. Before prisoners were examined under torture, too, it was usual to shave off all their body hair, although we cannot prove that this was generally done in the Pappenheimer case. From time immemorial, hair has been cut off whenever an individual submitted to a superior authority. The Roman vestal virgin dedicated herself to her goddess in this manner; nuns and monks thus declared themselves servants of Christ or of Mary. It is possible that cutting the hair of soldiers or convicted prisoners has the same unspoken justification as a symbolic gesture rather than as an ostensibly hygienic measure.

394

Thus, the barber who cut the prisoners' hair deprived the Devil of his power over them, while the authority that had ordered this procedure asserted symbolically its power over the bodies and souls of our vagrants. Like so much that was thought and done in those days, this act was performed on the basis of some dim presentiment and superstitious caution rather than for clear and rational motives. We may touch on a further, related motive, which may have played some subconscious part in engaging Zechetmair's services: it was customary to cut the hair of the dead—a noble, ethical form of that superstition that ascribes the power of the deceased to him who possesses parts of the body. In this way the dead man's soul was deprived of its magic power to harm others. Our commissioners might well have good reason to fear that the evildoers condemned by them might reappear in the form of ghosts to rob them of their sleep. This danger, too, the barber forestalled. That is why his fee—equivalent to a year's wages for a waitress—may have seemed cheap to the councillors.

In the early morning of 29 July, a whole group of visitors turned up at the Falcon Tower: Dr. Hannemann and another priest, Chief Justice Kulmer, Treasurer von Roming, and the clerk to the treasury. The worshipful gentlemen clambered noisily up the wooden stairs in the wake of Master Georg to pay a final visit to each of the condemned in their cells. The ironmaster would unlock the door and let the gentlemen into the gloomy, stuffy chambers, freeing the prisoners from their fetters so that they could stand up. There they would stand, washed, shorn, aware of their approaching end, listening with downcast eyes to the words of the confessor. These ran more or less on the following lines: It is the will of God that you will not live to see the coming evening, for you will be taken forthwith to an honorable court that will pass judgment on your evil and blasphemous deeds. But you, poor sinner, should not despair, for infinite is the Lord's mercy to him who opens his heart in remorse and contrition. But dire agonies awaited the unrepentant liar in Hell. In the face of imminent death, you, the accused, should take thought whether you have not done wrong to any of your accomplices or to any of the persons you have denounced. If so, you should say so without delay.

An agonizing dilemma. The revocation of confessions, as every prisoner knew from experience, might mean fresh agonies of torture: sustaining false accusations meant everlasting torment in Hell. Whom hadn't they accused of complicity and witchcraft! Was not everything said in the course of these proceedings a lie? Or was it all true? How could one draw a single strand from the net in which the commissioners had entangled their victims? The process of brainwashing so liberally and frequently applied had long since obliterated any clear distinction between nightmare and reality. It is hardly probable that the prisoners could recall all the names they had mentioned in the course of the interrogations. The clerk to the treasury with his list of those denounced would have had to prompt them. But he prudently refrained from reading out the list, for he had no wish to provoke the revocation of accusations at the last minute. And yet there was a revocation. At this late stage, Michel Pämb said that he had wronged Sugar Bun and the two tinker lads from the Bavarian Forest; even Jack the glazier and Augustin the bread carrier were innocent. Apart from Ulrich Schölz, who stuck to his denunciations to the last detail, the other prisoners also mentioned a few names, including some of their fellow prisoners. The clerk made a few notes. Such statements would have no influence on the proceedings and would certainly not bring about a postponement of judgment on those accomplices who had thus been declared innocent. The confessor's question was meant only to facilitate the salvation of the poor sinner's soul. Its judicial significance was of a purely negative kind: concerning those accusations which had not been revoked, it was said that those who had made them had "gone to their deaths on them" and had consequently underwritten the truth of the denunciations with their soul's salvation. We may assume that it was this argument that sealed the fate of the convent miller's family. None of those questioned on 29 July withdrew the charges brought against the people from the mill.

Following this early morning visit, the ironmaster's wife brought the prisoners something to eat for the last time, while the gentlemen refreshed themselves with a glass of wine in the ironmaster's quarters. A little later, the duke's constables entered the Falcon Tower and, with Master Georg's assistance, removed the prisoners from their cells. A procession formed in the lane outside, surrounded by a crowd of gaping onlookers. The chief justice and the clerk to the treasury emerged from the doorway first and mounted their horses, which were being held by grooms. The two clergymen followed on foot. The prisoners stumbled one by one into the open, blinking in the unaccustomed daylight, hampered by their heavy chains, encircled and followed by the duke's officers. The procession got underway. The ironmaster and his wife stayed behind; we can imagine them standing in front of the Falcon Tower, watching their prisoners depart and then turning to go back into their gloomy lodgings once the procession with its crowd of eager spectators had disappeared round the corner. There was a great deal to do. The six empty cells had to be cleaned out and aired. They would not remain empty for long.

THE CEREMONIAL OF ACCUSATION

From his window, Johann Baptist Fickler had a good view of the east side of the Marienplatz, the area just in front of the Town Hall. Since the first light of dawn, people had been pouring into the square; by eight o'clock it was densely packed. A hubbub of voices filled the air on this summer's day, more animated and louder than on market days. About thirty yards from the Town Hall a square space had been cleared of the surging crowds; the municipal grain stewards had formed a cordon with linked wooden staves, holding back the eager throng from the so-called "bench," which was reserved for the worshipful court. In the center of this enclosed area stood a long table covered with a black cloth that reached down to the cobbles of the square. On the table were several folio volumes bound in pigskin, and the staff of judgment: this was a wooden wand about a foot and a half long and as thick as a man's finger.

The clamor of voices suddenly rose to a climax as shouts heralded the appearance of the prisoners. From his vantage point, Fickler could see the little procession approaching down the Dienerstrasse from the direction of the Falcon Tower, pushing its way through the ever denser mob. It stopped right under his window. The two horsemen, whom the duke's archivist may have recognized as the ducal chief justice and the clerk to the treasury, were formally greeted by the chief magistrate of the city and one of the city councillors, who were also mounted. With the words prescribed for this ceremony, the duke's officers handed the prisoners over to the municipal authorities, whereupon the prisoners' guards were replaced by municipal constables. After this changeover, the procession moved on to the open square, to be greeted by the murmur of thousands of voices. The procession halted in front of the Town Hall.

The bell announcing a criminal session clanged out from the Fair Tower at the end of the Kaufingerstrasse as constables led the prisoners onto the steps of the Town Hall under the fascinated gaze of the thousands craning their necks to catch a glimpse of the proceedings. The prisoners could be seen easily enough from the square, but were now out of Fickler's sight, since the steps led up inside the arched doorway: they could be observed from the front but not from the sides.

That would not have troubled the spectator. In the performance of the public trial and sentence that was about to begin, our vagrants were merely extras. They stood silently in their chains, in the shadow of the archway, looking out onto the sunlit square. Then Christoph Neuchinger and his servant, both on horseback, forced their way through the crowd to the bench, where the executive justice dismounted. He handed his horse's reins to his groom, passed through the barrier, which the grain stewards opened for him, entered the enclosure, and was the first to sit down at the black-covered table, looking out over the Town Hall square. Immediately afterwards, the chief magistrate and the deputy magistrate of the city rode up, dismounted in front of the enclosure, approached the bench, and took their places on either side of the executive justice. The latter picked up the staff of judgment in his right hand and ordered the appointed bailiff to call for order in the square and to declare the criminal session open.

Whereupon, presumably from a window of the Town Hall, the following shout rang out over the Marienplatz: "Oyez! Oyez! Whosoever has a charge to bring before the court, let him bring it, in keeping with the law of criminal justice!"[137] The procedure was thus exactly as if the judge, as in ancient times, had made his appearance in the town to pronounce judgment there and then concerning grievances publicly laid before him by individuals from the ranks of the citizens. All those present were well aware that the summons to lay charges, in spite of its wording, was not issued to all and sundry but to a prosecutor long since appointed, the so-called procurator. This role had been assumed by one of the council's retainers, proud possessor of a stentorian voice, who now entered the enclosure, approached the somber magistrates' table, and, once silence had fallen on the square, began to declaim a text which he had learned by rote. Six offenders had lain for some time in the ducal prison of the Falcon Tower, he cried. He asked that these criminals, by name Paulus Gämperl, alias Pappenheimer, his wife Anna, and his sons Gumpprecht and Jacob, together with the farmer Ulrich Schölz and the tailor Georg Schmälzl, might be summoned to the bar of the court to answer for their misdeeds.

Whereupon Fickler could observe from his window how Neuchinger rose and ordered the first of those duly named to appear before the court. He behaved as if all six had not been standing the whole time in front of him on the steps of the Town Hall, and as if they had a choice. One of the constables guarding the prisoners called out loudly from the Town Hall that the accused had appeared before the court to answer the charges against them. Thereupon the prosecutor read out a power of attorney issued by the duke that empowered and entitled him to "charge" the six offenders before the court in the name of His Grace, Duke Maximilian, and "to seek redress." The document was handed to the executive justice, who made as if he had first to ensure what its contents were, before calling out: "I permit you to prosecute in criminal law, according to that law!" This was the cue for the prosecutor, now admitted in due form, to demand the public recital of the shrift.

And now the old councillor and all the other spectators heard a voice from a buttress high up on the Town Hall. It was the clerk to the chief justice, proclaiming the Pappenheimers' confessions—the lists that the prisoners had listened to on the morning of 26 July in the ironmaster's room, the lists to which they had given at least their tacit assent. Astonished or horrified "Oh's" and "Ah's" accompanied the revelation of their misdeeds.

Of Paulus Gämperl it was said that he had "crippled and slain one hundred young children and ten old people by dint of vile sorcery." The crowd also heard how "he had entered the cellars of innkeepers and other folk, shamelessly devouring such victuals and drink as he might lay his hands on." He had further confessed to having "committed ten robberies from churches, violently slain forty-four persons by his hand alone, set fire to homes or barns eight times, broken into houses by night fourteen times, pillaging and robbing the tenants, robbed wayfarers on the highway five times, and committed four other thefts."

"In like manner, his wife," the voice rang out over the square, "Anna Gämperl, being sixty years of age, has assailed one hundred infants and nineteen old people with her spells, crippling them and killing them in godless fashion; she has entered cellars on eight occasions, has committed one murder by her own hand, set fire twice to the homes of others, has caused four gales and hailstorms, and has poisoned meadows and afflicted cattle so often that she herself cannot tell the number."

The catalogue of crimes was lengthy, although we may note that by no means all the prisoners' admissions were taken into account. Only those were listed for which the court's investigation had elicited further evidence and which were thus, in the court's view, fully proven. "The elder of her two sons, called Gumpprecht," continued the voice from the heights of the Town Hall, "has caused the death of thirty children and adults by means of sorcery: has entered cellars on twelve occasions, burgled and robbed nine churches, committed twenty-four murders, set fire to nine homes, broken in by night and robbed folk six times. He has four times committed highway robbery, poisoned and ruined fields and cattle without number, and caused strife between God-fearing spouses on four occasions. The other, her son Jacob, aged twenty-one years, has slain sixty-five infants and five adults by sorcery, has ten times entered cellars, has committed five thefts from churches, has put to death and murdered thirty-three persons by his own hand, set five fires, broken in five times by night, committed four other thefts, caused ten gales and hailstorms, poisoned fields and beasts twenty-six times." Of the fifth accused it was said, "Ulrich Schältzbauer, sixty-eight years of age, . . . innkeeper of Tettenwang, . . . has slain seventy-one infants and thirty adults by sorcery, has entered cellars on seven occasions, has committed three murders by his own hand and forty times wrought evil on cattle and fields." And, finally, concerning the sixth culprit: "a tailor, called Georg Schmälzl, of Prunn, fifty years of age, has killed thirty-six infants and fifteen adults by sorcery, has six times entered cellars, has stolen four times from churches, and has committed two murders, laid two fires, brought about gales and hailstorms, and three times ruined meadows."

This was the gist of what was read out in ringing tones by the clerk. It is, at any rate, what has come down to us via an anonymous eyewitness who published his account of the trial shortly afterwards in the form of a broadsheet printed in Augsburg.[138] "No more than a summary of their crimes was read out," writes our source, "and yet this took more than two full hours." For "these six evil persons" had, "*in toto*," slain no fewer than "four hundred and one infants, and eighty-five adults by means of sorcery," and "entered cellars fifty-four times," had "committed twenty-eight thefts from churches and one hundred and seven murders, set twenty-six fires, broken into houses by night twenty-five times, perpetrated nine highway robberies, thirteen thefts, caused twenty-one gales and hailstorms, ruined untold numbers of cattle and fields, and brought strife into four marriages."

We may assume that the summary of all the crimes charged was also read out in this form by the clerk in the Marienplatz. The expectant crowd was once more to be reminded how alarming and dangerous the individuals up there on the Town Hall steps were. The sequence in which the chronicler lists the Pappenheimers' crimes was probably also based on the wording of the shrift. We may be struck by the totally haphazard mixture of "real" crimes, like murder, robbery, and arson, with the typical offenses of witchcraft. The list invariably opens with injuries done to people by means of sorcery, continues with entry into cellars, followed by murder, arson, robbery, and theft, and concludes with other forms of evil spells, such as those causing bad weather, harm to cattle, and "marital strife." Obviously the pact with the Devil and all its dire consequences were regarded as the major offense, ultimately subsuming all those felonies committed without the aid of sorcery. After all, the Fiend made his disciples injure their fellow men in every conceivable way. It must be brought home to everyone that the six accused had obeyed their master's orders with dreadful efficiency. Were they not indeed devils in human shape? A threatening murmur and loud cries of outrage no doubt accompanied the reading of the alleged crimes, even interrupting it from time to time.

From his vantage point, leaning from his open window, the aged councillor Johann Baptist Fickler, devotee of the midnight oil, watched the drama unfold. Even in those days an event of this kind was rarely seen and heard. It was no doubt idle curiosity rather than any deeper involvement that prompted the old man to watch. What did this rabble and their fate matter to him? He tended to divide mankind into devout children of the Catholic Church, on the one hand, and diabolical pests, on the other. Why should he be moved to pity the criminals over there on the Town Hall steps? Why should he, who had faith in God's justice in this world, feel the slightest doubt concerning the guilt of those who had been convicted? And yet he was linked in some odd way with these folk, for he was to be instrumental in rescuing them from oblivion. As he listened to the unending catalogue of their atrocities read out by the clerk, a thought occurred to him which ultimately gave birth to this book. He made up his mind to incorporate the transcript of the trial in the ducal archives as monstrous evidence of the Devil's depravity. Those records, bound in pigskin, containing the statements made by the convicted witches, would fit rather well into the duke's collection of curios, reflected the old man. And he took good care to see that the documents from the trial were lodged in the duke's art gallery. There they survived over the years, among pictures of bearded virgins, two-headed goats, dwarves, and deformed embryos, amid seashells, coral, antlers, stuffed birds, and a narwhal's fin.

THE JUDGMENT

After the shrifts had been recited, the prosecutor, played by the municipal retainer standing before the judges' bench, once more raised his stentorian voice, effortlessly silencing the incipient murmur of the crowd. Since everyone had now heard the evil deeds committed by the prisoners summoned to appear before the court, he, the procurator, enjoined the judges, in the name of His Grace, the Duke of Bavaria, "to give their judgment in law and pronounce that the delinquents thus charged had, by reason of the felonies committed and proved against them, forfeited their lives by irrevocable law and judgment, deserved death, and should hence be condemned to suffer that penalty as prescribed and ordained by statute." If this was a kind of motion by the public prosecutor, then the brief speech by the "advocate," who took the prosecutor's place in front of the judges' table, might be reckoned a plea by the defense. The actor given this minor part in the drama said nothing, in fact, concerning the nature of the case or the persons of the accused, but simply pleaded for a fair judgment and invoked the mercy of God. The accused themselves had no opportunity to speak. In keeping with their status in the preceding investigatory procedure, they were, even in this public spectacle, nothing but objects, with no choice other than to accept their fate. It was thought that their interests had been adequately served by the brief appearance of their advocate.

With that, the "prosecution" and "defense" were concluded. The executive justice declared that he would duly consider the prosecution brought by the duke and the reply of the defendants' advocate. He would also consult the deputy magistrate of the city, who had been appointed to serve with him, and would arrive "forthwith" at a judgment. That, too, of course, was nothing but play-acting: the judgment had been decided a week before. That is why the "consultation" between the judges probably amounted to little more than a nod of the head. Then Neuchinger raised his hand, which was the signal for the clerk, who was still standing on the buttress in front of the Town Hall window, to begin reading the judgment. It had been among his papers from the outset.

His voice rang across the square:[139] "Whereas Holy Scripture, no less than the common statutes of the Empire, especially the salutary Penal Code instituted by His Most Worshipful and Most Excellent Majesty, the Emperor Charles V, in the year of grace 1532, thereinafter promulgated and adopted in all parts of the Roman Empire, do verily state and ordain that the most heinous, abominable, and dreadful sin of witchcraft and sorcery, *a fortiori*, however, the denial and renunciation of God's Majesty and of all His Heavenly Host, be punished with the harshest and most fearful penalties as may be inflicted on man, viz. by burning, and in consideration that these six persons here presently arraigned, each serving as a public example, have in a detestable, godless, and unnatural manner proved themselves so lost to all sense of God's honor, to all natural affection, and to their own souls' salvation, as to indulge countless times in those abominable sins and vices of an infamous, unprecedented, and vile nature that have heretofore been set forth *in extenso*, flouting the Holy Commandments and, indeed, the sacred name of God himself, together with all the aforementioned salutary statutes, insofar as they have done to death and maimed a great number of persons, both young and old, by use of their accursed diabolical unguents, brought about gales and hailstorms, poisoned cattle and grazing-grounds alike, broken into cellars and other premises for the purposes of their unnatural revels and other ungodly and diabolical assemblies, likewise stealing the most Holy Sacrament from churches, many a time defiling the same in the most abominable, insolent, and inhuman manner, having moreover willfully committed many notable acts of murder and arson, likewise assaulting folk by night in a violent and murderous fashion, inflicting injury on them by fire, and wrenching their limbs asunder in unchristian fashion, as well as perpetrating robbery and theft upon the highway and elsewhere, all these being acts, vices, and atrocities of an unprecedented, to wit, unchristian, brutal, and detestable nature, such as are unlawful, yea, accursed, and liable to punishment, being such offenses as may, indeed, but rarely be discovered together in any company of persons, and these same persons not only having admitted and confessed to having perpetrated the same, both of their own free will, and under duress of examination under torture, as stated by word of mouth and recorded in writing, the same having also been found to be true by judicial investigation, and whereas His Grace, mindful of his sovereign office, and of his responsibility to discharge as a dutiful Prince and constituent member of our Holy Empire all such Edicts, Constitutions, and Decrees as require him to implant all manner of righteousness, chastising evil to the solace of the righteous, and as a deterrent to the wicked, does not mean, intend, or desire to proceed against or deal with the six persons here arraigned as criminals and evildoers publicly recognized as guilty of the aforesaid vices, otherwise than in accordance with and by virtue of the aforementioned common statutes and Imperial constitutional decrees, wherefore, upon due consideration of the dreadful acts and atrocities heretofore set forth, and confirmed by the irrevocable confession of those same six persons here arraigned, together with evidence of corroboration that they have in truth perpetrated such vile and abominable crimes of that kind on account of which, as witnessed in Holy Scripture, cities, realms, and nations alike are bound to suffer manifold tribulation, all manner of chastisement and misfortune being to this day visited upon us by Almighty God, so it behoves me, Christopher Neuchinger of Oberneuching, Executive Justice to His Grace, to declare as my irrevocable judgment that, in accordance with the abovementioned Imperial statutes and decrees, the aforementioned six culprits' lives are forfeit, they having incurred sentence of death by torment, namely that all six be placed publicly upon two carts, drawn in procession before their deaths to the place of execution, the body of each to be torn six times with red-hot pincers, the mother to have her breasts cut off, the five condemned males to have their limbs broken on the wheel, and Paulus Gämperle thereafter to be impaled upon a stake, all six persons then to be put to death by fire."

The resonant voice from the heights of the Town Hall fell silent, and the tense silence of the crowd doubtless gave way to a stir of excitement. What a judgment! It consisted of a single, monstrous sentence, a maze of logic, intricate, rambling, portentous in its introductory part, terse and chilly in what it really had to say. It was probably no easier for the listeners to follow the meanderings of this verbal monster than it is for us to read it. Its begetter was presumably none other than Dr. Wangereck; it was certainly not the executive justice, whose function was merely to lend his good name to the barbaric penalty. The contents reveal the author. In spite of its cumbersome grammar—even then, an educated German believed that the more complicated a sentence was, the profounder was its sense—and in spite of its traditionally formal phrases, the text of the judgment clearly demonstrates the motives behind the trial, and suggests its political justification. The duke's penal powers are explicitly derived from two sources: from

404

his "sovereign office," and from his responsibility toward the Empire as a whole. The aim of punishment by the state was to solace the righteous and to deter the wicked. This is a formula which, dispensing rather surprisingly with any religious circumlocution, demonstrates a very "modern" conception of the state. The principal justification for the draconian punishment is not retribution or atonement for the dreadful crimes, but prevention, the security of the state, deterrence. It is a matter of setting a "public example," not only the punishment of individual crimes but also a campaign against abominable misdeeds from which "cities, realms, and nations alike are bound to suffer manifold tribulation."

The thousands assembled on the Munich marketplace will scarcely have understood the complex syntax, although they listened with bated breath as the judgment was read out to them from a lofty bastion. The sanctimonious tone, certainly, was familiar enough to the townsfolk, the craftsmen, the peasants, and the courtiers. They imbibed from it a familiar mixture of exhortations and threats addressed to all and sundry. This final judgment was a theatrical performance produced for the benefit of the audience and intended to imply that a wise judge was pronouncing sentence in a case brought before him in keeping with ancient tradition and an "eternal" law, which he deduced solely from the people's wealth of experience. In fact, the text of the proclamation left no doubt that it was the authorities who were the source of all law. The crimes committed by the sovereign's subjects had incurred the wrath of God and moved the power of the state to retribution. The function of punishment was not so much to eradicate unlawfulness from the world as to show to the unruly the menacing fist of law and order. God, and hence the duke, felt themselves affronted, God and the duke were alike indignant. Both had to be placated by the ceremonious shedding of blood. Even if the listeners did not understand every word and phrase of the judgment, they nevertheless dimly sensed, with a thrill of fear, that this was the implicit purpose of the example set.

When the commotion that followed the announcement of the judgment had somewhat abated, the executive justice rose once more, seized the staff from the black-covered table with a theatrical gesture, and then, holding it at each end, raised it above his head and broke it. This was meant to indicate that the poor sinners' lives had suffered the same fate as the staff. The breaking of the staff was a symbolic anticipation of the execution, and a groan went up from the crowd as Neuchinger laid the broken pieces of the staff back on the table.[140] In the meantime, the Munich executioner, who had his own seat in the enclosure, had risen to his feet. He listened to the judge's order with an inscrutable face: "Executioner! I order you by the oath that you have sworn to the prudent, worshipful, and wise Council of the city of Munich to conduct the poor prisoners thus bound to the customary place of execution, there to carry out the sentence I have pronounced, in keeping with the law."

THE PROCESSION

The crowd of spectators began to stir. Two open, horse-drawn carts started to make their way through the throng, while constables led the "poor sinners" down the steps of the Town Hall. The executive justice and the deputy magistrate left the judicial enclosure and mounted their horses. Meanwhile, the executioner's assistants had fetched a brazier with glowing charcoal and placed it in front of the Town Hall, where it was cordoned off by bailiffs. The condemned prisoners were led into this open space. The executioner tested the pincers, large iron tongs, the ends of which had been plunged into the smoking brazier. Then he walked up to Anna Pappenheimer, seized her linen shift with both hands at the neck, and ripped it open with one powerful tug, pulling it down over the old woman's bony shoulders as far as her waist. The other prisoners were also stripped bare to the waist in similar fashion. Pale, eyes downcast or wide with terror, they stood there between their guards. The people in the square, of whom only those in the first few rows could see this part of the execution, craned their necks, surged toward the spot, and had to be forced back by mounted guards.

Among those spectators who became eyewitnesses was the eleven-year-old Hänsel Pämb. On the instructions of commissioner Wangereck, he was forced to watch his parents' execution— the councillor expected this to have a salutary effect on the boy. As soon as the prisoners had been brought from the Falcon Tower, the ironmaster handed the boy over to the sheriff of the city of Munich. The sheriff lifted the child onto his horse and rode off with him to the marketplace, where he mingled with the crowd, having been instructed to pay close attention to the vagrant boy's behavior, and to note carefully every word he said. For a long time Hänsel said nothing, but did not seem to be especially upset; on the contrary, in the sheriff's opinion, he appeared "lively enough."

The executioner drew the first of the red-hot pincers from the brazier and ripped six gaping wounds in the arms and torso of Paulus Pappenheimer, who uttered fearful screams of agony. In a moment, the executioner had the next pair of tongs in his hand and was carrying out the same cruel punishment on Gumpprecht. And so all the offenders were "ripped," one after another. Finally the executioner sliced off Anna Pappenheimer's breasts.

This harsh and repulsive punishment imposed on women was obviously intended to degrade the victim. At that time it was rarely carried out. In the most comprehensive manual of the time, which deals with all the customary "punishments to life and limb," it is mentioned only as a historical item—a form of torture practiced in the days when Christians were being persecuted.[141] "Anatomists unanimously agree that the female breasts are extremely sensitive, on account of the refinement of the veins, of which the heathen tyrants duly took note in their persecution of Christians, inflicting agonizing wounds to the breasts of those females that did stand by their Christian faith, ripping and tearing the same, and in the end even cutting them off." In Duke Maximilian's Bavaria, this punishment seems nevertheless not to have been altogether unusual. The regulations for the duke's executioner, drafted by Georg Hund in 1601, provide for it.

According to chroniclers' reports, the severed breasts were rubbed around Anna's mouth and around the mouths of her two sons.[142] Then constables seized the maimed criminals and thrust them onto the two carts, which were standing ready. Anna and her sons Gummprecht and Michel were put into the first cart; Paulus Pappenheimer, Ulrich Schölz, and Georg Schmälzl pushed onto the other. They sat on the planks which had been nailed from one side of the carts to the other to serve as benches. Then two priests clambered aboard and took their seats next to the condemned prisoners. Everything was then ready for the start.

In the meantime, a kind of procession had formed on the marketplace in a space that had been cleared of spectators.[143] At a signal given by the executioner's assistants, indicating that the poor sinners' carts were ready to set off, the procession got underway. It was headed by one of the Munich poor-law guardians carrying a large crucifix. Then came ducal and municipal constables, wearing side arms and leather belts to signify their authority. The mercenary troopers of the town watch followed, clanking in their gleaming armor, spiked helmets on their heads and long lances in their hands. Then came the legal officers of the city and the duchy in their short, red and blue tunics.

The clerk to the chief justice stalked by, dignified and alone, holding a folder with the fateful documents that had just been read out. Following him came the four so-called Kings of the Night: young men clad in blue and black, bearing lances and embodying allegorically the four districts of the city. There followed the grain stewards, who had cordoned off the judicial bench with their long wooden staves. They now formed the escort for the horse-drawn tumbrils that creaked along behind. The carts with the condemned prisoners were driven by the knacker and his mate; they were guarded on both sides by bailiffs and by the executioner's assistants. The executioner himself followed the second cart on horseback. Contingents of the Munich clergy—nuns, monks, chaplains to city and court—followed the carts, murmuring prayers. After them came a larger group of mounted participants: first the executive justice and his groom, then the chief magistrate of the city, the deputy magistrate, the ducal chief justice and the treasurer, city councillors and other dignitaries. Men, women, and children from the eager crowd of spectators brought up the rear. The procession was well over half a mile long: its tail was still forming in the marketplace long after the bearer of the crucifix at its head had passed the newly built Church of St. Michael.

The carpets of flowers, the sacred pictures, the altars with their birch branches, the ceremonial banners—all those were lacking, but otherwise the procession that moved westward through the city on that summer's day from the Town Hall via Kaufingerstrasse and Neuhauserstrasse was not unlike the festive Corpus Christi procession that had taken place six weeks earlier. At the end of the Kaufingerstrasse, bells rang out from the Fair Tower as the procession passed through its gateway. Certain groups in the parade sang hymns, others repeated the prayers recited by a precentor. But we also have to imagine the procession as being accompanied by the laughter and shouting of children chasing each other in and out of the festive crowd, the calls and sallies of neighbors greeting one another, the bawling of the beggars that we know so well. Peddlers raucously vaunted the virtues of the printed copies of the shrifts, offering them to such of the public as could read, while women and children collected money in their hats to pay for Masses for the souls of the condemned. Pickpockets darted through the serried ranks of gaping spectators, making a mockery in their own way of the educational function of this "exemplary punishment." And, of course, people stood in groups of three or half a dozen, supplementing from their own knowledge the cata-

408

logue of sins they had listened to just before the criminals were led off to execution.

The sheriff, carrying Hänsel Pappenheimer on his saddle in front of him, had forced his horse into the procession just behind the group of dignitaries that brought up the rear. As the pair of them reached the Fair Tower, where the spectators were most thickly crowded, the child turned around to his guardian and cried in delight: "Look, look! What a grand wedding for my father and mother! They've got so many men-at-arms—the duke doesn't have as many himself!" The official was shocked by these words. Far from regarding them as pathetically childish and naive, he considered them to be highly suspect, the work of the Devil, and noted them precisely for inclusion in the report he later submitted.

The portrals of the churches of Our Lady and St. Michel were thrown wide open. If any of the prisoners had succeeded in escaping from the cart, through the crowd and into one of the churches they passed, the bailiffs would not have been permitted to follow them. The victims might have cast longing glances from their lumbering carts into the dimness of St. Michael's Church, with its glints of gold within—there lay freedom, so near and yet so far. For heavy chains held the wretched creatures fast, the ranks of escorting guards to left and right of the carts offered no hope of escape, and their bodies, ripped with red-hot pincers, were weak. They probably sat there apathetically on their benches until the procession halted at the Neuhaus gate—now called the Charles Gate.

On the righthand wall of the gateway hung a wooden cross adorned with flowers.[144] According to ancient custom, criminals being led to the place of execution were supposed to say a prayer in front of the cross. The vagrants, the farmer, and the tailor were made to descend from the carts and were led in their clanking chains through the ranks of the procession, which had now halted in some confusion. The accompanying priests—presumably their confessor from the Falcon Tower, Dr. Hannemann, was among their number—instructed the condemned to clasp their hands in silent prayer, to think of their misdeeds, and to commit themselves to the Lord in remorse and humility. They then paused for a few moments in silent devotion with the condemned prisoners.

On their way back to the carts, the party was delayed, in keeping with ancient custom, by two municipal officials, who offered the chained prisoners wine from capacious bottles. The poor wretches presumably gulped it down eagerly. The gesture of compassion was no spontaneous impulse but a symbolic act, an institutionalized form of humanitarian sentiment, which stood in strange contrast to the cruelty of the execution. The custom of offering wine goes back to reports of Christ's crucifixion (Matthew 27:34; Mark 15:23), but it also served a practical purpose: the condemned prisoners were to be slightly intoxicated and hence better able to bear the agonies that awaited them. "Give strong drink unto them that are to die," urged Martin Luther, "so that they may drink and no more think of their plight." According to an instruction issued to judges, "those that are to be executed" should be given "wine mixed with incense or myrrh to drink, that they may be made either drunk or so fuddled in their thoughts, that they do not feel or heed the pain, but go the more serenely to their death. Or that they may be sustained, so as to bear the torture and the agony the longer."

Our prisoners, thus fortified in spirit and in body, were made to resume their places on the cart benches. The procession set off once more, leaving the confines of the city to the tolling of the "poor sinners' bell" and the strains of a hymn. The hooves of the horses echoed in the shady courtyard inside the gateway, the iron tires of the carts rumbled and crunched through the outer gateway and over the stone arch of the bridge. The great wooden cross swayed onward, as if this were a troop of devout pilgrims. It followed the gentle bends of a field path, past barns, summer meadows, fields of oats, across the broad, flat landscape bathed in the morning light. The road led westward along the highway to Pasing as far as the gallows hill, which rose up ahead in the haze. We can imagine our prisoners in their swaying carts occasionally turning to look back over the long procession behind them to the many towers that marked the city's precinct.

THE FIRE

Up on the gallows hill, the milling crowd was filled with a carnival spirit. Constables and grain stewards were hard put to it to hold back the curious from the six massive stakes and the "griddle." Even long after the tumbrils had reached the top of the hill, dense crowds of spectators were still streaming out from Munich; so the executive justice delayed the start of the execution. Among the crowd that stood jammed shoulder to shoulder was the sheriff from Munich on his horse, holding Hänsel in front of him. All around were the citizens of Munich, craftsmen, a farmer with a bushy black beard. The child bent down toward the latter and said: "Farmer, what a fine black beard you have! Give me your beard, I'd like to have one that color!" The man replied good-naturedly, jocularly, little suspecting whom he was talking to.

A shout of "Silence! Silence!" rang out over the place of execution. The tumult of the crowd, the shouting, singing, laughing, murmuring died down, and the attention of everyone present was focused on the summit of the gallows hill, which could be seen clearly from all sides. Christoph Neuchinger moved away from the group of horsemen waiting to the right of the stakes and guided his horse to the center of the hill. "I order the executioner to carry out his duty," he called in a voice that reached the very outskirts of the crowd, "and I warrant him peace and safe conduct, whatever may befall him!" With these words he placed the executioner under the protection of the court, in case he were to commit some blunder in carrying out the execution. It had been known for the frenzied spectators of a bungled execution to lynch the executioner. It was to forestall this kind of thing that the assurance of safe conduct was given.

"Look! Now they're bringing my father!" cried Hänsel to the folk standing round the sheriff's horse. The executioner and one of his assistants dragged Paulus Pappenheimer to the wooden grating, laid him on it, and bound his arms and legs. Then the executioner took up the wheel with his brawny arms and let it fall, first on the right arm, and then on the left arm of the condemned man. The bones snapped with a loud crack, and the victim groaned aloud. "Look how they're thumping my father's arms!" cried the horrified child on the sheriff's horse.

The other criminals suffered the same treatment. Only Anna was spared the wheel. For reasons that lie buried deep in the mystic symbolism of penal practices, women could not be broken on the wheel.[145] Possibly this punishment, which was usually continued until the battered victim died, was thought too cruel to be inflicted on the weaker sex. "Here in Germany," ran the general opinion, breaking on the wheel "is, apart from burning alive, the worst and most dreadful penalty, being imposed on murderers and highwaymen . . . , those who steal from churches and all who aid and abet them . . . , those who slay their parents or children . . . , assassins or hired killers . . . , witches and ogres, such as have committed barbaric crimes." In our case, in fact, the breaking on the wheel was not carried through to the end, for there was a risk that the victims might expire in the process when they were supposed to suffer to the bitter end the whole catalogue of penalties embodied in the sentence. The tearing of their flesh with red-hot pincers had already weakened the condemned criminals—full-scale breaking on the wheel would have put a premature end to their sufferings.

The masters of our vagrants' fate had no wish to risk that; so the executioner had been instructed to proceed with moderation. In order to set a sensational, terrifying example, the agony was piled on carefully to the utmost limit of what could be done to men without killing them outright. In the case of Paulus Pappenheimer, who was seen in some sense as the instigator and ring-leader of the gang, they had thought of something even more appalling: impalement. This was one of the most revolting punishments ever devised by the human imagination and even in those days was hardly ever used. The penal code of Charles V did not make provision for it. In the manual *Punishments of Life and Limb*, from which we have already quoted, we find the following: "In barbaric regions, particularly in Algiers, Tunis, Tripoli, and Salee, where inveterate pirates dwell, if a man is thought guilty of treason, he is impaled. This is done by inserting a sharply pointed stake into his posterior, which then is forced through his body, emerging through the head, sometimes through the throat. This stake is then inverted and planted in the ground, so that the wretched victims, as we may well imagine, live on in agony for some days before expiring . . . It is said that nowadays not so much trouble is taken with impalement as was once the case, but such criminals simply have a short spit thrust into their anus and are left to crawl thus upon the earth until they die." We may well imagine that such a barbaric punishment was calculated to arouse sympathy for the tormented victim among the spectators of an execution. This was no doubt the reason it was not generally employed. But Paulus Pappenheimer was forced to suffer it—apparently the authorities could think of no other way of enhancing the brutality of the proceedings. We shall spare the reader the description of his agony. But there is no doubt, according to statements in our sources, that he was indeed impaled. The victim's screams must have sent shivers down the spines of the spectators who crowded around on the summit of the gallows hill.

Two brawny retainers seized the victim as he writhed groaning on the ground and dragged him up the wooden planks that formed the ramp leading up to one of the central stakes. There they left him bound on top of the heap of brushwood. Then Anna was pulled up onto the pile alongside and tied to a wooden chair that had been secured among the bundles of faggots. Gumpprecht, Michel, Schölz, and the tailor were thrust onto the four other heaps of brushwood, where they were chained to the wooden stakes. Then the executioner's assistants dragged the gangways off the pyres. Pitch torches were lighted and thrust rapidly, one after the other, into the dry brushwood. Flames crackled and darted up to catch twigs and branches. Acrid smoke rolled up, blinding the victims, snatching their breath. The spectators' view of the culprits was increasingly obscured by smoke and leaping flames. The poor wretches could be dimly glimpsed, choking and writhing in the heat, as far as their bonds permitted. Hänsel, on the sheriff's horse, burst into heart-rending cries. "My mother is squirming!" he cried in despair.

Because it was such an uncommonly cruel punishment, burning alive was very rare. The screams of the suffocating victims, their appalling death agonies, had on similar occasions led to expressions of anger among the onlookers and to violent threats to the executioner. That is why William V's instructions regarding witchcraft recommended in cases of "execution by fire" that the poor sinner should "first be put to death by the rope, and then burned, unless there be special, momentous, and weighty reasons why the judges see fit to have the culprit punished and executed by burning alive, as an example and deterrent to others." This was precisely the reason in the case we are dealing with.

The strident, monotonous voices of those offering up prayers mingled with the crackling of the fire, the excited cries of the crowd, the screams and coughing of the agonized victims, which grew ever fainter: "Lord Jesus, for Thee I live! Lord Jesus, for Thee I die! Lord Jesus, I am Thine, dead and alive!" Thus a priest led the prayers, and a choir of the faithful repeated the words. It is possible that there was also singing—our source does not inform us on this point. There is, however, evidence that the boys of the Jesuit College, led by a teacher, took their places among the spectators at such executions and sang hymns during the proceedings.[146]

Soon, nothing more could be seen of the evildoers. The flames leapt high into the air, the heat in the immediate vicinity of the executions became unbearable. Thick clouds of smoke darkened the blue and white of the summer sky. One by one the piles of burning brushwood collapsed, and finally the glowing stakes in the center of each pile also crumbled. By that time the fire had burned down so far that the executioner could risk approaching it. He took up his position on the highest point of the hill and called out loudly across the grisly scene: "Worshipful Justice, have I properly executed sentence?" Whereupon Neuchinger, still mounted, replied: "Insofar as you have done execution as the law and the sentence demand, I declare that it remain so!"

With this act, the execution was completed. The crowd slowly dispersed and straggled back to Munich along the Pasing highway. Up on the hill, with its smoking embers, only the knacker remained with one or two of the excutioner's assistants, who were detailed to clear up the site. Soon new fires would be built here, for the trial of the rabble from Lower Bavaria was not yet concluded. In the Falcon Tower, Augustin Baumann (the "Bread Carrier"), the weaver Hans Stumpf ("Jack the Glazier"), "Sugar Bun," and two "tinker lads" from the Bavarian Forest still awaited sentence. The child, Hänsel Pappenheimer, was taken back to his cell by the sheriff. And a few days after the fire on the gallows hill, Alexander von Haslang's officers handed the Tettenwang miller's family over to Master Georg. New torture sessions were arranged in the vault of the Falcon Tower, Dr. Wangereck was to put a great many more searching questions, and the clerk to the treasury was to cover a great many more pages with his scurrying quill, before Hänsel Pappenheimer, Augustin Baumann, Jack the Glazier, and Agnes and Anna from the convent mill were also burned alive on 26 November 1600. And even then the case was not finished. The question whether three women denounced by the Pappenheimers should be arrested and tortured was to occupy the council of state for a further two years, to lead to a flood of learned legal opinions, but to remain unresolved. For the women thus incriminated were not riffraff from the highways or the cottages of smallholders; they included the respectable wife of a mayor, the wife of a wealthy innkeeper, a buxom farmer's wife. There were vehement protests against their arrest on the part of relatives, respected citizens, friends in high places. Whereupon the alleged witches were hurriedly released on bail, and the authorities began to bury their blunder under masses of paper, consigning the whole matter to oblivion.

People were to go on talking about the Pappenheimers and their associates for some years, however. A number of pamphlets describing their exploits and their punishment were circulated, not without financial aid from the authorities. The two sets of exemplary executions on the gallows hill were referred to from time to time in the taverns of Munich, until there was hardly a soul left

414

who could remember them. In the ducal archives, the transcript of the trial, preserved at the instigation of the long deceased Dr. Fickler, gathered dust over the years. When the "prevailing opinion" among lawyers began to swing round and belief in witchcraft was declared a superstitious fallacy, the files entitled "Pämb-Gämperl Case" were labeled "Witchcraft Files." They had become a historical curiosity, scarcely capable of arousing a flutter of interest.

Otherwise nothing was left of our vagrants. There was no need to bury them. The knacker stood guard and raked over the site of the fires until the ashes turned white, and only a dark cloud, drifting eastward with the wind across the blue sky of a summer afternoon, told of what had happened.

⋆ Notes

The interested reader will find a comprehensive bibliography and detailed references to sources and secondary literature in my dissertation
Der Prozess Pappenheimer ("The Pappenheimer Trial," Ebelsbach, 1981),
in which more detailed consideration is given to specific legal issues. The
following notes are consequently limited to an outline of the sources and
the most important secondary literature I have used. They may serve,
on the one hand, as a guide to the reader and, on the other, as an expression of gratitude to all the scholars who have made this book possible by
their work.

No special sources are quoted for historical facts that are generally accepted, or for features of cultural life that have been established by recognized authorities. Should the reader have further questions relating to the
account I have given of our vagrant family, then I would refer him to the
comprehensive apparatus appended to my dissertation.

The epigraph to my book is taken from an unjustly forgotten work by
Will-Erich Peuckert, *Die grosse Wende* (Hamburg, 1948), vol. 1, p. 121.

1. H. Dussler, "Reiseberichte über München und Oberbayern vom 16.
bis 19. Jahrhundert. Aus dem Tagebuch des Uditore Fantuzzi, Herbst
1652, MS, Rome, Archivio Segreto Vaticano, Misc. Arm. XV, 80," *Oberbayerisches Archiv*, vol. 93, pp. 34ff.

2. Munich City Museum, Print Collection, catalogue no. M-I 320.

3. *Häuserbuch der Stadt München*, vol. 1, Residenzstrasse 27. Nagler,
"Beiträge zur älteren Topographie Münchens," *Oberbayerisches Archiv*,
vol. 12, pp. 9ff. Gilardone, "Wälle und Mauern um München," *Bayerland*,
vol. 46, pp 673ff.

4. Model by Jakob Sandtner from about 1570. Bavarian National Museum, Munich.

5. *Häuserbuch der Stadt München*, vol. 1, Maximilianstrasse 44/45.
F. J. Lipowsky, *Urgeschichten von München*, part 2 (Munich, 1815), p. 500.

6. Court Chief Justice's Instruction, 1655, in G. K. Mayr, *Sammlung der Churpfalz-Baierischen allgemeinen und besonderen Landesverordnungen,* vol. 5 (Munich, 1797), pp. 720ff.

7. J. Döpler, *Theatrum poenarum,* vol. 1 (Sondershausen, 1693), p. 658.

8. G. Ferchl, "Bayerische Behörden und Beamte 1550–1804," *Oberbayerisches Archiv,* vol. 53 (Munich 1980), pp. 7f.

9. E. Rosenthal, *Geschichte des Gerichtswesens und der Verwaltungsorganisation in Bayern,* vol. 1 (1598–1745) (Würzburg, 1906), pp. 4ff. W. Leiser, *Strafgerichtsbarkeit in Süddeutschland* (Cologne-Vienna, 1971), pp. 81ff.

10. J. Steinruck, *Johann Baptist Fickler—ein Laie im Dienst der Gegenreformation* (Münster, 1973).

11. Bavarian State Library, Munich, Manuscripts Department 4° Cgm 3085, f. 117–160.

12. R. Heydenreuter, "Die Behördenorganisation im Herzogtum Bayern beim Regierungsantritt Maximilians I. (1598)," in *Um Glauben und Reich* (Munich, 1980), p. 249.

13. Council Instruction of 1590 (bound folio 1–56), contemporary manuscript, Bavarian State Archives, Court Registry ex. Fasc. 400. No. 1, Prod. 10.

14. S. v. Riezler, *Geschichte Baierns,* vol. 5 (Gotha, 1903), pp. 18ff.

15. F. Stieve, *Briefe und Acten zur Geschichte des Dreissigjährigen Krieges,* vol. 5 (Munich, 1883), pp. 1ff.

16. A. Perneder, *Von Straff vnnd Peen aller und yeder Malefitzhandlungen ain kurtzer bericht . . .* (Ingolstadt, 1544), fol. II.

17. G. Ferchl (see n. 8 above), pp. 734f. F. Stieve, *Briefe und Acten,* vol. 4 (1878), p. 191, nn. 3, 4. H. Dollinger, *Studien zur Finanzreform Maximilians I. von Bayern in den Jahren 1598–1618* (Göttingen, 1968), pp. 388, 418.

18. G. Frhr. von Pölnitz, ed., *Die Matrikel der Ludwig-Maximilians-Universität Ingolstadt—Landshut—München,* vol. 1, 1472–1600 (Munich, 1937), col. 1149.

19. B. Haendcke, *Deutsche Kultur im Zeitalter des Dreissigjährigen Krieges* (Leipzig, 1906), pp. 242ff. S. von Riezler, *Geschichte Baierns,* vol. 6 (Gotha, 1903), pp. 303f.

20. C. Prantl, *Geschichte der Ludwig-Maximilians-Universität,* vol. 1 (Munich, 1872), pp. 311ff. K. H. Burmeister, *Das Studium der Rechte im Zeitalter des Humanismus im deutschen Rechtsbereich* (Wiesbaden, 1974).

21. F. Stieve, *Briefe und Acten,* vol. 5, pp. 12f.

22. Cf. the view of the chief justice, Bernhard Barth, concerning a dispute in the council of state, Bavarian State Archives, Court Registry ex. Fasc. 401, Prod. 3.

23. Report by Councillor Hieronymus Auerbach, Bavarian State Archives, Court Registry ex. Fasc. 401, Prod. 3, no. 104.

24. *Häuserbuch der Stadt München,* vol. 1, Dienerstrasse 13.

25. F. C. B. Avé-Lallemant, *Das deutsche Gaunertum in seiner sozial-politischen, literarischen und linguistischen Ausbildung zu seinem heutigen Bestand* (1858–62; reprint, Wiesbaden, 1979), pp. 40ff.

26. Ä. Albertinus, *Der Welt Tummel- und Schauplatz* (Munich, 1612), pp. 385f.

27. Council ordinance of 28 July 1588, quoted from Avé-Lallemant (see n. 25 above), p. 42.

28. From the contemporary comedy *Frau Wendelgard*, by Nicodemus Frischlin.

29. *Lands- und Polizeiordnung der Fürstentumen Obern- und Nieder-bayern* (Munich, 1616), Title 5, Art. 1.

30. E. Schremmer, *Die Wirtschaft Bayerns* (Munich, 1970), p. 160.

31. Ibid., p. 171.

32. E. Gasner, *Zum deutschen Strassenwesen von der ältesten Zeit bis zur Mitte des 17. Jahrhunderts* (1889; reprint 1966).

33. *Lands- und Polizeiordnung der Fürstentumen Obern- und Nieder-bayern* (Munich, 1616), Title 10.

34. E. Friedell, *Kulturgeschichte der Neuzeit* (Munich, 1927), p. 123.

35. M. Kemmerich, *Kultur-Kuriosa* (Munich, 1920), vol. 1, pp. 190ff., vol. 2, pp. 266ff.

36. D. Albrecht, "Staat und Gesellschaft II (1500–1745)," in M. Spindler, (ed.), *Handbuch für Bayerische Geschichte*, vol. 2 (Munich, 1977), p. 560.

37. S. v. Riezler, *Geschichte Baierns*, vol. 6 (Gotha, 1903), pp. 209ff.

38. D. Stutzer, "Unterbäuerliche gemischte Sozialgruppen Bayerns und ihre Arbeits- und Sozialverhältnisse," in *Um Glauben und Reich* (Munich, 1980), pp. 264ff.

39. M. J. Elsas, *Umriss einer Geschichte der Preise und Löhne in Deutschland* (Leiden, 1936).

40. S. v. Riezler, *Geschichte Baierns*, vol. 5, pp. 38f.

41. J. Steinruck, *Johann Baptist Fickler* (Münster, 1965), p. 145.

42. Ibid., pp. 4ff. "A true and Circumstantial Record etc. . . . ," Bavarian State Library, Munich, Manuscripts Department 4° Cgm 3085, f.117ff.

43. M. Frhr. von Freyberg, *Sammlung historischer Schriften und Urkunden*, vol. 2 (Stuttgart-Tübingen, 1833), p. 147.

44. G. F. Chr. v. Zimmern and J. Müller, *Aus der Chronika deren von Zimmern*, ed. Bernh. Ihringer (Munich-Leipzig, 1911), pp. 366ff.

45. General decree of Duke Maximilian, dated 10 December 1610, Munich City Archives, Best. Bürgermeister und Rat, 60 A 1.

46. K. A. Hall, *Die Lehre vom Corpus Delicti: Eine dogmatische Quellenexegese zur Theorie des gemeinen deutschen Inquisitionsprozesses* (Stuttgart, 1933).

47. H. Dotterweich, *Der junge Maximilian* (Munich, 1962). F. Stieve, *Briefe und Acten zur Geschichte des Dreissigjährigen Krieges*, vol. 5 (1883). Fr. Schmidt, *Geschichte der Erziehung der Bayerischen Wit-*

telsbacher von den frühesten Zeiten bis 1750 (Berlin, 1892). K. Pfister, *Kurfürst Maximilian I. von Bayern und sein Jahrhundert* (Munich, 1949). Still indispensable is: S. v. Riezler, *Geschichte Baierns*, vols 4, 5, 6 (Gotha, 1903).

48. C.-J. Roepke, "Die evangelische Bewegung in Bayern im 16. Jahrhundert," in *Um Glauben und Reich* (Munich, 1980), pp. 101ff.

49. M. Ritter, *Deutsche Geschichte im Zeitalter der Gegenreformation und des 30jährigen Krieges*, 3 vols (1889–1908).

50. P. Ph. Wolf, *Geschichte Maximilians I. und seiner Zeit*, vol. 1 (Munich, 1807), pp. 397ff.

51. G. von Lojewski, *Bayerns Weg nach Köln* (Bonn, 1961).

52. L. Häusser, *Geschichte des Zeitalters der Reformation 1517–1648* (3rd printing, Berlin, 1903). Preferable to all other sources.

53. I owe this interpretation to the account of the Spanish style given by E. Friedell, *Kulturgeschichte der Neuzeit*, vol. 1 (1927), pp. 356ff.

54. A. Christl, "Der spanische Jesuit Gregor von Valentia, Deutschlands bedeutendster Kontrovertist im 16. Jahrhundert" (unpublished dissertation, Freiburg, 1921).

55. J. B. Fickleri epistolae 1560–1606, State Library, Munich, Manuscripts Department, 2° Clm 715a. The letters quoted are taken from the edition by Fr. Schmidt, *Geschichte der Erziehung der Bayerischen Wittelsbacher* (Berlin, 1892), pp. 349ff.

56. It should be borne in mind that this narrative, like all those relating to the fate of the accused in the trial, is taken from the statements made by the prisoners as recorded in the trial transcripts, State Archives, Munich, Hexenakten 2.

57. S. v. Riezler, *Geschichte der Hexenprozesse in Baiern* (Stuttgart, 1896), pp. 149ff.

58. Fr. Schmidt, *Geschichte der Erziehung der Bayerischen Wittelsbacher* (Berlin, 1892), p. 253. H. Dotterweich, *Der junge Maximilian* (Munich, 1963), pp. 123f.

59. Eb. Buchner, *Das Neueste von gestern: Kulturgeschichtlich interessante Dokumente aus alten deutschen Zeitungen*, vol. 1 (Munich, 1912), pp. 16ff.

60. Ibid., pp. 19f.

61. F. Chr. B. Avé-Lallemant, *Das deutsche Gaunertum* (1858), part 1, pp. 67ff.

62. Hans Jakob Christoffel von Grimmelshausen, *Abentheuerlicher Simplicius*, bk. 1, chap. 4. Quotation in the version by E. Hegauer.

63. The explanation of this and other dialect expressions I owe to the invaluable work by J. A. Schmeller, *Bayerisches Wörterbuch*, ed. K. Frommann (Munich, 1872–77); 3rd reprint, Aalen, 1973).

64. G. Liebe, *Das Judentum in der deutschen Vergangenheit* (Leipzig, 1903).

65. Jakob Twinger of Königshoven, quoted from J. Nohl, *Der schwarze Tod* (Potsdam, 1924), p. 156.

66. M. Doeberl, *Entwicklungsgeschichte Bayerns*, vol. 1 (Munich, 1906), p. 472.

67. *Lands- und Polizeiordnung* 1616, Bk. 5, Title 1, Art. 1.

68. J. Nohl, *Der schwarze Tod: Eine Chronik der Pest 1348–1720* (Potsdam, 1924). P. Ziegler, *The Black Death* (London, 1969).

69. "Mandat wie man sich in tempore pestis verhalten soll" of 5 September 1613, Munich City Archives, Best. Bürgermeister und Rat, no. 60 B/3, f.10 v.

70. G. Sticker, *Die Pest*, 2 vols (Giessen, 1908–10).

71. E. Nielsen, *Das Unerkannte auf seinem Weg durch die Jahrtausende* (Ebenhausen [near Munich], 1922). E. Buchner, *Das Neueste von Gestern*, vol. 1 (Munich, 1912).

72. F. Riemann, *Grundformen der Angst* (14th printing, Munich-Basel, 1979).

73. City Archives, Munich, Best. Bürgermeister und Rat, no. 60 A/1, 60 B/1, 2, 3.

74. D. Stutzer, "Unterbäuerliche gemischte Sozialgruppen Bayerns und ihre Arbeits- und Sozialverhältnisse," in *Um Glauben und Reich* (Munich, 1980), pp. 264ff. E. Schremmer, *Die Wirtschaft Bayerns* (Munich, 1970), pp. 211ff.

75. H. Bächtold-Stäubli, *Handwörterbuch des deutschen Aberglaubens* (Berlin-Leipzig, 1930–31), s.v. "Dämon," "Diebstahl."

76. A. Schöppner, *Bayrische Sagen*, 3 vols (reprint, Munich, 1979).

77. K. v. Leoprechting, *Bauernbrauch und Volksglaube in Oberbayern* (Munich, 1855), pp. 102ff.

78. *Lexikon für Theologie und Kirche* (Freiburg im Breisgau), s.v. "Teufel." Herbert Haag, *Teufelsglaube* (Tübingen, 1975).

79. A. Augustinus, *De Civitate Dei—Über den Gottesstaat* (Turnholti, 1955) ("Corpus Christianorum," Series Latina, vol. 48).

80. Caesarius von Heisterbach, *Wunderbare und denkwürdige Geschichten*, trans. E. Müller-Holm (Cologne, 1968).

81. Zähringer, *Handbuch theologischer Grundbegriffe*.

82. S. von Riezler, *Geschichte der Hexenprozesse in Bayern* (Stuttgart, 1896), pp. 149ff.

83. W.-E. Peuckert, *Die grosse Wende: Das apokalyptische Saeculum und Luther*, vol. 1 (Hamburg, 1948), pp. 152ff.

84. W.-E. Peuckert, in *Handwörterbuch* (see n. 75 above), s.v. "Endschlacht."

85. Pfister, in *Handwörterbuch* (see n. 75 above), s.v. "Gog und Magog." W.-E. Peuckert, *Die grosse Wende*, pp. 164ff.

86. N. Paulus, "Württembergische Hexenpredigten aus dem 16. Jahrhundert," *Diöcesanarchiv von Schwaben* 15, no. 6 (1897), p. 108.

87. J. W. R. Schmidt, trans., *Der Hexenhammer* (4th printing, Vienna-Leipzig, 1938). Schmidt's Introduction is the basis of my account of the work. The quotations from it are based on his translation.

88. J. Praetorius, *Blockes-Berges Verrichtung* (Leipzig, 1669; reprint Frankfurt, 1979), pp. 37f.

89. B. E. König, *Hexenprozesse* (Berlin-Friedenau, n.d.), pp. 96ff.

90. W. G. Soldan and H. Heppe, *Geschichte der Hexenprozesse*, ed. Max Bauer, vol. 1 (3d printing, Munich-Hanau, 1912), pp. 151ff.

91. J. Bodin, *De Daemonomania Magorum: Vom auszgelassenen Wütigen Teuffelsheer der Besessenen Unsinnigen Hexen und Hexenmeyster etc.*, trans. J. Fischart (Strasbourg, 1581).

92. W. Glauner, *Die historische Entwicklung der Müllerei* (Munich-Berlin, 1939).

93. O. Beneke, *Von unehrlichen Leuten*, 2d ed. (1882), pp. 79ff.

94. Jungwirt, in *Handwörterbuch* (see n. 75 above), s.v. "Mühle."

95. Bavarian State Archives, Munich, Generalregistratur, Fasc. 323/16, f. 23ff.

96. J. Brunnemann, *Tractatus Juridicus de Inquisitionis Processu*, 5th ed. (Wittenberg, 1679), p. 30.

97. A. Schoetensack, *Der Strafprozess der Carolina* (Leipzig, 1904), pp. 50ff.

98. Eb. Schmidt, *Inquisitionsprozess und Rezeption* (Leipzig, 1940). J. Hansen, *Zauberwahn, Inquisition und Hexenprozess im Mittelalter und die Entstehung der grossen Hexenverfolgung* (Munich, 1900).

99. *Handwörterbuch* (see n. 75 above), s.v. "Herd."

100. Fr. von Spee, *Cautio Criminalis*, quoted from the translation by J.-Fr. Ritter (Weimar, 1939), pp. 208ff.

101. K. Haberland, "Die Mittagsstunde als Geisterstunde," *Zeitschrift für Völkerpsychologie und Sprachwissenschaft*, 1882.

102. P. Laymann, *Juridicus Processus contra sagas et veneficos*, ed. Augsburg (1710; written in Cologne in 1629). Laymann's authorship is disputed.

103. L. Mejer, *Die Periode der Hexenprocesse* (Hannover, 1882). Id., "Hexenthum und Stechapfel," *Jahresberichte der Naturhistorischen Gesellschaft zu Hannover*, 1894.

104. H. P. Duerr, *Traumzeit: Über die Grenze zwischen Wildnis und Zivilisation*, 2d ed. (Frankfurt am Main, 1978), pp. 13ff.

105. L. Weiser, *Zum Hexenritt auf dem Stabe: Festschrift für Marie Andree-Eysn* (Munich, 1928).

106. S. Leutenbauer, *Hexerei- und Zaubereidelikt in der Literatur von 1450 bis 1550* (Berlin, 1972), pp. 18ff.

107. F. Byloff, *Das Verbrechen der Zauberei (crimen magiae)* (Graz, 1902), p. 5.

108. Quotations in the German text are according to the translation of Martin Luther, *Biblia: Das ist die gantze Heilige Schrift* (Wittenberg, 1545; repr. ed. H. Volz and H. Blanke, Munich, 1974). Quotations in the present English translation are from the King James version.

109. *Von rechtmässigen ordnungen inn Burgerlichenn und Peinlichen "Regimenten"* (Strasbourg, 1532), f. CXXV f.

110. K. Pfister, *Kurfürst Maximilian I von Bayern und sein Jahrhundert* (Munich, 1949), pp. 106ff.

111. K. Baschwitz, *Hexen und Hexenprozesse* (Munich, 1966), pp. 40ff.

112. J. C. Fickler, *Disputatio Juridica de maleficis et sagis . . .* (Ingolstadt, 1592).

113. J. Bodin, *Daemonomania*, trans. J. Fischart (Strasbourg, 1581), pp. 20ff.

114. R. Stintzing, *Geschichte der deutschen Rechtswissenschaft*, sec. 1 (Munich/Leipzig, 1880), p. 645.

115. J. Weyer, *De praestigiis Daemonum et Incantationibus ac veneficiis*, trans. J. Fuglinus (Frankfurt am Main, 1586; repr. Darmstadt, 1968).

116. Quotation taken from *Practica Nova Imperialis Saxonica Rerum Criminalium in Partes III Divisa*, 6th ed. (Wittenberg, 1670), Quaestio XLIX, notae 57s., p. 324.

117. Arts. 53, 54 of the penal code of Charles V, repr. of the edition by J. Chr. Koch (1787), ed. G. Radbruch (Stuttgart, 1962).

118. H. Fehr "Gottesurteil und Folter," *Festgabe für R. Stammler zum 70. Geburtstag* (Berlin/Leipzig, 1926). Id., "Zur Lehre vom Folterprozess," *Zeitschrift der Savigny-Stiftung für Rechtsgeschichte*, Germ. Abtl., vol. 53 (Weimar, 1933).

119. Decree of 13 June 1615, City Archives, Munich, Best. Bürgermeister und Rat, 60 B 2, f. 699 v.

120. *Cautio Criminalis*, German version by J.-F. Ritter (Weimar, 1939), pp. 123ff.

121. Becker, Bovenschen, Brackert, et al., *Aus der Zeit der Verzweiflung: Zur Genese und Aktualität des Hexenbildes* (Frankfurt am Main, 1977).

122. H. P. Duerr, *Traumzeit* (Frankfurt am Main, 1978), pp. 25ff.

123. S. v. Riezler, *Geschichte Baierns*, vol. 6 (Gotha, 1903), pp. 244ff. See also State Library, Munich, Manuscripts Department, Cgm 1967.

124. B. Carpzov, *Practica Nova*, 6th ed. (Wittenberg, 1670), part I, Quaestio XLIX, n. 61.

125. J. B. Fickler, Judicium generale de poenis maleficorum, Staatsbibliothek, Munich, Lib. impr. cum notis mss in 8°, No. 26, pars 2. See also P. Laymann, *Juridicus Processus contra sagas et veneficos* (Augsburg, 1710; orig. pub. Cologne, 1629).

126. G. Remus, *Nemesis Karulina* (Hessen-Nassau, 1594), Cap. CIX, pp. 100f.

127. W. Leiser, *Strafgerichtsbarkeit in Süddeutschland* (Cologne/Vienna, 1971), pp. 100f. State Archives, Munich, Best. Gerichtsliteralien, Fasc. 1657/52, 318/1 Prod. 4, 138/No. 106.

128. Neuchinger's letters in the Munich State Archives, Best. Gerichtsliteralien, Fasc. 138/no. 107, 3233/no. 48.

129. C. Manzius, *Summa Processus criminalis* (Ingolstadt, 1645), ad Art. 79 CCC.

130. "Ordnung des Malefizrechtens" of 1575, published by Hefner, *Oberbayerisches Archiv*, vol. 13, pp. 53f.

131. J. Striedinger, *Der Goldmacher Bragadino* (Munich, 1928), p. 123.

132. M. Schattenhofer, *Das alte Rathaus in München* (Munich, 1972), pp. 193ff.

133. J. M. Mayer, *Münchener Stadtbuch* (Munich, 1868), pp. 568ff.

134. City Archives, Munich, Ratsprotokolle 1600, Stadtschreiber- und Unterrichterserie, Best. Bürgermeister und Rat, nos. 54 A/22f 106 and 54 B/8 f. 26.

135. Bayerische Malefizprozessordnung of 1616, Title 6, Art. 1.

136. *Handwörterbuch* (see n. 75 above), s.v. "Haar."

137. Föringer, "Verhandlungsform des öffentlichen Malefizrechtstages nach altbayerischen Strafverfahren im XVI. Jahrhundert," *Oberbayerisches Archiv*, vol. 7 (Munich, 1846), pp. 431ff.

138. Munich City Museum, Print Collection, Inv. no. M. I/320.

139. State Archives, Munich, Hexenakten 4, Prod. 5.

140. E. v. Moeller, "Die Rechtssitte des Stabbrechens," *Zeitschrift der Savigny-Stiftung für Rechtsgeschichte*, Germ. Abt., vol. 21 (Weimar, 1900), pp. 27ff.

141. J. Döpler, *Theatrum poenarum*, vol. 1 (Sondershausen, 1693), p. 959.

142. Apart from the broadsheet already quoted (Munich City Museum, Prints Collection, Inv. no. M I/320), a contemporary poem published by C. A. Regnet, *München in der guten alten Zeit* (Munich, 1879), p. 122; also a reference in Johann Mayr's chronicle of 1604, and the diary of the contemporary musician Hellgemayr, published in *Oberbayerisches Archiv*, vol. 100, pp. 142ff.

143. A. Martin, "Über die ehemaligen Richtstätten der in München zur Todesstrafe Verurteilten und ihre Volkssagen," *Oberbayerisches Archiv*, vol. 31 (Munich, 1871), pp. 218ff.

144. W. Harke, "Das Strafrecht des Münchener Blutbannbuches unter Berücksichtigung der anschliessenden Malefitzprotokolle 1574 bis 1617," unpublished diss., Munich, 1950, p. 173.

145. K. v. Amira, *Die germanischen Todesstrafen* (Munich, 1922), pp. 176f.

146. J. Döpler, *Theatrum poenarum*, vol. 1 (Sondershausen, 1693), p. 457.